The HOK
Guidebook
to Sustainable
Design

The HOK Guidebook to Sustainable Design

Sandra Mendler, AIA
William Odell, AIA

Committed to Sustainable Humanistic Design
and Stewardship of the Environment

JOHN WILEY & SONS, INC.
New York • Chichester • Weinheim • Brisbane • Singapore • Toronto

Library of Congress Cataloging-in-Publication Data

Mendler, Sandra.
   The HOK guidebook to sustainable design / Sandra Mendler, William Odell
     p. cm.
   Includes bibliographical references and index.
   ISBN 0-471-37906-9 (cloth : alk. paper)
    1. Architecture—Environmental aspects. 2. Architecture—Environmental aspects—Case studies. 3. Architecture, Modern—20th century. 4. Architectural design—Methodology. 5. Hellmuth, Obata & Kassabaum. I. Hellmuth, Obata & Kassabaum. II. Odell, William. III. Title.
NA2542.35 .M445 2000
720'.47—dc21
                                                  00-022823

Printed in the United States of America.

10 9 8 7

Contents

Design Guidance

Case Studies

Foreword

Deep into his book *Ishmael*, author Daniel Quinn, speaking through the teacher Ishmael, likens our civilization, as it has arisen out of the first industrial revolution and the agricultural revolution before that, to one of those early attempts to build the first airplane, the one with the flapping wings and the guy pedaling away to make the wings go. You've seen them in old film clips. In Quinn's metaphor, the man and the plane go off a very, very high cliff; the guy is pedaling away, the wings are flapping, the wind is in his face, and this poor fool thinks he's flying. But in fact he is in free fall and just doesn't realize it because the ground is so far away. Why is his plane not flying? Because it isn't built according to the laws of aerodynamics, and it is subject, like everything else, to the law of gravity.

Quinn says that our civilization is in free fall, too, for the same reason: It wasn't built according to the laws of aerodynamics for civilizations that would fly. We think we can just pedal harder and everything will be okay; if we pedal still harder, we can even fly to the stars to find salvation for the human race. But we will surely crash unless we redesign our craft, our civilization, according to the laws of aerodynamics for civilizations that would fly.

In the metaphor, the very, very high cliff represents the seemingly unlimited resources we started with as a species and still had available to us when we threw off the habits of hunting and gathering, settled down to become farmers and later industrialists, and began to shape this civilization we have today. No wonder it took a while for the ground to come into sight.

But we are fortunate that there are people with better vision who have seen the ground rushing up toward us, perhaps sooner than most of us have, and others who have undertaken to discover those laws of aerodynamics for civilizations that would fly.

In the latter category is the Swedish endeavor, led by Dr. Karl-Henrik Robèrt, to achieve scientific consensus on the principles of sustainability. Reduced to four fundamental principles, they have become recognized as the first-order principles of sustainability. You might call them the consensus-derived, science-based laws of aerodynamics for civilizations that would fly—sustainable civilizations. The four principles are expressed as the system conditions for sustainability. The "system" is the ecosystem, that thin shell of life where we and all the other creatures live, also called the ecosphere and the biosphere, that is 8,000 miles in diameter but only about 10 miles thick. From sea level, it extends about 5 miles down into the depths of the ocean and about 5 miles up into the troposphere. Relative to a basketball-size Earth, it is tissue-paper thin, and oh so fragile! For practical purposes, it sustains all life, and today, worldwide, it is in decline. It is this decline that the principles of sustainability address.

The principles are based on scientific laws of nature that have been well understood for over a hundred years, the laws of thermodynamics. They are like the law of gravity. Someone has said, "They're not just a good idea, they are the law, the law of the universe."

The first law of thermodynamics says that matter and energy cannot be created or destroyed. This is the principle of conservation of matter. When we burn something, it doesn't cease to exist; it changes form. When an automobile turns into a pile of rust, it doesn't cease to exist; it changes form. Every atom in the universe has always been in the universe. Every atom has existed since the beginning of time and will exist until the end of time. It's true for matter; it's true for energy. Matter is energy. Neither can be created or destroyed.

The second law of thermodynamics says that matter and energy tend to disperse. A drop of ink in a bathtub disperses. It may seem to disappear, but that's through dilution; it's still there, dispersed. Every manufactured article, from the moment it takes its final form, begins to disintegrate and disperse. A simple water glass, through the concentration of energy and design and human labor, is transformed from a pile of sand into a container, but from the moment of its completion it begins to disintegrate. If I drop it, I will accelerate that disintegration. Another way to say it is that the arrow of time flies in the direction of entropy, from order toward disorder. In a closed system, everything runs down. Everything that is concentrated eventually disperses.

Matter and energy cannot be created or destroyed. Matter and energy tend to disperse. This means that any and all matter that is introduced into society will never cease to exist and will, sooner or later, find its way into our natural systems. It will find its way. It will disperse. Toxic materials are no exception. They, too, will disperse and find their way ultimately into our bodies. These are scientific principles. We can ignore them, but they will not go away.

With these two laws of thermodynamics for background (there are others, but these are enough for now), here are the scientifically derived (based on the laws of thermodynamics) principles of sustainability, the system conditions of sustainability published by Dr. Robèrt and his consensus-reaching Swedish peer group, and ratified by American peer review as well:

> *1.* Substances from Earth's crust must not systematically increase in the ecosphere. This means that fossil fuels, metals, and other minerals must not be extracted at a faster pace than they can be redeposited and reintegrated into Earth's crust, turned back into nature's building blocks. If

substances from Earth's crust systematically and inexorably accumulate, the concentration of those substances in the ecosphere will increase and eventually reach limits. We don't know what the limits are, but beyond the limits, irreversible changes will occur. So much radioactivity that we all die; so much lead in the water that we all become sterile; so much carbon dioxide in the atmosphere that the polar ice caps melt.

2. Substances produced by society (man-made materials) must not systematically increase in the ecosphere. This means that man-made materials must not be produced at a faster pace than they can be broken down and integrated back into the cycles of nature, or deposited into the earth's crust and turned back into nature's building blocks. If persistent man-made substances systematically and inexorably accumulate, the concentration of these substances in the ecosphere will increase and eventually reach limits. Again, we don't know the limits, but beyond those limits irreversible changes will occur. At some point, dioxins kill. Enough dioxins will kill us all. At some point, DDT, DDE, DES, mercury-containing compounds, and PCBs begin to disrupt endocrine systems. Endocrine systems keep our species going, and keep other species going as well.

3. The productivity and diversity of nature must not be systematically diminished. This means we cannot over-harvest or reduce our ecosystems in such a way that their productive capacity and diversity systematically diminish. We must certainly protect the small fraction of species that are capable of photosynthesis. We must not cut down the forests. They produce the oxygen that keeps us alive. Our health and prosperity depend on the capacity of nature to reconcentrate, restructure, and reorder building blocks into new resources. Rainforests and fisheries, farmlands and aquifers must not be pushed beyond their ability to recover. Species must be preserved; diversity in nature, protected. Why? Because we simply don't know all the interconnections in the web of life, but we know we are part of that web. It is foolish to say that we don't need this, or we don't need that. This and that lead to us.

4. Therefore, in recognition of the first three conditions, there must be fair and efficient use of resources to meet human needs. This means that basic human needs must be met in the most resource-efficient ways possible, and meeting basic needs for all must take precedence over providing luxuries for a few. Otherwise, we will reap a harvest of social as well as environmental instability. If people living in wooded or forested areas cut down all the trees for firewood because they don't have another source of fuel, all humanity suffers from the loss of biodiversity, and from the erosion, climate change, flooding, and desertification that follow. Fair is one thing; efficient is another, but they are intimately connected. How can we lift the lowest economically without dragging down the highest? The answer lies in resource efficiency. (Karl-Henrik Robèrt, Herman Daly, Paul Hawken, and John Holmberg, "A Compass for Sustainable Development," *The Natural Step News*, no. 1, winter 1996, p. 3.)

But how shall we reorganize businesses, industries, and communities to conform to these four systems' conditions for sustainability? How shall we rethink such subjects as architectural design and building construction? The system conditions will define sustainability when we get there, but of course we are not there; we have a very long way to go. How in the world do we get there when we as a civilization are headed in the other direction? How shall we heal and restore the biosphere?

As we reach for these system conditions, our organizations must systematically decrease their economic dependence on underground metals and fuels and other minerals; on the production of persistent, unnatural, man-made substances; on activities that encroach on the productive parts of nature; and on the use of unnecessary amounts of resources in relation to added human value. That is, they must systematically move toward fair and efficient use of resources to meet all basic human needs, and put people to work to raise their standards of living, too.

This is hard stuff. These are unrelenting principles, and they will not go away. Today we are violating every one of them in ways that must not go on. Species are disappearing at a rate unknown on Earth in the last sixty-five million years, and we are fouling our own nest, too. The laws of thermodynamics are undeniable, but no law says we must follow the principles of sustainability. That's a matter of choice. However, the principles are telling us, also in undeniable fashion, that we must, for the sake of humankind's future, fundamentally change our industrial system and all its components. There is a limit to what Earth can endure.

So that is the challenge, and with principles in hand, society's quest for sustainability becomes a design problem: How can we incorporate these principles into everything we do? Where are we in the process of designing, then building, the sustainable society? Just about where the Wright brothers were in 1901: just beginning, in field after field, with a rudimentary knowledge of the laws of aerodynamics for civilizations that would fly. It is a beginning.

Hellmuth, Obata + Kassabaum (HOK) has begun in its field, architectural design, and a very good place to begin this is. With some 40 percent of natural resource consumption being funneled into the construction industry to provide our built environment, sustainable design can make a very large difference in the use of finite, diminishing resources, as well as harmful materials.

In this guide, HOK has generously shared its current, state-of-the-art understanding of sustainable architectural design. The reader will find guidance toward best practices at every stage of the design process, from team formation to education and goal setting, gathering information, design optimization, documents and specifications, construction, and operation and maintenance.

A sustainable design checklist is provided, along with an introduction to the building rating system, created by the U.S. Green Building Council, upon which "green" certification is based. This is a bar that will be raised repeatedly as the art advances, moving us ever closer to the ultimate goal in building design and construction: zero footprint. The design guide begins with a list titled "Ten Simple Things You Can Do." This list is followed by concise summaries of goals and economics, and a description of the sustainable design process.

At the heart of the design guide is the Design Guidance section, providing guidance on what to do in terms of planning and site work, energy, building materials selection, indoor air quality, water conservation, recycling, and waste management. To bring the checklists and project actions to life, the design guide provides case studies, reflecting HOK's own application of sustainable design principles to real buildings, moving always toward satisfying the system conditions for sustainability.

Concluding with a detailed glossary of terms, and lists of other references, the HOK Design Guide makes a valuable statement for sustainability. It should take a prominent place in the library of every building owner and designer and of every teacher of those professions, and should become each one's most used reference book, for the sake of future generations. This entire community of interest owes a debt of gratitude to HOK for sharing its insights and practices.

Ray C. Anderson
CHAIRMAN AND CEO
INTERFACE, INC.

Preface

Hellmuth, Obata + Kassabaum is committed to increasing awareness of sustainable design issues and opportunities in the design professions. As a large international architecture/engineering/interiors/planning/consulting firm, HOK designs almost $5 billion in new construction and renovation each year. The impact of that construction on the environment is great; however, the ability to create meaningful improvements is even greater.

HOK has been engaged in an experiment over a period of seven years: to transform the practice of architecture, to truly be "leaders in innovation" for the built environment. HOK's goal is to influence their entire body of work as a firm, to move their projects and the profession as whole toward sustainable design. The goal is, quite fundamentally, to redefine design quality in the built environment. HOK's experience with real projects that are now complete affirms that sustainable design serves clients needs better, and that sustainable design is an economically viable approach.

It is exciting to see the change that has taken place in our industry in just seven years. Seven years ago the American Institute of Architects Committee on the Environment (COTE) was only a few years old, and had just embarked on the creation of the extensively researched Environmental Resource Guide (ERG). Since then COTE has created many programs and conferences, including hundreds of design charrettes across the country, to give professionals and the public a hands-on experience with the sustainable design process. This year, COTE is presenting a ten-point plan to integrate sustainable design into the center of the profession via our standard contract documents, model RFPs, targeted educational initiatives, research, and so on.

Seven years ago the U.S. Green Building Council (USGBC) was just forming. Now the USGBC has over four hundred member organizations representing the leading professional firms, building material manufacturers, developers, building owners, financial institutions, and others committed to transforming the building industry. This year, the USGBC has launched their LEED (Leadership in Energy and Environmental

Design) Green Building Rating System. LEED is a powerful tool that is defining "green buildings" for the market.

The federal government is taking an active leadership role in promoting sustainable design, as are many state and local governments. We have also seen that leading corporations are just as interested in sustainable design.

When clients understand that the goal is to provide more fresh air and daylight, eliminate toxic and irritating chemicals in the indoor environment, and reduce long-term operating costs—and oftentimes first costs as well—they say, "But of course we want you to do that. Why would you do it any other way?"

When we consider the environmental and health impacts of the building materials we specify, we think of that as "responsible," and building owners and occupants see it the same way. Why would we specify building materials that are detrimental to either building occupants or the natural environment? Once we have a greater understanding of how materials and products perform over their full life cycle and what the environmental and health impacts are from raw material acquisition, manufacturing, use, and disuse, it is natural that this new information will influence our decision making.

When we design our sites and landscaping to use natural stormwater strategies, native plantings, habitat restoration, and even natural wastewater treatment systems, we have found that we increase the natural beauty of the site while healing damaged ecosystems. And again, these strategies often reduce costs as well.

When we decide what to build, where to build, and how to interface with existing and newly forming communities, our sustainable design goals consistently echo the concerns of community groups. By embracing these goals proactively, our design solutions improve and the community review process becomes much simpler.

As we move toward sustainable design we find that the challenge is both more difficult and more rewarding than we imagined in the beginning. Some aspects of how we practice lend themselves to a simple fix that can be made once and then applied to all projects; however, many issues get right at the heart of how we think and how we evolve our design solutions.

While the kind of refinement that leads to incremental improvements has always been part of our practice, we have found that the best solutions—the ones that offer us an opportunity to radically change the way our buildings work—come from a different design process. The best solutions come from an integrated design process that allows us to discover design synergies that improve performance while reducing costs.

This book has been created to make the shift to sustainable design easier. It is a hands-on document for everyone involved with making buildings and communities. While it is primarily directed toward A/E professionals, facility managers, and building owners, it will also be useful to those who are more indirectly involved with the design process in government, academia, and the private sector.

Bill Browning of the Rocky Mountain Institute has often said that the value of sustainable design case studies lies in their ability to illustrate the "art of the possible." The case studies in this book, while not perfect, are part of a process. Most important, they are proof that the processes described in this book are possible, and in fact practical, cost-effective, and positive. We invite you to join us as we seek to create truly sustainable buildings and communities, because we believe that this work is essential to creating better environments for people—now and for future generations.

Sandra Mendler
CHAIR, AIA COMMITTEE ON THE ENVIRONMENT

Acknowledgments

We would like to acknowledge the many people who contributed to the development of this year 2000 edition of *The HOK Guidebook to Sustainable Design*. Katrin Scholz-Barth and John Gilmore contributed many hours of information gathering, writing, editing, and organizing material for this edition, and Mara Baum and Chris Sensening worked with the team to redraw and/or format all of the images in this edition.

The following HOK professionals contributed their knowledge and insights into the project case-study descriptions: Mark Husser, Sara Liss-Katz, Ripley Rasmus, Michelle Ludwig, Sam Spata, Walter Urbanek, Pam Light, Brian Fishenden, John Lawhon, Paul Henry, Rod Sheard, Alan Colyer, Robert Barringer, Debra Guenther, Nick Baylis, and Tim Blair. Albin Fai, Michele Fleming, and Lori Moran provided valuable assistance chasing down images, approvals, and photo credits.

We give special thanks to William Bobenhausen and Catherine Coombs at Steven Winter Associates for their review of and additions to the glossary, and to Michael Holtz of Architectural Energy Corporation for his input to the Energy Design Process and his review of the Energy Project Actions.

This guide has been issued twice before. In 1998, Sandra Mendler, Bill Odell, Sandra Leibowitz, and Joyce Yin updated and expanded the guide. A number of HOK professionals contributed to that effort, including Debra Guenther, Sigi Koko, Hal Kantner, and Mary Ann Lazarus.

The first edition, which was released in 1995 for in-house use by HOK employees only, was developed by Sandra Mendler, Chris Hammer, Mary Ann Lazarus, and Mark Bowers with the assistance of HOK professionals from all disciplines, including: Lisa Borowski, Phil Evans, Ken Hanser, Charles Howard, Dick Macias, Richard Saravay, Jamie Smith, Dave Troup, and Lou Williams.

Finally, we are grateful to the HOK leadership for recognizing the importance of this project and for supporting our work on it. We also want to thank our families for accommodating the many long days, nights, and weekends that were required to meet our schedule.

Introduction

Environmental issues have moved into the mainstream of our culture. Growing environmental challenges face each new generation. As we move toward greater awareness of these issues, we are slowly building a collective momentum, not only toward solving these problems, but toward recognizing the opportunities they offer us. These opportunities can lead us to a new generation of buildings and communities that are healthy, productive, and enhance our quality of life. It is an exciting time—many of the things that we strive to do to move toward a truly sustainable built environment are practical and feasible today. Perhaps the biggest challenge is simply to get started. This guide is designed to help you do just that.

What Is Sustainable Design?

Sustainability represents a balance that accommodates human needs without diminishing the health and productivity of natural systems. The American Institute of Architects defines sustainability as "the ability of society to continue functioning into the future without being forced into decline through exhaustion or overloading of the key resources on which that system depends."

In these times of rapidly rising world population, increased demand on scarce resources, and continued pollution, sustainability is quickly becoming the dominant issue of our time. It is an issue that each of us, individually and as institutional representatives, can and should address in our daily work.

Unfortunately, our current economic accounting system does not recognize the value of depleted resources or the cost of pollution and diminishing biodiversity. If it did, our current practices would no longer appear to be economically justifiable. However, the search for sustainability highlights waste and lost opportunities in our current prac-

DID YOU KNOW...?

How fast is nature disappearing from the Earth? From 1970 to 1995—the space of one generation— the world has lost 30 percent of its natural wealth of forests, wildlife, and marine and freshwater species.

—World Wildlife Fund, "Living Planet Report 1999," WWF International, 1999.

tices that can serve as the engine for the development of improved solutions. Increasingly, people are realizing that environmental and economic sustainability go hand in hand.

While environmental and economic sustainability is the goal, sustainable design is the means we as designers have to contribute to that goal. Sustainable design moves away from extractive and disposable systems that are energy intensive, resource inefficient, and toxic toward cyclical, closed-loop systems that are restorative, dynamic, and flexible.

Environmental Impacts of Buildings and Construction

DID YOU KNOW...?

Every day the worldwide economy burns an amount of energy the planet required 10,000 days to create—the stored solar energy is burned and released by utilities, cars, houses, factories, and farms.

—Paul Hawken, *The Ecology of Commerce* (New York: HarperCollins, 1993), 21–22.

Buildings and construction contribute directly and indirectly to most of our environmental problems. Buildings are tremendous consumers of resources and generators of waste, and the industrial processes used to manufacture building materials and equipment contribute to waste and pollution as well. Buildings and the infrastructure that supports them consume open space and displace habitat. The quality of our indoor environments can inhibit productivity, and in some cases can even threaten our health.

According to the Worldwatch Institute, buildings in the United States use 17 percent of the total freshwater flows and 25 percent of harvested wood; they are responsible for 50 percent of CFC production, use 40 percent of the total energy flows, generate 33 percent of CO_2 emissions, and generate 40 percent of landfill material as a result of construction waste.

The environmental impacts of buildings are eroding our very quality of life. Our open space is being consumed by sprawl, and our communities are being overcome with traffic and congestion. According to the U.S. Environmental Protection Agency (EPA), nearly one-third of all buildings suffer from "sick building" syndrome.

Opportunities for Improvement

The good news is that there are many ways to improve our work without increased costs or program sacrifices. By embracing sustainable land-use planning, habitat can be preserved and enhanced, and our communities made more livable. Sustainable design in buildings and construction requires a holistic view of land, infrastructure, and buildings in order to use material, energy, and water resources efficiently, improve the health of ecosystems, and address health issues relating to the indoor environment. For nearly every conventional building product and system used today there are environmentally preferable alternatives. In most cases, there are practical and affordable choices with significantly improved environmental performance.

Economic Benefits

Sustainable design can lead to a variety of economic benefits. These include the economic benefits of energy, water, and materials savings as well as reduced maintenance and other operational costs. There are also numerous studies that connect healthy buildings to increased productivity, with green buildings producing increases of from 2 percent to 15 percent. Environmentally friendly buildings provide additional benefits to building owners and occupants by limiting risks, such as liability due to poor indoor air quality. Finally, environmentally friendly buildings can contribute to positive public relations. Public concern about these issues will continue to grow, and with it will come increasing demand for solutions and support for those who are seeking those solutions.

Why We Wrote This Book

The HOK Guidebook to Sustainable Design was written to serve as a desktop reference for design professionals, including architects, MEP engineers, interior designers, site planners, landscape architects, civil engineers, and facility consultants. The guide was created by and for design professionals, to support our project work. As such, it is an ongoing work in progress that represents our evolving knowledge of these issues.

As we have been working to address sustainable design issues and opportunities in our work, we have come to understand that we need two things: a greater base of information to inform our decision making, and a revised and expanded design process. Both are needed; without a deeper understanding of the myriad impacts our buildings have on the global environment, our communities, and our homes and workplaces, we are unable to see where the opportunities are for improvement. Likewise, without a design process that is more inclusive and more rigorous in the pursuit of integrated design solutions that require multidisciplinary collaboration, sustainable design cannot be realized and developed fully.

We hope that this book will demystify the sustainable design process and make it more tangible to designers, facility managers, and owners alike. We have outlined a process for all members of the design team that provides specific guidance at each stage of the design process and highlights the collaboration required to create an integrated response.

How to Use This Book

The material in this book has been organized to allow for easy use as a reference document. This Introduction provides an overview of issues that includes "Ten Simple Things You Can Do," a list summarizing the broad range of issues designers should consider as part of a sustainable design approach. The following chapters describe sustainable design goal setting, the economics of green design, and the sustainable design process.

The second part of the book contains design guidance information, which is organized as a series of checklists and project actions. The checklists identify what needs to be done, phase by phase, to meet the project's sustainable design goals. The checklists enable all team members to keep track of issues; project managers can use the checklists to organize the design effort.

The project actions, on the other hand, provide detailed information on how each of the issues on the checklist should be implemented. A graphic key indicates which team members would typically be responsible for implementing the action. Actions that identify more than one responsible team member indicate that collaboration is called for to address the issue properly.

The third part of the book contains case studies of HOK projects in a uniform format that mirrors the format of the design guide. The projects that were selected represent both new construction and renovation projects for a broad range of project types, including office buildings, interiors, research laboratories, courthouses, museums, a stadium, a resort, and urban planning. While most of the projects are built, some of them are still in design or under construction at the time of this printing.

The last part of the book contains a detailed glossary and references for further research. The reference list of books, periodicals, and Internet sources is intentionally concise, to provide readers with our recommendation of the best and most accessible resources currently available.

 TEN SIMPLE THINGS YOU CAN DO

① Select and Develop Sites to Promote Livable Communities
Consider regional land-use patterns and impacts to the watershed and wildlife habitat when selecting sites. Seek out opportunities to redevelop existing sites, structures, and infrastructure. Develop links to public transit and strategies to develop pedestrian-friendly, mixed-use communities. Provide areas of dedicated open space, and greenways and flyways for wildlife.

② Develop Flexible Designs to Enhance Building Longevity
Consider future needs and design in the flexibility to accommodate them through the use of modular planning and flexible building infrastructures for HVAC, power, and communications. Design for ease of expansion.

③ Use Natural Strategies to Protect and Restore Water Resources
Design the site to limit disruption to existing vegetated areas, and use natural stormwater treatment systems such as bioretention, bioswales, pervious paving, and vegetated rooftops to purify runoff and promote groundwater recharge.

④ Improve Energy Efficiency While Ensuring Thermal Comfort

Improve the building envelope and develop passive solar strategies to improve comfort and reduce energy demand first; then optimize energy efficiency of HVAC systems. Use energy analysis to refine the design, and utilize full systems building commissioning to ensure that systems perform as designed. Coordinate daylighting with high-efficiency electric lighting and smart controls.

⑤ Reduce Environmental Impacts Related to Energy Use

Explore opportunities to reduce reliance on fossil fuels and to use cleaner sources of power. Consider cogeneration, fuel cells, photovoltaics, solar hot water, and other renewable energy sources, and explore opportunities to use green power. When evaluating building systems options, consider overall source energy usage.

⑥ Promote Occupant Health and Well-being in the Indoor Environment

Enhance the indoor environment by providing a connection to nature and daylight, improved lighting and acoustics, and improved indoor air quality. Develop systems and detailing to ensure thermal comfort and avoid future microbial contamination. Use natural ventilation and/or HVAC systems that promote effective ventilation, and consider systems that promote occupant control.

⑦ Conserve Water and Consider Water Reuse Systems

Conserve water with the use of low-flow plumbing fixtures and water-efficient appliances and HVAC equipment. Consider collection of rainwater, reuse of gray water for nonpotable uses, and constructed wetlands for natural wastewater treatment.

⑧ Use Environmentally Preferable Building Materials

Evaluate the environmental impacts, resource efficiency, and performance of proposed building materials over their full life cycle. Seek out nontoxic materials from local, renewable, sustainably acquired resources that minimize waste and pollution from manufacturing, installation, and maintenance. Use wood products from independently certified sustainably managed sources.

⑨ Use Appropriate Plant Material

Use plant material native to the region's climate, soils, and water availability to ensure survival while reducing maintenance and irrigation requirements. Use native species to the greatest extent possible. Explore opportunities to provide habitat for wildlife and to restore degraded site areas.

⑩ Plan for Recycling During Construction, Demolition, and Occupancy

Provide collection bins for recyclable materials at the point of use on each floor, and a staging area for materials collection at the loading dock. Where appropriate, consider vertical chutes to make collection easier. Require contractors to develop a construction waste management plan prior to construction that identifies licensed companies to recycle materials.

Goals

Sustainable Design Goals for Facilities

Our current standard design practices work against sustainability and fall short in terms of quality. Norms in our industry for thermal comfort, indoor air quality, access to daylight, and long-term durability, for example, can certainly be improved upon. Sustainable design goals provide an alternative vision for the built environment.

Sustainable design recognizes the interdependence of the built and natural environments; it seeks to harness natural energy flows and biological processes, eliminate reliance on fossil fuels and toxic materials, and improve resource efficiency. Because sustainable design is concerned with the quality of our environment as a whole, issues related to land use and community planning are also of primary importance.

Six overarching goals for the environmental improvement of facilities are:

- Protect ecosystems and support restoration of natural systems
- Promote development of livable communities
- Use resources efficiently, including energy, water, land, and materials
- Create healthy indoor environments
- Move toward eliminating waste and pollution
    - in the production of material used in the project
    - in the construction of the project
    - in the use of the project
    - in the ultimate disposal of the building and its components
- Move away from fossil fuels
    - to reduce the use of fossil fuels
    - to increase the use of sustainable resources

Sustainable design goals are essential to guiding the design process, because they define the challenge to the design team by holding up an image of what success would be like. Quantifiable goals can also be used

The HOK Guidebook to Sustainable Design

to target an anticipated level of achievement and serve as motivators for the design team. Without the need to be explicit about the methods that may be used, goal statements establish the metric for success.

- The goal for the S. C. Johnson Wax, Commercial Products Headquarters, was to create the most advanced, environmentally responsible building possible without adding to the overall cost.
- The World Resources Institute's goal was to create a showcase sustainable design project that would demonstrate the potential for improvement within the context of an interior office fit-out. Specifically, the team's goal was to seek out materials, products, and building systems from around the world that represent promising alternatives to typical unsustainable practices—that preserve biological resources, reduce the threat of climate change, and recognize manufacturers and suppliers that are leaders in industry.
- The goals for the University of Wisconsin, Green Bay, project included a reduction of energy consumption by 50 percent compared to comparable buildings, and a goal to demonstrate the latest in photovoltaic technology.
- The General Services Administration (GSA) set as a goal for the expansion of the U.S. Federal Courthouse in Denver to "use the latest available proven technologies for environmentally sensitive design, construction, and operation. It should set a standard and be a model of sustainable design."
- The design goal for the Fort Bonifacio new city master plan was to create an environmentally sensitive metropolis for the twenty-first century and to reduce sprawl, traffic congestion, and reliance on the automobile.
- Monsanto set as a goal that the new Nidus Center for Scientific Research should reflect the commitment to innovation housed within the facility. The team was charged with using cost-effective materials and technologies to create a cutting-edge green building that would earn a rating from the USGBC's LEED Green Building Rating System.
- The design goal for Edificio Malecon, a new office building in Buenos Aires, Argentina, was to create "the most technologically advanced" office building in the city within the context of a traditional speculative building pro forma.

The case studies section of this guide contains descriptions of each of these projects and others that have embraced sustainable design goals in planning, architecture, engineering, interiors, and site design.

Ten Simple Things You Can Do

This list translates the overarching sustainable design goals identified above into a set of issues that are more tangible in terms of how the architecture and planning would be affected. These goals can be used as a framework for preliminary discussions with the design team. A concise version of this list was presented on pages 4–5; following is a more detailed discussion.

1. Select and Develop Sites to Promote Livable Communities

Consider regional land use patterns and impacts to the watershed and wildlife habitat when selecting sites. Give preference to options that redevelop existing sites and structures, and make use of existing infrastructures. Develop links to public transit and strategies to develop pedestrian-friendly, mixed-use, livable communities. To encourage use of mass transit, locate higher-density mixed-use developments around transit nodes, and seek a balance of homes to jobs within communities to reduce commuting distances. To encourage pedestrian circulation, animate streets with retail space at street level, and promote the use of pedestrian networks that connect neighborhoods, offices, schools, and shopping centers.

Respond to the historical and cultural context, to maintain local cultural resources. Look for opportunities to redevelop existing sites and structures, to reduce undisturbed land and the negative effects of suburban sprawl. Provide parks, recreational areas, and conservation easements, to protect open space, and provide greenways and flyways for wildlife.

See Planning and Site Work Checklist and Project Actions for more information.

2. Develop Flexible Designs to Enhance Building Longevity

Design for ease of expansion and reconfiguration. Consider future needs and design in flexibility to accommodate them through the use of modular planning and flexible building infrastructures for HVAC, power, and communications. Avoid the use of fixed cabling, ductwork, and chases that are embedded into the building structure, which can be difficult and costly to change.

Consider the appropriate longevity of the proposed facility, and design accordingly. If the anticipated life span is short, consider possible future uses for the facility and/or design for disassembly. For facilities with a long anticipated life span, design to ease periodic refurbishment and selective replacement of building systems.

See Material Resources Checklist and Project Actions for more information.

3. Use Natural Strategies to Protect and Restore Water Resources

Design the site to limit disruption to existing vegetated areas, and use natural stormwater treatment systems such as bioretention, bioswales, pervious paving, and vegetated rooftops to purify runoff and promote groundwater recharge. Make use of pervious materials and the existing drainage patterns wherever possible. Where space permits, minimize the creation of concentrated stormwater flows by using grassy swales instead of curb and gutter, to encourage water to flow across vegetated areas and improve groundwater recharge.

Consider the impact on water flows on the site when locating buildings, roadways, and site infrastructure to limit disruption to existing natural site drainage patterns. Identify the hundred-year floodplain, wetlands, stream corridors, and aquifer recharge zones as open space preservation areas. Use this understanding to protect wildlife habitat, and provide for natural stormwater treatment.

See Planning and Site Work Checklist and Project Actions for more information.

4. Improve Energy Efficiency While Ensuring Thermal Comfort

Improve the building envelope and develop passive solar strategies to improve comfort and reduce energy demands first; then optimize the energy efficiency of HVAC systems. Engage in energy analysis to refine the design, and full systems building commissioning to ensure that systems perform as designed. Coordinate daylighting with high-efficiency electric lighting and controls.

The key to understanding building performance as a whole is to understand and maximize integration among the various building systems. Begin by carefully and systematically reducing the overall building loads. When all loads have been lowered, then look at mechanical systems. By reducing overall building loads first, you can reduce not only the operational costs but also the first capital costs, as smaller equipment is specified.

A good practice is to work on the orientation and massing of architectural elements first, the building skin second, and finally the glass itself. Consider the use of "super-windows," which can achieve an insulative value of R-12, and new insulation products with low infiltration rates. Make maximum use of building orientation, shading, exterior landscaping, and other passive solar opportunities to reduce overall heating and cooling loads while admitting beneficial daylight.

There have been substantial advances in the efficiency and the quality of lamps and ballasts. Electronic ballasts with T-8 or T-5 lamps or compact fluorescent PLs should be used for standard building lighting. The coloration of fluorescent lamps has improved markedly, so designers no longer need to use incandescent lighting to create a "warm" interior. With incandescent lamps, only 10 percent of the energy emitted is in the form of light—the other 90 percent is heat. LED (light-emitting diode) exit lamps should also be used as a building standard.

Evaluate the lighting efficiency of each program area in terms of watts per square foot (W/SF). Use of daylight combined with occupancy and daylight sensors, dimmable ballasts, and task lighting with reduced ambient light levels can achieve substantial savings not only in the energy required for lighting but also in the cooling that is required as a result of the lighting. General office lighting should be less than 1.1 W/SF connected, and with lighting controls, it may be as low as 0.5 W/SF actual.

Energy analysis should be incorporated into the process from the very beginning of conceptual design to allow the team to understand the energy design challenge that is specific to their building type, program requirements, and climate zone. At this point in time, the use of energy analysis is rare in all but government work, and even then it is rarely used as a design tool. This lack of knowledge is in part a result of the legacy of the separation of architectural and engineering efforts. If your engineering team doesn't regularly use energy modeling, hire a separate energy consultant to work with the team.

See Energy Checklist and Project Actions for more information.

5. Reduce Environmental Impacts Related to Energy Use

Explore opportunities to reduce reliance on fossil fuels and to use cleaner sources of power. Consider use of cogeneration, fuel cells, photovoltaics, solar hot water, and other renewable energy sources. Thermal energy storage systems (such as ice storage) do not contribute to energy efficiency; however, they provide benefits by shifting energy loads to non-peak hours. Load shifting also produces environmental benefits when it reduces reliance on older, dirty power plants that are used during peak hours in many parts of the country.

When evaluating building systems based on energy use and energy cost, consider the overall source energy usage. Source energy reflects the fuel used and pollution generated by the electricity provider, as compared to other fuel source options. Depending on whether the utility uses coal, oil, natural gas, or nuclear energy sources, the environmental impacts will vary substantially. Deregulation complicates the issue; however, in many parts of the country it enables the building owner to choose "green power."

See Energy Checklist and Project Actions for more information.

6. Promote Occupant Health and Well-being in the Indoor Environment

Consider opportunities to enhance the indoor environment by providing building occupants with a connection to nature and natural daylight, improved lighting and acoustics, and improved indoor air quality. Consider use of gardens, landscaped courtyards, green roofs, and views to landscapes beyond. Use natural ventilation and/or HVAC systems that promote ventilation effectiveness, such as underfloor air distribution systems, and consider systems that promote occupant control.

Locate building intake and exhaust locations carefully to avoid contamination. Protect indoor air quality through careful selection of building materials and attention to the way they are installed, finished, and maintained. Good ventilation is also required during installation as well as during the life of the building to avoid the buildup of contaminants. Develop HVAC systems and building detailing to ensure thermal comfort and avoid future microbial contamination by eliminating fleecy materials, including insulations exposed to the airstream and internal duct linings.

See Indoor Environmental Quality Checklist and Project Actions for more information.

7. Conserve Water and Consider Water Reuse Systems

Conserve water with the use of low-flow plumbing fixtures and water-efficient appliances and HVAC equipment, including water-efficient cooling towers. The Energy Policy Act of 1992 outlines current requirements for low-flow fixtures; however, use of aerators and self-closing or electronic faucets and ultra-low-flow fixtures provides additional water savings. Consider the use of waterless fixtures such as waterless urinals and composting toilets where appropriate.

Consider collection of rainwater and reuse of gray water for nonpotable uses. For very large projects, or in areas without existing sewage treatment infrastructure, consider use of on-site constructed wetlands for biological wastewater treatment.

See Water Checklist and Project Actions for more information.

8. Use Environmentally Preferable Building Materials

Evaluate the environmental impacts and resource use of proposed building materials over their full life cycle. Raw material sources, production, and transport to the site, installation and use, and finally disposal or reuse should be questioned and evaluated prior to making a selection. Select preferred materials and products, and require compliance with environmental improvements in the specification, such as VOC limits, minimum recycled content, and avoidance of toxic materials and admixtures.

Seek out nontoxic materials from local, renewable, sustainably acquired resources that minimize pollution from manufacturing, installation, and maintenance. Consider use of regionally appropriate biobased materials such as wheat straw, brick, and wood. Require that all wood used in the project originate from sustainably managed sources that have been independently certified by the Forest Stewardship Council (FSC).

See Material Resources Checklist and Project Actions for more information.

9. Use Appropriate Plant Material

Use plant material adapted to the region's climate, soils, and water availability to ensure survival while reducing maintenance and irrigation requirements. Use native species to the greatest extent possible. Limit use of high maintenance landscaping and maximize the area of natural settings. Overall, protect the natural features of the site. If necessary, restore those that had been previously destroyed. Explore opportunities to provide habitat for wildlife and to restore degraded site areas.

See Planning and Site Work Checklist and Project Actions for more information.

10. Plan for Recycling During Construction/Demolition and Occupancy

It is a matter of experience and perhaps of human nature that if recycling is made easy and convenient, it will probably happen. Provide facilities for recycling at the point of use on each floor (e.g., galleys and copy rooms) and at the loading dock. Commonly recycled materials include white paper, newspapers, aluminum, plastic, glass, and cardboard. Less common but desirable materials to recycle include mixed paper, organic matter, miscellaneous metals, and wood. Consider use of vertical chutes to make collection easy. Plan and allow space for recycling and composting, even if the local recycling industry is not yet ready to accept all of the materials.

Like building waste, construction and demolition waste can be cost-effectively reduced with care and planning. Experience has shown that it

DID YOU KNOW...?

We have decimated 97% of the ancient forests of North America, and globally we are losing 27,000 species a year largely due to the 500,000 trees that are cut every hour in tropical forests.

—Paul Hawken, *The Ecology of Commerce* (New York: HarperCollins, 1993), 29.

is possible to reduce construction waste by 90 percent or more, with corresponding savings to the project. The first step is to contact local waste authorities to identify companies to recycle materials. The second is to calculate the cost of recycling and disposal. The third is to establish procedures to accommodate the existing recycling industry and to expand upon the range and scope of materials recycled. This can be as simple as separate Dumpsters for woods, metals, and drywall scraps, or the use of scrap gypsum as a soil amendment. There are several good construction waste specifications to guide the effort.

See Material Resources Checklist and Project Actions for more information.

Economics

The reason we have seen such a tremendous surge of interest in sustainable design is that it is the right thing to do, it improves building performance, *and* it also makes sense economically.

Many of the projects featured as case studies in this book have been done on very modest budgets. We have found that sustainable design does not have to cost more. Using the design guidance in the checklists and project actions in this book, design teams will be able to identify many opportunities for improved building performance and reduced environmental impacts that are cost neutral and do not impact the economics of the project at all. It is just a matter of developing an increased awareness of sustainable design issues and opportunities.

This guide also provides numerous examples of projects where sustainable design strategies have led the design teams to discover synergies that result in first cost savings *and* operational cost savings. However, when the owner has the ability to make decisions based on life cycle economics, the range of opportunities does expand. We strongly advocate for a life cycle approach to decision making wherever possible.

We have also found that the sustainable design strategies add real value to the projects. Each of the case studies included in this book contains a section on the economics surrounding the project, and each concludes with a section on the benefits of the design. Many of these provide insights into the broad range of benefits that result from a sustainable approach.

Sustainable Design Does Not Have to Cost More

First, there is a lot that can be done within traditional first cost constraints. Integrated design solutions allow for cost shifting to occur within a conventional budget envelope. For example, increased expenditures on the building envelope and improved lighting can lead to reductions in the size and therefore the cost of mechanical systems.

A design process that is more rigorous in seeking out efficiencies and eliminating waste also provides economic benefits. Many of these savings are small when considered in terms of the overall budget; however, they can allow for meaningful upgrades in other areas. For example, low-impact site development leads to reduced earthwork and more balanced cut and fill, elimination of irrigation systems, and reduced stormwater requirements. The funds that would have gone to installation of an irrigation system, for instance, can be shifted to another part of the budget.

EXAMPLES

- *S. C. Johnson Wax, Commercial Products Headquarters, in Racine:* Reduced energy consumption saved more than $100,000 per year, and use of indigenous, low-maintenance landscaping saves more than $3,000 per acre in annual maintenance costs. Energy-efficient design strategies did not add to the project's cost; in fact, at $139/SF, the project is 10–15 percent below the U.S. average cost for traditional lab and office buildings.

- *Federal Reserve Bank of Minneapolis:* Most of the sustainable design features added no cost to the project, and many of them led to reduced first cost. The use of triple-paned high-performance glass, for example, not only reduced long-term energy use, but allowed for downsizing of HVAC systems and a reduction in the building's overall capital cost by eliminating almost all perimeter radiant heating systems.

- *Sam M. Gibbons United States Courthouse in Tampa:* This courthouse, at just $146/SF, is one of the most cost-effective courthouses built in recent years. The design team was able to free up funds for building enhancements by reducing cost in other areas. For example, sun shading and low-E glazing at the new courthouse reduced the peak load for cooling by 180 tons, which enabled the team to reduce the size of the mechanical plant.

- *Monsanto Company A3 Leadership Team offices in St. Louis:* Approximately 50 percent of the ceiling grid and tile from the existing office space was salvaged during demolition, cleaned, and reused. This saved resources, reduced waste, and reduced project costs as well.

- *National Wildlife Federation in Reston:* Bioretention areas in the parking lot naturally treat stormwater and contribute to a network of rich and diverse wildlife habitat areas on the site. It did not, however, add cost to the project, because the bioretention areas enabled the team to build a much smaller stormwater retention area, or dry pond.

A Shift to Life Cycle Economics Expands Opportunities

Even though it is not necessary to spend more to create a green building, a shift to life cycle economics does expand the opportunities for improving our buildings. By considering first cost together with operating and maintenance costs, periodic replacement, and residual value, designers help their clients choose options that make sense over the long term.

Long-term owner-occupants of buildings clearly have an interest in life cycle economics, and speculative builders can also benefit from increased life cycle value, provided the added value can be measured and translated into increased market value.

Before the project budget is fixed, the issue of life cycle economics should be clearly addressed. Will decision making be based on life cycle costing or first cost economics? This is a fundamental distinction. Then, if life cycle costing will be used, assumptions regarding the life cycle, discount rates, fuel cost escalations, and so on need to be clearly established.

If life cycle costing is going to be used to justify decision making, it is very useful to have a mechanism to increase funding for the project if it is warranted. In some cases life cycle costing is used within fixed budget constraints. Another approach is to work within a fixed budget that has a contingency amount set aside to pay for life cycle cost-effective upgrades. Yet another approach is to secure special financing for life cycle cost-effective upgrades through energy service contractors (ESCOs).

EXAMPLES

- *Stadium Australia:* Use of innovative, ecological design strategies reduced energy use by over 30 percent and potable water use by over 50 percent, and boosted the recycling of waste streams. These strategies required some additional first cost investment; however, the payback for this project will provide significant economic benefits for years to come.

- *U.S. Federal Courthouse Expansion in Denver:* In planning for the courthouse expansion, the GSA made a conscious decision to challenge conventional thinking about building economics in order to improve the building in terms of both conventional and environmental performance. While not every green design feature provides a payback, in aggregate all of the sustainable design measures together produce life cycle cost savings that pay back the initial investment within twenty-five years.

- *U.S. Environmental Protection Agency campus in Research Triangle Park:* Cost-effective energy efficiency measures are expected to save more than $1 million per year overall. The lighting design alone saves approximately $200,000 per year, with a payback of less than one year. Water-efficient cooling towers that reduce chemical use and save over 4 million gallons of water per year have a payback of less than two years.

Sustainable Design Improves the Value of Buildings

In addition to reduced construction, operating, and maintenance costs, sustainable design produces buildings that are more valuable to owners and occupants. As a rule of thumb, reductions in annual operating costs can be multiplied by 10 (capitalization rate) to estimate increased building value.

While some of the benefits can be easily quantified, others are more qualitative. The sustainable design features tend to produce a better indoor environment that improves productivity and employee retention. Improved indoor air quality reduces the risk of future liability and also contributes to happy, productive building occupants. Finally, the buildings are easier to lease and sell because they are viewed very positively by the public.

- *The Nature Conservancy in Arlington:* Their new headquarters building transformed an underutilized site with contaminated soils in a quickly emerging inner-ring suburb into an amenity for the community. The real estate values adjacent to the new Nature Conservancy headquarters have increased by 10–15 percent in less than one year since the project has been completed.
- *University of Wisconsin, Green Bay:* Extensive daylighting will create energy savings in excess of $18,000 per year, providing an economic payback in approximately five years. The real benefit, however, is the greatly enhanced interior environment, which provides a much better environment for learning.
- *The World Resources Institute (WRI) in Washington, D.C.:* The office lighting selected for WRI provides comfortable direct/indirect lighting, and integral lighting controls for occupancy sensing, daylight dimming, and personal dimming. At about 0.4 watts per square foot, the system also provides energy savings of 77 percent compared to the building standard. This high-performance lighting system, which was equivalent in cost to the standard 2 × 2 recessed fluorescent downlighting and more energy efficient, produced much better lighting. Staff appreciate the aesthetics as well as the ability to set lighting levels based on their personal preferences.

Many Creative Financing Options Currently Exist for Green Buildings

Many design professionals see cost as the primary impediment to green design. In fact, in some ways green buildings are easier to finance than standard buildings. A number of creative financing mechanisms are available to teams that are willing to seek them out. Some of these include utility incentive programs, manufacturer discounts, government programs, and energy service contractors (ESCOs).

- *Federal Office Building at Foley Square in New York:* At $3 million, the rebate paid in recognition of the Foley Square building's energy savings to the General Services Administration (GSA) was the largest rebate ever provided by a U.S. utility.
- *Smithsonian Institution, National Air and Space Museum, Dulles Center:* Because the use of photovoltronics could not be justified on conventional life cycle economics, a separate fund-raising effort was initiated to support their use. BP Solarex has donated photovoltaic cells and inverters for the building, and the Virginia Initiative for Solar Energy, a partnership between state utilities and the photovoltaic manufacturers located in the state, will provide for some additional cost sharing.

The case studies in this book verify that the economic benefits of sustainable design are real. The next section of this book will provide insight into *how* to do it.

Process

Designing Sustainability

The model for sustainable design is nature itself. Nature is efficient and effective by design, essentially producing no waste. As we seek to reshape our own processes to eliminate waste, nature is a logical model to study.

To adopt nature as our model, we need to convert our linear processes to cyclical processes. The cyclical model of production, for example, has been adopted by the German automotive industry. All materials for a new car are coded to allow easy identification for recycling. When its useful life is finished, a car is returned to disassembly plants, where it is broken down into component parts to be reprocessed and reassembled into a new car. BMW expects 99.9 percent reuse of material when today's cars are recycled. The German electronics industry is following a similar course. This use of closed-loop systems is being repeated in a growing number of industries that are involved with the building industry, including carpet, furniture, and some equipment manufacturers. The next challenge is to reformulate the way buildings and communities are designed, constructed, and operated, to ensure that the entire building process is itself cyclical.

A green building or community may not necessarily look much different; however, it relates to the world around it in new and more benign ways. At the least, it does a minimum of damage to the world in its construction, use, and ultimate reuse. At their best, such buildings and communities help heal the damage that has already been done. See the case studies section of this guide for examples of projects that have embraced these goals in terms of planning, architecture, engineering, interiors, and site design.

The new sustainable design process demands that every product, process, and procedure be questioned and reviewed from a new perspective that includes the ecological and human health impact of decisions. Doing so can result in substantial improvement from an environmental point of view, and it can also lead to more pleasing and productive environments for users combined with savings for the owner.

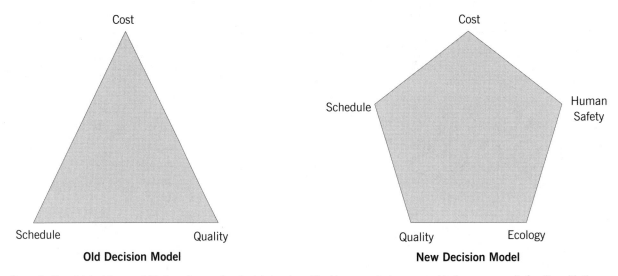

Figure 1. *The old decision model is based on cost, schedule, and quality. However, designers need to become equally familiar with the effect decisions have on the environment and human health. The new decision model integrates human health and safety as well as ecology as deliberate considerations for the decision-making process.*

The process outline below is intended to help you to systematically change the way you and your organization go about the business of designing and delivering the buildings and communities of the future.

Going Beyond the Minimums

Our communities have been formed by minimal, and sometimes nonexistent, planning requirements that frequently ignore the complex interrelationships between the built environment and the natural world or the long-term implications of the decisions that they influence. Building performance has also been measured almost exclusively by minimum code requirements. In other words, the minimum has also been seen as the maximum. Nonetheless, an inefficient building will put thousands of tons of pollutants into the air, a site that doesn't manage its stormwater effectively will cause off-site problems, and communities that do not offer transportation alternatives will continue to suffer from automobile congestion and pollution.

By going beyond minimum requirements and focusing instead on optimum performance, we redefine our design problems in a way that opens up many exciting possibilities. We need to challenge ourselves to search for creative solutions that will continue to move beyond minimum performance. The use of integrated design opens the door to solutions that can provide synergistic benefits. Once the shift has been made to a design process based on optimization instead of minimum performance, the design task becomes much more open-ended.

Most of the procedures listed in the design guidance section of this guide are easily accomplished within the framework of existing technologies and budgets. Fully implemented, these will significantly improve the environmental performance of our buildings and the livability of our communities, while also lowering overall costs. However, the incremental improvements that can be easily accomplished at this point in time should be taken as our new "minimums."

In energy use, for example, the initial goal is to use less energy, to be more efficient. The long-term goal, however, is to move from the use of fossil fuels to the efficient use of renewable energy sources. Great advances have been made in the last decade in both the efficiency and the cost of photovoltaics and wind power. It is now possible to think of buildings and communities that are not only efficient but energy neutral to the world around them; in some cases, buildings and communities can become net *producers* of energy.

The Need for Integrated Design

We should not expect to produce fundamentally new buildings using the same traditional design process. In order to effect change in our building designs, the project delivery process itself must change from a serial collection of discrete tasks performed with little interaction between players to a collaborative and self-conscious effort to integrate design strategies between all disciplines and all players in the project delivery process.

To best achieve the goal of integrated design, the definition of the building team needs to expand in order to overcome the lack of communication present in the traditional design process. Integrated design demands a more inclusive team working much more closely together than is traditionally the case. Community representatives, future users, contractors and subcontractors, and future maintenance staff can all add considerably to the success of the final design solution. For example, when the contractor has been included in the design phase and understands the goals of the project, challenges and calls for substitutions can be reduced because the overall design strategies will be better understood. On the other hand, when the overall project goals are understood, the contractor can often offer creative solutions that will limit environmental impacts during construction.

To improve overall performance, the team needs to improve not just the functioning of the individual parts but the functioning of the whole as a system. Integrated design means capturing the benefits of multiple systems designed to work effectively together rather than separately. For example, overall comfort can be raised and energy consumption reduced if site design, lighting, window fenestration, air delivery systems, and furniture are thought of together rather than as discrete parts of the project. However, to capture multiple benefits requires the engineers, architects, and interior designers to work *together* to design these components of the system. The result of such coordination can frequently lower the first cost as well as long-term cost.

Integrated design leads to the discovery of design synergies that multiply benefits. For example, integration between mechanical engineers, civil engineers, traffic engineers, and architects can lead to successful low-impact site development that preserves more open space while also reducing costs for stormwater management. And a raised-floor air distribution system can lower long-term operating costs while also providing for wire management and improved thermal comfort. When the budget is evaluated from a holistic perspective, rather than simply line by line, the raised-floor distribution system can also reduce first costs when it is integrated with the design of HVAC and furniture systems.

Measuring Performance

Benchmark values allow the entire design team to better understand the value of proposed design solutions. A variety of benchmarking systems have been developed to track typical and improved performance in terms of sustainable design, and many of them are referred to in the project actions sections of this design guide. One very useful tool for evaluating environmental performance is the LEED Green Building Rating System.

LEED Green Building Rating System

In 1993, the U.S. Green Building Council was formed by a consortium of building owners, suppliers, contractors, governmental agencies, architects, engineers, and others involved in the business of creating buildings. The purpose was to promote a mainstream change in the industry toward sustainable facilities. One of the first steps the Council took was the development of a green building rating system. That system is LEED, which stands for Leadership in Energy and Environmental Design. It has been in development for the last several years and was formally introduced to the public in the spring of 2000. However, it has been envisioned as a living document that will be updated every three years.

LEED was created through a consensus process involving many stakeholders. It is seen as a transition document to help move the U.S. building industry toward more sustainable practices. It is rigorous, transparent, and easy to use. Design team members can track their progress toward earning a LEED rating throughout the course of the project themselves, without the need for specialty consultants. As such, it can be used as a tool to introduce, promote, and guide comprehensive and integrated green building design.

The rating system is based on a series of prerequisites and credits. The design team must verify that all of the prerequisites and at least 40 percent of the credits have been met to get a bronze rating. Likewise, 51–60 percent of the credits earns a silver rating, 61–80 percent earns a gold rating, and 81 percent or more earns a platinum rating. Most of the credits are performance-based, which means that they measure the degree of improvement relative to a recognized standard, rather than requiring the use of specific design strategies or technologies.

DID YOU KNOW...?

Taken as a whole, climate-sensitive design using available technologies in the US could cut total energy use by 60% in commercial buildings.

—Worldwatch Paper 124 David Malin Roodman and Nicholas Lessen, "Building Revolution: How Ecology and Health Concerns Are Transforming Construction" (Washington, DC: Worldwatch Institute, 1995), 38.

For more information on LEED and a copy of the rating system to download, see the USGBC website at http://www.usgbc.org.

The New Design Process: Seven Key Steps

At the moment, the impacts of the built environment on the natural world are not well understood, and the best sustainable design solutions cannot be determined based on intuition alone. This new design process has been shaped to help ensure that sustainable design issues will be understood by all team members, the issues addressed, and solutions found. Awareness of these issues is new, the relationships are new, the holistic view of the built environment is new, and many of the products and materials going into our built environment are new. It would be easy to miss many problems and opportunities without an extra measure of care in the way we approach the planning, design, and construction process.

All of the issues relating to team formation, communication, design procedures, and design tools should be reexamined and reevaluated. There are seven key steps in the revised facility delivery process where this extra care and deliberation are called for.

1. Team formation
2. Education and goal setting
3. Gathering information
4. Design optimization
5. Documents and specification
6. Bidding, construction, and commissioning
7. Operations and maintenance

1. Team Formation

The first task is to assemble the full design team, including consultants and others. Ideally, you will be able to put together an entire team of individuals already experienced in and committed to sustainable design and experienced in working collaboratively. As with most ideals, this is not likely to be the case for some time. In most cases, the team will be made up of individuals and firms with little prior experience with sustainable design and a great deal of uncertainty about how to proceed. This lack of experience should not dissuade anyone. Most pioneering green projects—including many of the case studies in this book—were done by teams who were learning as they went. What matters most is a commitment to improve the design, and care in the approach to each aspect of the project.

This having been said, there are some things that can be controlled in assembling teams.

- *Experience.* Demonstrated experience in sustainable design is highly desirable and should be sought out wherever possible. The experience may reside not within a firm as a whole but only with some

Assembling the Team

individuals within a firm. If this is the case, make sure that these people will actually be available for the project.

- *Attitude.* The next most important thing to experience is attitude. A positive attitude toward creating a truly new and innovative project is an extremely important part of moving toward sustainable design solutions. While there are increasingly more resources to help along the way, there will be frequent frustrations, dead ends, and pressure to fall back on the tried-and-true. The willingness to persevere through these obstacles is critical.

- *Energy modeling.* Good energy modeling capacity within the team is essential for nearly every project, and ideally this capability resides within the engineering team. Most engineering firms, however, rely exclusively on energy modeling software supplied by equipment manufacturers. Those programs are intended primarily to size equipment and do not adequately model the complex interactions that influence the overall performance of the design. If the engineering design firm doesn't have the capability to use advanced energy modeling tools in-house, an energy modeling specialist should be enlisted to work with the entire team as the design develops.

- *Specialty consultants.* There are many other specialty consultants who should be considered to supplement the team, depending on the project and the expertise within the core team. An expert in native plantings may supplement the knowledge of the landscape planners. Experts in constructed wetlands may help the civil engineers and the site designers. Specialists in daylighting design might supplement a more conventional lighting designer.

- *Help getting started.* If the team is completely new to the issues of sustainable design, consider retaining expertise to help get the team off on the right foot. There are many resources to choose from, including nonprofit organizations, sustainable design consultants, and design firms that offer this service. Initial help could be as simple as an hourlong overview of issues and opportunities, or it could be a more involved effort that helps the team define goals and objectives for the project and sets the initial direction. The goal is to lower the learning curve for everyone involved.

Sustainable Design Champions on the Team

For any project to be successful, many team members will need to contribute their expertise and insights to the development of environmentally preferable solutions. Sustainable design advocates should be identified to oversee the effort to improve environmental performance and to help coordinate the contributions of all members of the team. Ideally, a sustainable design advocate should be recruited from within the A/E team to focus the design effort, and one should also be recruited from within the ranks of the owner's team to represent the owner's perspective and to assist with design reviews.

Collaborative and Inventive Working Environment

Once the team is assembled, the next step is to ensure that the team works collaboratively and inventively from the beginning. This is critical to achieving integrated design. The objective is to create a working atmosphere that challenges conventional thinking and standard solutions.

By including a larger group of participants from the beginning of the project, we can hope to achieve the degree of understanding, consensus, and cooperation that is required to provide integrated and optimal solutions. Only by working consciously and deliberately at improving environmental performance can the design and construction industry begin to acquire an intuitive approach to these issues over time.

EXAMPLE

- In the S. C. Johnson Wax Commercial Products Headquarters, the entire team was largely in place from the early programming stage of the project. This included the construction manager staff, key subcontractors and suppliers, and the eventual building manager and his staff, as well as the traditional design team and the owner. Very few of the team members had any previous knowledge of these issues. Initially, many attended the early work sessions with little understanding and perhaps little enthusiasm. In time, however, the atmosphere changed as individuals began to see not only how they could contribute, but that their help was welcome. Many of the ultimate successes of the project came from the often unexpected interactions between team members who would traditionally never have gotten to know each other. For example, the furniture supplier and the field superintendent found a way to deliver new furniture to the site without packaging. In another instance, the piping subcontractor was able to make recommendations to the plumbing designers and the structural engineers that made it easier to use standard-length material and thus eliminated a large percentage of the usual waste.

2. Project Initiation: Education and Goal Setting

Project initiation is the start-up phase of the project for the design team. It is the time when design consultants, including architects, engineers, and interior designers, are introduced to the project requirements. It is an ideal time to focus on educating the team about sustainable design issues and opportunities, and on setting goals.

Education

Education of the entire team is critical to achieve a common understanding of sustainable design issues. Use the LEED system as one basis for discussion and evaluation. In whatever form it takes, the educational session must cover the basic environmental problems. Opportunities related to design and construction should precede the discussion of environmental goals. Time with the entire team should be taken to share information on environmental issues and their impact on the project as a whole. This phase should include an extensive review of similar projects so that everyone can quickly see what others are doing and how to bridge the gap between theory and practice. Once the team has built a common vocabulary and an understanding of the issues involved, it is ready to develop environmental goals.

Goal Setting

The next step is to establish the goals themselves. While goal setting at the beginning of a project is common, sustainable design goal setting is not. Sustainable design goals should be identified as distinct from other project goals so that they receive the attention they deserve. In years to come, we can expect that project goals and sustainable design goals will be one and the same. This is clearly not the case today, when merely the term "sustainable design goals" will be new to most people in the industry. Sustainable design goals should have their own focus to allow the entire team to arrive at a common understanding.

Goals will tend to be very broad at the beginning—protection of the existing natural environment, for example. Wherever possible, these goals can and should be specific. Water usage, construction waste recycling, VOC emissions, and energy use are all easily quantifiable. Part of the education process should be designed to allow benchmark comparisons on these and other items. In this way, the team can be challenged to set appropriately aggressive goals. By setting specific numeric goals, we can create the necessary yardsticks by which to measure the progress of the design and overall performance. See the checklists in this guide as lists of issues to be considered during project goal setting.

EXAMPLES

- A goal for the new academic building at University of Wisconsin at Green Bay was to use less than 50 percent of the energy of a comparable building that met the stringent Wisconsin Commercial Buildings energy code.
- A goal for Monsanto's Nidus Center was to achieve a rating from the U.S. Green Building Council's LEED Green Building Rating System.

3. Gathering Information

At the outset of the project, the team should organize the base of information that will be used for decision making. This requires some focused research time, clear discussion of the preferred method for evaluating cost-effective options, and a comprehensive review of the design criteria.

Clarify Decision-making Criteria

Design criteria are the set of requirements and standards that guide the design. Typically these criteria are accepted as givens, and design options are explored only within those parameters. However, many of the solutions that reduce cost *and* environmental impacts come about by challenging basic design criteria, such as lighting power densities, plug loads, parking requirements, stormwater guidelines, and so on. Voluntary industry guidelines produced by the American Society of Heating, Refrigerating, and Air Conditioning Engineers (ASHRAE), the U.S. Green Building Council, and other organizations should be sought out and incorporated into the design criteria where appropriate.

Life cycle cost analysis should be strongly encouraged to determine the highest-value solutions. The team needs to define the duration of the life cycle to be used for economic analysis and the discount rate that will be used for considering the time value of money.

Start early to identify resources needed to inform the development of the project along the way. See the lists of resources at the end of this guide for suggestions of useful books, periodicals, and Internet resources.

Sustainable design requires the design team to consider a larger number of issues in the decision-making process. Supplemental research is required to understand the environmental impacts associated with design options and to identify preferred approaches. In some areas, such as energy and water conservation, the ongoing research required is minimal once the design issues and methodology have been established; however, ongoing research into green building materials selection and specification and emerging technologies is required because the products, technologies, and associated costs change rapidly.

Of particular note should be local or regional resources. These can be invaluable and time-saving assets to the project. For example, a growing number of states and local communities have published guides identifying firms that will take various components of the construction waste stream for recycling. Some utilities have incentive programs in place encouraging new technologies, energy conservation initiatives, and demonstration projects.

- Research by the team led to a partnership and cost-sharing agreement with the Wisconsin Public Service Corporation, the local utility for the University of Wisconsin, Green Bay, project, as the utility is looking toward a future involving distributed power generation and wanted an opportunity to test photovoltaics.

EXAMPLE

4. Optimization

Optimization is the process of questioning each component and process to achieve the most with the least expenditure of resources. Design optimization involves the careful evaluation of a broad range of solutions so that the best can be discerned from other, less promising options. The best solutions will contain synergies between design disciplines, where a single strategy will provide multiple benefits.

We are familiar with this process in terms of a financial budget through the normal process of systematic cost estimating and value engineering employed throughout the design process. Generally, the profession is not at all familiar with this process as a method for meeting environmental goals. For example, while we cannot imagine starting a project without a clear understanding of the financial budget, an energy budget is rarely understood and even less commonly discussed and evaluated as part of the design process. One can imagine what would happen if the financial budget was not discussed until the project was complete; it certainly would not be optimized. The same is true of energy use, water use, or any of the other resource conservation measures quantified in the goal-setting phase.

Furthermore, optimization should be considered for systems rather than simply for components. For example, energy minimization must include an active and informed integration of internal equipment loads, lighting, exterior shape and massing, exterior skin, landscaping, and site work. Because the many refinements that lead to an optimized design cannot be determined intuitively, simulation tools are needed to predict future performance.

A process is outlined below for optimizing energy use. This process is designed to get beyond standard solutions. A similar process should be applied to other aspects of the project, including water use, waste generation, materials, site impacts, and indoor environmental quality, where appropriate. The key to improving the overall environmental performance of the facility is to follow a deliberately self-conscious process to question each component of the design.

See the project actions in this guide for specific recommendations on how to achieve design optimization.

Energy Optimization Process

Energy consumption in buildings is the result of a complex set of interrelationships between the external environment, the shape and character of the building components, its equipment and other internal heat sources, and finally the occupant density and patterns of use of the building. Understanding and manipulating these interrelationships is the key to reducing energy use while also improving comfort for the building's users. The following energy optimization process has been developed so that information will be available to the design team when it is most useful, to guide decision making as the building and its HVAC systems are developed.

The best way to understand the complex interactions in a building is through the use of a dynamic energy model, such as the U.S. Department of Energy's DOE-2 building energy analysis simulation. It is one of the most sophisticated building energy analysis software tools now available, and it has spawned a number of user-friendly commercial interface programs such as VisualDOE, EZ DOE, and Power DOE. DOE-2 allows the user to model all aspects of the building, including form, orientation, equipment loads, patterns of use, and the like. A dynamic model, it calculates the complex interactions between these various elements on a 24-hour, 365-day basis, allowing the design team to understand relationships that are impossible to see in most other predictive systems.

The key to optimizing building performance as a whole is to carefully and systematically reduce the overall building loads and then to maximize the integration of the various building systems. Generally, the first place to look is the overall architectural organization, orientation, massing, roof forms, and so on. Second, look at the building envelope. Third, carefully look at and reduce all interior cooling loads. When all loads have been lowered, then look at mechanical systems. By reducing overall building loads first, you can reduce not only the operational costs, but also the first capital costs, as smaller equipment is specified.

The following steps summarize the process for systematically reducing overall energy consumption. A more detailed description of this process follows in the Energy Project Actions.

Step 1. Gather Information

Collect programmatic information, such as space use, population, hours of occupancy, expected equipment, et cetera. Also collect climate data, utility rate structures, energy code requirements, site information, and any preliminary building assumptions, such as high-rise versus low-rise and floorplate configuration.

Step 2. Create Base Case Energy Model

Use DOE-2 or other dynamic energy model to create a base case energy model that is specific to the program and the site, and that reflects a design that is minimally compliant with the energy code requirements. Because the design is not very developed at this stage, many assumptions are made by default positions within the program.

Step 3. Characterize Energy Use and Energy Cost

Using the base case energy model, generate simple pie charts that describe the energy consumption and energy cost by end use for the building. It is important to understand where energy is being used in the facility. For example, buildings can be dominated by internal loads, envelope loads, or ventilation requirements, among others.

Then develop a set of elimination parametrics so that the interaction between components can be seen and the largest targets for energy improvement can be identified. In this analysis, selected components of the energy model are "turned off" one by one. To demonstrate the potential impact of each factor on overall energy use, the equipment load is hypothetically set at zero, occupancy is set to none, glazing is eliminated, the exterior wall is set to an infinite R-value, and so on. This information provides the design team with some base information on potential energy and cost savings that can be used to guide the development of proposed energy efficiency measures (EEMs).

Step 4. Develop Alternative Design Solutions

Identify strategies to reduce the energy loads for all components of the project, with the major energy uses as the first targets. If lighting and cooling are significant loads, daylighting strategies will be of primary interest. If solar gain is a critical factor, site orientation, landscaping, and building-integrated shading devices should be looked at carefully. Use the DOE-2 energy model to determine the energy savings that result from each alternate compared to the base case. Then analyze the cost and benefits of these strategies to identify the best options.

Because the most valuable solutions capture the benefits of synergies between components, evaluate whole building systems, not just individual strategies. Use this early analysis of potential energy design features to inform the development of the architecture and HVAC systems.

Step 5. Repeat the Process

Because the design process is iterative, the energy analysis needs to be repeated several times to achieve the best results. With various energy conservation measures now incorporated into the design, the relative balance of loads will have changed, and a new set of energy use characterization needs to be developed. The newest iteration will show that the energy loads and costs, which had once been the most significant, may be reduced, with other loads taking their place as the primary targets. A new set of energy conservation strategies needs to be developed to reduce these new loads, and new design synergies may suggest themselves at this point.

This process of (1) identifying the major loads, (2) identifying energy reduction strategies to reduce these loads, and (3) refining the design is done repeatedly until no more savings can be found. Throughout this process, the team should challenge the conventional "law of diminishing returns" and seek out solutions based on design synergies to reduce or even eliminate costly mechanical systems. When this design effort is complete, a final DOE-2 run is made incorporating all of the energy efficiency measures included in the design.

Step 6. Follow Up

Just as with a cost model, it is important to follow the progress of the design with periodic updates to the energy model to ensure that the energy budget is maintained. At appropriate stages in the development of contract documents, the various energy-saving design strategies should be reviewed, the DOE-2 energy model modified if necessary, and new runs made to evaluate the status of the design. If new energy efficiency measures can be identified, these may be reviewed and incorporated if the schedule permits.

5. Documents and Specifications

Once a set of design decisions has been made, it is necessary to record these in the contract documents and specifications. While this is familiar and common, we can face some difficulties with sustainable design strategies that make use of new products and processes that will require the development of new specifications. Specifications for the handling of construction waste, for example, will be new to many communities. It will be necessary to tailor the specifications to the local community to avoid misunderstandings and costly misinterpretations. Other examples include the allowable VOC emissions of paints and other products, avoidance of toxic materials, and sequencing of finish installation to guard against the introduction of contaminants into the completed building. Materials specifications are particularly dependent upon the dynamics of the current market of environmentally preferable products, requiring continuous updating for each new project. See the project actions in this guide for recommendations on documentation and specification language.

A parallel concern is that the number of people involved in producing the documents will generally expand. It is particularly important that the overall goal of the project be systematically communicated to the new players and that the individual technical strategies be understood. Extra care needs to be taken to ensure that the selected solutions are detailed properly.

6. Bidding, Construction, and Commissioning

Bidding, buyout, procurement, construction, and commissioning are particularly important steps in delivering an environmentally responsible facility. The process can become complicated simply because the number of people involved suddenly expands greatly as suppliers, subcontractors, and others enter the picture. With each new player, we likely face a new lack of understanding of the project environmental goals and the established process. Some of the materials and methods may be new and little understood. Substitutions, many not meeting the basic requirements, will be offered as a matter of course. Likewise, many of the construction procedures, while not difficult or more expensive in themselves, may be new to the larger construction team.

The value of the initial team formation and goal-setting sessions becomes evident at this phase. The construction professionals become the first line of defense in sorting out viable alternatives from those that are not practical. Where possible, ongoing education and explanation of goals should be incorporated for new members of the team, subcontractors, suppliers, and the construction workers themselves. Just as there are sessions for new workers concerning job site procedures and safety, there should be sessions on environmental goals. The greater the understanding of the overall goals, the greater will be the effort to understand and incorporate the products and procedures called for in the project. Unlike many topics, protection of the environment has the capacity to quickly command the attention, respect, and help of most people. This can only happen, however, if information is shared and the help requested. See the project actions in this guide for recommendations on issues to consider during construction.

Commissioning is a systematic process for ensuring that all building systems perform interactively, as a system, according to the contract documents, the design intent, and the owner's needs. Commissioning is increasingly becoming a common part of the start-up of a new building. Ideally the commissioning process begins early in design and continues through construction, acceptance, and the warranty period to be truly effective. See the project actions in this guide for recommendations on commissioning.

7. Operations and Maintenance

The typical project ends for most professionals shortly after the opening festivities are over. Yet in many ways things are just beginning. Studies show that if buildings were only operated as they were originally designed, on average a 20 percent savings in energy could be achieved. Often this does not happen because those operating the building systems were generally not part of the design process and were not properly informed of the design intent (i.e., how the various systems were intended to operate). Additionally, those who designed the systems may not stay in touch to make sure that the system is being operated properly. This is the case for the operation of conventional mechanical systems. As we proceed toward newer, innovative systems and products, the need for education and follow-up becomes even more critical. Once again, the issue of team formation and the early involvement and education of those ultimately responsible for the operations and maintenance of the facility becomes critical. See the project actions in this guide for recommendations on issues to consider during operations and maintenance.

EXAMPLE
- At the S. C. Johnson Wax, Consumer Products Headquarters, the overall energy consumption of the building was very good, lower than expected. Here the building manager had been part of the design team from early in the process. Had he not been part of the process, he might very well have been satisfied with the low energy bills. However, he knew that although the overall energy numbers were very good, consumption of electricity was higher than originally anticipated. In investigating why this might be the case, it was discovered that a blind system designed to lower glare on the lower vision glass had been placed above the upper daylighting glass. When monitors detected that glare was a problem, the shades were lowered, blocking not only the glare but also the light that was supposed to provide much of the illumination in that portion of the building. The result was that the electric lighting was on for a much greater portion of the day than originally anticipated. This used more electricity and also raised the cooling load in the building. Without follow-up, the problem with the daylighting system would have been missed, masked by the already low energy numbers.

Life Safety Analogy

Until the nineteenth century we built buildings, communities, and cities without the help of building codes, life safety codes, zoning regulations, or any of the myriad of other restrictions that guide us today. As the industrial revolution spread in Europe and North America, the nature of buildings began to change, the use of buildings began to change, and the kinds of buildings necessary to accommodate the new industrial processes began to change as well. These changes quickly led to a series of building disasters of an unprecedented order—fires, structural failures, decayed neighborhoods, and pollution of all kinds. Much of the history of building in the nineteenth century is one of trial and error as people struggled to understand these problems and arrive at solutions. It took about a hundred years to arrive at a generally accepted set of rules to deal with basic issues of safety in modern buildings. Those rules are the basis for today's collection of building and safety codes.

Today, we follow the much improved version of those rules, but we do so in an almost automatic way. It is second nature to us because society agrees on the necessity for safe buildings and communities. Designers, builders, owners, and operators know instinctively the "right" way to approach things. There is no debate about the goals of having safe buildings; rather, there is a constant upward cycle of improvement in the safety performance of our buildings.

Figure 2. *Today, the Crystal Palace outside of London is known as one of the icons of modern architecture because of the exhibition center's early use of metal and glass for the exterior walls. At the time it was built—the mid-nineteenth century—however, it was known as one of the first fireproof buildings, as iron and glass do not burn. They forgot, of course, that the wood exhibits inside would burn. The building was destroyed by fire shortly after it opened.*

We now must move forward by focusing on environmental issues, on moving toward sustainable design in the twenty-first century, just as our nineteenth-century predecessors focused on life safety. Just as they struggled with their issues, so too are we struggling with ours. We are only now beginning to see our problems and starting to look for the solutions. Like them, we need to be self-conscious, careful, and deliberate about this effort.

Design
Guidance

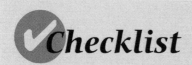 **Checklist**

General Issues

Team Building

❏ 1. Seek out individuals for the A/E team (planners, architects, engineers, landscape architects, and interior designers) who express a strong interest in sustainable design, as well as those who have proven experience whenever possible.

❏ 2. Encourage the owner to involve contractors and future operations and maintenance personnel on the project team.

Education and Goal Setting

❏ 3. Educate the team about the impact of buildings and construction on the environment, and the opportunities for improvement.

❏ 4. Identify overall project sustainable design goals.

❏ 5. Make a commitment to achieve a LEED rating.

Gathering Information

❏ 6. Clarify decision-making criteria for the project.

❏ 7. Identify local sustainable design resources.

Optimization

❏ 8. Explore opportunities to meet requirements of the LEED Green Building Rating System.

❏ 9. Explore opportunities to enhance flexibility and future adaptability.

❏ 10. Seek out design synergies.

Documents and Specifications

❏ 11. Review progress toward meeting the requirements of the LEED Green Building Rating System.

❏ 12. Clearly document sustainable design goals and strategies in the contract specifications.

Bidding, Construction, and Commissioning

❏ 13. Hold an educational session for all contractors and subcontractors.

Operations and Maintenance

❏ 14. Offer to educate the owner, maintenance professionals, equipment managers, and occupants about the sustainable design goals and the design strategies that have been incorporated into the design to meet those goals.

❏ 15. File for LEED rating. As-built drawings will need to be submitted.

❏ 16. Assemble lessons learned from the project.

Project Actions

General Issues

The General Issues Project Actions are recommendations organized by project phase and by topic that should be considered during the design process. When relevant, actions are followed by further explanations in italics and a notation in brackets indicating the potential effect on time, construction cost, energy cost, and maintenance cost or fee.

Team Building

1. Seek out individuals for the A/E team (planners, architects, engineers, landscape architects, and interior designers) who express a strong interest in sustainable design, as well as those who have proven experience whenever possible.

   P|A|I|E|L|O 1.1. Seek out team members who are willing to work toward development of successful sustainable design solutions.

   P|A|I|E|L|O 1.2. Depending on the level of expertise within the core team and the complexity of the project, consider the use of specialty consultants such as energy modelers, lighting/daylighting designers, indoor air quality (IAQ) consultants, natural wastewater treatment consultants, and so on. [$F]

   P|A|I|E|L|O 1.3. Identify sustainable design advocates on the project team. Ideally, the owner and the A/E should each designate a point person to track progress toward meeting the project's environmental goals.

2. Encourage owner to involve contractors and future operations and maintenance personnel on the project team.

   P|A|I|E|L|O 2.1. Invite contractors, subcontractors, and future operations and maintenance personnel to participate in goal-setting sessions and early design sessions, to gain their input on potential design strategies. When possible, keep them involved as participants and/or reviewers throughout the design process. [T, $M]

| P = Planner | A = Architect | I = Interior designer | E = Engineer | L = Landscape architect | O= Owner consultation |

[T] = Could affect length of construction (+ or –), [$C] = Affects construction costs (+ or –), [$E] Affects energy costs, [$F] = Affects fees (+ or –), [$M] = Affects maintenance costs (+ or –).

| P | A | I | E | L | O | 2.2. Encourage owner to consider design/build, negotiated construction contracting, or predesign construction services to engage the contractor's participation in development of creative sustainable design solutions, and to increase understanding and support for design strategies. [T, $C]

Education and Goal Setting

3. Educate the team about the impact of buildings and construction on the environment, and the opportunities for improvement.

| P | A | I | E | L | O | 3.1. Review the information contained in the "Goals" section of this guide with the team.

| P | A | I | E | L | O | 3.2. Invite a sustainable design expert, either from within the project team or from government, a nonprofit organization, or a university, to make a presentation on sustainable design to the team.

| P | A | I | E | L | O | 3.3. Review examples of successful green buildings that have similar requirements, so that the team can learn from other successful projects.

4. Identify overall project sustainable design goals.

| P | A | I | E | L | O | 4.1. Make a commitment to optimize the design rather than rely on minimum code-mandated requirements. [$C, $E]

| P | A | I | E | L | O | 4.2. Consider the value of identifying the project as a showcase project, to educate building occupants, visitors, and the public about sustainable design.

5. Make a commitment to achieve a LEED rating.

| P | A | I | E | L | O | 5.1. Conduct a preliminary assessment to determine the relative difficulty of earning a LEED rating, based on the region, the site location, and the building type, and set a goal for the project of either a bronze, silver, gold, or platinum rating. (See the U.S. Green Building Council website at http://www.usgbc.org for a copy of the most recent version of the LEED rating system.)

Gathering Information

6. Clarify decision-making criteria for the project.

| P | A | I | E | L | O | 6.1. Encourage the owner and design team members to make decisions based on life cycle costing. Establish methodology for life cycle cost analysis, including the length of the life cycle, discount rates, and so on. [$C, $E, $M]

| P = Planner | A = Architect | I = Interior designer | E = Engineer | L = Landscape architect | O= Owner consultation |
[T] = Could affect length of construction (+ or –), [$C] = Affects construction costs (+ or –), [$E] Affects energy costs, [$F] = Affects fees (+ or –), [$M] = Affects maintenance costs (+ or –).

`P|A|I|E|L|O` 6.2. Carefully review proposed design criteria from the owner, design team members, and consultants to seek out assumptions that may work against sustainable design solutions, and suggest alternative criteria where appropriate.

`P|A|I|E|L|O` 6.3. Identify voluntary standards that improve environmental performance and advocate for their use as design guidance for the project. The LEED Green Building Rating System identifies many useful voluntary design standards, as do the individual Project Actions in this guide.

7. Identify local sustainable design resources.

`P|A|I|E|L| |` 7.1. Seek out local green building organizations. Also, contact the U.S. Green Building Council (USGBC) and the AIA Committee on the Environment (COTE) for information on local resources, and to see if there is an active local chapter there.

`P|A|I|E|L| |` 7.2. Contact local architecture schools within colleges and universities to see if they have resources that can support the team, such as energy modeling, daylighting analysis, and so on.

Optimization

8. Explore opportunities to meet requirements of the LEED Green Building Rating System.

`P|A|I|E|L| |` 8.1. Use the LEED Green Building Rating System as a design guidance tool throughout the design process. Develop a scorecard to track progress toward earning a LEED rating, and assign oversight of individual credits to appropriate team members.

9. Explore opportunities to enhance flexibility and future adaptability.

`P|A|I|E|L|O` 9.1. Plan for future growth as well as for other potential future uses.

`P|A|I|E| | |` 9.2. Develop modular design solutions that can be reconfigured easily to enhance long-term flexibility.

10. Seek out design synergies.

`P|A|I|E|L|O` 10.1. Encourage whole-team design meetings throughout the design process to encourage cross-disciplinary collaboration.

`P|A|I|E|L| |` 10.2. Compare design performance to benchmark values for standard performance.

`|A|I|E| | |` 10.3. Seek out opportunities to offset improved performance with reductions and/or simplifications in other areas. For example, improvements in building envelope and lighting usually allow for smaller HVAC systems.

Documents and Specifications

11. Review progress toward meeting the requirements of the LEED Green Building Rating System.

[A | I | E | L] 11.1. Educate new team members about the sustainable design goals for the project and the requirements of the LEED rating system. Review progress toward earning a LEED rating at regular intervals in the project.

12. Clearly document sustainable design goals and strategies in the contract specifications.

[A | I | E | L] 12.1. Describe sustainable design goals in division one of the specifications, and identify special requirements.

[A | I | E | L] 12.2. Require that all construction meetings include an agenda item to review progress toward meeting sustainable design requirements.

[A | I | E | L] 12.3. Develop new specification sections as needed to address construction waste recycling, environmental certification of materials, sequence of finishes installation (for IAQ), and so on. See the project actions for guidance on recommended specifications.

Bidding, Construction, and Commissioning

13. Hold educational sessions for all contractors and subcontractors.

[A | I | E | L] 13.1. Educate all members of the construction team about sustainable design and their role in making the project successful. Describe specific design elements that may be unfamiliar. [T]

[A | I | E | L] 13.2. Highlight the importance of sustainable design in the preconstruction conference. Highlight requirements for site protection, erosion control, integrated pest management, waste minimization, construction waste recycling, and hazardous materials handling.

[A | I | E |] 13.3. Review commissioning requirements in the preconstruction conference, and describe the process that will be followed throughout construction.

Operations and Maintenance

14. Offer to educate the owner, maintenance professionals, equipment managers, and occupants about the sustainable design goals and the design strategies that have been incorporated into the design to meet those goals.

[A | I | E | L | O] 14.1. Consider developing display materials for the building lobby or other public area that describe the sustainable design features and the benefits of the design.

[A | I | E | L | O] 14.2. Offer to provide a comprehensive operations and maintenance manual. The manual should include a plan to minimize indoor air quality hazards from cleaning and

| P = Planner | A = Architect | I = Interior designer | E = Engineer | L = Landscape architect | O= Owner consultation |

[T] = Could affect length of construction (+ or –), [$C] = Affects construction costs (+ or –), [$E] Affects energy costs, [$F] = Affects fees (+ or –), [$M] = Affects maintenance costs (+ or –).

maintenance products, strategies to minimize waste from building refurbishment, including lighting waste disposal, a recycling and composting plan, etc. [$F, $M]

|A|I|E|L|O| 14.3. Ensure that the building owner, occupants, and maintenance staff understand the cleaning and maintenance requirements for all equipment, materials, finishes, landscaping, etc.

15. File for LEED rating. As-built drawings will need to be submitted.

|A|I|E|L|O| 15.1. An official LEED rating can only be received from the U.S. Green Building Council. The fee for filing is nominal. Submit required documents and as-built drawings to the USGBC for their review and approval. For a modest fee, the USGBC can provide technical support to help teams with the paperwork.

16. Assemble lessons learned from the project.

|A|I|E|L|O| 16.1. Offer to conduct a postoccupancy evaluation. Evaluations can very tremendously in complexity, from a comprehensive survey of occupant satisfaction across the organization to a follow-up interview one year later with the owner or project manager. [$F]

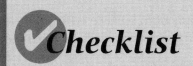 **Checklist**

Planning and Site Work

Team Building

❑ 1. Seek out planners, architects, and landscape architects experienced with ecological urban and community planning, site planning, and landscape design.

❑ 2. Identify community groups that can contribute to the design process.

Education and Goal Setting

EDUCATION

❑ 3. Educate the team about the importance of the interface between the built and natural environments, and the impact that individual facilities have on their larger communities and natural systems.

GOAL SETTING

❑ 4. Make a commitment to develop regional and community planning projects to promote livable communities, based on the Ahwahnee Principles (see pages 48–49).

❑ 5. Make a commitment to create positive connections between the new or renovated facility and its community.

❑ 6. Place priority on development of an urban infill site and/or rehabilitation of an existing building.

❑ 7. Encourage the owner to develop a master plan for the site, to plan for future growth and protect natural site features.

Gathering Information

SITE ANALYSIS

❑ 8. Analyze the regional impacts of the proposed development on the watershed, flooding, wetlands, wildlife habitats, and transportation.

❑ 9. Study the microclimate, geology, hydrology, and ecology of the site, and document findings in site analysis drawings.

❑ 10. Survey existing plants and wildlife on the site.

❑ 11. Test site for possible contamination.

❏ 12. Identify elements of the site that represent cultural and/or historical resources that should be preserved.

RESEARCH

❏ 13. Identify existing pedestrian, bicycle, and transit networks in the community and on the site.

❏ 14. Research local native plant species and invasive plants to avoid.

❏ 15. Consider holding an environmental design charrette to solicit input on the needs and concerns of the community.

Optimization

MASTER PLANNING

❏ 16. Develop transit, pedestrian, and bicycle networks.

❏ 17. Develop networks of open space, with agricultural greenbelts, wildlife corridors, and stream corridors permanently protected from development.

❏ 18. Develop livable, mixed-use communities, based on the Ahwahnee Principles (see pages 48–49).

SITE PLANNING

❏ 19. Preserve natural site features and restore degraded site areas.

❏ 20. Minimize impervious surface areas on the site.

❏ 21. Manage stormwater by working with natural systems to the greatest extent possible.

❏ 22. Maximize positive effects of solar orientation and wind patterns; minimize the urban heat island effect.

LANDSCAPE DESIGN

❏ 23. Develop self-sustaining landscapes based on plants tolerant of soils, climate, and water availability; maximize use of native plants.

❏ 24. Maximize efficiency of irrigation systems and consider water reuse strategies.

❏ 25. Utilize trees and other landscape features to create habitat for wildlife.

Documents and Specifications

DETAILING

❏ 26. Identify composting facilities for organic waste to reduce solid waste while producing a nutrient-rich soil amendment.

❏ 27. Optimize the energy efficiency of site lighting; consider use of photovoltaics.

❏ 28. Develop a site lighting design that minimizes light pollution.

❏ 29. Consider recharge stations for alternative-fuel vehicles and signage for carpooling.

❏ 30. Select and specify environmentally preferable materials for site development.

❏ 31. Explore opportunities to reuse on-site materials.

SPECIFICATIONS

❏ 32. Evaluate erosion control requirements and consider opportunities for improvements.

❏ 33. Develop specifications and design detailing based on integrated pest management (IPM).

❏ 34. Include tree preservation easements in contractor specifications.

Bidding, Construction, and Commissioning

❏ 35. Consider a plant "rescue" to transplant trees and other vegetation.

❏ 36. Protect on-site soil and vegetation during construction.

❏ 37. Phase excavation and construction to limit soil erosion.

❏ 38. Treat land-clearing debris as a resource; find high-value use for large timber, shred remaining wood waste for use as mulch, and stockpile soil and rock for reuse.

Operations and Maintenance

❏ 39. Assist the owner in developing a maintenance program that reduces impact on the environment by utilizing organic fertilizers, integrated biological pest control, and water-conserving irrigation measures.

❏ 40. Quantify operational waste. Publicize and reward recycling efforts.

Project Actions

Planning and Site Work

The planning and site work project actions are recommendations by phase and topic that should be considered during the design process. When relevant, actions are followed by further explanations in italics and a notation in brackets indicating the potential effect on the time, construction cost, energy cost, maintenance cost, or fee.

Team Building

1. Seek out planners, architects, and landscape architects experienced with ecological urban and community planning, site planning, and landscape design.

   `P|A| | | |O` 1.1. Seek out planners experienced with urban and community planning organized around pedestrian and public transit systems.

   `|A| |E|L|O` 1.2. Seek out architects, landscape architects, and engineers experienced with low-impact development, natural strategies for stormwater management, and native plantings.

   `|A| |E|L|O` 1.3. Add team members with experience in biodiversity protection and integrated coastal zone management and planning, where appropriate. [$F]

2. Identify community groups that can contribute to the design process.

   `P|A| | | |O` 2.1. Seek out community groups active in the vicinity of the proposed project and solicit their input on the project. [T, $F]
   Contact with the community early on in the project's life can elicit valuable input while also building goodwill for future approvals that may be required.

   `P|A| | | |O` 2.2. If no community groups have organized in the vicinity of the proposed project, consider contacting the local government planning office, school district, or business association to solicit input. [T, $F]

Education and Goal Setting

Education

3. Educate the team about the importance of the relationship between the built and natural environments, and the impact that individual facilities have on their larger communities and natural systems.

| P|A| | |O | 3.1. Invite an environmental specialist (could be a team member, or someone from a local university or environmental group) to make a presentation to the team. Include information on the impact of the built environment on the local watershed, wildlife habitat corridors and flyways, air quality, and other locally relevant environmental issues to help the team understand the impact of their project on larger ecosystems.

| P|A| | |O | 3.2. Invite local community groups to share information and resources with the team, and to consider the particular needs and concerns of the community.

| P|A| | |O | 3.3. Invite representatives from the Department of Transportation and alternative transportation advocacy groups to share short- and long-range transportation planning goals for the region with the design team.

Goal Setting

4. **Make a commitment to develop regional and community planning projects to promote livable communities, based on the Ahwahnee Principles.**

| P|A| | |O | 4.1. Adopt the Ahwahnee Principles, developed by the Center for Livable Communities, as a set of guiding principles for the design (see box on pages 48–49).

5. **Make a commitment to create positive connections between the new/renovated facility and its community.**

| P|A| | |O | 5.1. Make a commitment to reinforce pedestrian networks or to begin to establish them if none exists.

| P|A| | |O | 5.2. Make a commitment to reinforce greenways and/or wildlife corridors or begin to establish them if none exists.

| P|A| | |O | 5.3. Make a commitment to reinforce local mass transit and transit reduction strategies. Consider both current conditions and long-range planning for the region.

| P|A| | |O | 5.4. Make a commitment to protect and enhance cultural and historical resources.

6. **Place priority on development of an urban infill site and/or rehabilitation of an existing building.**

| P|A| | |O | 6.1. Seek out an existing urban infill area for rehabilitation or redevelopment rather than disturbing open space or a virgin site. [T, $C]

| P|A| |E| |O | 6.2. Explore opportunities to reuse and renovate existing structures in lieu of demolition. To determine whether a building can be reused, critically evaluate structural integrity, building skin, HVAC system, functional suitability, compliance with current codes, historical significance, and other aspects to determine whether the existing building can be reused. [$C, $F]

| P|A| |E| |O | 6.3. Explore opportunities to redevelop a site that was classified as a brownfield by the EPA. There are tax incentives associated with redevelopment of a brownfield. In gen-

| P = Planner | A = Architect | I = Interior designer | E = Engineer | L = Landscape architect | O= Owner consultation |

[T] = Could affect length of construction (+ or –), [$C] = Affects construction costs (+ or –), [$E] Affects energy costs, [$F] = Affects fees (+ or –), [$M] = Affects maintenance costs (+ or –).

eral, brownfields are abandoned sites that were previously industrial and commercial urban areas, where redevelopment is complicated by real or perceived environmental contamination. [$C, $F]

For more information on brownfields, see EPA's Brownfields Initiative, which was established to restore contaminated urban land, bring back to community use, and put land to productive use. Contact EPA at http://www.epa.gov for brownfield updates and brownfield contacts, or your state environmental agency about local brownfield programs.

7. Encourage the owner to develop a master plan for the site, to plan for future growth and protect natural site features.

The ability of the facility to adapt and change to accommodate future requirements is a central priority of sustainable development, because it extends the life of the facility and the materials it is built from, reducing waste and pollution associated with demolition and rebuilding.

| P | A | | | O | 7.1. Encourage the owner to develop a master plan for the site that documents all sensitive site systems that should be off-limits to future development, including wetlands, stream corridors, floodplains, sensitive habitat areas, historic elements, and so on. [T, $F]

| P | A | | | O | 7.2. Encourage the owner to identify zones for future structures as well as future site design elements such as linkages to pubic transit, on-site power generation, constructed wetlands, and so on. [T, $F]

Gathering Information

Site Analysis

8. Analyze the regional impacts of the proposed development on water quality and flooding, wetlands, wildlife habitats, and transportation.

| P | | E | | | 8.1. Identify watersheds, drainage areas, stream corridors, wetlands, aquifer recharge zones, and hundred-year floodplains.

Development of floodplains and other hydrological features should be avoided. Fill should not encroach upon wetlands, watercourses, floodplains, or constructed channels. Changing water flow patterns through these areas may change water temperatures, in turn adversely affecting wildlife habitat. Development of floodplains may increase the risk of flooding by raising the elevation of the floodplain.

| P | | | | L | 8.2. Identify wildlife habitat and nesting areas in the surrounding area and consider methods to mitigate any negative impacts from the project.

| P | | | E | | 8.3. Investigate demographics of the users of the proposed project and the need for and availability of public transportation facilities. Evaluate the impact of the project on the existing transportation infrastructure and explore potential expansion of existing services or the addition of new services.

9. Study the microclimate, geology, hydrology, and ecology of the site.

| P | | | E | L | 9.1. Study the microclimate of the site and identify zones best suited for development based on temperature, humidity, wind, solar orientation, and solar access. Evaluate

Ahwahnee Principles

In 1991 Peter Katz, author of The New Urbanism, *Andres Duany, Elizabeth Plater-Zyberk, Stefanos Polyzoides, Elizabeth Moule, Peter Calthorpe, and Michael Corbett were asked to develop a set of community principles that express what new planning ideas—from neotraditional planning to sustainable design—have in common. The architects' ideas were presented in the fall of 1991 to about a hundred local elected officials at a conference at the Ahwahnee Hotel in Yosemite. There they received both a highly enthusiastic response and their title—the Ahwahnee Principles.*

Preamble

Existing patterns of urban and suburban development seriously impair our quality of life. The symptoms are: more congestion and air pollution resulting from our increased dependence on automobiles, the loss of precious open space, the need for costly improvements to roads and public services, the inequitable distribution of economic resources, and the loss of a sense of community. By drawing upon the best from the past and the present, we can plan communities that will more successfully serve the needs of those who live and work within them. Such planning should adhere to certain fundamental principles.

Community Principles

1. All planning should be in the form of complete and integrated communities containing housing, shops, work places, schools, parks and civic facilities essential to the daily life of the residents.
2. Community size should be designed so that housing, jobs, daily needs and other activities are within easy walking distance of each other.
3. As many activities as possible should be located within easy walking distance of transit stops.
4. A community should contain a diversity of housing types to enable citizens from a wide range of economic levels and age groups to live within its boundaries.
5. Businesses within the community should provide a range of job types for the community's residents.
6. The location and character of the community should be consistent with a larger transit network.
7. The community should have a center focus that combines commercial, civic, cultural and recreational uses.
8. The community should contain an ample supply of specialized open space in the form of squares, greens and parks whose frequent use is encouraged through placement and design.
9. Public spaces should be designed to encourage the attention and presence of people at all hours of the day and night.

the site for the potential to generate alternative forms of electricity, such as solar, wind, and geothermal. (See also the Energy Project Actions in this design guide.)

| P | | E | L | 9.2. Study the geology and hydrology of the site to identify soil characteristics, drainage capacity, and groundwater flow direction, as well as possible water contamination issues.

| P | | E | L | 9.3. Review environmental impact assessment and environmental impact statement or other related environmental quality studies, including existing environmental, noise, air and water quality studies, if available. Check with local governmental units to see if

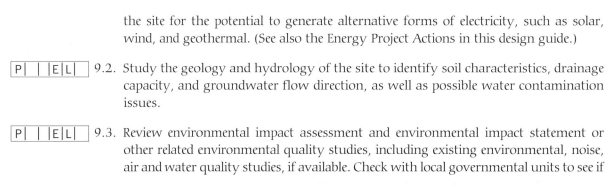

| P = Planner | A = Architect | I = Interior designer | E = Engineer | L = Landscape architect | O= Owner consultation |

[T] = Could affect length of construction (+ or –), [$C] = Affects construction costs (+ or –), [$E] Affects energy costs, [$F] = Affects fees (+ or –), [$M] = Affects maintenance costs (+ or –).

10. Each community or cluster of communities should have a well-defined edge, such as agricultural greenbelts or wild-life corridors, permanently protected from development.

11. Streets, pedestrian paths and bike paths should contribute to a system of fully-connected and interesting routes to all destinations. Their design should encourage pedestrian and bicycle use by being small and spatially defined by buildings, trees and lighting; and by discouraging high speed traffic.

12. Wherever possible, the natural terrain, drainage and vegetation of the community should be preserved with superior examples contained within parks or greenbelts.

13. The community design should help conserve resources and minimize waste.

14. Communities should provide for the efficient use of water through the use of natural drainage, drought tolerant land-scaping and recycling.

15. The street orientation, the placement of buildings and the use of shading should contribute to the energy efficiency of the community.

Regional Principles

1. The regional land-use planning structure should be integrated within a larger transportation network built around transit rather than freeways.

2. Regions should be bounded by and provide a continuous system of greenbelt/wildlife corridors to be determined by natural conditions.

3. Regional institutions and services (government, stadiums, museums, etc.) should be located in the urban core.

4. Materials and methods of construction should be specific to the region, exhibiting a continuity of history and culture and compatibility with the climate to encourage the development of local character and community identity.

Implementation Principles

1. The general plan should be updated to incorporate the above principles.

2. Rather than allowing developer-initiated, piecemeal development, local governments should take charge of the planning process. General plans should designate where new growth, infill or redevelopment will be allowed to occur.

3. Prior to any development, a specific plan should be prepared based on these planning principles.

4. Plans should be developed through an open process and participants in the process should be provided visual models of all planning proposals.

Source: Local Government Commission's Center for Livable Communities, http://www.lgc.org/clc/

reports have been previously generated for the site. Check to see if the site is located in an environmentally sensitive area or near lakeshores, rivers or potable water sources.

P| | |E| | 9.4. Generate a complete soil report, including the physical and chemical soil characteristics of the proposed site, to determine bearing, compaction, and infiltration rates. This will help to identify design and construction limitations and help to prepare for potential mitigation requirements. Identify all areas that are prone to erosion and do everything possible to protect the existing vegetation cover.

P| | |E| | 9.5. Generate a tree survey (include location, genus, and species) of all trees sized 15 cm DBH (diameter breast height) or greater.

P| | |E|L| 9.6. Identify sites with habitat for threatened and endangered species. Determine if development is possible on the site, and what preservation and/or mitigation measures are required. Document all information on site analysis drawings and continue using information throughout planning process and project life.

10. Survey existing plants and wildlife on the site.

`P| | |L|` 10.1. Conduct a qualitative inventory of the site's natural features, plant species, and wildlife habitats, and identify native species. [$F]

`P| | |E|L|` 10.2. Identify characteristic site features, and include them as base information on the site plan, such as large boulders and trees, natural water bodies, and prairie lands.

11. Test site for possible contamination.

`P| | |E| |` 11.1. Test the site for radon levels if the region has been identified as one with potential for radon contamination. (See the Indoor Environmental Quality Project Action in this design guide for details.) [$F]

`P| | |E| |` 11.2. Perform soil tests to identify contaminants from past agricultural or industrial uses, unauthorized dumping and so on. Check site for arsenic, pesticides, lead, other heavy metals, petroleum, dry cleaning fluids, and other hazardous substances. [$F]

12. Identify elements of the site that represent cultural and/or historical resources that should be preserved.

`P|A| | | |` 12.1. Identify existing historical features that should be preserved.

`P|A| | | |` 12.2. Identify sites, buildings, and/or building elements that are registered as special cultural, historical, or archaeological sites.

`P|A| | | |` 12.3. Explore architectural styles prevalent in the area as well as building types that are common in the region. Consider adoption or adaptation of the historical styles prevalent in the area, to reinforce the cultural heritage of the region.

Research

13. Identify existing pedestrian, bicycle, and transit networks in the community.

`P|A| | | |` 13.1. Map the existing traffic patterns for pedestrians, bicycles, automobiles, public transit, and other modes on the site and identify neighboring destinations.

14. Research local native plant species and invasive plants to avoid.

`| | | |L|` 14.1. Identify plant species that are native to the state for the best adaptation. Use of plants native to the United States (or other country, depending on project location) and adapted to the region will extend the palette of plant materials available to the design team.
Contact the local Native Plant Society—nearly every state has one, and many of them have local chapters—for information on native plant species. See http://207.13.80.6/ wildflower/native1.html for a detailed state-by-state listing of native plant organizations, courtesy of the Lady Bird Johnson Wildflower Center.

| P = Planner | A = Architect | I = Interior designer | E = Engineer | L = Landscape architect | O= Owner consultation |

[T] = Could affect length of construction (+ or –), [$C] = Affects construction costs (+ or –), [$E] Affects energy costs, [$F] = Affects fees (+ or –), [$M] = Affects maintenance costs (+ or –).

`[ | | | |L| ]` 14.2. Check federal, state, and local restrictions on regulated invasive species. Adopt voluntary restrictions on invasive plants that are not regulated, to encourage a balanced plant community on the site. [$M]

Many municipalities have lists of preferred plants for the area and may have specific landscape requirements. There are also species that are prohibited in certain regions because they are invasive to the area and displace native species—for instance, purple loosestrife (Lythrum salicaria), buckthorn (Rhamnus cathertica), and reed canary grass (Phalaris arundinacea). Contact the Soil and Water Conservation Service, the county extension agent, or local urban forester. Also see "Invasive Plants" in Reference Section.

15. Consider holding an environmental design charrette to solicit input on the needs and concerns of the community.

`[P|A| | |O| ]` 15.1. For projects that provide services to the community (retail, public housing, schools, municipal buildings, etc.) or that have a large impact on the community because of their size and/or location, consider holding a environmental design charrette to solicit input from the community. [T]

> ## What Is an Environmental Design Charrette?
>
> The charrette process combines brainstorming methods with "future search" processes. Brainstorming involves letting ideas flow in an open way, with each idea building upon the suggestions of all participants, whereas "future search" processes create time lines and issue maps and diagrams to help individuals, groups, and communities visualize design alternatives and discuss and evaluate best choices.
>
> Environmental design charrettes build upon the thirty-year history of the American Institute of Architects R/UDAT (Regional and Urban Design Assistance Teams) process, in which expert design and planning professionals consult with communities about long-range strategies. Environmental design charrettes provide a first step in acting locally while thinking globally, by considering the views of all community members who will be affected in the present and the future. The primary issues that environmental design charrettes focus on are:
>
> • Energy and resource conservation
>
> • Building ecology
>
> • Environmental approaches to landscaping
>
> • Waste prevention and reclamation
>
> • Cultural change and behavioral Issues
>
> • Regional scale planning
>
> *Source: Environmental Design Charrette Workbook, AIA Press, 1996.*

Optimization

Master Planning

16. Develop transit, pedestrian, and bicycle networks.

`[P|A| | |L| ]` 16.1. Provide convenient walkways linking all major destinations on the site. [$C]

| P|A| | |L| | 16.2. Support use of mass transit by providing pedestrian-friendly physical linkages, such as covered or enclosed access to subway, bus, or trolley stops or stations. [$C]

| P|A| | |L| | 16.3. Explore potential for sharing parking areas and shuttle services to public transit with neighboring facilities. [$C]

| P|A| | |L| | 16.4. Support use of bicycles for transportation by providing conveniently located bicycle racks, and showers and changing facilities for cyclists where appropriate. [$C]

| P|A| | |L| | 16.5. Make provisions to support carpooling. For example, design the parking lot with preferred parking areas for high-occupancy vehicles (HOVs).

17. Develop networks of open space, with agricultural greenbelts, wildlife corridors, and stream corridors permanently protected from development.

| P|A| | |L| | 17.1. Identify adjacent open spaces and explore opportunities to connect them with the proposed green space on the site, to provide habitat corridors and to stimulate healthy microclimates.

18. Develop livable, mixed-use communities, based on the Ahwahnee Principles.

| P|A| | |L|O| | 18.1. Determine community size based on the ideal of providing housing, jobs, and daily needs for a diversity of socioeconomic groups, within easy walking distance of each other and local transit stops.

| P|A| | |L|O| | 18.2. Develop communities that have an edge well defined by agricultural greenbelts or wildlife corridors that are permanently protected from development. Provide a central focus that combines commercial, civic, cultural, and recreational uses, as well as specialized open space in the form of squares, greens, and parks.

| P|A| | |L|O| | 18.3. Develop streets, transit routes, pedestrian paths, and bike paths that contribute to a system of fully connected and inviting routes to all destinations that encourage transit, pedestrian, and bicycle use.

Site Planning

19. Preserve natural site features and restore degraded habitat areas.

| P|A| |E|L| | 19.1. Coordinate building and site design with required infrastructure. Cluster underground utilities, such as telephone, cable, electric, water, wastewater, and fire lanes in same or nearby conduits to minimize site disturbance and to preserve open space.

| P|A| |E|L| | 19.2. Work with the existing topography. Design building, parking, and roadways to complement existing site contours by limiting cut and fill. [$C]

| P|A| |E|L| | 19.3. Minimize disruption to existing hydrological features, such as creeks, streams, ponds, lakes, and/or wetlands. Contact the U.S. Army Corps of Engineers and local ordinances for watershed protection requirements.

| P = Planner | A = Architect | I = Interior designer | E = Engineer | L = Landscape architect | O= Owner consultation |

[T] = Could affect length of construction (+ or –), [$C] = Affects construction costs (+ or –), [$E] Affects energy costs, [$F] = Affects fees (+ or –), [$M] = Affects maintenance costs (+ or –).

`P|A| |E|L|` 19.4. Implement a stormwater management plan that includes groundwater recharge and stream channel protection strategies resulting in no net increase of stormwater runoff from existing to developed conditions. When building on a site with an existing building, parking, or other impervious cover, attempt to develop a stormwater management plan that represents no net increase of runoff relative to the forested or precolonial conditions.

`P| | |E|L|O` 19.5. Consider creating or restoring wetlands on site. "Banking" of wetland credits can benefit the owner either for mitigation of impacted wetlands or offered for sale to others that need to mitigate wetlands. The economic benefits of banked wetland credits can offset some project costs. [$C]

Creation or restoration of wetlands involves creation of three wetlands characteristics: soil, vegetation, and hydrology. Created wetlands need to be certified and approved by the U.S. Army Corps of Engineers and local environmental agencies before wetlands credits can be banked. Wetland credits can be traded only within the same region or watershed. Therefore, the value of wetland credits is site specific.

`| | | |L|` 19.6. Restore the surface cover of impacted areas. Use topsoil, which should be stockpiled before construction, to restore disturbed areas. Topsoil is fertile and contains nutrients that support plant life; it also filters contaminants and neutralizes or binds many air and water pollutants.

20. Minimize impervious surface areas on the site.

Open space and undeveloped areas should be treated as assets, because pervious surface areas provide for infiltration of rainwater, reducing stormwater management requirements and recharging groundwater aquifers. Preserve the maximum area of a development as permanent open space to keep the on-site hydrology in balance.

`P|A| |E|L|` 20.1. Avoid expansive parking areas; they create concentrations of contaminated runoff, reduce infiltration, create "heat islands," and are aesthetically unpleasing. Instead, consider structured parking and incentives to reduce parking to provide more green space on the site. In required surface parking lots, use parking islands that are at least 10–15 feet wide to allow for healthy plantings and filtration of stormwater. [$C]

`P|A| |E|L|` 20.2. Consider water-permeable materials such as porous asphalt or concrete, open-celled pavers, reinforced turf, concrete or plastic grids, or stabilized aggregate in light-traffic areas such as emergency-access lanes and overflow parking lots. [$C]

`P|A| |E|L|` 20.3. Consider water-permeable materials for pedestrian pathways, such as loose aggregate, wooden decks, mulch pathways, or paving stones. [$M]

21. Manage stormwater by working with natural drainage systems to the greatest extent possible.

`P|A| |E|L|` 21.1. Work with natural drainage systems, using swales and native vegetation cover of soils, to the greatest extent possible to naturally absorb and filter runoff and promote infiltration. These strategies reduce the need for artificially constructed drainage channels and stormwater piping. [$C, $M]

`P|A| |E|L|` 21.2. Use vegetated buffers to treat stormwater runoff from parking lots, streets, and rooftops. Vegetated buffers, in the form of rain gardens or shallow vegetated swales, and bioretention are low-cost alternatives to curb and gutter that naturally filter gasoline, oil and grease, herbicides, fertilizers, and other pollutants suspended in stormwater runoff. [$C, $M]

P|A| |E|L| 21.3. Use open vegetated swales for infiltration where space permits. The recommended minimum area is 15 feet by 40 feet. Open drainage increases vegetative variety, filters contaminants, reduces the need for irrigation of landscaped area, reduces drainage velocity and erosion, supports wildlife, and requires little maintenance. [$C, $M]

P|A| |E|L| 21.4. Consider biofiltration of runoff from impervious areas to improve water quality. Runoff from parking areas picks up petroleum, oil and grease, and other contaminants during a rainfall. The system should be designed such that runoff is filtered and infiltrated on-site and only overflow is drained away. Evaluate the sensitivity of the site and surrounding areas, depth to groundwater table, and local regulations when determining whether to recommend on-site pretreatment strategies or discharge to a stormwater system. [$C, $M]

P| | |E|L|O   21.5. If natural infiltration systems are insufficient to handle runoff due to limited open space or impermeable soils, accommodate this deficiency by planning on-site

---

What Is Bioretention?

The bioretention concept was developed by the Department of Environmental Resources in Prince George's County, Maryland, in the early 1990s as an alternative to traditional best management practice (BMP) structures. Bioretention is the management and treatment of stormwater runoff within a shallow depression, using a conditioned soil bed and plant materials to reduce runoff and to treat and infiltrate it where it originates. The method combines physical filtering and adsorption with biological water treatment processes. The system consists of:

- Flow regulation structure
- Pretreatment vegetated filter strip or channel
- A shallow ponding area, maximum of 6–8 inches high
- An overflow system above the maximum ponding depth
- A surface layer of organic mulch
- Plant material
- A planting soil bed, minimum 4 feet deep
- A sand bed, 12 inches deep, under the soil bed
- Pea gravel curtain drain
- Pea gravel with underdrain system at the base of the trench

Bioretention can be applied to almost all development situations, except in urban conditions where pervious surfaces are limited to 5 percent or less. The practice is applicable for treating runoff from parking lots and roadways, as well as pervious areas such as golf courses.

Source: The Center for Watershed Protection, Ellicott City, MD (410) 461–8323.

| P = Planner | A = Architect | I = Interior designer | E = Engineer | L = Landscape architect | O= Owner consultation |

[T] = Could affect length of construction (+ or –), [$C] = Affects construction costs (+ or –), [$E] Affects energy costs, [$F] = Affects fees (+ or –), [$M] = Affects maintenance costs (+ or –).

stormwater retention and detention strategies to minimize reliance on stormwater systems. [$C]

`P| |E|L|O` 21.6. On tight sites, where little pervious surface areas remains, consider the use of pervious concrete or pervious asphalt paving systems. Gravel beds beneath the paving serve as stormwater detention areas. Porous concrete and asphalt require periodic vacuuming to remove silt and small particles that can clog the systems over time. [$C, $M]

`P|A| |E| |O` 21.7. Consider use of vegetated rooftops, which serve as a water quantity control to absorb the majority of water from a normal storm event. These measures reduce runoff and thus the size and costs of stormwater collection systems. [$C, $M]

22. Maximize positive effects of solar orientation and wind patterns, and minimize the urban heat island effect.

`P|A| |E|L|` 22.1. Coordinate the site design with building energy design strategies to support and enhance the energy performance of the building. (See the Energy Project Actions in this guide.) [$E]

`P|A| | |L|` 22.2. Utilize trees to act as a channel for summer breezes or to shield against winter winds. [$E]

`P|A| | |L|` 22.3. In general, orient buildings along an east-west axis, with the long sides facing north and south, to provide access to beneficial daylight and minimize difficult-to-control low-angle sun. [$E]

`P|A| |E|L|` 22.4. Use light-colored, reflective materials throughout the design of the facility and the site to minimize contribution to the urban heat island effect. Particularly in warm climates, light-colored, low-albedo finishes also tend to lower building energy loads. [$E]

`P|A| |E|L|` 22.5. Consider use of green roofs, which have excellent insulative values, absorb the sun's heat, and provide cooling through evapotranspiration. Green roofs reduce building energy loads and minimize contribution to the urban heat island effect (see box on page 56). [$C, $E]

`P|A| |E|L|` 22.6. Consider impacts on building peak loads when orienting buildings. In warm climates, shading and insulation on west-facing walls can reduce the peak cooling requirements. [$E]

Landscape Design

23. Develop self-sustaining landscape designs based on plants tolerant of soils, climate, and water availability; maximize use of native plants.

`| | | |L|` 23.1. Select plants based on species diversity, wildlife habitat, and companion planting. Refer to local ordinances for preferred plant lists, but be aware of adapted plants that are invasive and may outcompete natives.
Many municipalities have lists of preferred plants for the area and may have specific landscape requirements. Contact the Soil Conservation Service, county extension agent, or local urban forester.

Green Roofs: Innovative Ecological Stormwater Management Solutions

As open space and pervious area give way to urban sprawl and development, ever increasing amounts of stormwater runoff become a challenge for local governments, municipalities, and developers alike. Stormwater runoff, whether from parking lots, conventional roofs, or other impervious surfaces, is a source of pollution into receiving streams.

Vegetated roof surfaces provide an innovative alternative that tackles a number of challenges related to stormwater runoff. An extensive green roof, consisting of a thin soil and vegetation layer, acts as a pervious surface. Although water is not infiltrating into the ground, through their water absorption capacity Green Roofs store and recycle rainwater that otherwise would run into overloaded sewer or stormwater systems. Green Roofs reduce and delay stormwater runoff, which also helps to avoid pollution of surrounding water bodies. In addition to the direct benefits of reduced runoff and improved water quality, the advantages of a Green Roof include:

- Reduced urban heat island effect through a reduction of the surface temperature of the roof
- Extended lifetime of the roofing system by protecting roof against direct sun exposure and extreme temperatures
- Moderated extremes in roof surface temperature
- Increased insulation and thus reduced energy use for heating and cooling
- More stable indoor temperature and humidity
- Substitute for lost open space and wildlife habitat
- Aesthetics

Extensive Green Roofs add between 15 and 40 pounds per square foot to roof loading, depending on the soil mix and thickness of the soil layer. To support a healthy species variety, 3 to 6 inches of soil is recommended. A drainage layer is needed for flat roofs. Green Roofs are economically and environmentally sound stormwater management strategies that provide creative and aesthetically pleasing strategies for meeting regulatory requirements.

Source: Katrin Scholz-Barth and re∗natur, Germany. Information can also be obtained from Roofscapes, Inc. (www.roofmeadow.com), and the Toronto Rooftop Gardens Resource Group (www.peck.ca).

| | | | L | 23.2. Place a priority on the use of native species. Native plant materials are adapted to the local climate and regional ecosystem, promise low maintenance requirements, and usually do not require irrigation. [$M]

| | | | L | 23.3. Consider the negative effects of monoculture when selecting plant materials. Species diversity better maintains an ecological balance and diminishes future biological problems.
As an example, Dutch elm disease seriously affected many street trees in our nation due to a lack of species diversity.

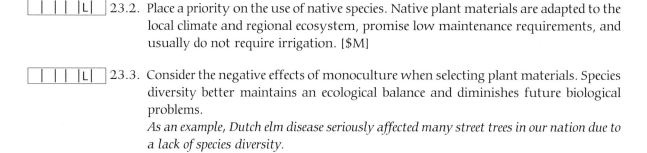

| P = Planner | A = Architect | I = Interior designer | E = Engineer | L = Landscape architect | O= Owner consultation |

[T] = Could affect length of construction (+ or –), [$C] = Affects construction costs (+ or –), [$E] Affects energy costs, [$F] = Affects fees (+ or –), [$M] = Affects maintenance costs (+ or –).

[| | | |L|] 23.4. Elect to cluster rather than scatter site plantings. For instance, create larger but fewer planting islands. This type of planting promotes large common root systems, helps to protect other plants from wind, sun, and reflected heat, and prevents erosion. [$C]

[| | | |L|] 23.5. Reduce areas using water-intensive plantings, such as turf grass. Instead, select native shrubs, ground covers, and grasses with water requirements that are equal to natural precipitation patterns in the region. This will help to reduce irrigation requirements as well as water pollution from pesticides, herbicides, and fertilizers that may be required. [$M]

[|A| |E|L|] 23.6. Consider a plant's root system and allow for growth as the design of buildings, utilities, and site features are developed.

[| | | |L|] 23.7. Consider the microclimate of the streetscape when selecting street trees, and select species that can survive the stressful environment. [$M]

24. Maximize efficiency of irrigation systems and consider water reuse strategies.

[| | |E|L|] 24.1. Consider eliminating permanent irrigation systems through the exclusive use of plant materials suited to the site's climate, soil, and water availability. Accommodate temporary irrigation requirements with "quick coupler" systems for use during the establishment period and extreme drought. [$C, $M]

[|A| |E|L|] 24.2. If a permanent irrigation system must be provided, consider the following:
- Limit the use of irrigation to defined areas by grouping plants with similar water requirements.
- Develop zones for the irrigation system based on water use requirements, and clearly identify them on the site plan drawings.
- Design the irrigation system to make the most of the natural flow of water along topographic planes.
- Avoid irrigating steep slopes to discourage additional runoff.
- Avoid high-pressure misting sprinklers, which are inefficient due to high evaporation rates and wind.
- Consider use of soaker hoses.
- Automate the irrigation system to increase efficiency.
- Consider use of solar-electric power to operate controls.
- Submeter irrigation systems that use potable water, to monitor water use.

[|A| |E|L|O|] 24.3. Consider the use of harvested water for irrigation. Using municipal water for irrigation is a waste of a resource. Plants do not require potable water and are often sensitive to chlorine. Where water costs are high, rainwater harvesting can provide significant savings. (See the Water Project Actions in this design guide for more information on rainwater harvesting and water reuse systems.) [$C, $M]

[|A| |E|L|O|] 24.4. Consider use of a gray water system for landscape irrigation that collects, filters, and reuses gray water from sinks, showers, and other sources. Ideal applications are sites where some landscape irrigation is desirable within regions with limited water availability. Identify the personnel who will operate and maintain the treatment system, and obtain their input before selecting a system. (See the Water Project Actions in this design guide for more information on gray water reuse systems.) [$C, $M]

Since gray water reclamation and wastewater treatment facilities require regulatory authority approval, initiate the permitting process as soon as the requirement is known.

| | | E | L | 24.5. If irrigation is provided, ensure that the design and layout of the system are efficient and site specific. Factor in the topography, surrounding structures, water bodies, and soil characteristics. Consider precipitation and evaporation rates when planting on south-facing slopes.

| | | E | L | 24.6. Promote the use of efficient drip irrigation systems instead of spray irrigation systems. If spray systems are used, ensure that the direction, height, and coverage of spray sources are coordinated with site conditions to avoid waste.

| | | E | L | 24.7. Use timers for irrigation systems, which allow for a fixed amount of water to be distributed for a fixed amount of time; sensors can override the system in cases of rain or extreme wind.

25. Utilize trees and other landscape features to create habitat for wildlife.

| A | | L | 25.1. Consider opportunities to provide habitat for wildlife when developing landscape design. Use of native plantings that provide food and shelter for wildlife, together with a source of water that is not chemically treated, can support a diversity of wildlife, even in urban areas.

| A | | L | O | 25.2. Consider participating in the National Wildlife Federation's (NWF) Backyard Habitat program, to create a certified wildlife habitat on the site.

Documents and Specifications

Detailing

26. Locate composting facilities for organic waste to produce nutrient-rich soil amendment. *Compost adds organic matter to soil. In sandy soils, compost helps retain water; in clay soils, compost helps add porosity to the soil. Compost also inoculates the soil with beneficial microbes that help plants to extract nutrients.*

| A | | L | O | 26.1. Explore the potential for continuous composting of organic waste (food and soiled paper and/or landscaping debris) on-site, or off-site by others. Identify local composting facilities, or set aside a place for on-site composting. [$C, $M]

| A | | L | 26.2. Review local requirements that govern use of composting systems.

| A | | L | 26.3. For on-site composting, seek a location with easy access and correct environmental conditions for composting. Temperature control is not required; however, it is important to ensure adequate aeration, or composting will become slow and odorous. Provide a mix of dry bulky ingredients, such as straw, dry brown weeds, and

| P = Planner | A = Architect | I = Interior designer | E = Engineer | L = Landscape architect | O= Owner consultation |

[T] = Could affect length of construction (+ or –), [$C] = Affects construction costs (+ or –), [$E] Affects energy costs, [$F] = Affects fees (+ or –), [$M] = Affects maintenance costs (+ or –).

The National Wildlife Federation's Backyard Habitat Program

The Backyard Wildlife Habitat program was started in 1973 by the National Wildlife Federation (NWF) to encourage individuals and organizations to create and maintain landscapes with suitable habitat for wildlife, and to acknowledge their efforts through a national certification program.

NWF provides information and assistance to schools, businesses, homeowners, and community groups that are interested in enhancing habitat for wildlife and creating environmentally friendly landscapes. Wildlife Habitats at the Workplace is a special initiative of the Backyard Wildlife Habitat program that provides guidelines for businesses and other organizations interested in creating a Backyard Wildlife Habitat project on workplace grounds.

What Is a Backyard Habitat?

Restoration of native plant communities is the main emphasis of the backyard habitat program. This is especially important since our native plants and wildlife have coevolved and depend on each other for survival. All wildlife species have four basic requirements for survival: food, water, cover, and places to raise young.

Food

Select plants that provide natural foods such as fruits, seeds, nuts, pollen and nectar. Choose your plants to provide food for wildlife throughout the year. Butterflies and hummingbirds can easily be attracted to your yard by planting native trees, shrubs, and perennials that suit them and their young. Bird feeders should only be used as a supplement to foods provided by native plants.

Water

Wildlife needs water for drinking, bathing, and in some cases breeding. Preserve or restore natural ponds, streams, vernal pools, or other wetland on the site, as these can be excellent aquatic habitats. Water can also be supplied in a birdbath, small pond, recirculating waterfall, mister, or shallow dish. Consider providing a source of water through all four seasons.

Cover

Include clumps of dense vegetation, native to your area, to provide year-round protective cover from weather and predators. Examples of these may be native grasses, cacti, or evergreen shrubs and trees. Dense deciduous plants also make excellent cover. Rock, log, and brush piles can also offer cover for small mammals, birds, reptiles, amphibians, and a great variety of insects.

Places to Raise Young

Native vegetation also provides great nesting areas for wildlife. Some wildlife species have very specific plants they prefer to nest in. Cacti and dead or dying trees (called "snags") provide nesting sites for owls, flying squirrels, and other cavity-nesters. Native grasses, ground dens, rock, log, and brush piles also provide nesting sites for a variety of wildlife. Some aquatic animals deposit their eggs in or near ponds, vernal pools, and other wetlands. Butterflies require specific "host" plants on which to lay their eggs.

Source: National Wildlife Federation. For more information about National Wildlife Federation's Backyard Wildlife Habitat program, see http://www.nwf.org/habitats/backyard/basics/provide.cfm/

autumn leaves, and moist ingredients, such as food scraps and green leaves; otherwise provide a mechanical method for mixing the material. Proper moisture is also required: Provide cover from rain in wet climates, and a source of water in dry climates. Consider use of enclosed containers or worm bins for composting of food waste. [$C, $M]

Worm bin composting can be accomplished on many scales. Small systems can accommodate a household or small office, whereas large-scale systems can service a large building or a campus of buildings. The EPA campus in Research Triangle Park is planning a vermiculture system for their 1,000,000 SF facility.

|A| |E|L| 26.4. If an off-site facility is used, identify a temporary holding area and ensure proper access to the pickup location. If off-site composting of food waste is accommodated, provide refrigerated storage at the pickup location.

27. Optimize the energy efficiency of site lighting; consider use of photovoltaics.

|A| |E|L|O| 27.1. Use efficient light sources, and explore the possibility of reducing the extent of site lighting. [$E]

|A| |E|L|O| 27.2. Consider using PVs for all outdoor lighting, including parking lots, walkways, garages, and the like. To evaluate the cost of the system, consider the following: [$C]
- Study lighting photometrics and the number of fixtures required. PV parking lot lighting typically uses a 36W compact fluorescent lamp (mounted 20 feet high), whereas metal halide or high-pressure sodium (HPS) uses 250 or 400W lamps.
- Calculate the winter sun hours of collection (will vary for flat or tilted panels) to determine the required storage capacity for the batteries.
- Determine the cost difference for special fixtures and lamps, with batteries and PV panels, versus conventional fixtures and lamps. The installation costs for the two types of fixtures are the same.
- Determine the cost savings for trenching and conduit that is typically required for electric lighting.

28. Develop site lighting that minimizes light pollution in the sky.

|A| |E|L| 28.1. Consider use of motion sensors so that site lighting is used only when needed. [$C, $E]

|A| |E|L| 28.2. Select exterior light fixtures that have a lighting cut-off angle that prevents light spill to the sky.

|A| |E|L| 28.3. Reduce the height of exterior light fixtures where possible to reduce overall lighting output required. Study photometrics to ensure that lighting distribution is adequate.

29. Consider recharge stations for alternative-fuel vehicles and signage for carpooling.

|A| |E|L|O| 29.1. Consider installation of refueling facilities for alternative-fuel vehicles using, for example, electricity, natural gas, or methanol/ethanol. Where appropriate, recharge stations for electric vehicles may be incorporated into parking garages and/or other locations on the site at minimal cost. Liquid or gaseous fueling facilities must be separately ventilated or located outdoors. [$C, $M]

P = Planner	A = Architect	I = Interior designer	E = Engineer	L = Landscape architect	O= Owner consultation

[T] = Could affect length of construction (+ or –), [$C] = Affects construction costs (+ or –), [$E] Affects energy costs, [$F] = Affects fees (+ or –), [$M] = Affects maintenance costs (+ or –).

Materials Selection

30. **Select and specify environmentally preferable materials for site development. (See also the Material Resources Project Action section of this design guide.)**

    |A| | |L| 30.1. Select and specify wood products from certified sustainable forests. [$C]
    Wood should be independently certified by an organization recognized by the Forest Stewardship Council (FSC).

    |A| | |L| 30.2. Select and specify wood products treated with an environmentally safe wood preservative such as ammoniacal copper quaternary (ACQ) instead of chromated copper arsenate (CCA) pressure-treated wood. [$C]

    |A| | |L| 30.3. Specify fungicide- and biocide-free paint.

    |A| | |L| 30.4. Consider use of salvaged materials such as used bricks or timbers.

    |A| | |L| 30.5. Consider use of materials made from recycled content, such as recycled plastic benches and planters.

    |A| | |L| 30.6. Consider use of biodegradable materials for soil stabilization, such as hydromulch, instead of asphaltic tackifiers.

31. **Explore opportunities to reuse on-site and demolition materials.**

    |A| |E|L| 31.1. Retain and protect native soil. Write specifications that require stockpiling of all excavated soil for redistribution and landscaping after construction.

    |A| |E|L| 31.2. Identify reusable salvaged materials.

Specifications

32. **Evaluate erosion control requirements and consider opportunities for improvements. (*See LEED prerequisite for landscaping and erosion control.*)**

    | | |E|L| 32.1. Check ordinances for erosion control requirements. Consider the adoption of more stringent requirements if necessary to protect the site and surrounding areas. [$C, $M]
    The Maryland Model Erosion and Sediment Control Ordinance is widely recognized as an exemplary model ordinance. It outlines basic required erosion control measures and storm-water runoff management practices that should be followed during construction, and suggests additional procedures that can be implemented to minimize disturbance of the site.

    | | |E|L| 32.2. Retain and protect as much on-site vegetation as possible, and restore degraded areas where possible. Vegetation, mature vegetation in particular, not only filters pollutants and absorbs runoff, but also maintains the stability of the soil, thereby reducing erosion from both wind and water.

    | | |E|L| 32.3. Stabilize soil and avoid invasion by weeds using filtration barriers (straw bale dams, filter-fabric fences), soil tackifiers, jute netting, hydroseeding with quick-sprouting plants like annual ryegrass, or mulch.

| | |E|L| 32.4. For more permanent soil stabilization, consider geotextiles (fabrics designed to filter soil from water); soil cells separated with masonry, wood, or fabric; and crib or retaining walls.

| | |E|L| 32.5. Protect storm sewer inlets from carrying sediment into receiving streams. Install silt fences or straw bales prior to grading and construction to minimize washout of topsoil and to filter out fine particles before water drains into the storm sewer.

33. Develop design and specifications that require integrated pest management (IPM).

|A| | |L| 33.1. Utilize biological controls to combat pests. Examples for IPM include companion planting, creating favorable environments for natural predator insects, and pheromone traps. As a secondary defense, apply natural pesticides, and only as a last resort, use carefully timed and targeted chemical pesticides. [$M]

|A| | |L| 33.2. Develop detailing with barrier controls for pests.

34. Include tree and soil preservation easements in contract drawings and specifications.

|A| |E|L| 34.1. Outline the limits of construction clearly in the construction documents, and develop a specification section clearly defining tree preservation requirements. Coordinate tree preservation areas with all utility lines and construction staging areas.

| | | |L| 34.2. Map the driplines of existing trees to be retained. A tree grown in open soil may have a root system covering an area two to three times the spread of its crown. Effects of damage to a tree's root system often does not show up for 5–10 years.

|A| |E|L| 34.3. If on-site wastewater treatment is being considered, identify suitable soils for infiltration of pretreated effluent and fence off the area to protect soil structure and natural percolation rates from compaction during construction.

Bidding, Construction, and Commissioning

General

35. Consider holding a "plant rescue" prior to clearing the site.

| | | |L|O| 35.1. Encourage the owner and contractor to organize a "plant rescue" to transplant existing trees, shrubs and perennials. Plant material can be relocated on-site or donated to others in the community. Plant rescues can involve volunteers from the community to dig and "adopt" unwanted plants. [T]

36. Protect on-site soil and vegetation during construction.

|A| | |L| 36.1. Protect on-site vegetation. Employ an arborist or urban forester to assist in tree preservation techniques. [$C, $F]

| P = Planner | A = Architect | I = Interior designer | E = Engineer | L = Landscape architect | O= Owner consultation |

[T] = Could affect length of construction (+ or –), [$C] = Affects construction costs (+ or –), [$E] Affects energy costs, [$F] = Affects fees (+ or –), [$M] = Affects maintenance costs (+ or –).

|A| |L| 36.2. Establish staging areas, travel routes, and parking areas for construction vehicles. Compaction or contamination from construction activities may render the soil lifeless.

|A| |L| 36.3. Identify safe holding areas for hazardous materials and hazardous waste during construction to protect soil from contamination.

|A| |E|L| 36.4. Schedule construction to take advantage of natural weather conditions to the maximum extent possible. Strip sites in early spring or late winter and revegetate in late spring or early winter, as possible.

37. Phase excavation and construction to limit soil erosion.

|A| |E|L| 37.1. Only the smallest practical area of soil should be exposed at any one time during development. Exposure should be kept to the shortest practical period of time. Temporary plantings should be used to stabilize exposed soil areas during construction.

|A| |L| 37.2. Schedule the installation of permanent vegetation immediately upon completion of improvements such as streets, storm sewers, or other features of the development if at all possible.

|A| |L| 37.3. Scarify soils prior to the addition of mulch to increase water retention capacity and soil permeability.

38. Treat land-clearing debris as a resource, stockpile soil and rock for reuse, and find high-value use for large timber and shred remaining wood waste for use as mulch.

|A| |E|L| 38.1. Stockpile topsoil on-site after excavation, cover it, and reuse for landscaping.

|A| |E|L| 38.2. Crush excavated rock material for reuse on site.

|A|I| |L|O 38.3. Consider milling wood from land-clearing debris into building materials and/or furnishings.

|A| |L| 38.4. Use a portable tub grinder to shred wood waste for use as mulch. [$C]

Operations and Maintenance

General

39. Assist the owner in developing a landscape maintenance program that utilizes organic fertilizers and water-conserving irrigation measures.

| | | |L|O 39.1. Educate building maintenance staff on irrigation requirements and monitor water consumption. For example, if irrigation is necessary, irrigate in the early morning or late afternoon to avoid loss of water from evaporation. Encourage root growth and drought tolerance by applying at least ½ inch of water only on designated irrigation days. Small quantities of water applied frequently may lead to shallow root systems and weak plants. [$F, $M]

☐ | | |L|O| 39.2. Educate building maintenance staff on preferred landscape maintenance. Require proper pruning of shrubs and trees. Improper pruning techniques may lead to disease or insect infestation. Maintain landscape to protect wildlife habitats. Use organic compost, mulch, humus, sand or gravel, lime, or pH modifiers. Check local composting facilities as a source, or provide a composting area on site. [$F, $C]

40. Assist the owner in developing an integrated biological pest control management program.

☐ | | |E|L|O| 40.1. Assist the owner in developing an IPM program that uses biological controls as a first defense; include insects, pheromone traps, natural pesticides such as pyrethrum, and companion planting. If nontoxic controls fail, use chemical pesticides carefully targeted to a narrow range of plant species. The chemicals should be carefully screened and EPA certified. [$C, $F, $M]

☐ | | |E|L|O| 40.2. Train workers in proper application of low-volume, targeted pesticide application. [$F]

| P = Planner | A = Architect | I = Interior designer | E = Engineer | L = Landscape architect | O= Owner consultation |

[T] = Could affect length of construction (+ or –), [$C] = Affects construction costs (+ or –), [$E] Affects energy costs, [$F] = Affects fees (+ or –), [$M] = Affects maintenance costs (+ or –).

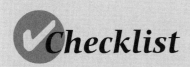 **Checklist**

Energy

Team Building

❑ 1. Establish energy design team; consider use of specialty consultants for energy analysis, lighting, and daylighting.

❑ 2. Suggest that the client include the future building operator responsible for energy management on the team, as a participant in the design process.

Education and Goal Setting

EDUCATION

❑ 3. Educate the team about the importance of design optimization instead of code-minimum design.

❑ 4. Educate the team about the various methods for assessing life cycle costs, and select the preferred method.

GOAL SETTING

❑ 5. Identify energy performance goals and develop a strategy for meeting them.

❑ 6. Make a commitment to commission the building.

❑ 7. Make a commitment to engage in future energy management.

❑ 8. Consider participation in voluntary incentive programs (such as Energy Star and Green Lights) and adoption of voluntary design standards.

Gathering Information

PROGRAMMING

❑ 9. Review design criteria carefully, including temperature and humidity requirements, ventilation rates, and occupancy schedules.

SITE ANALYSIS

❑ 10. Gather information on the local climate.

❑ 11. Analyze site microclimate to identify features that will impact energy design.

❏ 12. Explore potential for utility rebates for energy efficiency and/or renewable energy.

❏ 13. Research performance benchmarks.

PRELIMINARY ENERGY MODELING

❏ 14. Select energy analysis tools, including computer analysis and physical models.

❏ 15. Develop a base case energy model.

Optimization

SITE AND BUILDING DESIGN

❏ 16. Integrate energy analysis into the design process; review and monitor energy analysis methodology as the design progresses.

❏ 17. Integrate passive solar design strategies into the design of the site and building.

❏ 18. Optimize design of the building envelope, including insulation, glazing, and sun shading devices.

LIGHTING

❏ 19. Maximize the controlled use of daylight for ambient lighting using a holistic approach that considers heat gain and loss, and reduced reliance on electric lighting.

❏ 20. Select efficient electric lighting systems.

❏ 21. Consider use of lighting control technologies, such as occupancy sensors and daylight dimming.

MECHANICAL, ELECTRICAL, AND PLUMBING (MEP) SYSTEMS

❏ 22. Explore efficient HVAC system alternatives; avoid oversizing, which can reduce efficiency.

❏ 23. Balance energy efficiency goals with consideration of the environmental impacts of fuel type and refrigeration selection.

❏ 24. Maximize efficiency of electric power and distribution.

❏ 25. Maximize efficiency of service water heating.

❏ 26. Consider potential for use of renewable energy strategies.

Documents and Specifications

SITE AND BUILDING DESIGN

❏ 27. Use the energy model to refine the design.

❏ 28. Develop architectural detailing to support energy design strategies.

❏ 29. Clearly document energy performance requirements for equipment, lighting, insulation, and glazing, to guard against inferior substitutions.

❑ 30. Optimize performance of individual components of the MEP systems.

❑ 31. Provide a direct digital control energy management and control system.

❑ 32. Clearly document energy performance requirements for equipment, lighting, and control systems to guard against inferior substitutions.

❑ 33. Develop clear and comprehensive commissioning specifications for inclusion in the contract documents.

Bidding, Construction, and Commissioning

❑ 34. Confirm compliance with all energy requirements in the contract documents.

❑ 35. Encourage the contractor to conserve energy during construction.

Operations and Maintenance

❑ 36. Offer to provide a comprehensive operations and maintenance manual for the facility.

❑ 37. Offer to assist with ongoing monitoring.

❑ 38. Recommend that the owner establish educational and promotional programs.

➔ *Project Actions*

Energy

The Energy Project Actions are recommendations by phase and topic that should be considered during the design process. When relevant, actions are followed by further explanations in italics and a notation in brackets indicating the potential influence on the time, construction cost, maintenance cost, or fee.

The information in the second part of this section (see pages 93–101) provides a detailed discussion of energy design optimization in a narrative format with accompanying graphs and tables.

Team Building

1. **Establish energy design team; consider use of specialty consultants for energy analysis, lighting, and daylighting.**

   |A| |E| |O| 1.1. Include engineers on the design team who have expertise in energy design and analysis. Consider the use of an energy specialist for advanced energy analysis using DOE-2, Power DOE, or VisualDOE (see page 78), or computational fluid dynamics. [$E, $F]

   |A|I|E| |O| 1.2. Include a lighting designer with expertise in the integration of daylighting with energy electric lighting and controls (includes daylight dimmers, occupancy sensors, time clock controls, etc.). [$E, $F]

   |A|I|E| |O| 1.3. Consider the use of a daylighting specialist. The daylighting specialist should work with both physical models and computer models to refine daylighting design options. [$E, $F]

   |A|I|E| |O| 1.4. Consider the use of a third-party commissioning agent, to participate during design construction, start-up, and postoccupancy reviews. [$E, $F]

   |A|I|E| |O| 1.5. Clearly document energy design expectations for all consultants and subconsultants in contractual agreements. [$E, $F]

2. **Include the future building operator responsible for energy management on the team, as a participant in the design process.**

P = Planner	A = Architect	I = Interior designer	E = Engineer	L = Landscape architect	O= Owner consultation

[T] = Could affect length of construction (+ or –), [$C] = Affects construction costs (+ or –), [$E] Affects energy costs, [$F] = Affects fees (+ or –), [$M] = Affects maintenance costs (+ or –).

|A| |E| |O| 2.1. Suggest that the future building operator responsible for energy management participate as a member of the design team. The energy manager will benefit from an understanding of the design and may also propose refinements that will make the system easier to use in the future. The energy manager should also participate in building commissioning.

Education and Goal Setting

Education

3. **Educate the team about the importance of design optimization instead of code-minimum design.**

|P|A| |E|L|O| 3.1. Define a design methodology for the team based on energy analysis, integrated design, and design optimization rather than code-minimum performance. See the second part of this project action (page 93) for detailed guidance on energy analysis. [$E]

|A| |E| |O| 3.2. Define the measures that will be used to evaluate options and optimize the design. Typically, energy cost is used as the metric. Recommend that options be evaluated based on source energy consumption as well, so the environmental impacts associated with various options can be more accurately understood.
Source energy (as opposed to site energy) is a more holistic measure based on the total energy resources expended. For example, source energy recognizes energy lost in the production and transmission of electricity. Solar energy, on the other hand, has a source energy value of 0.

4. **Educate the team about the various methods for assessing life cycle costs, and select the preferred method.**

|P|A| |E|L|O| 4.1. Define the life cycle for the team as an assessment of the expected life span of the facility and/or the duration of the owner's financial interest in the property. Life cycle cost analysis will make use of discount rates to adjust for the value of money over time. The life cycle may be twenty-five, thirty, or fifty years for long-term owner-occupants of buildings, whereas the life cycle for tenant work may only be five or ten years. [$C, $E]

|P|A| |E| |O| 4.2. Define the various approaches for assessing the economics of design options. While simple payback analysis can provide a quick indication of the value of various design options, the results can be misleading. Life cycle costing calculates the first cost of building and equipment plus projected maintenance costs and energy costs over a designated life cycle. Other factors include financing costs, utility rebates, fuel escalation, inflation, facility repair and replacement costs, facility alteration and improvement costs, and salvage value at the end of the life cycle. [$C, $E]
For detailed evaluations, see the Life Cycle Costing Manual for the Federal Energy Management Program. *Life cycle costing tools are also available on the Internet at http://www.eren.doe.gov/femp/greenfed/2.2/2_2_economic_analysis.htm.*

|P|A| |E| |O| 4.3. Consider establishing an overall budget for building construction and operations, to provide a mechanism for supplementing the construction budget to pay for cost-effective energy efficiency upgrades. [$C, $E]

`|A|I|E| |O|` 4.4. Determine the client's interest in the use of third-party-financed energy-saving performance contracts to finance cost-effective energy efficiency improvements by energy service companies (ESCOs).

Goal Setting

5. Identify energy performance goals and develop a strategy for meeting them.

`|P|A|I|E|L|O|` 5.1. Hold a goal-setting session, with all team members participating, to determine project energy goals or targets. The goals will be preliminary and may be revised as the design progresses, based on the design investigations and energy analysis; however, they will serve as a point of departure for the team.
In general, it is possible to reduce energy use 30–50 percent compared to an ASHRAE 90.1-1989 baseline using cost-effective, off-the-shelf technologies. In mild climates, the goal may be to eliminate reliance on mechanical systems for air conditioning; or the team may attempt to eliminate all reliance on fossil fuels, by reducing energy loads, and using only renewable energy sources.

`|P|A|I|E|L|O|` 5.2. Integrate time for energy studies into the overall project schedule. To be most effective, energy studies need to be integrated into the design process from the outset of design.

6. Make a commitment to commission the building.

`|P|A| |E| |O|` 6.1. Strongly recommend full systems commissioning services to the owner. For large buildings use either the GSA or the Portland Energy Commission's (PECI) Model Commissioning Plan and Guide Specifications. For buildings less than 50,000 SF, consider using the Bonneville Power Administration's Building Commissioning Guidelines, second edition. [T, $C, $F, $E, $M]
Full systems commissioning includes HVAC, electrical, and life safety systems. It is good practice to include all systems in commissioning; this has generally proven to be an excellent investment toward future owner and occupant satisfaction.

`|P|A| |E| |O|` 6.2. To help clarify specific commissioning requirements and identify sources of model documents, review the commissioning prerequisites and credits in the LEED Green Building Rating System. The LEED system has prioritized the commissioning requirements in the guidelines identified above, in response to the realities of many project budgets. A basic level of commissioning that is simpler and less costly than full compliance has been identified, and the remaining beneficial procedures have been identified as "optional." [T, $C, $F, $E, $M]

`|P|A| |E| |O|` 6.3. If full systems commissioning cannot be agreed upon, recommend HVAC commissioning based on ASHRAE Guideline 1. [T, $C, $F, $E, $M]
- Includes on-site services to assist in the proper sequencing and start-up of mechanical systems to verify that specified IAQ has been achieved at the completion of construction.
- Confirms HVAC systems are installed as per design documents.
- Provides the owner with clear operating documentation, maintenance procedures, and enhanced operator training.

| P = Planner | A = Architect | I = Interior designer | E = Engineer | L = Landscape architect | O= Owner consultation |

[T] = Could affect length of construction (+ or –), [$C] = Affects construction costs (+ or –), [$E] Affects energy costs, [$F] = Affects fees (+ or –), [$M] = Affects maintenance costs (+ or –).

7. **Make a commitment to engage in future energy management.**

P | | E| |O 7.1. Recommend compliance with the Department of Energy's International Performance Measurement and Verification Protocol (IPMVP). IPMVP has been created to help ensure that projected energy savings due to design and engineering improvements are realized in actual operations. [T, $C, $E, $F]

P | | E| |O 7.2. Plan for submetering of electricity. Submetering by tenant, department, or organizational group allows energy managers to track energy usage and identify potential areas for improvements in efficiency. Separate accounting or billing can also be implemented to provide a financial incentive for energy conservation. [$C, $E]

8. **Consider participation in voluntary incentive programs (such as the U.S. DOE/EPA's Energy Star and Green Lights) and adoption of voluntary design standards.**

P|A|I|E| |O 8.1. When involved with building renovation projects, consider participating in the DOE/EPA's Green Lights and Energy Star Buildings Program, a voluntary program for lighting and energy efficiency upgrades. Green Lights, which refers exclusively to

Green Lights and Energy Star Buildings

The program asks U.S. commercial building owners to survey their existing facilities and to voluntarily make cost-effective improvements over a specified time period. EPA provides a range of support systems to help participants obtain information on financing options and energy-efficient technologies that support the Green Lights and Energy Star Buildings upgrade strategies. EPA also provides public recognition through EPA-generated news articles, media events, and public service advertisements. Energy Star Buildings use a five-stage approach for energy-efficiency upgrades:

> *Stage one*: Green Lights
>
> *Stage two*: Building tune-up
>
> *Stage three*: Other load reductions
>
> *Stage four*: Fan system upgrades
>
> *Stage five*: Heating and cooling system upgrades

Benefits

- Green Lights participants, on average, can expect to cut their electricity bills for lighting in half and to generate an internal rate of return of 30 percent or more, oftentimes improving lighting quality in the process.

- Energy Star Buildings participants, on average, can expect to reduce their energy bills by 43 percent and earn internal rates of return of 58 percent on their investments in these upgrades.

For more information: http://www.epa.gov/buildings/esbhome/

lighting upgrades, represents the first tier of issues to consider in the overarching Energy Star Buildings Program. [T, $C, $E, $F]

P|A| |E| |O 8.2. For new construction of commercial office buildings, consider participating in the DOE/EPA's Energy Star Building Label Program, a voluntary incentive program that recognizes exemplary building performance. Buildings that are among the top 25 percent nationwide in energy performance (based on DOE's benchmarking tool) and that maintain good indoor air quality become eligible for designation as an Energy Star Building. [T, $C, $E, $F]

P|A|I|E| |O 8.3. Recommend that all appliances and office equipment meet the DOE/EPA Energy Star guidelines. The guidelines specify efficiency ratings that exceed minimum federal standards yet are widely available in the marketplace. Energy Star products are available nationwide, and a detailed list of compliant products is available on-line at http://www.energystar.gov/products. [$E]

P|A| |E| |O 8.4. Adopt ASHRAE 90.1-1999 as an energy design standard in locations where this revised edition has not yet been adopted by the local energy code. This revised edition of the 1989 standard reflects the improvements in glazing and lighting technologies

| P = Planner | A = Architect | I = Interior designer | E = Engineer | L = Landscape architect | O= Owner consultation |

[T] = Could affect length of construction (+ or –), [$C] = Affects construction costs (+ or –), [$E] Affects energy costs, [$F] = Affects fees (+ or –), [$M] = Affects maintenance costs (+ or –).

Energy Star Buildings Label

The U.S. Environmental Protection Agency (EPA) and the U.S. Department of Energy (DOE) have established the Energy Star Label initiative to enable benchmarking of commercial building energy consumption on a 0–100 scale. Buildings that are among the top 25 percent nationwide in energy performance (equal to a score of 75 or greater) and maintain an indoor environment that conforms to industry standards can qualify for designation as an Energy Star Building.

Benchmarking Tool

The benchmarking tool is an on-line interactive software tool that evaluates the energy performance of a building against similar-use buildings in the United States. The comparisons are made on a scale of 0–100, in terms of energy cost as well as energy use intensity (BTU/SF/year or kWh/SF/year). As the tool makes use of a national database of building energy performance, the comparison accounts for factors that cannot be controlled, such as location and weather, as well as factors that are a reflection of the building's activity, such as occupant density, hours of occupancy, and building space use.

Inputs Required for Benchmarking

- Primary heating energy source
- Primary cooling energy source
- Floor area of office areas, computer rooms
- Area of parking garages and open parking lots
- Weekly hours of operation
- Number of occupants
- Number of computers
- Location (choose from fifty cities)

Indoor Environment Requirements

- Indoor air pollutants properly controlled
- Adequate outside air ventilation provided
- Interior thermal conditions provided
- Adequate illumination provided

For more information: http://www.epa.gov/buildings/label/

that have occurred over the past ten years. Building energy performance under this new standard will be approximately 15–20 percent better than it would have been under the old standard. [$E, $C]

P|A|I|E| |O 8.5. Consider adopting California Title 24 lighting design requirements for projects outside of California. Title 24 establishes limits for W/SF, requires dual-level switching, and establishes zones for lighting controls in daylit areas. [$E, $C]

Gathering Information

Programming

9. Review design criteria carefully, including temperature and humidity requirements, ventilation rates, plug loads, and occupancy schedules.

   Design criteria fundamentally drive energy performance. Assumptions need to be carefully reviewed so that energy use is neither under- nor overestimated.

   |A|I|E| |O| 9.1. Verify expected occupancy schedules, and determine the extent to which these are subject to change over time. If hours of occupancy are difficult to determine, consider defining a range of the potential hours of occupancy. Buildings with a high percentage of off-hours operations where the building is only partially occupied will benefit from highly flexible HVAC systems with high part-load efficiencies. [$E]

   |A|I|E| |O| 9.2. Confirm that ventilation rates meet the minimum standards set by ASHRAE 62-1999 and that the ventilation assumptions used for energy analysis are based on this standard program, as ventilation requirements vary depending on the space type. Consider adding 10–20 percent extra ventilation capacity and variable-speed drives to the system to allow for potential changes in the use of the space over time. [$E]

   |A|I|E| |O| 9.3. Opinions vary on what constitutes an acceptable comfort range. ASHRAE 55-92 (Thermal Environmental Conditions for Human Occupancy) cites a range of approximately 30–60 percent, which varies depending on dry bulb temperature, whereas some feel that a range of 20–60 percent is acceptable. Excess humidity is a problem during the cooling season and low humidity is a problem in the heating season. Humidification and dehumidification strategies can be energy intensive. [$E, $C, $M]

   |A|I|E| |O| 9.4. Determine the winter and summer temperature set points for occupied and unoccupied areas, as these can very considerably. Verify that energy loads calculations are based on the correct set points.

   |A|I|E| |O| 9.5. Review plug load assumptions, and recommend that the owner monitor existing facility plug loads if possible. Plug load requirements are commonly overestimated. Differentiate between electric capacity (represented by nameplate values on equipment), which is mandated by code, versus anticipated usage, which is based on the user's requirements. [$E]

   |A|I|E| |O| 9.6. Determine lighting levels for all programmed areas based on current Illuminating Engineering Society (IES) standards. Recommend use of task-ambient lighting systems. When task lighting is anticipated, reduce ambient lighting levels accordingly. [$C, $E, $M]

   Current thinking on recommended lighting levels has changed. For example, older standards called for as much as 100 foot-candles of illumination on the workplane in office areas. Current standards call for 50 foot-candles on the workplane and 15–20 foot-candles of ambient light in office areas when task lighting is anticipated.

| P = Planner | A = Architect | I = Interior designer | E = Engineer | L = Landscape architect | O= Owner consultation |

[T] = Could affect length of construction (+ or –), [$C] = Affects construction costs (+ or –), [$E] Affects energy costs, [$F] = Affects fees (+ or –), [$M] = Affects maintenance costs (+ or –).

The HOK Guidebook to Sustainable Design

Site Analysis

10. Gather information on the local climate, to inform the design process.

   Source for climate information is the Climatic Atlas of the United States, *by the National Oceanic and Atmospheric Administration (NOAA), for "Local Climatological Data summaries" (called LCDs). NOAA's National Climate Data Center (NCDC) provides access to climate data over the Internet at www.ncdc.noaa.gov/ol/climate/climatedata.html. ASHRAE's* Fundamentals Handbook and Applications Handbook *and AIA's* Architectural Graphic Standards *also contain some of this information.*

   |A| |E| | 10.1. Collect information on local temperature means and extremes. The ASHRAE Fundamentals Handbook lists summer values as 1 percent, 2.5 percent, and 5 percent, and winter values as 95 percent and 97.5 percent for almost eight hundred locations in the United States. A diurnal temperature swing (temperature swing that occurs on a twenty-four-hour cycle) of 20 degrees F or higher indicates that thermal mass storage or night ventilation could be an effective strategy.

   |A| |E| | 10.2. Collect information on available solar radiation. Direct, diffuse, and reflected daylight all contribute to incident solar radiation, or insolation. The ASHRAE Fundamentals Handbook measures this heat energy in terms of BTU/SF/hr or Langleys/hr. The LCDs provide data on daily hours of sunshine and the "percent of possible sunshine" likely to be available based on the average number of clear and cloudy days.

   |A| |E| | 10.3. Collect information on humidity. The LCDs provide morning and afternoon data on relative humidity. Based on the stated design criteria, an estimate of the number of days that would require humidification or dehumidification can be calculated.

   |A| |E| | 10.4. Collect information on prevailing wind direction and velocities. The LCDs present wind data in terms of monthly average speed and prevailing direction, as well as the fastest speed recorded and its direction. Wind patterns will influence the amount of air infiltration that will contribute to the heating and cooling load. Wind patterns (direction and velocity) also inform the development of natural ventilation strategies.

11. Analyze site microclimate to identify features that will impact energy performance. Document findings on site analysis drawings.

   |P|A| |E|L| 11.1. Consider the impact of topography. Elevation, hills and valleys, slopes, and aspects contribute to energy performance by draining cool air at night, contributing to lower temperatures. Surface conditions, including color and reflectivity, can modify prevailing climatic conditions by retaining and/or rejecting heat from the sun.

   |P|A| |E|L| 11.2. Consider the impact of existing vegetation. Trees can reduce exposure to sunlight, reducing temperatures by as much as 15 degrees F. Trees and other vegetation control the wind by obstructing, deflecting, or guiding its flow, and can reduce wind speeds by up to 90 percent.

   |P|A| |E|L| 11.3. Consider the impact of bodies of water. Water moderates extreme temperature variations. Water features such as ponds or fountains can raise temperature lows in winter and lower temperature highs in summer.

`[P|A| |E|L|]` 11.4. Consider the impact of adjacent buildings, walls, and fences. These can act as wind-breaks and deflectors, and affect solar access by casting shadows and providing reflective surfaces.

`[ |A| |E| |]` 11.5. Consider the extent to which the ground can act as a heat sink, based on the elevation of the water table relative to the frost line, and the soil structure.

Research

12. **Explore potential for utility rebates for energy efficiency and/or renewable energy.**

`[ | |E| |]` 12.1. Evaluate potential for utility rebates. Check the local utility rate structure as well as state programs to determine if the particular building type is a candidate for receipt of rebates for energy-efficient design, or for cost savings due to reduced energy use at peak hours. If peak hour demand charges apply, this may provide financial incentive for using time-lag and thermal cooling storage techniques. [T, $C, $F]

`[ | |E| |]` 12.2. Evaluate potential rebates for use of renewable energy such as solar-electric, solar-thermal, geothermal, and wind. Look for local allowances for "net metering," which runs the utility meter backward for all energy generated on-site, thereby providing a much greater cost benefit for renewable energy. [$C, $F, $M]

13. **Research performance benchmarks.**
    Performance benchmarks provide the team with a point of reference to develop energy performance goals and to evaluate performance as the design evolves.

`[ |A| |E| |]` 13.1. Evaluate energy performance against benchmark values for gross energy intensity, a measure of total site BTUs per SF per year. See the Department of Energy (DOE) publication Commercial Buildings Energy Consumption and Expenditures for average building energy consumption by building type, region, size, and vintage.

`[ |A| |E| |]` 13.2. Review building performance relative to the DOE benchmarking tool. This on-line interactive tool is available at http://www.epa.gov/buildings/label. The benchmarking tool makes use of the *Commercial Buildings Energy Consumption and Expenditures* database of building energy statistics, and normalizes for factors such as location, climate, occupant density, hours of occupancy, and building space use. Comparative data are provided for energy use and energy cost for fifty cities in the United States.

`[ |A| |E| |]` 13.3. Search for other performance benchmarks that can be used to evaluate your building during the design phase. The following benchmark data were developed by the Rocky Mountain Institute in Boulder, Colorado.

Example: Benchmark values for a large office building (>100,000 SF) in a temperate climate such as Washington, D.C.:

- *Total site BTU/SF/year (gross energy intensity)*
  - Average = 100,000
  - Good practice = 40,000–60,000
  - Advanced practice = 10,000–20,000

| P = Planner | A = Architect | I = Interior designer | E = Engineer | L = Landscape architect | O= Owner consultation |

[T] = Could affect length of construction (+ or –), [$C] = Affects construction costs (+ or –), [$E] Affects energy costs, [$F] = Affects fees (+ or –), [$M] = Affects maintenance costs (+ or –).

Benchmarking

The U.S. Department of Energy publishes *Commercial Buildings Energy Consumption and Expenditures,* which provides benchmark information on total energy consumption, in BTU per SF per year, which is called gross energy intensity. It is a ratio of the total amount of net energy ("site energy"), including heating, cooling, fans, motors, lighting, and plug load, to the total gross floor area of the building. This measure is climate dependent as well as program dependent and has improved over time. Some of the statistics are as follows:

Average for all office buildings	104.2
Average for all educational buildings	87.2
Average for all health care buildings	218.5
Average for all laboratory buildings	319.2
Average for all office buildings built 1990–1992	87.4
Average for all educational buildings built 1990–1992	57.1
Average for all parking garages built 1990–1992	24.5
Average for large office buildings in the Northeast in 1992	100.6
Average for large office buildings in the Midwest in 1992	110.0
Average for large office buildings in the South in 1992	76.3
Average for large office buildings in the West in 1992	84.1

Source: U.S. DOE *Commercial Buildings Energy Consumption and Expenditures.*

- *Connected Interior Lighting Load (W/SF)*
  The National Electric Code requires that all buildings be designed with a minimum capacity of 3.5 W/SF. The connected lighting load reflects use; it measures equipment efficiency and is an indicator of operational savings. Operational savings can be further quantified by measuring as-used lighting load, which factors in savings due to daylighting, controls, and use patterns.
  - Average = 1.5–2.0
  - Good practice = 1.0
  - Advanced practice = 0.65–0.7
- *Plug load, as used (W/SF)*
  The plug load represents energy use for equipment. Plug load requirements generally range between 3 and 6 W/SF. The as-used plug load reflects the diversification that accrues from energy saving (Energy Star) equipment with smart controls, auto-off switching for copiers, and so on.
  - Average = 3–6
  - Good practice = 1–2
  - Advanced practice = 0.
- *Mechanical-cooling sizing (SF/ton)*
  This measure is climate and program dependent.
  - Average = 250–350
  - Good practice = 500–600
  - Advanced practice = 1000–1200

- *Whole system cooling and air handling intensity (kW/ton)*
  Includes chiller, supply fan, chilled water pump, condenser water pump, and cooling tower at design conditions. This is a measure of the overall efficiency of the system. The best chiller available on the market today operates at 0.5 kW/ton.
    - Average = 1.9
    - Good practice = 1.5
    - Advanced practice = 0.9–1.1

Preliminary Energy Analysis

14. **Select energy analysis tools, including computer analysis and physical models.**

|A| |E| |O| 14.1. Review options for energy analysis and select computer analysis tools appropriate to the project. The best type of energy analysis software for the project will depend on the building type, size, and complexity, and the energy design goals. Energy simulations, such as DOE-2 and its associated graphic interface editions, provide

---

Building Energy Analysis Tool Options

- **TRACE 600**—TRACE 600, developed by Trane, produces accurate room load calculations and HVAC system design criteria based on ASHRAE algorithms. Can model advanced options such as free cooling and heat recovery, thermal storage, cogeneration, and chilled-water piping arrangements, including series, parallel, and decoupled; however, modeling of some architectural features is limited. TRACE Economics uses energy consumption numbers, utility rate structures, and other parameters to perform life-cycle cost analyses such as simple and life-cycle paybacks and internal rates of return.

- **HAP v4.0**—Hourly Analysis Program (HAP), developed by Carrier, is an energy simulation module that performs a true 8,760-hour energy simulation of building heat flow and equipment performance using typical meteorological year (TMY) climate data and the transfer function method to calculate building heat flow. Many types of air-handling systems, packaged equipment, and plant equipment can be simulated; however, modeling of some architectural features is limited. Costs can be computed using complex utility rates. Version 4.0 provides a Windows-based graphical user interface.

- **DOE-2**—Detailed, hourly, whole-building energy analysis of multiple zones in buildings of complex design; widely recognized as the industry standard. It calculates energy performance and life cycle cost of operation. This base program, developed by the U.S. Department of Energy, has been repackaged with graphical interfaces by commercial vendors (see below). It strength is in accurate whole-building analysis, including detailed simulation of architectural design elements.

- **Power DOE**—Power DOE has a graphical interface running under Microsoft Windows, making it easier to use than DOE-2 while retaining DOE-2's calculating power and accuracy. It has menu-driven input, on-line help, building component libraries, links to CAD packages, and the option to generate a building description automatically from type and vintage.

P = Planner | A = Architect | I = Interior designer | E = Engineer | L = Landscape architect | O= Owner consultation
[T] = Could affect length of construction (+ or –), [$C] = Affects construction costs (+ or –), [$E] Affects energy costs, [$F] = Affects fees (+ or –), [$M] = Affects maintenance costs (+ or –).

- **VisualDOE**—VisualDOE is a Windows graphical interface for the DOE-2 calculation engine. High-level concepts are used to minimize the time needed to enter data and to construct a model, as the geometry of an entire floor can be drawn with a CADD-like interface or imported through a .DXF file. A system of smart defaults fills in information gaps, and up to twenty design alternatives can be created to evaluate different design strategies and energy efficiency measures. Libraries are provided for construction assemblies, fenestration products, HVAC components, utility rates, and climate data. VisualDOE can use either the DOE-2.1E or DOE-2.2 calculation engines.

- **BLAST**—Building Loads and System Thermodynamics (BLAST) performs hourly simulations of buildings and central plant equipment. Zone models based on the fundamental heat balance method allow for analysis of thermal comfort, passive solar structures, high- and low-intensity radiant heat, moisture, and variable heat transfer coefficients—none of which can be analyzed in programs with less rigorous zone models. BLAST output may be utilized in conjunction with the LCCID (Life Cycle Cost in Design) program to perform an economic analysis of the building/system/plant design.

- **BDA**—Building Design Advisor (BDA) allows use of sophisticated analysis tools from the early, schematic phases of building design, without requiring in-depth knowledge of the linked tools. BDA acts as a data manager and process controller, allowing building designers to benefit from the capabilities of multiple analysis and visualization tools throughout the building design process. BDA is implemented as a Windows-based application with links to DOE-2, a daylighting analysis tool, and databases of prototypical values and case studies. The program is PC compatible, and uses Windows 3.x or higher.

- **System Analyzer**—System Analyzer is a powerful, interactive presentation tool with graphical interface that allows those with minimal HVAC experience to develop energy and economic analyses in as little as ten minutes in a Windows-based environment. It can be used either as a scoping tool to select systems for an initial design or to determine how one system/equipment combination performs versus another. Libraries and templates can be customized to fit the requirements of the project. System Analyzer interfaces with TRACE 600 and System Speculator for more intricate design and analysis results.

- **ENER-WIN**—ENER-WIN is an energy design tool for large commercial buildings with input through a sketching interface. It performs whole-building energy analysis for 8,760 hours/year for up to ninety-eight zones and twenty different wall and window types, making generous use of default values to speed schematic level design studies. The software calculates transient heat flows, daylighting, energy consumption, demand charges, and life cycle costs. This is best used for building design studies—it is not recommended for testing differences in HVAC systems (only nine available).

- **ESP-r**—Primarily used in Europe, ESP-r is a CADD-compatible program that supports early through detailed design stage appraisals. It has a powerful capability to simulate many innovative or leading-edge technologies, including daylight utilization, combined heat and electrical power generation via photovoltaic facades, CFD, multigridding, and complex control systems. ESP-r comprises a central Project Manager around which is arranged support databases, a simulator, various performance assessment tools, and a variety of third-party applications for CADD, visualization, and report generation.

- **TRNSYS**—TRNSYS (TRaNsient System Simulation Program) is used for HVAC analysis and sizing, solar design, daylighting, building thermal performance, analysis of control schemes, and so on, with component routines to handle input of weather or other time-dependent forcing functions and output of simulation results. Due to its modular approach, it is extremely flexible for modeling a variety of thermal systems in differing levels of complexity; supplied source code and documentation provide an easy method for users to modify or add components not in the standard library. It can be used on any platform supporting standard FORTRAN 77 (DOS, UNIX, VMS).

- **Energy 10**—This energy analysis program is appropriate for buildings less than 10,000 SF in size. Easy-to-use graphical interfaces, extensive library of default values, and detailed graphical output make this a good tool for small buildings.

Existing Buildings Energy Analysis

- **ASEAM**—A Simplified Energy Analysis Method (ASEAM), version 5.0, automatically creates DOE-2 input files. It evaluates high-potential, cost-effective energy-efficiency projects in existing federal buildings, and calculates results that are within 4–5 percent of DOE-2 annual energy results; using quick input routines, it permits evaluation of a 10,000 SF building in about ten minutes.

Lighting/Daylighting Analysis

- **Lumen Micro**—This is a relatively simple-to-use tool for daylighting and electric lighting analysis. Lumen Micro calculates interior illuminance levels and produces graphical outputs; however, complex building forms need to be simplified.

- **SuperLite**—A sophisticated tool for daylighting and electric analysis, SuperLite calculates interior illuminance levels in complex building spaces. Its analysis accounts for direct, externally reflected, and internally reflected light.

- **Lightscape**—Lightscape incorporates both radiosity and ray tracing technologies to simulate the physical properties of daylight, electric lighting, and materials. Lighting effects such as indirect illumination, soft shadowing, and color bleeding produce photorealistic images. Lightscape 3.2 is interoperable with AutoCAD, 3D Studio VIZ, and 3D Studio MAX, and includes an extensive library of hundreds of ready-to-use luminaires, blocks, and materials featuring products from leading manufacturers.

- **Radiance**—Radiance is a complex yet highly accurate program for use on a UNIX-compatible workstation. A more user-friendly PC-compatible version has recently been released. An advanced lighting simulation and rendering package creates photorealistic images and animation, and calculates spectral radiance values (illuminance and color) and spectral irradiance (illuminance and color) for interior and exterior spaces considering electric lighting, daylight, and interreflection. The package predicts illumination levels, visual quality, and appearance of design spaces.

- **ADELINE**—Advanced Day- and Electric Lighting Integrated New Environment (ADELINE) is used primarily for large commercial building applications. It provides 3-D CAD modeling of a space, automatically generates SuperLite and Radiance input files, calculates interior illuminance levels in complex building spaces, and graphically displays analysis results.

- **CEL-1**—Conservation of Electrical Lighting (CEL-1) is a lighting program that has been modified to operate as a lighting simulation subprogram of BLAST to create the hybrid program BLAST/CEL-1.

- **Physical Models**—Scale models are the best way to make qualitative assessments of lighting schemes. Light-meter values taken within a physical model can be highly accurate if glazing transparency can be simulated.

Water Conservation/Energy

- **Watergy**—This simple spreadsheet model screens sites for potential water conservation opportunities and illustrates the energy savings that result from water conservation activities. The user inputs site-specific data, including utility bill information; water usage; water, sewer, treatment, and energy costs; and numbers and kinds of water-using fixtures. Watergy then gives the user various conservation opportunities, the direct and indirect water and energy savings from these options, costs, and the payback period. It runs on an Excel or Lotus spreadsheet, Mac or PC.

> ## Renewable Energy
>
> - **FRESA**—Federal Renewable Energy Screening Assistant (FRESA) is useful for determining which renewable-energy applications require further investigation; however, it requires a high level of knowledge about energy audits and the limitations of the program. FRESA technologies represented include active solar heating, active solar cooling, solar hot water, daylighting with windows, daylighting with skylights, photovoltaic, solar thermal electric (parabolic dish, parabolic trough, central power tower), wind electricity, small hydropower, biomass electricity (wood, waste, etc.), and cooling load avoidance (multiple glazing, window shading, increased wall insulation, infiltration control). Life-cycle cost calculations comply with 10 CFR 436. FRESA is PC-compatible, 286 or better, and operates under DOS.
>
> - **Solar-Pro**—Solar-Pro simulates the operation of a solar hot water heating system, hour by hour, for one year based on TMY information available from the National Renewable Energy Lab (NREL). Hundreds of customizable variables are incorporated into the simulation. Runs under Windows 95 with MS-Excel 7.0.
>
> - **T*SOL**—T*SOL is software for the planning, analysis, and simulation of thermal solar heating systems. A user-friendly professional tool for planners, engineers, and energy specialists, it requires no training for use. Five classic solar water heating systems, two of which include space heating, can be tested under varying parameters, with the results (temperature, energies, efficiencies, and solar fraction) easily saved to file and presented in graph or chart form. It is primarily used in Europe; however, version 2.0 is in English. Uses Windows 3.1 or higher.
>
> For more information on available tools, see the Building Energy Tools Directory, http://www.eren.doe.gov/buildings/tools_directory, which lists more than 110 software tools, from research-grade software to commercial products. The listing includes descriptions, strengths, and weaknesses, and information on where you can get them.

excellent analysis of architectural and site design options, whereas other programs focus more exclusively on systems options and have limited capability to analyze innovative architectural strategies. In some cases, it will be best to use more than one program. [T, $F]

|A| |E| |O| 14.2. Plan for the use of physical models to complement and enhance energy analysis. Detailed daylighting analysis is best done with both computer and physical models. Wind tunnel testing is valuable for the development of natural ventilation strategies. [T, $F]

15. Develop a base case energy model.
See the second part of this project action (page 93) for detailed guidance on energy analysis.

|A| |E| | | 15.1. Develop a base case reference building that represents code-minimum design to provide a datum or benchmark against which energy design options can be measured. [$F]

|A| |E| | | 15.2. Identify and prioritize building energy requirements. Before energy design strategies can be developed, a clear picture of the building's most significant energy requirements should be developed. These statistics can be documented in energy cost and energy consumption pie charts. The ranking of energy cost components for a given building are generally not identifiable by intuition. The largest annual energy cost component may be lighting, cooling, heating, or ventilation. [$E]

Optimization

Site and Building Design

16. Integrate energy analysis into the design process; review and monitor energy analysis methodology as the design progresses.
    See the second part of this project action (page 93) for detailed guidance on energy analysis.

    |A| |E| | 16.1. Reduce energy requirements first, using architectural and site design strategies; then analyze HVAC systems options based on the reduced requirements.

    |A| |E| | 16.2. Categorize energy strategies in terms of whether they affect peak energy loads, energy use, energy cost, and/or demand cost.

    |A| |E| | 16.3. Separate design sizing function from energy analysis function, and develop diversity factors to reflect actual usage patterns to model energy-efficient design options.

    |A| |E| | 16.4. Use an energy analysis method that takes into account building overhangs and sunshading (not all of them do).

    |A| |E| | 16.5. Use an energy analysis method that takes into account heat gain avoidance from daylighting (not all of them do).

17. Integrate passive solar strategies into the design of the site and building.

    |A|I|E|L| 17.1. Explore opportunities for passive solar heating where appropriate. Passive or "natural" heating options involve the coordination of glazing, thermal mass, and surface reflectance. A passive heating system is divided into five elements: collector, absorber, storage, distribution, and heat regulation. Avoid overheating from solar gain in large commercial buildings, which already have considerable internal heat loads from body heat, equipment, and lighting.

    |A|I|E|L| 17.2. Explore opportunities for passive solar cooling where appropriate. Passive or "natural" cooling systems require an environmental heat sink for rejection of excess heat. Four commonly available heat sinks are the sky, heat absorptance that occurs during evaporation, cool night air, and cool ground temperatures. Simple natural cooling options include sun shading, building reflectance, insulation, and natural ventilation.

    |A|I|E|L| 17.3. Consider the impact of landscaping on passive solar strategies. Trees can provide shade, and ground vegetation reduces reflected light into and onto the building. Vegetation can act as a buffer, reducing wind speeds by up to 90 percent, or vegetation can guide air flows and contribute to natural ventilation strategies.

18. Optimize design of the building envelope, including insulation, glazing, and sun shading devices.

    |A| |E| | 18.1. Optimize building insulation. More insulation is usually, but not always, better. In temperate climates, where rejection of heat from interior sources is most critical, insulation can impede beneficial heat transfer from the inside to the outside of the building. Use energy modeling to determine the optimal, cost-beneficial R-value of

| P = Planner | A = Architect | I = Interior designer | E = Engineer | L = Landscape architect | O= Owner consultation |

[T] = Could affect length of construction (+ or –), [$C] = Affects construction costs (+ or –), [$E] Affects energy costs, [$F] = Affects fees (+ or –), [$M] = Affects maintenance costs (+ or –).

the roof, wall, and slab insulation, and the appropriate quantity and type of insulation. Factor in the effect of thermal bridges to determine the effective R-value of the overall system for energy modeling. [$C, $E]

Cross-reference with the Material Resources Project Actions (page 138) for information on the environmental impacts associated with various types of insulation.

|A| |E| | 18.2. Use light-colored roofing. Light-colored roofing reflects light and heat, reducing cooling requirements and diminishing the building's contribution to heat islands. Metal, tile, and even some membrane roofing are available in a range of colors. ASTM formulas are currently being developed to factor light reflectance (albedo) of building surfaces into energy performance calculations. [$C, $E]

|A| |E| | 18.3. Optimize building glazing. Evaluate U-value, visible light transmittance, and shading coefficient of the glass. Consider impact of orientation and exterior and interior sun shading on performance of glazing. High-performance glazing offers a high ratio of visible light transmittance to shading coefficient (called the coolness index, or CI), together with high insulative value (R-value). Give preference to glass with a Coolness Index greater than 1.2. Many options are now available, including: [$C, $E]

- Double- or triple-glazed insulating units
- Spectrally selective tinted glass
- Low-emissivity coatings (called low-E glass)
- "Heat mirror" (incorporates a thin plastic film within the airspace to effectively create two airspaces)
- "Superwindows" (incorporate multiple thin plastic films within an enlarged airspace); can have a center-of-glass R-value as high as 12

Reflective coatings have low visible light transmittance relative to their shading coefficient and are not generally a good solution for schemes that incorporate daylighting into their energy strategy. Highly reflective building skins may also be considered "bad neighbors," reflecting glare and heat to neighboring structures.

|A|I|E|L| 18.4. Consider use of exterior shading and sun control. Exterior shading and sun control can dramatically influence solar heat gain and therefore both the sizing of the cooling system (first cost) and the energy required to cool the building. Develop sun control to suit facades based on their orientation. Explore both natural and architectural options, including trees and other vegetation, as well as interior and exterior building overhangs, fins, shades, and the like. Coordinate with interior shading requirements and daylighting strategy. Some examples are: [$C, $E, $M]

- Horizontal projections
- Vertical projections
- Sunscreens
- Shutters
- Shades
- Awnings
- Trellises, to direct the growth of shading vegetation
- Photovoltaic (PV) sunshades, which incorporate PV panels into the exterior sunshades; PV glazing is now available in a wide range of light transmissivity

Give priority to exterior sun control over interior strategies to control both light and heat gain before penetrating the building envelope.

|A|I|E| | 18.5. Consider options for interior sun shading that improve visual comfort and energy performance. Finishes with high light reflectivity perform best. Interior shading devices include: [$C, $E, $M]

- Opaque and semiopaque shades (semiopaque roller shade manufacturers claim that energy use can be reduced by as much as one-third)
- Draperies
- Venetian blinds (two-tone venetian blinds are available for applications where some heat collection is desirable—one side reflects light and heat out, the other side absorbs heat and reradiates it to the space)
- Motorized blinds on photocell controllers (used in areas where individual control is not desired)

|A| |E| |O 18.6. Consider dynamic building envelope components. Envelope components have been developed to respond dynamically to changing climatic conditions. Examples are motorized shading for walls, windows, or skylights, movable shutters or insulation, and mirror systems that adjust to optimize daylighting systems according to outdoor sky conditions. [$C, $E, $M]

|A| |E| | 18.7. Consider the impact of thermal lag associated with heavy mass construction. [$C, $E]
Thermal loads can be less with heavy mass than with light walls of equal U-value, due to the time lag associated with heat transfer through a heavy mass wall. Consider the location of insulation when designing with thermal mass, because it affects the time lag. Thermal mass saves energy in regions where the outdoor air temperature fluctuates daily above and below the comfort range, and can also provide peak shaving in hot climates. Thermal mass can also act as a heat sink for direct or indirect passive solar heating strategies.

Lighting

19. Maximize the controlled use of daylight for ambient lighting requirements using a holistic approach that considers heat gain and loss, and reduced reliance on electric lighting.
   A computer modeling program for daylighting, such as Lumen Micro, is an effective and efficient tool for evaluating most daylighting systems. The use of scale models may be preferred for especially complex spaces, and for a qualitative evaluation of the daylighting scheme.

|A| | | | 19.1. Prepare a detailed analysis of the of the sun's position relative to the site and possible building forms during schematic design.
   To ensure success, the daylighting strategy must be established early in schematic design, as it will influence decision making related to the site plan, building orientation, building massing, and fenestration.

|A|I| | |O 19.2. Where possible, locate program areas that benefit most from daylight at perimeter zones with northern and southern exposures. Eastern and western exposures require more careful sun control strategies to control glare and overheating.

|A|I|E| | 19.3. Identify daylighting zones within the building. Typically the perimeter 15 feet of space can be entirely lit by daylight during daytime hours. Use of optical light

| P = Planner | A = Architect | I = Interior designer | E = Engineer | L = Landscape architect | O= Owner consultation |

[T] = Could affect length of construction (+ or –), [$C] = Affects construction costs (+ or –), [$E] Affects energy costs, [$F] = Affects fees (+ or –), [$M] = Affects maintenance costs (+ or –).

shelves integrated with the fenestration, glass type, and sun shading can extend the daylight zone up to 45 feet deep.

|A|I|E| | 19.4. Consider use of monitors, clerestories, and skylights to provide daylight in the building interior zone. [$C, $E]

|A|I|E| | 19.5. Consider use of light shelves to project light deep into the space. Coordinate with space planning, interior shading requirements, and finishes. [$C, $E]

|A| |E| | 19.6. Carefully design skylight areas to avoid overlighting and overheating. Overlighting in skylit areas, such as building atria, creates discomfort from contrasting light levels, glare, and overheating. Use a lighting analysis tool as well as physical models to evaluate light qualitatively and quantitatively.

|A| |E| | 19.7. Consider the use of light transport systems, such as light pipes or fiber optics, where access to natural light is limited due to site constraints, limited access, or security requirements. [$C, $M]

20. Select efficient electric lighting systems.

|A|I|E| | 20.1. Develop a lighting strategy for each space type based on the use of the space and the quality of lighting desired (direct, indirect, task, combination). Separate lighting systems into task and ambient applications wherever possible. Maximize the use of borrowed light for ambient lighting in interior areas.

|A|I|E| | 20.2. Choose fixtures that combine high lighting efficiency with high visual comfort protection (VCP). Baffles and other glare reduction features reduce light output efficiency yet are necessary in many applications.

|A|I|E| | 20.3. Use high-efficiency lamps and ballasts, including fluorescent, high-intensity discharge (HID), and sulfur lighting. Use electronic ballasts wherever possible. [$E]
Sulfur lighting (also called fusion lighting) uses a light pipe to distribute focused light from a high-powered sulfur lamp over large areas to create a high-efficiency, low-UV, low-maintenance indirect light source. The light pipe distribution system also requires many fewer lamps, and those lamps can be positioned for ease of maintenance.

|A|I|E| | 20.4. Avoid incandescent lighting whenever possible. Compact fluorescent lamps, which typically are four times more efficient and last ten times longer than incandescents, can be used in almost all applications where incandescents have been used.

|A|I|E| |O| 20.5. Use task lighting to supplement moderate ambient light levels.

|A|I|E| | 20.6. Always use Energy Star–rated LED exit signs. A typical long-life incandescent exit sign consumes 40W and must have the lamps replaced every eight months. A typical LED exit sign consumes less than 5W and has a life expectancy of more than eighty years. [$E, $M]

21. Consider use of lighting controls.

|A|I|E| | 21.1. Consider the use of occupancy sensors for all new buildings. Occupancy sensors, which automatically shut off lighting in unoccupied areas, are an inexpensive tech-

nology that can save up to 75 percent of energy usage, depending on the application. [$E, $C]

Care must be taken to specify sensors compatible with each other and with the automated building control system. The most reliable (and expensive) occupancy sensors are dual-technology sensors, utilizing both ultrasonic and infrared technologies. They are available in ceiling mount only and have adjustable settings.

|A|I|E| | 21.2. Consider use of occupancy sensors that control plug loads in workstation areas, including task lighting, computers, and other miscellaneous loads within the workstation. [$E, $C]

|A|I|E| | 21.3. Consider the use of daylight dimming sensors that dim electric lighting levels in response to daylight. Coordinate ballasts with dimming requirements in the daylighting zones. Combination dimming and occupancy sensors are available. [$E, $C]

|A|I|E| | 21.4. Consider the use of time clock controls that turn off lighting during hours when the building is unoccupied. [$E]

|A| |E|L| 21.5. Consider using solar-powered exterior lighting, particularly where the costs of wiring to the building's power supply and/or the utility grid would be high. [$C]

MEP Systems

22. Use high-efficiency HVAC systems. Avoid oversizing, which can reduce efficiency.

|A| |E| |O| 22.1. Consider use of separate HVAC systems to serve areas expected to operate on widely differing operating schedules or design conditions, constant and weather-independent areas, and perimeter spaces. [$C, $E, $M]

- Provide controls to allow systems to operate in occupied and unoccupied modes
- Reset supply air temperature to extend economizer operations
- Control equipment loads generated by HVAC systems

|A| |E| | 22.2. Use the highest-efficiency energy transport system that complements other system parameters. The following options are listed in order of efficiencies from most to least efficient: [$C, $E, $M]

- Electric wire or fuel pipe
- Two-phase fluid transfer (steam or refrigerant)
- Single-phase liquid fluid (water, glycol, etc.)
- Air

| | |E| | 22.3. Use high-efficiency heating and cooling equipment, pumps, and motors. Use premium-efficiency motors for all motors over 1 hp. Consider primary heating equipment based on the 97½ percent design temperature values, with a target load safety factor of no more than 10 percent, and a heating pickup load factor of less than 30 percent. [$C, $E, $M]

Avoid oversizing of heating and cooling equipment, fans, and motors, which can reduce efficiency and increase operating costs.

| P = Planner | A = Architect | I = Interior designer | E = Engineer | L = Landscape architect | O= Owner consultation |

[T] = Could affect length of construction (+ or –), [$C] = Affects construction costs (+ or –), [$E] Affects energy costs, [$F] = Affects fees (+ or –), [$M] = Affects maintenance costs (+ or –).

| A | E | | 22.4. Verify that the following equipment options have been included in the design, as they result in cost savings in almost every application: [$C, $E, $M]

- Primary heating equipment
  - High-efficiency boilers
  - Supply water temperature reset
- Primary cooling equipment
  - High-efficiency chillers
  - Direct or indirect evaporative chillers (as appropriate to climate conditions)
  - Heat pumps, water-source and air-source
  - Supply water temperature reset
- Fans and air distribution systems
  - Variable air volume
  - Variable frequency drives
  - High-efficiency motors
  - Airside or waterside economizer cycle
- Pumps and hydraulic distribution systems
  - Variable-flow pumping
  - Variable-frequency drives
  - High-efficiency motors
  - Low-flow plumbing fixtures

| | | E | | 22.5. Develop design so that reheating of conditioned air streams for comfort control is minimized. All fans and air distribution systems should utilize temperature reset controls. [$E]

| | | E | | 22.6. Use variable-frequency drives for pumps and fans, and variable-air-volume boxes for air distribution, unless the design analysis clearly demonstrates that other equipment is more cost-effective over the life cycle.

| A | E | | 22.7. Consider the following equipment and measures as upgrades to basic systems. These options may require life cycle cost analysis to determine cost-effectiveness. [$C, $E, $M]

- Primary heating equipment
  - Renewable resources, such as solar, wind, geothermal
- Primary cooling equipment
  - Chiller heat recovery
  - Waterside economizer cycle
  - Low approach temperature for water in cooling towers
  - Desiccant dehumidification
  - Evaporative versus air-cooled condensers
  - Indirect and direct evaporative cooling
  - Cogeneration
- Fans and air distribution systems
  - Air-to-air heat recovery
- Low duct velocities
  - Optimal duct design (to improve air delivery and reduce fan power requirements)
  - Low-temperature air distribution
  - Underfloor air distribution
- Pumps and hydraulic distribution systems
  - Radiant ceilings

|A|I|E| | 22.8. Locate mechanical equipment to maximize the efficiency of distribution. Consider the use of an underfloor air delivery system. Equipment rooms should be located to minimize the length of travel, so as to reduce losses. Distributed systems can lower energy usage by allowing unused areas to be isolated. [$C, $E]

|A| |E| | 22.9. Explore options to reclaim waste heat from equipment and return air and water. [$C, $E]

23. Balance energy efficiency goals with consideration of the environmental impacts of fuel type and refrigeration selection.

| | |E| | 23.1. Consider alternatives to HVAC equipment that uses HCFC refrigerants, such as natural gas engine chillers. For existing buildings, develop a phase-out plan for any CFC equipment, and consider phasing out HCFC equipment as well. [$C, $E]

|A| |E| | 23.2. Consider the primary source energy when determining what type of energy should be used on site. To determine the overall environmental impact of a building's energy consumption, the site energy can be converted into primary source energy to recognize the transformations and transportation it undergoes from the extraction site to delivery. For example, electricity generated from coal creates more pollution and is ultimately less energy efficient than natural gas. [$F, $C, $M]

24. Maximize efficiency of electric power and distribution.

| | |E| | 24.1. Size transformers and generating units as close to the actual anticipated load as possible. [$C, $E]

| | |E| | 24.2. Distribute electric power at the highest practical voltage and load at the maximum power factor consistent with safety.

25. Maximize efficiency of service water heating and cooling. Consider use of solar hot water heating.

|A| |E| | 25.1. Consider point-of-use hot water heaters. [$C, $E, $M]

|A| |E| | 25.2. Consider the use of centralized chillers for water cooling in place of individual electric water coolers. [$C, $E, $M]

| | |E| | 25.3. Fully insulate hot water distribution piping. Recirculating systems should have pumps with automatic control to cycle pumps off during hours of nonuse. [$C, $E]

| | |E| | 25.4. Consider the use of low-temperature water heating systems.

|A| |E| | 25.5. Consider the use of solar hot water heating. [$C, $E, $M]
Solar hot water systems are particularly beneficial for building types that use high volumes of hot water, such as hospitals, apartment buildings, health clubs, restaurants, and similar places. For best efficiency, locate the solar panels, water storage tank, and backup water heater near the fixtures or equipment using hot water.

| P = Planner | A = Architect | I = Interior designer | E = Engineer | L = Landscape architect | O= Owner consultation |

[T] = Could affect length of construction (+ or –), [$C] = Affects construction costs (+ or –), [$E] Affects energy costs, [$F] = Affects fees (+ or –), [$M] = Affects maintenance costs (+ or –).

26. Consider the potential for on-site power generation.

|A| |E| | 26.1. Consider the potential for use of combined heat and power systems (CHP, also known as cogeneration) such as microturbines, fuel cells, absorption chillers, and engine-driven chillers. [$C, $E, $M]
CHP systems generate electricity and use the waste heat that would conventionally be discarded for making steam, heating water, chilling water, or compressing air. Interest in the potential for CHP has been further heightened by the introduction of absorption chillers that have expanded the range of cost-effective CHP applications. For more information, see http://www.oit.doe.gov/chpchallenge/vision.html.

|A| |E| | 26.2. Consider the potential for use of fuel cells, especially for projects having continuous power requirements.

|A| |E| | 26.3. Consider the potential for use of photovoltaics, especially in areas remote from electricity infrastructure, or where electricity costs and sun availability are high. [$C, $E]
Building-integrated photovoltaics (PVs) can be integrated into the building envelope as metal roofing, spandral glazing, or semi-transparent vision glazing. The PV installation as a whole can either be grid-connected or stand-alone (which requires use of batteries). Check status of net metering legislation in the state to see if excess power can be stored in the power grid.

|A| |E| | 26.4. Consider potential for use of wind turbines where space allows and wind access is good. Wind power can be cost-effective, as it can be produced for as little as 5 cents per kW. [$C, $E, $M]

|A| |E| | 26.5. Consider potential for use of ground-source heat pumps, particularly for low-rise buildings. Verify that subsurface conditions allow for the use of geothermal. See http://www.geothermal.org/index.html. [$C, $E]

Documents and Specifications

Site and Building Design

27. Use the energy model to refine the design.
See the second part of this project action (page 93) for detailed guidance on energy analysis.

|A| |E| | 27.1. Update the energy model to reflect the design as it has developed. Verify that energy model inputs for building massing, fenestration, overhangs and sun shading, glass types and insulation values, and electric lighting are consistent with the design.

28. Develop architectural detailing to support energy design strategies.

|A| |E| | 28.1. Minimize air infiltration, which is caused by wind pressure and the stack effect. Heating loads due to infiltration of unconditioned air can exceed transmission losses, and fan energy consumed in pressurizing buildings is considerable. Proper sealing of joints and the use of airlock entryways are essential. [$E]

| A | E | | 28.2. Provide an adequate air barrier and vapor retarder. Correct placement of the vapor barrier (at point where cool surfaces meet warm, moist air) and design of a tight exterior wall are key in preventing microbial contamination. [$C, $E, $M]

| A | E | | 28.3. Minimize unintentional or uncontrolled thermal bridges. Thermal bridges can radically alter the conductivity of the building envelope. Detail carefully to avoid cold spots, which cause discomfort and can lead to condensation on the cold surfaces. Condensation can lead to mold and to microbial growth, even though the relative humidity of the room air may remain within the range prescribed by ASHRAE 55-1992. Examples include wall studs, balconies, ledges, and extensions of building slabs. [$E]

29. Clearly document energy performance requirements for equipment, lighting, insulation, and glazing, to guard against inferior substitutions.

| A | E | | 29.1. When specifying equipment, document the kW requirements, and the power factor or efficiency rating wherever possible.

| A | E | | 29.2. When specifying lighting, document the lamp (type, wattage, and color), ballast, and control requirements, in addition to the fixture.

| A | E | | 29.3. When specifying insulation, document the type of insulation, the thickness (minimum thickness for tapered installations), and the R-value per inch.

| A | E | | 29.4. When specifying glazing, document the R-value, shading coefficient, and visible light transmittance.

MEP Systems

30. Optimize performance of individual components of the MEP systems.

| A | E | | 30.1. Use the energy model to evaluate alternative designs and refine energy performance.

| | E | | 30.2. Optimize ventilation system design through careful sizing and locating balancing dampers to reduce pressure losses. Use effective sealing methods and good insulation to reduce leakage. Select diffusers with high induction ratios, low pressure drop, and good airflow at part load.

| | E | | 30.3. Reduce pressure losses in piping by sizing piping carefully. Insulate piping.

| | E | | 30.4. Use high-efficiency pumps and motors, and variable-speed drives.

31. Provide a direct digital control energy management and control system.

| | E | O | 31.1. Recommend use of a direct digital control energy management and control system. An energy management and control system should be considered in any building exceeding 40,000 SF of gross area. [$C, $E, $M]
A good energy management and control system (EMCS) offers the potential to increase the efficiency of all the systems that it controls. Building systems start-ups, shutdowns, and operation can be fine-tuned to meet and anticipate loads, and can be optimized for comfort and energy conservation. It can also offer diagnostic and energy use analysis informa-

| P = Planner | A = Architect | I = Interior designer | E = Engineer | L = Landscape architect | O= Owner consultation |

[T] = Could affect length of construction (+ or –), [$C] = Affects construction costs (+ or –), [$E] Affects energy costs, [$F] = Affects fees (+ or –), [$M] = Affects maintenance costs (+ or –).

tion. See ASHRAE/IES Standard 90.1-1999 for guidance on the use of central monitoring and control systems.

| | |E| | 31.2. Integrate the operation of individual components (such as boilers, chillers, fans, pumps, motors, lighting, lighting controls, security, etc.) into a centralized computer interface program to ease operations.

32. Clearly document energy performance requirements for equipment, lighting, and control systems to guard against inferior substitutions.

| | |E| | 32.1. Include energy efficiency ratings for all equipment in the specifications.

| | |E| | 32.2. Verify that lighting control systems are fully documented and coordinated with the specified fixtures.

33. Develop clear and comprehensive commissioning specifications for inclusion in the construction documents.

| | |E| | 33.1. Include documentation of HVAC system design criteria, ventilation criteria, and the building program requirements in the commissioning specifications.

| | |E| | 33.2. Develop specifications that describe a detailed plan for the commissioning process, with roles and responsibilities clearly described.

Bidding, Construction, and Commissioning

34. Confirm compliance with all energy requirements in the contract documents.

| | |E| | 34.1. Verify that a maintenance plan for HVAC equipment has been provided. [$F, $E]

| | |E| | 34.2. Verify that the commissioning agent has developed a detailed commissioning plan, including any required one-time (static) or dynamic tests.

| | |E| | 34.3. Confirm that specified equipment efficiencies have been met.

35. Encourage the contractor to conserve energy during construction.

| | |E| | 35.1. Require the contractor to pay for electricity costs during construction, to provide an incentive for energy conservation.

| | |E| | 35.2. Encourage the contractor to install motion sensors for security lighting. [$C, $E]

| | |E| | 35.3. Request that the contractor use compact fluorescent lamps for temporary lighting and energy-efficient HVAC equipment for temporary systems. [$C, $E]

Operations and Maintenance

36. Offer to provide a comprehensive operations and maintenance manual for the facility.

|A| |E| |O| 36.1. Offer to provide a comprehensive operations and maintenance manual for the facility. The manual should include operation instructions, performance verification procedures and results, equipment inventory, and the recommended maintenance program. Consider including the following as requirements and/or recommendations: [$F, $E, $M]

- Verify that heating and cooling are operated on an accurate schedule that coincides with the occupancy schedule. Scheduled overrides should be limited to night setback temperatures, and based on a duration of one hour.
- Operate large recirculating systems on a time-of-day schedule that coincides with the occupancy schedule only.
- Set domestic hot water temperatures as low as possible, that is, 110°F (43°C), except for food service areas, where a local booster heater shall be used.
- Turn off all equipment when not in use and keep refrigerator doors closed.
- Perform periodic reviews to ensure proper operation of equipment, including lighting sensors, controllers, air economizer dampers, and automatic temperature control dampers. Recalibrate as required.
- Periodically verify the status of control setpoints and confirm they are reasonable.
- Periodically review automatic start/stop and reset schedules for equipment to confirm that they coincide with current building operation and occupancy patterns.
- Periodically revise set points for controls and verify correct automatic responses by system components.
- Perform recommended preventative maintenance on valves, actuators, and other control devices.
- Purchase equipment with the EPA's Energy Star label.
- Select energy-efficient replacements for electric motors.
- Clean equipment and appliances regularly.
- Ensure that lamp, ballast, and fixture replacements meet or exceed the efficiencies of the original specification.

37. Offer to assist with ongoing monitoring.

| | |E| | | 37.1. Offer to assist with ongoing monitoring to verify that projected energy savings are being met. [$F, $E]

| | |E| |O| 37.2. Ensure that required personnel have been properly trained on equipment operation and maintenance on the specific equipment in the facility. [$M]

| | |E| | | 37.3. Suggest a lamp maintenance program that ensures proper cleaning of lamps and fixtures and maintains a proper lamp replacement schedule. [$M]

38. Recommend that the owner establish educational and promotional programs.

|A|I|E| |O| 38.1. Recommend that the owner establish educational and promotional programs that encourage staff to turn off lights and equipment whenever practical. [$M]

| P = Planner | A = Architect | I = Interior designer | E = Engineer | L = Landscape architect | O= Owner consultation |
[T] = Could affect length of construction (+ or –), [$C] = Affects construction costs (+ or –), [$E] Affects energy costs, [$F] = Affects fees (+ or –), [$M] = Affects maintenance costs (+ or –).

A SYSTEMATIC APPROACH TO ENERGY DESIGN OPTIMIZATION

The design of energy-efficient, environmentally responsive commercial and institutional buildings is as much art as it is science. There is no one best solution or one best approach; rather, it is a collaborative search by the project design team for the most appropriate solution within the economic, site, and functional constraints of the project. How the information is gathered, analyzed, and presented, however, will significantly influence the design and the ultimate energy and environmental performance of the building.

The purpose of this energy optimization process is to assist the project design team in making decisions by providing the appropriate information at the right time and in the right form. These activities are designed to be an integral part of the architectural design process and to support, complement, and enhance the creative process of design. This process has been adapted from research managed by Architectural Energy Corporation's Michael Holtz and the Solar Energy Research Institute as part of the Passive Solar Commercial Building Demonstration Program, funded by the U.S. Department of Energy.

Activity 1: Gather Information

Prior to the outset of design, the team will develop or verify an architectural program that summarizes the client's goals, functional requirements, site conditions, budget, and so on. The building's total conditioned floor area and the floor area devoted to each functional activity are needed as well as the energy use in terms of lighting power, equipment, occupancy, ventilation, and so on. Site information should include the location and height of adjacent structures, landscape plantings, and ground surface materials. Meteorological data and information on the utility rate structure need to be collected at this time as well, for use in energy modeling.

Activity 2: Create Base Case Energy Model

Based on the program information, an initial building form concept can be established that is representative of the functional relationships, floor area, and volume of the actual building. Specific attention should be given to the functional requirements of the building, so that the energy design characteristics assumed in the reference building are appropriate. Initial form-giving constraints such as building footprint, number of floors, orientation with respect to the cardinal directions, and so on provide information from which a starting point for the analysis can proceed. If the design team has few preconceived notions about the design, then estimates are made for the initial analysis.

Next, the initial concept of the building is integrated with prescriptive requirements from an energy standard to produce a "base case" or "reference building" energy model. The energy standard can be the local energy code, current practice, or some nationally recognized standard, such as ASHRAE 90.1-1989. The reference building computer model uses prescriptive criteria specified in the code for opaque shell construction, percent fenestration, glazing characteristics, lighting power budget, equipment loads, mechanical equipment performance, and so on.

While accuracy in defining the reference building is helpful at this stage of the process, it should not become a deterrent to proceeding with development of the base case model. Because the model will be continuously updated during the design process, it is more important to make educated guesses to fill in gaps in information, so that the process can move forward.

To perform the base case analysis, the annual energy performance of the reference building is simulated and presented in pie chart form. One is created to describe the annual operating costs for electricity consumption, electric peak demand, and gas according to the applicable utility rate structure for the facility, and another is created to describe the energy consumed in BTUs for each end use, including heating, cooling, lighting,

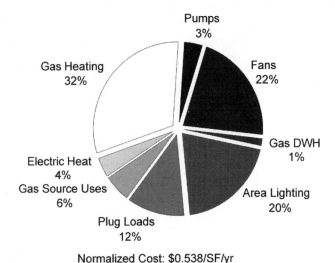

Normalized Cost: $0.538/SF/yr
Total Cost: $25,661/yr

West Jefferson Schematic Design. As-designed building.

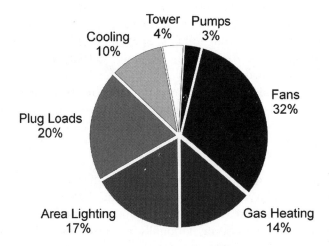

Normalized Cost: $1.513/SF/yr
Total Cost: $262,451

Denver Federal Courthouse. As-designed building.

Figure 3. Energy Cost Breakdown by End Use. *These energy cost pie charts are for baseline building design conditions, for different projects in the same climatic zone. These pie charts show the variability of end-use energy costs driven by building function, occupancy and lighting schedules, and design requirements. The first is a 47,000 SF elementary school that does not contain air-conditioning. The second is a 160,000 SF federal courthouse facility in downtown Denver.*

TABLE 1
ELIMINATION PARAMETRICS (FROM REFERENCE BUILDING MODEL)

Elimination Parametric Category	Input Change
1. Illumination	Lighting W/SF = 0
2. Occupants	Number of people = 0
3. Equipment	Equipment power = 0
4. Ventilation	Outside air = 0
5. Internal loads	Combination of 1 through 4
6. Opaque envelope conduction	R wall >100
7. Glazing conduction	Glazing U = value = 0
8. Solar gain on glazing	Glazing shading coefficient = 0
9. Infiltration	Infiltration air = 0
10. Envelope loads	Combination of 6 through 9

and so on. As is shown in Figure 3 below, the distribution of building energy loads for different building types can vary significantly.

Activity 3: Characterize Energy Use and Energy Cost

The purpose of energy use characterization is to identify energy problems and opportunities and inform the development of design solutions. The characterization involves a series of energy simulation runs that are performed on the base case energy model described above, to provide some insight into the relative impact of each individual component.

One by one, each component of overall building energy consumption listed in Table 1 is eliminated from the simulation, and the annual energy consumption, demand, and cost for each run is calculated. The components having significant impact on overall energy consumption will show a significant reduction in the annual energy cost when eliminated from the simulation. The energy model is evaluating not just the impact of individual components being manipulated, but the interrelationship between that component and the rest of the building.

This exercise identifies the most important factors in overall building energy consumption and points the design team toward solutions that can make the greatest impact on reducing energy consumption, demand, and operating costs. It also provides the design team with an indication of the range of economic benefit that could be derived from each of the individual strategies. Figure 4 is an example of elimination parametric results from the Federal Courthouse in Denver, Colorado.

Activity 4: Develop Alternative Design Solutions

The design optimization process is exploratory and begins with the project team formulating and evaluating a large number of whole-building design options. The goal is to search out those site and functional factors or determinants that will shape the design. Energy-related issues, such as the use of daylighting or natural ventilation, can represent powerful form determinants. Additional sets of computer runs estimate the impact of energy design options on the reference building. Throughout the analysis, three types of energy performance measures should be evaluated.

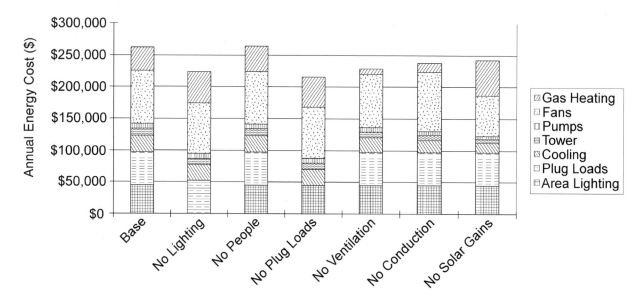

Figure 4. *Example of elimination parametric results for the U.S. Federal Courthouse Expansion in Denver, Colorado. The base case is a minimally compliant building, based on 10 CFR 435. As design parameters—solar gain, outside air, envelope conduction, and so on—were eliminated from the energy analysis, the annual energy cost impact was shown. The interactive influence of the various design parameters is apparent in the changing size of the end-use energy cost bars.*

1. Energy conservation
2. Energy cost reduction
3. Peak demand reduction

Each of these measures represents a different energy performance target. Reductions in energy cost and peak demand provide a direct economic benefit in terms of reduced operating cost and reduced system size. It must be remembered, however, that energy cost is a function of the existing regulatory and legislative environment, and could change at any point in time. Too heavy a reliance on energy cost and peak demand alone can lead to strategies that may make little sense under another regulatory environment. The overall annual energy consumption of a building design, however, will be unaffected by rate structures and regulations. All three measures need to be evaluated and considered before final decisions are made on energy strategies.

Activities during this phase of the design process need to be interactive and iterative. Exploration of energy design features that may influence architectural form, such as integration of daylighting apertures in the building skin, are of primary importance during this phase. Once major form decisions are made, it is unlikely that they will be reconsidered or revised based on energy reasons alone. Therefore, it is essential that considerable interaction be maintained between the architects, engineers, landscape architects, energy modelers, and others influencing the form of the building early in the design process.

Typically, design alternatives are organized by building/system components—lighting, HVAC, appliances, shell, and so on—whereas energy

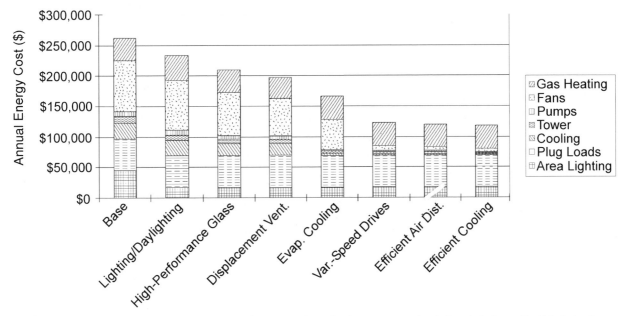

Figure 5. *This bar chart displays the cumulative annual energy savings of various energy-saving design strategies on the U.S. Federal Courthouse expansion in Denver, Colorado.*

use is projected in terms of end uses such as heating, cooling, and lighting. As energy design options are generated, the magnitude of potential energy and cost savings identified through the parametric analysis should be used to focus the effort on end uses and design alternatives that will have the most significant impact on those end uses first. However, before the optimization process is complete, energy-saving design options should be developed for all of the energy end use categories.

Figure 5 illustrates this approach to developing and evaluating energy design options. The example shown is from the U.S. Federal Courthouse in Denver. Energy costs for the reference design meet ASHRAE 90A-1980, the existing energy code at the time of the study.

Activity 5: Daylighting Design and Analysis

Where daylighting is a viable and desirable energy-saving design strategy, additional analysis and scale model testing is recommended. The use of daylighting may significantly impact the architectural form of a building, as well as many of the design details. To begin with, Lumen Micro is a good tool because it is easy to use and provides quantitative information on light levels in spreadsheet form, as well as a graphic image. Because Lumen Micro can model only the simplest of daylighting apertures, many times it is necessary to construct a scale physical model of the building design and obtain measurements of interior and exterior illuminance.

Scale models of proposed design options are built to serve both as an analytical tool for calculating the daylighting performance of the design and as a qualitative tool for observing the luminous environment created by the daylighting design. The model is built to a large enough scale to permit observation and allow sufficient space for illuminance sensors and

Figure 6. *Lumen Micro rendering of an open office area under design in the U.S. Federal Courthouse in Denver, Colorado. Glazing has been divided into a daylight portion and vision portion, and the interior offices have glass walls to obtain some "shared" daylighting.*

a video camera for later testing. Representative colors and reflectances are used for interior surfaces, and representative visible light transmittances are used to simulate the glazed surfaces.

The model is tested under natural light conditions for both the quantity and quality of daylight. Information such as brightness ratios, variability in light levels across the space, aesthetics during clear and overcast skies, light levels in the darkest spaces, and so on are obtained from the model. This level of testing usually does not involve gathering a large quantity of data, but rather provides the opportunity to evaluate the performance and characteristics of the daylighting design before detailed data are collected. The photograph shown in Figure 7 is illustrative of the interior of the scale model for the S. C. Johnson Wax, Commercial Products Headquarters.

To aid the quantitative analysis, a grid pattern is overlaid on the model interior. Measurements of exterior and interior horizontal illuminance are taken to develop a relationship between interior illuminance and the exterior (ambient) horizontal illuminance for both overcast sky and clear sky conditions. The measurements are used to identify the areas in

Figure 7. *Model of the atrium of the S. C. Johnson Wax, Commercial Products Headquarters, which was built to study the daylighting in that space.*

the model that have the lowest illumination, to define lighting zones and control points for electric lighting controls. Daylight factors are developed for each control point to calculate the contribution of daylight at each point. The measurements are made outdoors under natural sunlight as the model is tilted and rotated on a gimbaled stand to simulate sun angles representative of various hours of the day and months of the year.

A computer model of the building design is also created. Daylight factors calculated from the scale model tests are incorporated into the computer analysis. The DOE-2 building energy analysis simulation program has the capability to use these daylight factors to calculate hourly interior illuminance from daylighting and the hourly electric lighting loads required to supplement the daylight to meet the design criteria for illumination. The hourly electrical lighting values are summed on a monthly and annual basis to estimate the total annual requirement of electrical lighting energy. The electric lighting loads also generate heat, which impacts the total hourly internal heat gains used in the calculation of total heating and cooling loads, and subsequently system and plant requirements. In this way, the illumination measurements made in the scale model are linked to the thermal performance calculation methods.

Once the conceptual energy design options have been developed, the energy model needs to be revised and updated based on the package of energy features that have been incorporated in the design. For details of construction that have not been decided, default values are used. A new energy model is created, and key energy performance measures—energy consumption, demand, and energy cost—are calculated by end use. These measures can then be compared to the base case design to establish energy, demand, and cost savings.

Activity 6: Energy and Economic Analysis

The DOE-2 program is used to calculate the performance of each energy design alternative and to compare its performance to the base case. Combinations or packages of energy design features are evaluated so that the synergies between individual components can be understood. The bar chart in Figure 8 shows the relative impact of individual design options, and the chart in Figure 9 shows "packages" of design options that have been bundled together.

The life cycle cost of each energy-saving design alternative or package of alternatives can then be established, based on first cost, maintenance cost, operational cost, and replacement cost. If the life span of the system is less than the life cycle that has been established for the building, then replacement cost needs to be factored into the analysis as well. Because the design alternatives can impact the peak load and therefore the size of the system required, both the architectural and MEP design options will impact the installed first cost and replacement cost of the system. Operational cost savings for each option include energy savings as well as reduced demand charges. "Peak shaving" strategies refer to design options that may have little impact on energy consumption overall but have a larger impact on demand charges.

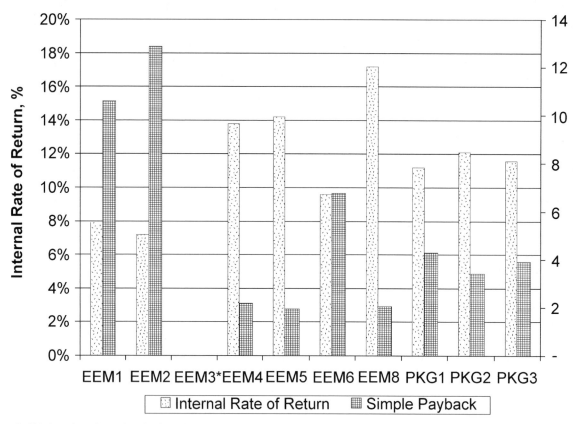

Figure 8. *This bar chart shows the simple payback and calculated internal rate of return (IRR) for both a series of individual energy efficiency measures (EEMs) and a series of packages. *EEM 3 has a reduction in the first cost that correlates to an immediate payback and return.*

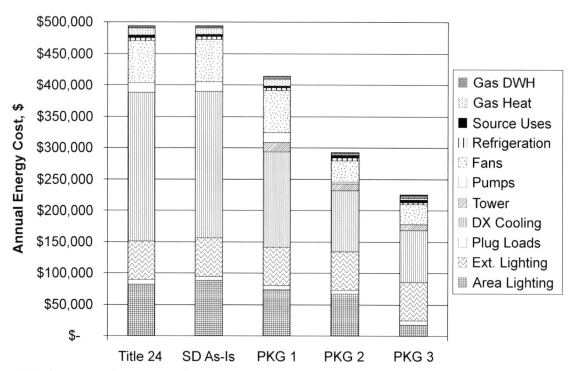

Figure 9. *This bar chart details the energy performance of several packages of EEMs and compares them to the baseline design.*

The process needs to be iterative. With various energy conservation measures now incorporated into the design, the relative balance of loads will have changed. A new energy use characterization needs to be developed. The new study will show that the loads that had once been the most significant have now been reduced, and others will take their place as the primary energy loads. A new set of energy conservation strategies needs to be developed to reduce these new loads. This process of (1) identifying the major loads, (2) identifying energy reduction strategies to reduce these loads, and (3) refining the design is done repeatedly until no more savings can be found.

This refinement phase is also exploratory but at a greater level of detail than before. Many options are evaluated for each building component. The goal is to identify a subset of options that perform best, and then select the final option based on performance, costs, and aesthetic objectives of the project. Once a final design solution meeting the overall building design objectives is selected, a final energy run is made incorporating all of the energy-conserving measures.

Just as with a cost model, it is important to follow the progress of the design through the construction documents phase with periodic updates to the energy model to ensure that energy performance is maintained. At appropriate stages in the development of contract documents the status of the energy conservation strategies should be reviewed, the energy model updated to reflect design modifications that may have occurred, and corrective actions taken if performance has deteriorated. A final energy run is made at the end of the construction documents phase to confirm that energy design objectives are being met.

Evaluating the building after occupancy is essential for improving the quality and performance of future buildings; however, postoccupancy evaluations are rarely included in the architectural design process. As a consequence, little is learned about how the building is actually performing, how satisfied the occupants are, or what preventative actions are needed to ensure proper future operation. Postoccupancy evaluations make use of qualitative and quantitative methods, including questionnaires, monitoring, and detailed energy analysis, to evaluate building performance and occupant satisfaction, to resolve any outstanding problems, and to improve the design of subsequent buildings.

Activity 7: Repeat the Process

Activity 8: Follow Up

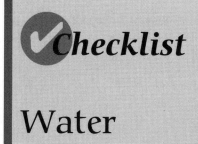

Water

Team Building

☐ 1. Seek out plumbing engineers, HVAC engineers, and civil engineers experienced with water conservation and reuse, and natural wastewater treatment systems.

☐ 2. Consider enlisting a specialty consultant to evaluate the feasibility of on-site natural wastewater treatment, and to design the system if appropriate.

Education and Goal Setting

EDUCATION

☐ 3. Educate the team about the importance of water conservation, water reuse opportunities, and the ecological value of natural wastewater treatment systems.

GOAL SETTING

☐ 4. Define project goals for water as a team—include consideration of water conservation, water reuse, and natural wastewater treatment.

☐ 5. Recommend that the owner plan for future water management.

Gathering Information

PROGRAMMING

☐ 6. Estimate water use requirements.

SITE ANALYSIS

☐ 7. Test quality of potable water sources.

RESEARCH

☐ 8. Identify local water and sewer network, and rate structures.

☐ 9. Collect information on precipitation.

☐ 10. Explore local codes regarding water reuse systems and alternative waste treatment systems.

☐ 11. Identify incentive programs for water conservation and water quality.

Optimization

BUILDING AND SITE DESIGN

❏ 12. Zone water-using areas within the building and the site.

MEP DESIGN

❏ 13. Engage in water-use analysis to develop cost-effective water conservation and reuse strategies.

❏ 14. Explore opportunities to improve water efficiency of HVAC equipment. (Coordinate with Energy Project Actions.)

❏ 15. Explore opportunities to reuse rainwater and/or gray water.

❏ 16. Explore opportunities to provide natural wastewater treatment systems for black water on site.

Documents and Specifications

DESIGN DETAILING

❏ 17. Consider use of alternative ultra-low-flow or waterless plumbing fixtures.

❏ 18. Explore opportunities to improve the water efficiency of cooling towers.

❏ 19. Consider alternative treatment systems for swimming pools that are less chemically intensive.

❏ 20. Eliminate need for landscape irrigation to the greatest extent possible, and maximize water efficiency of required irrigation systems.

SPECIFICATIONS

❏ 21. Specify water-efficient plumbing fixtures.

❏ 22. Specify water-efficient appliances.

Bidding, Construction, and Commissioning

❏ 23. Enforce the protection and preservation of water sources during construction.

❏ 24. Encourage the contractor to consider water reuse strategies during construction.

Operations and Maintenance

❏ 25. Assist the owner or management company in developing a maintenance program.

❏ 26. Educate users about water conservation.

Project Actions

Water

The Water Project Actions are recommendations by phase and topic that should be considered during the design process. When relevant, actions are followed by further explanations in italics and a notation in brackets indicating the potential effect on the time, construction cost, energy cost, maintenance cost, or fee.

Team Building

1. Seek out plumbing engineers, HVAC engineers, and civil engineers experienced with water conservation and reuse, and natural wastewater treatment systems.

   | |A| |E| |O| 1.1. Select plumbing engineers familiar with developing a water budget analysis, to explore the cost and life cycle benefits associated with water conservation and reuse strategies.

   | |A| |E| |O| 1.2. Select HVAC engineers who will consider water conservation issues when evaluating equipment options.

   | |A| |E| |O| 1.3. Select civil engineers with experience in evaluation of alternative waste treatment options, including constructed wetlands.

2. Consider enlisting a specialty consultant to evaluate the feasibility of on-site natural wastewater treatment, and to design the system if appropriate.

   | |A| |E| |O| 2.1. For large projects or projects remote from existing waste treatment infrastructure, recommend that a specialty consultant join the team to help evaluate the feasibility of using an on-site natural wastewater treatment system. [$F]

Education and Goal Setting

Education

3. Educate the team about the importance of water conservation, water reuse opportunities, and the economical and ecological value of natural wastewater treatment systems.

P = Planner	A = Architect	I = Interior designer	E = Engineer	L = Landscape architect	O= Owner consultation

[T] = Could affect length of construction (+ or –), [$C] = Affects construction costs (+ or –), [$E] Affects energy costs, [$F] = Affects fees (+ or –), [$M] = Affects maintenance costs (+ or –).

P|A|I|E|L|O 3.1. Invite an environmental specialist (either a member of the design team or someone from a local university, nonprofit environmental organization, or local government agency) to speak to the design team about local watershed issues. Discuss the extent of water scarcity in the region, the percentage of regional water use for buildings and for irrigation, and the necessity for improvement.

P|A|I|E|L|O 3.2. Define terms for the design team:

- *Rainwater harvesting* refers to the collection of rainwater runoff from rooftops, paved surfaces, and/or landscaped areas for future reuse. After simple filtration water can be reused for toilet flushing and other nonpotable uses.
- *Gray water* is collected wastewater from building-related uses such as sinks, showers, and air conditioning equipment (condensate). Treatment is required prior to reuse.
- *Black water* is wastewater from building-related uses containing human fecal waste. Treated effluent from black water systems can be used for irrigation of landscaped areas.

P|A| |E|L|O 3.3. Educate the team about biological wastewater treatment alternatives.

Why Use Constructed Wetlands for Wastewater Treatment?

Constructed wetlands provide wastewater treatment through natural biological processes. There are two forms of constructed wetlands: open water wetlands and subsurface flow wetlands. Open water constructed wetlands are used primarily in temperate zones, but subsurface flow constructed wetlands can be used in any climate. Because subsurface flow constructed wetlands are safer, are odor and nuisance free, and have wider application, they are preferred over open water wetlands.

Centralized sewage treatment plants in large urban areas are typically mechanical plants that are energy and chemical intensive. They produce large quantities of by-product, which must be further treated before disposal. For large populations mechanical plants are a necessity; however, constructed wetlands are an alternative for flows ranging in size from that generated by an individual home to that of communities generating 100,000 gallons per day.

After wastewater treatment, disposal of the treated water can be through soil infiltration or surface water discharge. Subsurface flow constructed wetlands can use both disposal alternatives, whereas mechanical plants are usually limited to surface water discharges.

Standard septic systems, such as drain fields and mounds, are commonly used in nonurban areas. These septic systems, after settling out solids in a septic tank, discharge partially treated water directly into the soil. Soil bacteria provide the treatment. Over time, the soil is damaged by a buildup of bacteria and partially treated water is released into the environment, where it can cause surface and groundwater pollution. Therefore, there are advantages to providing a greater degree of treatment before introducing wastewater to the soil for disposal.

Constructed wetlands, in contrast to standard septic systems, pretreat water in a lined treatment bed before it is released into the environment, thus protecting the soil. Constructed wetlands are very effective in removing nutrients (nitrogen and phosphorus). It is therefore considered an advanced waste treatment technology and a more suitable wastewater treatment alternative in environmentally sensitive locations such as lakeshores and sensitive groundwater recharge areas.

Constructed wetlands are biological treatment systems because bacteria provide the majority of treatment. Plants provide aesthetically pleasant surroundings while they assimilate nutrients and consume water. Treating wastewater in a constructed wetland allows the treated water to be recycled by irrigating landscaped areas and recharging groundwater resources.

Subsurface flow constructed wetlands for wastewater treatment have been used in Europe and the United States for more than twenty years. Constructed wetlands are reliable, are easy to monitor and operate, and are an economical and effective technology for waste decomposition and nutrient reduction.

Source: North American Wetland Engineering, P.A., (888) 433-2115, nawe@visi.com

Goal Setting

4. **Define project goals for water as a team—include consideration of water conservation, water reuse, and natural wastewater treatment.**

P|A|I|E|L|O 4.1. Make a commitment to reduce potable water use.

P|A| |E|L|O 4.2. Make a commitment to explore landscape design options that will eliminate the need for irrigation or to irrigate only with treated effluent from the on-site wastewater treatment system (coordinate with Planning and Site Work Project Actions). [$C, $M]

P|A| |E|L|O 4.3. Make a commitment to explore water reuse opportunities. [$C, M]

P|A| |E| |O 4.4. Make a commitment to install dual plumbing systems for gray water recycling opportunities. [$C]

P|A| |E|L|O 4.5. Make a commitment to consider natural wastewater treatment on-site, especially for large projects or projects remote from existing waste treatment infrastructure, where the economics can be very favorable. [$C, $M]

5. **Recommend that the owner plan for future water management.**

P|A| |E| |O 5.1. Recommend submetering of water use. Potable water use for irrigation should be discouraged, but if it is needed, it should always be submetered. Consider submetering of other large water uses and/or tenant groups within a facility. [$C]

P|A| |E| |O 5.2. Recommend adoption of the Department of Energy's International Performance Measurement and Verification Protocol (IPMVP), which encourages owners to monitor and measure actual water consumption after occupancy of the building. Periodically, starting after one year of occupancy, water use should be compared to estimates to ensure compliance with the specified water conservation design. If water use exceeds initial estimates, corrective action measures are recommended to reduce the water use in the building. [$C]

Gathering Information

Programming

6. **Estimate water use requirements.**

P|A| |E|L|O 6.1. Obtain projected water use from the owner for activities that will occur on-site. Include water use for non-building-related uses such as irrigation, vehicle washing, laundry facilities, and so on. Involve engineers to assist with estimates of water use from plumbing fixtures (toilets, sinks, showers) and mechanical equipment. Identify

P = Planner	A = Architect	I = Interior designer	E = Engineer	L = Landscape architect	O= Owner consultation

[T] = Could affect length of construction (+ or –), [$C] = Affects construction costs (+ or –), [$E] Affects energy costs, [$F] = Affects fees (+ or –), [$M] = Affects maintenance costs (+ or –).

The HOK Guidebook to Sustainable Design

downtime, such as weekends at office buildings or weekdays at parks and resorts. *This information is critical to calculate sewer requirements and can be used to efficiently size on-site treatment and disposal systems. It also provides a tool to consider flow equalization to compensate for days without flow, which can significantly reduce the required area. Refer to the EPA design manual* On-site Wastewater Treatment and Disposal Systems *(EPA 625-1-80-012) for information on water use estimation.*

| P | | E | O | 6.2. Separate water use requirements into potable and nonpotable to identify portion of water use that could be satisfied by collected rainwater or gray water reuse systems. Potable water use includes water for drinking and cooking, whereas water that need not be from potable sources includes water used for irrigation, cooling towers, toilet flushing, and the like.

Site Analysis

7. Test water quality of potable water sources.

| P | | E | | 7.1. When working with existing buildings, verify compliance with EPA's Lead in Drinking Water Protocol, which requires the use of lead-free plumbing in facilities connected to a public water system.
Solders and flux are considered lead free when they contain less than 0.2 percent lead, and pipes, pipe fittings, faucets, and other fixtures are considered lead free when they contain less than 8 percent lead. The EPA Publication #812-B-94-002, "Lead in Drinking Water in Schools and Non-residential Buildings," April 1994, can be obtained by calling (800) 276-0462 and requesting Publication G158.

| P | | E | | 7.2. In rural areas and areas without a water main, explore potable water sources. Identify underlying aquifers and have a well driller perform a test boring. All encountered aquifers should be tested to determine whether the well water can be used as drinking water.
Water should be tested for health hazards, such as fecal coliform bacteria; for contaminants, such as petroleum, heavy metals, dry cleaning chemicals (if a potential source is within a 1-mile radius of the well head); and for nutrients, such as phosphorus and nitrogen. Water should also be tested for total suspended solids (TSS) and biological and chemical oxygen demand (BOD and COD).

Research

8. Identify local water and sewer network, and rate structures.

| P | | E | | 8.1. Contact local municipalities or the city engineer to determine availability and capacity of local water and sewer network.

| P | | E | | 8.2. Request information about the local rate structures for water and sewer usage to determine the cost of potable water and charges for water discharge. This information will help the team determine the economic value of water conservation, water reuse strategies, and on-site sewage treatment.

9. Collect information on precipitation.

| P | | E | | 9.1. Determine average monthly rainfall. Local climatological data summaries (called LCDs), available from the National Oceanic and Atmospheric Administration

(NOAA), include data on monthly averages and extremes for rain and snow. ASHRAE's *Fundamentals Handbook* and *Applications Handbook* and AIA's *Architectural Graphic Standards* also contain some of this information.

| P | | E | | 9.2. Evaluate the impact of air quality on the quality of rainwater sources. Regions with poor air quality may not be well suited for rainwater collection systems.

10. Explore local codes regarding water reuse systems and alternative waste treatment systems.

| P | | E | | 10.1. Review local codes to assess if water reuse and alternative wastewater treatment technologies are permitted, or if special permits and/or variances are required. [T, $F]
Early research and feasibility studies prior to design combined with cost analysis can help ensure successful, cost-effective integration of proven and accepted alternative technologies. Codes vary widely across the country; however, some regions not only allow but promote the use of such systems. Consider acquiring special permitting and/or variances when utilization of alternative technologies provides significant benefit in terms of resource conservation and capital, operation, maintenance, and replacement costs.

11. Identify incentive programs for water conservation and water quality.

| P | | E | | 11.1. Search for government, utility, and private-sector incentive programs to conserve water and reduce discharge to sewage treatment facilities. Contact the local state Department of Natural Resources, water utilities, and environmental organizations representing the regional watershed or water bodies for information. [T, $F]

| P | | E | | 11.2. For large projects, consider programs that provide support for improvements to water quality in communities, urban areas, and waterfronts, such as EPA's Better America Bonds. [T, $F]

Optimization

Building and Site Design

12. Zone water-using areas within the building and the site.

| A | E | O | 12.1. Co-locate water using program areas to minimize piping and pumping requirements. Domestic water use will benefit from decreased heating and pumping requirements. If recycling of gray water or rainwater catchment has been identified as a possible strategy, co-location of water-using functions will ease collection, treatment, and reuse.
Because gray water systems require dual-system plumbing to separate gray water from black water, the cost-effectiveness of gray water systems depends on the ability of the design team to effectively co-locate sources of gray water, treatment and holding tanks, and reuse sites.

| P = Planner | A = Architect | I = Interior designer | E = Engineer | L = Landscape architect | O= Owner consultation |

[T] = Could affect length of construction (+ or –), [$C] = Affects construction costs (+ or –), [$E] Affects energy costs, [$F] = Affects fees (+ or –), [$M] = Affects maintenance costs (+ or –).

MEP Design

13. Engage in water use analysis to develop cost-effective water conservation and reuse strategies.

| | |E|L| 13.1. Develop a water budget that tracks the cost associated with all projected water uses and discharges, including mechanical equipment, plumbing fixtures, food service areas, process water use, irrigation, and so on.

| | |E| | 13.2. Engage in cost modeling of various alternatives to determine which is most cost-effective. Depending on water use patterns and the billing rate structure, the project will benefit most economically from either reductions in water use, reductions in effluent, or a combination of the two.

| | |E|L| 13.3. Reduce water use requirements first, to determine true requirements for nonpotable water, then explore water reuse strategies. For example, explore opportunities to reduce or eliminate water use for irrigation before evaluating the benefits associated with a water reuse system.

| | |E|L| 13.4. Monitor and analyze water use monthly instead of annually, because some water demands vary seasonally (such as water use for cooling towers and irrigation).

| | |E| | 13.5. Identify secondary benefits of water collection and recycling, such as secure water supplies in regions subject to water use restrictions.

14. Explore opportunities to improve water efficiency of HVAC equipment.

| | |E| | 14.1. Disallow the use of "one pass" cooling units that use potable water and discharge it to a drain, such as those used for computer room installations and supplementary space cooling. These units waste water and consume energy for pumping and wastewater treatment. [$C, $E]

| | |E| | 14.2. Consider the pros and cons of evaporative cooling strategies in regions with scarce water resources. When using evaporative cooling, consider using nonpotable water from rainwater or treated gray water. [$C, $M]

15. Explore opportunities to reuse rainwater and/or gray water.

High-quality potable water is needed only for drinking, washing, and cooking. Rainwater and/or gray water can be reused for toilet flushing, process water, cooling towers, irrigation, and the like. Water reuse systems, which provide the double benefit of reducing the potable water demand while reducing wastewater flows, are common in many parts of the world and are strongly encouraged in parts of the United States where water shortages are becoming acute. See the Planning and Site Work Project Actions section of this design guide for recommendations on stormwater management and landscape design.

|A| |E| | 15.1. Consider installing a dual plumbing system for gray water reuse. [$C]
Simple, inexpensive rainwater collection systems that require a minimal amount of filtration can be used to provide water for nonpotable uses such as irrigation and toilet flushing, and can be cost-justified in most parts of the United States. Water can also be stored in open ponds for firefighting. Greater filtration and purification are required for systems used to provide potable water. At this point in time, rainwater collection and

gray water systems for potable use will be cost-justifiable only in remote areas, in areas where potable water supplies are scarce, or where financial incentives are in place.

|A| |E| | | 15.2. Integrate design of water collection systems closely with the architecture, so that rainwater is collected from clean surfaces that are as close as possible to the points of distribution. The cleanest collection areas will be the roof and plaza areas designed for pedestrian use only. Metal roofing is generally the best; however, lead, copper, or tern roofing can contaminate water sources. Install screening to keep debris out of the system, and consider installing devices that divert the first flush of rainwater from the collection system.

|A| |E| | | 15.3. Identify potential sources of gray water (sinks, showers, dishwashers, condensate from cooling towers, drinking fountains, etc.), and place priority on those that generate the greatest quantity of water and are co-located to minimize piping requirements.

|A| |E|L| | 15.4. Evaluate a range of options for the reuse of rainwater and treated gray water when evaluating costs and benefits. For example, toilet flushing will require pumping and nonpotable water supply piping, whereas irrigation does not require dual piping, and it can be gravity fed if cisterns are integrated appropriately into the landscape design.

|A| |E|L| | 15.5. Integrate the design of water reuse systems closely with the landscape design. Collection of rainwater will reduce stormwater discharge; however, release of treated gray water will increase overall water flows on the site. The benefits of water reuse will be best realized when the selection and placement of landscape planting are closely coordinated with the design of water collection and reuse systems.

16. **Explore opportunities to provide natural wastewater treatment systems for black water on site.**
"Black water" refers to wastewater generated from toilet flushing, which cannot be reused in the building because it contains fecal coliform bacteria. Black water can be reclaimed by natural, biological on-site wastewater treatment systems and then recycled to irrigate landscaped areas and to recharge the aquifer. If the cost of water and/or sewage is high, these systems will also be economically beneficial. Small-scale systems can be used for individual buildings; large-scale systems can work for an entire community.

|A| |E| |O| 16.1. In unsewered areas, encourage use of biological on-site wastewater treatment, such as constructed wetlands, over a standard septic system, such as drainfields or mounds. Constructed wetlands are usually more effective and less mechanically complex than conventional wastewater treatment plants. This type of treatment can also be extremely cost-effective, as first costs can be less and long-term maintenance costs are vastly reduced. [$C, $M]

|A| |E| |O| 16.2. Where facilities have high water use demand and/or are located in municipalities where water treatment capacity is limited and/or costly, consider use of an on-site wastewater treatment system using alternative technologies. The resulting effluent can be used for nonpotable water use demand, such as irrigation.

P = Planner	A = Architect	I = Interior designer	E = Engineer	L = Landscape architect	O= Owner consultation

[T] = Could affect length of construction (+ or –), [$C] = Affects construction costs (+ or –), [$E] Affects energy costs, [$F] = Affects fees (+ or –), [$M] = Affects maintenance costs (+ or –).

|A| |E| |O| 16.3. Identify the type of treatment system best suited to the project. Options for waste water treatment include the following: [$C, $F, $M]

- *Open water constructed wetlands:* As wastewater slowly flows through an open wetland bed or open channels, microbes break down the waste and plants take up nutrients from the water. Waste is removed in a tiered system of sedimentation, treatment, and infiltration ponds that simulate a wetland environment.

- *Subsurface-flow constructed wetlands:* As wastewater slowly flows through a subsurface wetland bed, microbes break down the waste and plants take up nutrients from the water. The advantage of this system is that the treatment occurs underground. The treatment and infiltration beds are covered with a soil layer that provides three functions: (1) planting media for wetland plants that drive their root system into the treatment bed; (2) insulation against freezing; and (3) protection against waste exposure, undesirable odor, and nuisance mosquitoes.

- *Sand or peat filters:* Single-pass sand and peat filters are two additional low-cost technologies. Wastewater flows vertically through a sand or peat layer and is collected in drainage pipes. Water is treated in the upper layer, where most of the biological treatment occurs. The biomat needs to be periodically scraped away. Those systems still require waste disposal.

- *Anaerobic wastewater treatment:* Anaerobic digestion occurs within a mechanical treatment plant that makes use of microorganisms to process food waste, sewage, and landscape waste without oxygen. The advantage of this method is that it requires less space and includes the production of three usable by-products:
  - Biogas (methane), which can be used for heating, to offset energy costs
  - A nutrient-rich, solid organic fertilizer
  - A diluted liquid organic fertilizer

- *Aerobic treatment:* Aerobic waste treatment also occurs within a mechanical treat-ment plant that makes use of microorganisms. In this system, however, oxygen is a key component in the treatment process. The advantages include a shorter process time, less treatment area, and very little odor. To maintain the flow of oxygen, however, additional power is required to operate a blower. Consider solar, wind, or thermal-powered equipment.

- *Aquaculture systems:* Aquaculture systems use wastewater as a food source for plants and fish, producing food and fertilizer while purifying wastewater. Main-tenance requirements for this type of system are high.

| | |E| | | 16.4. To design the natural wastewater treatment system, identify pollutants to be removed from water, required area and detention time necessary to achieve desired treatment level, and integrated aesthetics.

Documents and Specifications

Design Detailing

17. Consider use of ultra-low-flow or waterless plumbing fixture alternatives.

How Does a Subsurface Flow Constructed Wetland Work?

There are two types of subsurface flow constructed wetland treatment systems: horizontal flow wetlands and vertical flow wetlands. Both types provide treatment underground in an engineered gravel bed. There is no open water surface to allow exposure to infectious waste. There are no undesirable odors and nuisance mosquitoes. Year-round operation is secured through an insulating organic mulch layer on top of the gravel bed.

If space is limited, the subsurface flow constructed wetland can be designed as a vertical flow recalculating filter. By adding a tank and pump to recirculate water over the treatment bed, the biological process occurs in a much smaller area.

An impervious liner is covered with gravel; bacteria attached to the gravel provide the primary treatment. On top of the gravel organic material such as compost or peat is used for insulation, for odor control, and to be the growing media for wetland plants. Wetland plants play an important role in the treatment process. They introduce fungi and other bacteria associated with the plant root systems. This increases the diversity of the microbial population in the treatment bed and enables this natural system to withstand shock loads and to quickly rebound from adverse conditions. The plants introduce oxygen into the treatment zone through their root system and take up nitrogen and phosphorus. Through evapotranspiration plants consume and recycle water, which significantly reduces the amount of water to be discharged.

The land required for the treatment area varies in size, depending on the flow rate and the strength of water to be treated. Where soil infiltration is used, the infiltration area is proportional to the soil texture, structure, and percolation rate. The primary treatment area can be located almost anywhere because it is lined with an impermeable membrane that confines the wastewater in a treatment zone.

Infiltration alternatives include wetland infiltration beds, at-grade beds, conventional drainfields, mounds, or drip irrigation. Treated water can also be discharged to surface water.

Successfully applied at homes, resorts, industrial parks, cluster residential developments, and other projects, constructed wetlands provide cost-effective treatment of wastewater using a natural biological process that is easy to operate, simple to maintain, and attractive in appearance.

Source: North American Wetland Engineering, P.A., (888) 433-2115, nawe@visi.com.

|A| |E| |O| 17.1. Consider use of ultra-low-flow toilets. These fixtures require more maintenance than the standard 1.6–gallon-per-flush models, so their use is best suited to regions where water conservation is especially important. [$C, $M]

|A| |E| |O| 17.2. Consider the use of waterless urinals. Waterless urinals are odor free and low maintenance and are installed to a typical drain line. A small quantity of "blue seal" liquid of biodegradable oils and alcohol isolates urine from room atmosphere. Periodic replenishment of the blue seal liquid is necessary; however, no water supply plumbing or valves are required.

|A| |E| |O| 17.3. Consider the use of composting toilets, also called dry toilets, particularly in remote locations. Composting toilets either are self-contained units or have separate,

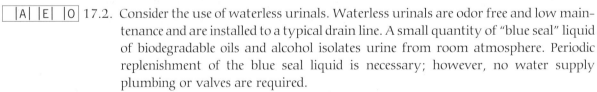

| P = Planner | A = Architect | I = Interior designer | E = Engineer | L = Landscape architect | O= Owner consultation |

[T] = Could affect length of construction (+ or –), [$C] = Affects construction costs (+ or –), [$E] Affects energy costs, [$F] = Affects fees (+ or –), [$M] = Affects maintenance costs (+ or –).

The HOK Guidebook to Sustainable Design

remote storage tanks. Composting toilets should be approved by the National Science Foundation (NSF). [$C, $M]

|A| |E| |O| 17.4. Consider using seawater for toilet and urinal flushing in coastal developments. Due to the corrosive nature of seawater, material selection in piping, plumbing, pumping, and treatment systems must be addressed, because it will limit options for on-site wastewater treatment. [$C, $M]

18. Explore opportunities to improve water efficiency of cooling towers.

| | |E| | 18.1. To manage water usage for the cooling tower, provide metering for both the makeup and the blowdown rate. [$C, $M]

| | |E| | 18.2. Install cooling tower systems designed with delimiters to reduce drift and evaporation.

| | |E| | 18.3. Minimize blowdown for cooling towers through the use of dynamic water analysis programs. Use of this type of system allows for cycles of concentration to be increased from the industry standard of 12–14 cycles of concentration to 6–8 cycles of concentration. [$C, $M]
A dynamic water analysis system allows the quantity of blowdown to be minimized. Regular monitoring of water quality allows the dosage to be reduced because there is no need for a safety factor to accommodate days when water quality may be atypical. This system conserves waste, while also reducing chemical use.

19. Consider alternative treatment systems for swimming pools that are less chemically intensive.

| | |E| |O| 19.1. Consider water-conserving options for the operation of swimming pools. Where possible, use seawater to reduce potable water demand and/or continuously cycle water through a filtration/disinfection system. Typically, about 10 percent of the water is bled off the system as blowdown and replaced with freshwater with each cycle. [$C, $M]

| | |E|L|O| 19.2. Consider the use of biological filtration (i.e., constructed wetlands) followed by an ultraviolet light (UV) disinfection unit. This approach uses no toxic chemicals at all, which means the blowdown water can be treated by the suggested wastewater treatment system and just a minimal amount of potable water requires disinfection before reentering the pool. [$C, $M]

| | |E| |O| 19.3. Consider the use of bromine (available in liquid or tablet form) as an alternative to chlorine. Bromine is not as irritating and toxic as chlorine. [$C, $M]
Chlorination for disinfecting swimming pool water is bad environmental practice. While it is very effective in killing the germs, it introduces irritants into the water that many people are sensitive to. The chemical itself (sodium hypochlorite), whether in gas form or in liquid form, is very toxic. Residual chlorine, which is left over after bacteria are killed, can be removed using sulfur dioxide (another toxic gas). However, all dissolved oxygen is removed from the water, and the water needs to be re-aerated.

|A| | |L|O| 19.4. Consider measures to reduce evaporation from pool surfaces in warm climates. [$M]

| | |E|L|O| 19.5. Coordinate design of pool and filtration systems with the landscape design.

20. **Eliminate need for landscape irrigation to the greatest extent possible, and maximize water efficiency of required irrigation systems.**
See the Planning and Site Work Project Actions section of this design guide for recommendations on water-efficient landscaping and water-efficient irrigation systems.

Specifications

21. Specify water-efficient plumbing fixtures.

| | |E| | 21.1. Meet the water efficiency requirements as mandated by the Energy Policy Act of 1992 (42 USC Section 6295 (j)), and consider opportunities to improve upon those federally mandated standards.

|A| |E| |O| 21.2. For building renovation projects with existing plumbing fixtures in good working condition, consider replacing older fixtures as a water conservation measure. The benefits from water conservation far outweigh the resource conservation benefits from reusing the fixtures. [$C]

| | |E| |O| 21.3. Consider using aerators on lavatory faucets to reduce water flow from 2.5 GPM (the federal standard) to 0.5 or 1.0 GPM. Lavatories used primarily for hand washing function very effectively at the lower flow rate.
Note: Some state and municipal regulations have lower GPM limits than the federal EPACT standard. Some are as low as 1.5 GPM for lavatory faucets and 2.0 GPM for shower heads.

EPACT Requirements for Plumbing Fixtures

The maximum flow rates for fixtures manufactured after January 1, 1994, are listed below. Units are in gallons per minute (GPM), gallons per cycle (GPC), or gallons per flush (GPF).

Lavatory faucets	2.5 GPM @ 80 PSIG
Lavatory replacement aerators	2.5 GPM @ 80 PSIG
Kitchen faucets	2.5 GPM @ 80 PSIG
Kitchen replacement aerators	2.5 GPM @ 80 PSIG
Shower heads	2.5 GPM @ 80 PSIG
Metering faucets	0.25 GPC @ 80 PSIG
Gravity-tank-type toilet	1.6 GPF
Flushometer tank toilets	1.6 GPF
Electromechanical HYD toilets	1.6 GPF
Blowout toilets	3.5 GPF
Urinals	1.0 GPF

| P = Planner | A = Architect | I = Interior designer | E = Engineer | L = Landscape architect | O= Owner consultation |

[T] = Could affect length of construction (+ or –), [$C] = Affects construction costs (+ or –), [$E] Affects energy costs, [$F] = Affects fees (+ or –), [$M] = Affects maintenance costs (+ or –).

| | |E| |O| 21.4. Specify automated controls for lavatory faucets for *water conservation*, such as infrared sensor faucets, delayed action shutoff, or automatic mechanical shutoff valves, particularly for high-use public rest rooms. [$C, $M]

| | |E| |O| 21.5. Avoid automatic flush toilets and urinals, except for large, high-volume public facilities such as stadiums, airports, and the like, where their use may be justified. Otherwise, specify manual flush valves. [$M]

22. Specify water-efficient appliances.

|A| |E| | 22.1. Specify water-saving dishwashers. Because most of the energy consumed by dishwashers is used to heat water, the energy efficiency of a dishwasher is a good measure of its water efficiency. Require that dishwashers meet the Energy Star standard, and consider specifying a minimum energy factor that surpasses the standard. [$C]

The U.S. EPA and U.S. DOE–sponsored Energy Star program rates the energy efficiency of appliances, including dishwashers, and provides listings of all manufacturers that meet their standard. National standards require an energy factor of at least 0.46 for dishwashers; however, Energy Star–qualified dishwashers must have an energy factor of at least 0.60 to qualify. The most efficient models on the market have energy factors of over 0.90.

|A| |E| | 22.2. Specify efficient horizontal-axis washing machines as opposed to top-loading machines. Horizontal-axis machines use much less water and detergent, and because they spin faster, more moisture is removed, shortening the required drying time. First costs are higher; however, the payback period is short. Require that washing machines meet the Energy Star standard, and consider specifying a minimum energy factor that surpasses the standard. [$C]

|A| |E| |O| 22.3. Consider eliminating all in-sink garbage disposals and provide for composting of organic waste as an alternative. This will reduce the organic load of wastewater and greatly reduces the size of the wastewater treatment system. Some garbage disposals filter and separate organic material so that it can be collected for composting from a holding tank under the sink. [$M]

Bidding and Construction

23. Enforce the protection and preservation of water sources during construction.

|A| | | | 23.1. Enforce the protection of on-site water sources, such as drinking water well heads and reservoirs, from contamination at all times during the construction process.

|A| | | | 23.2. Enforce *water conservation*, and avoid unnecessary use of water during construction.

24. Encourage the contractor to consider water reuse strategies during construction.

|A| | | | 24.1. Encourage the contractor to consider water reuse during construction. Use of settling tanks for wash water has the double benefit of conserving water and reducing

erosion and contamination. Water reuse can be especially beneficial for on-site concrete production facilities.

| A | | | | 24.2. Encourage the contractor to direct rainwater and/or filtered wash water toward landscaped areas for irrigation but avoid flooding.

Operations and Maintenance

25. Assist the owner or management company in developing a maintenance program.

| | | E | L | O | 25.1. Develop a schedule for regular water meter readings and maintenance of irrigation systems, plumbing, and equipment to maintain efficiency. [$F, $M]

| | | E | L | O | 25.2. Document all water-conserving devices and systems. Ensure that future modifications to landscaping, plumbing fixtures, and building systems follow low-water-use goals.

| | | E | L | O | 25.3. Establish water leak detection programs.

26. Educate users about water conservation.

| A | | E | L | O | 26.1. Educate facility users about water conservation goals and the application of conservation devices and systems. Inform owners and users of actual and potential water savings and their role in achieving them.

| P = Planner | A = Architect | I = Interior designer | E = Engineer | L = Landscape architect | O= Owner consultation |

[T] = Could affect length of construction (+ or –), [$C] = Affects construction costs (+ or –), [$E] Affects energy costs, [$F] = Affects fees (+ or –), [$M] = Affects maintenance costs (+ or –).

The HOK Guidebook to Sustainable Design

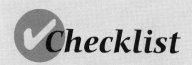
Checklist

Indoor Environmental Quality

Team Building

❑ 1. Recommend that the client include future building operators and maintenance staff on the design team, and that one of them be designated the "indoor air quality manager."

❑ 2. Consider hiring an IAQ consultant, particularly if any of the building occupants suffer from chemical sensitivities.

Education and Goal Setting

EDUCATION

❑ 3. Educate the team about the importance of indoor environmental quality (IEQ), including lighting and acoustics, thermal comfort, access to daylight, connection to nature, and good indoor air quality (IAQ).

❑ 4. Educate the team about the cost and schedule implications of design strategies to protect IAQ.

GOAL SETTING

❑ 5. Develop IEQ goals, including performance objectives for lighting, acoustics, thermal comfort, access to daylight, connection to nature, and IAQ.

Gathering Information

PROGRAMMING

❑ 6. Document all programming information that affects IEQ; identify any chemical sensitivities.

SITE ANALYSIS

❑ 7. Document IAQ-related site and building characteristics prior to acquisition.

❑ 8. Determine if radon is present on the site, and if prevention measures should be taken.

DESIGN CRITERIA

❑ 9. Recommend a nonsmoking building.

❏ 10. Adopt appropriate voluntary standards, such as ASHRAE 62-1999 for ventilation, ASHRAE 55-1992 for thermal comfort, and IES guidelines for lighting.

❏ 11. Establish ventilation, humidification/dehumidification, and filtration requirements.

❏ 12. Consider permanent air quality monitoring.

Optimization

BUILDING AND SITE DESIGN

❏ 13. Design the building and site to promote the effective use of daylight and a sense of connection to the natural environment.

❏ 14. Protect IAQ by carefully locating building fresh air intakes and exhaust locations.

❏ 15. Protect building openings from vehicle pollution and contaminants from landscaped areas.

MEP DESIGN

❏ 16. Develop design to promote effective ventilation systems.

❏ 17. Isolate all interior pollutant-generating sources (such as copy machines, chemical storage areas, etc.) to avoid contamination of indoor air quality.

❏ 18. Design for easy access to and maintenance of HVAC equipment; eliminate internal duct liners.

Documents and Specifications

DETAILING

❏ 19. Develop glazing and sun control strategies to provide comfortable natural daylight without glare.

❏ 20. Develop detailing to control air and moisture flows and improve comfort.

❏ 21. Provide appropriate acoustical separation between sources of noise inside and outside the building.

❏ 22. Develop detailing to reduce cleaning requirements during occupancy by using walk-off mats at building entries and low-maintenance finishes.

MATERIALS SELECTION

❏ 23. Limit the use of fibrous materials, which have potential for microbial contamination.

❏ 24. Select materials that are low in emissions of particulates, total VOCs (volatile organic compounds), and toxic components.

❏ 25. Consider engaging in emissions testing of building materials and products to screen out those with toxic and/or irritating compounds.

❏ 26. Develop an IAQ management plan for the construction process. Specify the sequence of finish installation, temporary ventilation, and baseline air quality testing.

❏ 27. Protect IAQ in occupied areas from contamination during renovation or phased construction.

Bidding, Construction, and Commissioning

❏ 28. Include IAQ in the agenda of regularly scheduled construction meetings.

❏ 29. Review submittals, samples, and product literature to determine compliance with IAQ standards.

Operations and Maintenance

❏ 30. Offer to assist the owner in developing an indoor air quality manual to guide operations.

❏ 31. Recommend that the IAQ manager remain active in the postoccupancy IAQ program.

 *Project Actions*

Indoor Environmental Quality (IEQ)

The Indoor Environmental Quality Project Actions are recommendations by phase and topic that should be considered during the design process. When relevant, actions are followed by further explanations in italics and a notation in brackets indicating the potential effect on the owner, time, construction cost, energy cost, maintenance cost, or fee.

Team Building

1. Recommend that the client include future building operators and maintenance staff on the design team, and that one of them be designated the IAQ manager.

   | A | E | O | 1.1. Recruit future building operators and maintenance staff to participate in the design process.

   | A | E | O | 1.2. Suggest that the owner designate an indoor air quality manager as part of the owner's team. The IAQ manager provides continuity from design to operations, to ensure a thorough understanding of the building space usage, ventilation system design, and monitoring capabilities of the HVAC system. It is a recommended practice in the EPA document *Building Air Quality: A Guide for Building Owners and Facility Managers* (1991).

2. Consider hiring an indoor air quality (IAQ) consultant, particularly if any of the building occupants suffer from chemical sensitivities.

   | A | | | O | 2.1. For new buildings, where there is owner agreement to a thorough assessment of building materials and product options, consider hiring a consultant with experience in materials emissions testing and analysis. [$C, $F]
   Selection of building materials and furnishings that contribute as little as possible to indoor air pollution is a complex task. Emissions information is not often readily available, and choices can involve difficult trade-off decisions.

   | A | | | O | 2.2. For existing buildings that have a history of substandard indoor air quality, hire a specialist to perform a building evaluation, and if necessary, engage in tracer gas testing to evaluate the performance of the ventilation systems. [$C, $F]

| P = Planner | A = Architect | I = Interior designer | E = Engineer | L = Landscape architect | O= Owner consultation |

[T] = Could affect length of construction (+ or –), [$C] = Affects construction costs (+ or –), [$E] Affects energy costs, [$F] = Affects fees (+ or –), [$M] = Affects maintenance costs (+ or –).

| A | | | O | 2.3. Consider hiring a consultant to provide input on cleaning requirements and selection of building materials that have lower and more compatible maintenance requirements. By designing for ease of maintenance, chemical use can also be reduced. [$F]

| A | | | O | 2.4. Consider hiring a consultant to develop future housekeeping procedures during the building design process. Such procedures should include recommendations for low-VOC nontoxic cleansers and consideration of strategies to simplify future cleaning requirements. [$F]

Education and Goal Setting

Education

3. **Educate the team about the importance of indoor environmental quality, including lighting, acoustics, thermal comfort, access to daylight, connection to nature, and good indoor air quality.**

| P | A | I | E | L | O | 3.1. At the outset of the project, hold a full team meeting to discuss the factors that contribute to good IEQ.

| P | A | I | E | L | O | 3.2. Define IAQ terminology for the design team, including "source control," "source isolation," and "source dilution."
Source control eliminates potential contaminants at the source, preventing their entry into the building. Source isolation physically separates potential sources of contaminants from the airstream. Source dilution utilizes ventilation and filtration to dilute contaminants in the airstream.

4. **Educate the team about the cost and schedule implications of design strategies to protect IAQ.**

| P | A | I | E | | O | 4.1. Describe potential IAQ design strategies and the long-term cost and benefits of these strategies. Consider life cycle costs and the benefits of improved air quality, reduced health risks, and increased productivity. Consider the following: [T, $F, $E, $C]
   - Site investigations
   - Design, construction, and commissioning consultant costs
   - Design and installation costs of enhanced HVAC system components
   - Increase in duct size from elimination of internal duct liner
   - Potential cost premiums for low-emission building materials, finishes, and furnishings (low-emission materials have reduced quantities of formaldehyde (VOCs) and other compounds that are toxic and/or irritating in the indoor environment)
   - Costs for emissions testing of building materials as required
   - Premium for special indoor air quality procedures during construction such as requirements for sequencing of finish installation and temporary ventilation
   - Baseline indoor air quality testing at initial occupancy

☐P☐A☐I☐E☐ ☐O☐ 4.2. Discuss with the owner the possible schedule implications of IAQ design strategies. [T, $C]

- Commissioning
- Sequence of finish installation
- Flush-out of building prior to and during installation of furniture and finishes
- Baseline air quality testing

Goal Setting

5. **Develop IEQ goals, including performance objectives for lighting, acoustics, thermal comfort, access to daylight, connection to nature, and IAQ.**

☐P☐A☐I☐E☐L☐O☐ 5.1. Involve all parties, including designers, the building's owner and operators, contractor, and tenants, in an integrated approach to IEQ goal setting.

☐P☐A☐I☐E☐L☐O☐ 5.2. Determine performance objectives for lighting, acoustics, thermal comfort, access to daylight, connection to nature, and IAQ.
The team will need to consider the building type, location, budget, and other factors when determining these goals. Based on the goals of the client, make clear statements to guide the design effort, such as "Provide natural daylight and views in every continuously occupied workspace" or "Provide personal environmental controls for all building occupants."

☐P☐A☐I☐E☐L☐O☐ 5.3. Make a commitment to engage in full systems commissioning services. If full systems commissioning cannot be agreed upon, recommend HVAC commissioning based on ASHRAE guidelines. See the Energy Project Actions for more information on building commissioning. [T, $C, $F, $E, $M]

Gathering Information

Programming

6. **Document all programming information that affects IEQ, and identify occupants with chemical sensitivities.**

☐P☐A☐I☐E☐ ☐O☐ 6.1. Clearly document program requirements, especially in multiuse or multitenant situations where the use of the space is likely to change over time. Provide clear, detailed descriptions, and distribute copies to the owner. Documentation should include the following:

- Building size and location
- Types of occupants (note any special concerns regarding susceptibility to indoor air contaminants)
- Anticipated occupant densities, activities, and use patterns

Because the use of a building may change over time, it is important to clearly document design assumptions that can affect indoor air quality. Future modifications can then be made in ways that do not adversely affect the health and safety of the building occupants.

| P = Planner | A = Architect | I = Interior designer | E = Engineer | L = Landscape architect | O= Owner consultation |

[T] = Could affect length of construction (+ or –), [$C] = Affects construction costs (+ or –), [$E] Affects energy costs, [$F] = Affects fees (+ or –), [$M] = Affects maintenance costs (+ or –).

`P|A|I| |O` 6.2. Determine from the owner any special requirements regarding occupants and their susceptibility to indoor air contamination. For instance, it is becoming increasingly common to find occupants who suffer from multiple chemical sensitivity.

`P|A|I|E| |O` 6.3. Obtain from the owner information on any planned activity, equipment, or material usage that may impact indoor air quality (e.g., smoking, copy center, or chemical supply storage).

Site Analysis

7. Document IAQ-related site and building characteristics prior to acquisition.

`P| | |E| |` 7.1. Identify current and zoning-approved uses for nearby sites. Investigate and plot polluting characteristics of neighboring buildings and sites.

`P| | |E| |` 7.2. Obtain a history of prior site uses through permit authorities.

`P| | |E| |` 7.3. Obtain ambient air quality data from the EPA, National Ambient Air Quality Standards (NAAQS), or local sources. Depending on the site, it may be valuable to test ambient air quality on-site in the probable location(s) of outside air intakes. [$F]

`P| | |E| |` 7.4. For existing buildings, evaluate the HVAC systems to determine whether adequate outside air is being provided.

8. Determine with the owner if radon prevention measures should be taken.

`P| | |E| |O` 8.1. Have soils tested for radon if the building is located in a region where radon occurs. Radon gas is not just an issue for residential construction; the EPA has determined that radon can present a health risk in commercial buildings as well. See http://www.radon.com/radon/radon_map.html for maps showing U.S. regions with elevated risk of radon-contaminated soils. [$F]

`P| | |E| |O` 8.2. Determine with the owner if radon prevention measures should be taken. If required, radon prevention for commercial buildings generally follows these three strategies: [$C, $F]
  • Installation of an active soil depressurization system
  • Pressurizing the building using the HVAC system
  • Sealing major radon entry routes

Design Criteria

9. Recommend a nonsmoking building.

`P|A|I|E| |O` 9.1. Strongly recommend to the owner that the building be designated a nonsmoking building. Inform the owner of local ordinances that prohibit smoking indoors where appropriate.
EPA has declared environmental tobacco smoke to be a Group A carcinogen. Prohibiting smoking will minimize building occupants' exposure to environmental tobacco smoke.

10. Adopt appropriate voluntary standards, such as ASHRAE 62-1999 for ventilation ASHRAE 55-1992 for thermal comfort, and IES guidelines for lighting.

`P|A| |E| |O|` 10.1. Designate ASHRAE Standard 55-1992 for thermal comfort and ASHRAE Standard 62-1989 for ventilation as minimum design standards.

- *ASHRAE 55-1992:* Many IAQ complaints have been traced to thermal control problems involving building mechanical equipment. ASHRAE Standard 55-1992: Thermal Environmental Conditions for Human Occupancy identifies the range of design values for temperature, humidity, and air movement that will provide a satisfactory thermal environment for 80 percent or more of the building occupants.
- *ASHRAE 62-1999:* Standard building codes generally prescribe minimum outdoor air ventilation rates for mechanically ventilated spaces. In many cases, these rates are adopted from ASHRAE Standard 62. However, because of time lags inherent in code amendment, the building codes that apply to your project may not reflect the most recent version, Standard 62-1999. ASHRAE 62-99 includes important requirements such as minimum ventilation rates and the need to document HVAC design assumptions thoroughly to provide clear, detailed descriptions of building systems.

`P|A|I|E| |O|` 10.2. Use the ninth edition of the Illuminating Engineering Society of North America's (IESNA) *Lighting Handbook* for information on the revised industry standards for lighting. The ninth edition replaces the former illuminance recommendation table with chapter 10, which is entitled "Lighting Design Guide."

11. Determine ventilation, humidification/dehumidification, and filtration requirements.

`P|A| |E| |O|` 11.1. Require ventilation rates prescribed by ASHRAE 62-1999 at a minimum. Take into account maximum potential occupancy in calculating outside air in all spaces, including programmed number of occupants plus visitors. Plan for possible future requirements. [$E, $C, $M]

`P|A| |E| |O|` 11.2. Where possible, exceed ASHRAE recommendations for outside air per person for buildings with a low density of occupancy. Assume a population of no fewer than five persons for each 1,000 SF for the purposes of outside air calculation even where the estimated population is less than this figure. [$E, $C, $M]

`P|A| |E| |O|` 11.3. Require HVAC systems to maintain adequate ventilation rates even at minimum settings at all times during all hours of operation. [$E, $C, $M]

`P| | |E| |O|` 11.4. Determine humidification and/or dehumidification requirements based on the building type and the local climate. Systems that will maintain a range of 30–60 percent will enhance comfort. Humidification systems that will need to operate only a small portion of the year may not be justifiable, as they can be costly and difficult to maintain. [$C, $M, $E]
Occupant comfort can be adversely affected if relative humidity levels are either too high or too low. Excess indoor relative humidity can also contribute to the development of microbial growth, a problem both in hot, humid climates and in colder climates, where condensation can occur on building surfaces or within building envelope components.

| P = Planner | A = Architect | I = Interior designer | E = Engineer | L = Landscape architect | O= Owner consultation |

[T] = Could affect length of construction (+ or –), [$C] = Affects construction costs (+ or –), [$E] Affects energy costs, [$F] = Affects fees (+ or –), [$M] = Affects maintenance costs (+ or –).

`P| |E| |O` 11.5. Assess filtration requirements. Determine the impact of outside air quality in the design of air filtration and treatment. Outside ambient air quality should be evaluated at the location of the building fresh air intakes, not based on generalized data for the region. [$C, $E, $M]

`| |E| |` 11.6. Consider requiring installation of an alarm or sensor to notify building maintenance of the need to change air filters, to minimize the buildup of static pressure in the system. [$C, $E, $M]

12. Consider permanent air quality monitoring.

`P| |E| |O` 12.1. Consider designing ventilation rates based on indoor carbon dioxide (CO_2) monitoring. The ventilation rate should maintain a dilution of indoor CO_2 levels that does not exceed outdoor levels by more than 530 parts per million (ppm) at any time. In addition, the indoor-to-outdoor differential should be less than 50 ppm in the early morning, prior to occupancy. The early morning level verifies that the overnight purge successfully cleared the building of human effluents from the previous day. [$E, $C, $M]

Optimization

Building and Site Design

13. Design the building and site to promote the effective use of daylight and a sense of connection to the natural environment.

`|A|I|E| |` 13.1. See the Energy Project Actions section of this book for detailed information on the use of daylight and sun control strategies.

`|A|I|E|L|` 13.2. Develop building design to maximize views from the building to outdoor green spaces.

14. Protect IAQ by carefully locating building fresh air intakes and exhaust locations.

`|A| |E| |` 14.1. Locate outside air intakes upwind and away from potential pollutants/contaminants such as loading docks, standing water, sanitary vents, building exhausts, vehicular exhausts, generator exhausts, parking garages, and street traffic.

`|A| |E| |` 14.2. Locate cooling towers distant from air intakes to avoid entrainment of drift containing water-treatment chemicals or microbial contaminants.

`|A| |E| |` 14.3. Prevent reentrainment of building exhaust back into the building.

15. Protect building openings from vehicle pollution and contaminants from landscaped areas.

`P|A| |L|` 15.1. Employ building setbacks and landscaped buffers to prevent vehicle emissions or other off-site sources of pollution from entering the building.

`|A| |E| |` 15.2. In buildings with internal parking, provide a pressurized air lock at access to building elevators or stairways continuing up through the building. [$C, $E, $M]

`| | |E|L|` 15.3. Avoid the use of sporulating plants (plants that shed spores that are irritating to people with allergies) or plantings that may require use of chemical treatments, especially near building openings such as air intakes, entries, or operable windows.

MEP Design

16. **Develop design to promote effective ventilation systems.**

`|A|I|E| |` 16.1. Explore opportunities to use natural ventilation. [$C, $M]
To optimize natural ventilation, buildings should ideally be long and narrow and provide either cross ventilation or a solar chimney that draws air up and out of the building. The inlet window openings should face within 45 degrees of the prevailing wind direction. If the outlet opening is larger than the inlet opening, the wind velocity will increase slightly as it moves through the space.

`|A|I|E| |` 16.2. Analyze the impact of air supply and return locations on airflows to eliminate short circuiting and dead air zones. Use the most appropriate diffusers for the space.
Short circuiting of airflow can be a problem even where adequate air quantities are provided. This is of particular concern in office buildings, with the use of interior panel-based systems that extend to the floor.

`|A|I|E| |` 16.3. Consider the use of an underfloor air distribution system. Underfloor air systems can achieve 100 percent effectiveness, whereas traditional overhead systems rarely exceed more than 85 percent effectiveness due to short circuiting between intake and exhaust diffusers. [$C]

`|A|I|E| |` 16.4. Incorporate flexibility into the HVAC design to allow for ease of future change in the building layout, use patterns, and occupancy types. [$C]
The degree of flexibility built into the HVAC system will have a potential cost impact on the building systems, and should be determined with the owner early in the design process.

17. **Isolate all interior pollutant-generating sources (such as copy machines, chemical storage areas, etc.) to avoid contamination of indoor air quality.**

`|A| |E| |` 17.1. Provide dedicated exhaust for high-volume copy machines, and locate return air diffusers no more than 10 feet from desktop convenience copiers and printers, to provide dilution of the emissions.

`|A| |E| |` 17.2. If smoking is permitted, provide designated smoking areas within the building with 100 percent of return air exhausted directly to the outside, and ventilation rates providing a minimum of 60 CFM per person.

`|A| |E| |` 17.3. Provide 100 percent return air exhausted directly to the outside for pollutant-generating activities, such as printing equipment and food preparation. [$C]

`|A| |E| |` 17.4. Locate central storage and distributed janitor's closets with sinks and drains plumbed for appropriate disposal of waste products, with rooms under negative pressure and 100 percent return air exhausted directly to the outside. [$C, $M]

P = Planner	A = Architect	I = Interior designer	E = Engineer	L = Landscape architect	O= Owner consultation

[T] = Could affect length of construction (+ or –), [$C] = Affects construction costs (+ or –), [$E] Affects energy costs, [$F] = Affects fees (+ or –), [$M] = Affects maintenance costs (+ or –).

18. Design for easy access to and maintenance of HVAC equipment; eliminate internal duct liners.

|A| |E| | 18.1. Confirm that proper and adequate access is provided for all ventilation equipment. [$C]

IAQ problems can be caused by building equipment maintenance issues (e.g., problems with filters or microbiological contamination). Ease of access is important for the reduction of maintenance problems and long-term effectiveness of the building systems.

|A| |E| | 18.2. Design to eliminate use of internal duct liners. Ductwork commonly uses fleecy acoustical liners to deaden the sound associated with high-velocity airflows. Use of larger-section ductwork, which can accommodate airflows at slower velocities, can eliminate the need for acoustical lining. Mylar-coated sound attenuators can be used to accommodate sections of ductwork that require additional sound deadening to meet ASHRAE acoustical criteria. [$C, $M]

Exposed fiberglass internal duct lining can be a source of several IAQ-related problems. It can release fibers into the airstream, act as a sink for other emissions, may promote microbial growth, and is very difficult to maintain and clean. Air quality is further compromised by the rapid transfer of microbes/emissions throughout the building's air supply. This issue is of particular concern in hot, humid climates.

Documentation and Specifications

Detailing

19. Develop glazing and sun control strategies to provide comfortable natural daylight without glare.

|A| |E| | 19.1. See the Energy Project Actions section of this book for detailed information on the use of daylight and sun control strategies.

20. Develop detailing to control air and moisture flows and improve comfort.

|A| |E| | 20.1. Develop the building envelope design to provide an adequate air barrier and vapor retarder to control air and moisture flow through the exterior wall. Provide a vapor barrier at the point where cool surfaces meet warm, moist air (on the outside in hot, humid climates, and on the inside in cold climates). [$E]

The correct placement of the vapor barrier and design of a tight exterior wall are major contributing factors in the prevention of microbial contamination, particularly in hot and humid climates and microclimates.

|A| |E| | 20.2. Detail the building envelope with thermally broken windows to eliminate cold drafts and moisture accumulation from condensation. [$C, $E]

|A| |E| | 20.3. In hot, humid climates, design the HVAC system to effectively remove moisture loads, including both internally generated moisture as well as moisture entering the building by infiltration. Maintain positive building pressurization to inhibit water vapor infiltration from outdoors to the indoors. [$C, $E, $M]

The HVAC system should complement the building envelope design by properly conditioning the building's interior and envelope and pressurizing the building with dehumidified air. This may require sizing systems beyond average capacities. If negative pressurization occurs, the results can quickly lead to moisture and mildew problems.

| A | E | | | 20.4. Develop detailing to maintain mean radiant temperatures within ASHRAE's comfort ranges.

21. Provide appropriate acoustical separation between sources of noise inside and outside the building.

| A | | | | 21.1. Consider the sound transmission coefficient (STC rating) of building materials or assemblies to satisfy acoustical separation requirements.

| A | | | | 21.2. Consider the benefit of using a green roof to provide acoustical separation for sites with noise problems. See the Planning and Site Work Project Actions in this design guide for more information on green roofs. [$C]

22. Develop detailing to reduce cleaning requirements during occupancy by using walk-off mats at building entries and low-maintenance finishes.

| A | | | | 22.1. Provide an entryway walk-off system at all major entryways to catch and hold dirt and moisture before it is tracked into the building interior. Permanent, cleanable systems such as recessed grilles or grates are preferred. [$C, $M]

| A | I | | | 22.2. Specify easily maintained and durable surfaces, especially where traffic is greatest. Keep carpet away from entrances, where it can be contaminated from the outside, and away from water sources. [$M]
Designing for ease of maintenance at high traffic areas will help to eliminate the potential for buildup of particulates and microbiological growth. It is also important to consider the frequency and nature of the materials and processes required to perform maintenance. Surfaces requiring the frequent use of solvents in the cleaning process are the least desirable.

| A | I | | | 22.3. Require manufacturers to make recommendations in writing for their preferred maintenance methods that have a minimal impact on building air quality.
Maintenance can introduce high levels of VOCs into the building on a regular basis.

Materials Selection

23. Limit the use of fibrous materials, which have potential for microbial contamination.

| A | I | | | 23.1. Avoid the use of fleecy materials (such as fiberglass or mineral wool insulation) in plenum areas that are exposed to the airstream. In addition to the fact that the fibers can get loose in the airstream, the material can harbor mold and microbial growth if exposed to moisture.

| A | I | | | 23.2. Consider specification of antimicrobial treatments where microbial contamination is of particular concern—for example, in carpet, textile or vinyl wall coverings, ceiling tiles, or paints. Antimicrobial agents in products must be EPA registered and have an EPA-accepted Technical Data Sheet for the specific application. [$C]
Microbial growth can be inhibited through the use of antimicrobial additives either as part of the manufacturing process or as a topical treatment.

| P = Planner | A = Architect | I = Interior designer | E = Engineer | L = Landscape architect | O = Owner consultation |

[T] = Could affect length of construction (+ or –), [$C] = Affects construction costs (+ or –), [$E] Affects energy costs, [$F] = Affects fees (+ or –), [$M] = Affects maintenance costs (+ or –).

Building Materials with Potential IAQ Impact

Panel-based furniture systems

Floor coverings: carpet, carpet padding

Resilient flooring: rubber, vinyl, linoleum

Wood and composite wood products: particleboard, laminated wood, plywood

Acoustic ceiling and wall panels

Gypsum board

Paint and wall coverings

Preservatives and finishes

Adhesives: flooring, wallcovering, casework

Insulations: thermal, fire, acoustic

Sealants

Control joint fillers

Glazing compounds

---

24. Select materials that are low in emissions of particulates, total VOCs, and toxic components.

|A|I| | | 24.1. Specify low-VOC-emitting materials. See the Material Resources Project Actions in this guide for specific recommendations.

|A|I| | | 24.2. Avoid the interior use of engineered wood products that are high emitters of formaldehyde. Specifically, look for no- or low-formaldehyde substrates for casework such as MDF by Medite, or wheat straw substrates. If standard particleboard (which contains urea formaldehyde) is used as a substrate for casework, specify that exposed surfaces of substrate be sealed or encapsulated and unused assembly holes be plugged during manufacture. [$C]

|A|I| | | 24.3. Request MSDSs (Material Safety Data Sheets) from manufacturers and eliminate from consideration products with significant quantities of toxic, flammable, corrosive, or carcinogenic material. Manufacturers are required to provide information for each product according to OSHA (Occupational Safety and Health Administration) regulation, including: chemical identification, hazardous ingredients, reactivity, physical/chemical characteristics, fire/explosion data, potential health hazards, spill and leak procedures, necessary protection, and special precautions. [$F, $C]

MSDSs do not list all product ingredients, only those hazardous materials present in levels above 1 percent. Carcinogens, however, are listed if present above 0.1 percent. Furthermore, some materials, such as carpet, do not require an MSDS. Though they provide very limited information regarding IAQ properties, MSDSs are often the sole source of information on this subject.

25. Consider engaging in emissions testing of building materials and products to screen out those with toxic and/or irritating compounds.

| A | I | | O | 25.1. While emissions testing of building materials provides important information about product performance, it is particularly important for projects where people with chemical sensitivities may be users of the building. Materials that should be targeted for particular attention to IAQ considerations are:

- Those used in large quantities
- Those having potentially high emission rates
- Those located near the occupants' breathing zone or exposed directly to the ventilation air [$F, $C]

| A | I | | | 25.2. Request and evaluate available emissions and total volatile organic compound (TVOC) test results for high-priority materials and furniture items. To best analyze the emissions data for material selection, request the following information from testing agencies: [$F, $C, T]

- Description of the material that was tested, including its origin and history.
- Clear specification of test methods, conditions, and parameters.
- Emissions rates for individual VOCs and TVOC as a function of time. Be sure to use the same units when comparing like products. VOCs are often expressed as percentages of the total product: amount of volatiles per amount of product.
- Presence of heavy metals in the material.
- Identification of hazardous VOCs and chemicals included in any of the following regulatory and guidance lists. Carcinogenic and teratogenic potentials are considered especially unacceptable.
  - California Environmental Protection Agency, Air Resources Board, list of toxic air contaminants (California Air Toxics)
  - California Health and Welfare Agency, Safe Drinking Water and Toxic Enforcement Act of 1986 (Proposition 65), which lists carcinogens and teratogens, chemicals known to cause cancer and reproductive toxicity
  - International Agency on Research of Cancer (IARC), which classifies known and probable human carcinogens
  - National Toxicology Program, which lists known carcinogens
  - Chemical Cross Index, Chemical List of Lists, a compilation of state- and federally regulated hazardous chemicals

In general, materials with lowest emissions based on a thirty-day decay curve and lowest toxicity are to be selected. The thirty-day decay curve allows for products with high initial emissions and fast decay rates, in combination with moderate to low toxicity, to be considered acceptable. Where possible, document the selected product performance in terms of these variables. Document extent of test results on which selection was based.

Specifications

26. **Develop an IAQ management plan for the construction process. Specify the sequence of finish installation, temporary ventilation, and baseline air quality testing.**

| A | I | | | 26.1. Document the requirements of an IAQ management plan for the construction process clearly in division one of the project specifications.

| P = Planner | A = Architect | I = Interior designer | E = Engineer | L = Landscape architect | O= Owner consultation |

[T] = Could affect length of construction (+ or –), [$C] = Affects construction costs (+ or –), [$E] Affects energy costs, [$F] = Affects fees (+ or –), [$M] = Affects maintenance costs (+ or –).

Common Substances to Avoid in Materials Selection

Volatile organic compounds (VOCs)		Heavy metals (and their compounds)
Formaldehyde	Isophorone	Lead
Vinyl chloride	Methylene chloride	Mercury
4-phenylcyclohexene (4-PC)	Ethylbenzene	Cadmium
Styrene	Naphthalene	Chromium
Benzene	Phthalate esters	Antimony
Methyl ethyl ketone	Acrolein	Nickel
Methyl isobutyl ketone	Acrylonitrile	
Toluene	1,2-dichlorobenzene	
Xylenes	Acetone	
1,1,1-trichloroethane	Carbon tetrachloride	
Trichloroethylene	Tetrachloroethane	

See the Sheet Metal and Air Conditioning Contractors National Association's (SMACNA) "IAQ Guidelines for Occupied Buildings Under Construction" for more guidance on procedures to protect the building during construction. While the guide is written for renovation projects, the principles are equally applicable to new construction.

|A|I| | | 26.2. Require the contractor to include construction-related IAQ procedures on the agenda for the pre-construction meeting, and for regular progress meetings.

|A|I|E| | 26.3. Consider making construction sequencing a requirement in the specifications. Include a sample sequence of finish installation that illustrates the application of wet and/or odor-emitting materials, such as paint, coatings, sealants, and solvent-based materials, before the installation of dry "sink" materials, such as carpet, ceiling tile, fabric wall covering, and upholstered furnishings, that can adsorb contaminants. Require that the contractor submit a schedule of finish installation following those principles prior to the start of construction. [$C]
Wet materials tend to be short-term high emitters of VOCs. Installing wet materials early while providing maximum ventilation will reduce the amount of adsorption onto fleecy sink materials. Adsorption is defined as the adhesion of molecules to the surface of a solid substance. These molecules can later be reemitted into the building atmosphere.

|A|I|E| | 26.4. Consider making temporary ventilation a requirement in the specifications. Specification would require that 100 percent outside air be provided twenty-four hours a day during installation of materials and finishes. Temporary ventilation should begin after the building is substantially enclosed, and a minimum rate should be set at no less than one air change per hour. Require that air be exhausted directly to the outside, and that permanent return air ductwork be sealed off to prevent contamination. Temporary ventilation systems should be designed by the contractor and must not cause damage from high humidity. [$C]
Use of the permanent return air ductwork (that will be used for recirculating air in the finished project) during construction is to be avoided because it can easily become contam-

inated with dust, dirt, and chemical emissions, and it is difficult and expensive to clean. If the return air ductwork must be used for ventilation during construction, require that the contractor clean the ductwork prior to occupancy, using EPA duct cleaning guidelines.

|A|I|E| | 26.5. Require the use of separate filtration media on all permanent HVAC equipment during construction. Change out media to provide clean, new media before occupancy and verify that all air filters, casing, coils, and fans are in a clean condition. This should be done before testing and balancing commences and before baseline air quality tests are conducted. [$C]

|A|I|E| |O| 26.6. Consider specifying a requirement to conduct baseline air quality tests immediately prior to occupancy. The specifications should require testing for CO, CO_2, airborne mold and mildew, total volatile organic compounds (TVOC), formaldehyde, 4-PC, total particulates, and other pollutants. See chart below for maximum allowable indoor air concentrations of each. If the maximum threshold limits are not met, consider requiring the contractor to ventilate the building until the building complies. [$C, $F]

|A|I|E| | 26.7. Consider specifying preoccupancy ventilation or flush-out using 100 percent outside air ventilation, twenty-four hours per day. In typical new buildings the flush-out should be two to four weeks long, or until baseline IAQ testing measurements indicate that allowable air quality levels have been met (see below). Maximum achievable outside air ventilation rate should not exceed the capacity of heating or cooling equipment and should not exceed allowable indoor humidity levels, especially in humid climates. [$C]
Use of low-emission materials, and continuous ventilation during construction, lessens the need for postconstruction flush-out.

|A|I|E| |O| 26.8. If bake-out procedures are raised as a possibility, recommend against them.
Bake-out procedures involve elevating the building temperature during preoccupancy for a length of time in order to accelerate emissions. Studies have shown that damage may occur to the structure and equipment and that the potential benefits can be achieved through increased ventilation alone.

27. **Protect IAQ in occupied areas from contamination during renovation or phased construction.**

|A|I|E| | 27.1. Protect occupied areas from contamination during renovation or phased construction by isolating construction areas and return air ducts and by temporarily venting to the outside. [$C]
See the Sheet Metal and Air Conditioning Contractors National Association's (SMACNA) "IAQ Guidelines for Occupied Buildings Under Construction." The goal is to operate the HVAC system continuously when finishes and furnishings are applied or installed, and before and during initial occupancy. Increasing ventilation will accelerate the off-gassing process of newly installed materials and thus reduce residual airborne VOC concentrations. It will also minimize the adsorption of emitted VOCs on fleecy materials such as carpet, wall covering, and upholstery.

P = Planner	A = Architect	I = Interior designer	E = Engineer	L = Landscape architect	O= Owner consultation

[T] = Could affect length of construction (+ or –), [$C] = Affects construction costs (+ or –), [$E] Affects energy costs, [$F] = Affects fees (+ or –), [$M] = Affects maintenance costs (+ or –).

Bidding, Construction, and Commissioning

28. Include reporting on the IAQ management plan (see above) in the agenda of regularly scheduled construction meetings.

   |A|I|E| | 28.1. Confirm that special construction-related IAQ procedures, such as sequence of finish installation, temporary ventilation, and so on, are being met as required by the specifications.

29. Review submittals, samples, and product literature to determine compliance with IAQ standards.

   |A|I|E| | 29.1. Review submittals, samples, and product literature to determine compliance with specified IAQ standards. Verify that proposed material substitutions meet IAQ standards set by the specified products.

   |A|I|E| | 29.2. Verify that all proposed material substitutions meet IAQ standards.

Operations and Maintenance

30. Offer to assist the owner in developing an indoor air quality manual to guide operations.

   |A|I|E| |O| 30.1. Offer to assist the owner in developing an indoor air quality facility operations manual. Include educational materials, documentation of IAQ decision making, and scheduling of periodic maintenance, flush-outs, and monitoring. Consider the following for inclusion in the manual: [$F, $E, $M]

   • Educational materials that explain the importance of maintaining the building and its systems and describe major maintenance issues
   • Documentation of all design decisions with a potential impact on IAQ
   • Schedule for periodic measurement of indoor air quality to allow for comparison with baseline indoor air quality test results
   • Schedule for periodic inspection of mechanical ventilation and air conditioning ductwork where fitted to ensure that there is no visible freestanding water
   • Schedule for maintenance of HVAC system to ensure proper ventilation (include inspection of the filter fitted to the air-conditioning system)
   • Schedule for flush-outs of the building at frequent intervals and during a generally unoccupied time, such as early morning hours prior to normal daily occupancy and before reoccupancy after any period of vacancy, especially weekends or holidays
   • Recommendation that materials replacement or repair be made with low-emission materials and products
   • Recommendation that if partitions or furniture-related panel locations are changed during the life of the building, changes will be reviewed by an engineer to consider the effect on airflow and the area rebalanced

31. Recommend that the IAQ manager remain active in the postoccupancy IAQ program.

|A| | |O| 31.1. Recommend that the owner's designated IAQ manager remain active in managing an ongoing IAQ program once the facility is occupied, to provide informed guidance on potential IAQ problems that may arise during occupancy.

Because the IAQ manager understands the design of the facility and the design and construction strategies that were developed to protect IAQ, keeping this manager involved makes it much less likely that changes will be made over time to that approach.

|A| | |O| 31.2. Recommend that the IAQ manager be involved in developing the building cleaning and maintenance program, to advocate for the use of nontoxic, low VOC cleaning materials, and to ensure that cleaning and maintenance are coordinated with ventilation schedules.

| P = Planner | A = Architect | I = Interior designer | E = Engineer | L = Landscape architect | O= Owner consultation |

[T] = Could affect length of construction (+ or –), [$C] = Affects construction costs (+ or –), [$E] Affects energy costs, [$F] = Affects fees (+ or –), [$M] = Affects maintenance costs (+ or –).

134   The HOK Guidebook to Sustainable Design

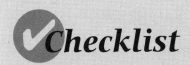 *Checklist*

Material Resources

Team Building

❑ 1. Seek out architects, engineers, landscape architects, and interior designers who can evaluate environmental and health impacts of the building materials and systems they specify over their full life cycle; or consider hiring a consultant to help with this task.

Education and Goal Setting

EDUCATION

❑ 2. Educate the team about the importance of design flexibility to enhance the longevity of buildings and infrastructure.

❑ 3. Educate the team about the environmental and health impacts of building materials over their full life cycle, from raw materials acquisition to production processes, packaging and shipping, installation and use, and ultimate resource recovery.

GOAL SETTING

❑ 4. Consider opportunities to reuse an existing building over new construction.

❑ 5. Make a commitment to consider environmental and health impacts over the full life cycle when selecting materials and products; identify which of these issues is of highest priority for the project, based on the building type and location.

❑ 6. Make a commitment to reduce waste and promote recycling; establish and quantify waste reduction goals.

Gathering Information

PROGRAMMING

❑ 7. Explore opportunities to reduce building area requirements through consolidation, shared uses, telecommuting, and the like.

❑ 8. Identify the desired life span of buildings and/or building components, and the rate of churn in interior spaces.

❑ 9. Develop space requirements for operational recycling and composting.

❏ 10. Identify locally manufactured building materials and products.

❏ 11. Research local recycling requirements and local infrastructure to support recycling beyond the mandated minimums.

Optimization

❏ 12. Explore opportunities to enhance flexibility and future adaptability.

❏ 13. Evaluate and select building materials and systems that reduce impacts to the environment and the health of building occupants, over the full life cycle of each.

❏ 14. Explore opportunities to use locally available materials and products and salvaged materials.

❏ 15. Design for disassembly of materials and systems.

❏ 16. For projects that involve demolition, propose salvage, reuse, and recycling of demolition materials.

❏ 17. Integrate requirements for materials collection systems for recycling into the building design.

Documents and Specifications

CONSTRUCTION DOCUMENTS

❏ 18. Develop resource-efficient design detailing based on material modules.

❏ 19. Develop design detailing that minimizes impacts on indoor air quality.

SPECIFICATIONS

❏ 20. Document detailed environmental performance criteria for the environmental performance of materials in the specifications.

❏ 21. Develop construction waste recycling section for specification; include a salvage and reuse plan for demolition of existing construction.

❏ 22. Develop specifications for appropriate handling of hazardous waste materials, such as oil, paint, and lighting.

❏ 23. Specify reuse of on-site materials to the greatest extent possible; shred wood for use as mulch, and crush rock for gravel.

Bidding, Construction, and Commissioning

❏ 24. Include waste management as an agenda item in the pre-start meetings.

❏ 25. Enforce special environmental requirements related to use of environmentally preferable materials.

❏ 26. Encourage vendors to reduce packaging, to use reusable packaging, and to transport materials to the site efficiently.

Operations and Maintenance

☐ 27. Offer to provide a comprehensive operations and maintenance manual with a plan that minimizes indoor air quality hazards from cleaning and maintenance products and minimizes waste from building refurbishment, including lighting waste disposal.

☐ 28. Quantify operational waste. Publicize and reward recycling efforts.

Project Actions

Material Resources

The Material Resources Project Actions are recommendations organized by project phase and by topic that should be considered during the design process.

When relevant, actions are followed by further explanations in italics and a notation in brackets [ ] indicating the potential effect on time, construction cost, energy cost, maintenance cost, or fee.

The information in the second part of this section (see pages 151–171) provides a summary listing of specific materials recommendations organized in accordance with the sixteen-division, five-digit specification number system of the familiar Construction Specifiers Institute (CSI) Master Format. Emphasis is placed on the proper selection, use, and application of environmentally preferable materials.

Team Building

1. Seek out architects, engineers, landscape architects, and interior designers who can evaluate environmental and health impacts of the building materials and systems they specify over their full life cycle, or consider hiring a consultant to help with this task.

   |A|I|E|L|O| 1.1. Seek out team members with interest in and understanding of life cycle environmental performance issues related to the materials and systems they specify.

   |A|I|E|L|O| 1.2. Seek out team members with interest and understanding of the health impacts related to materials and systems they specify.
   Most wet materials off-gas chemical emissions as they cure, and some materials will off-gas chemicals for extended periods of time. Other health concerns include contaminants in cleaning and maintenance compounds, potential sites of mold and microbial growth, and respirable fibers. Some materials release toxic and potentially lethal gases in a fire, posing health risks to occupants and firefighters.

   |A|I|E|L|O| 1.3. Select team members with knowledge of the durability and maintenance requirements of the materials and systems they specify.
   The goals of high durability and low maintenance are central to sustainable design; however, they are not well integrated into standard design decision making.

   |A|I|E|L|O| 1.4. Seek out team members familiar with the use of regionally appropriate materials and materials available in the local market.

   | P = Planner | A = Architect | I = Interior designer | E = Engineer | L = Landscape architect | O= Owner consultation |

   [T] = Could affect length of construction (+ or –), [$C] = Affects construction costs (+ or –), [$E] Affects energy costs, [$F] = Affects fees (+ or –), [$M] = Affects maintenance costs (+ or –).

|A|I|E|L|O| 1.5. If team members are not experienced in selecting and specifying environmentally preferable products, consider hiring a consultant. [$F]

Education and Goal Setting

Education

2. **Educate the team about the importance of design flexibility to enhance the longevity of buildings and infrastructure.**

|P|A|I|E|L|O| 2.1. In terms of resource efficiency, extending the life of buildings and infrastructure is of primary importance. Buildings and sites that can adapt to changing requirements do not become obsolete.

|P|A|I|E|L|O| 2.2. Consider future uses for the facility. Considerations about potential future uses can enhance the long-term value of the asset.

|P|A|I|E|L|O| 2.3. Discuss the impact that flexible design solutions will have on the design.
Design solutions should isolate permanent building elements, such as structure and enclosure, from those that will be replaced or modified over time, such as power, data, or HVAC systems. Interior planning modules should be coordinated with building structural systems.

3. **Educate the team about the environmental impacts of building materials over their full life cycle, from raw materials acquisition to production processes, packaging and shipping, installation and use, and ultimate resource recovery.**

|P|A|I|E|L|O| 3.1. Discuss the importance of selecting and specifying environmentally preferable products during goal setting sessions. Describe life cycle assessment of materials as a tool for decision making (see box on next page).

Goal Setting

4. **Give priority to reuse of an existing building over new construction.**

|P|A|I| | |O| 4.1. When evaluating potential sites, consider options that involve renovation or adaptive reuse of existing buildings. Factor in the value of salvage and reuse of building elements into the economic analysis. [$C]

5. **Make a commitment to consider environmental and health impacts over the full life cycle when selecting materials and products; identify which of these issues is of highest priority for the project, based on the building type and location.**

|P|A|I|E|L|O| 5.1. Establish a preference for building materials and products that are made from nontoxic or low-toxicity, renewable, sustainably acquired raw materials; have recycled content; are durable and low maintenance; are low polluting in manufacture, shipping, and installation; and are recyclable.

Life Cycle Assessment of Materials

Issues that should be considered when evaluating products include the following:

Raw Materials

- Is the raw material nontoxic?
- Does the raw material come from a renewable source?
- Does the raw material come from a certified sustainable source?
- Is the raw material an agricultural or industrial by-product?
- Does the product or material come from a salvaged source?
- Does the product have recycled content (either postconsumer and/or postindustrial)?

Production Processes

- How much energy is used in manufacturing?
- Is the manufacturing plant energy efficient, or does it use alternative or renewable resources?
- How much water is used in manufacture?
- Does the manufacturing plant conserve or reuse water?
- How much solid, aqueous, and gaseous waste is associated with manufacture?
- Have toxic emissions and effluents been eliminated from the production process?
- Have ozone-depleting materials been eliminated from the production process?
- Is manufacturing waste reused or recycled?

Packaging and Shipping

- Is the product or material locally manufactured?
- Does the product or material use minimal, reusable, or recycled packaging?
- Does the manufacturer use efficient shipping methods?

Installation and Use

- How durable is the product?
- Does the product off-gas VOCs, formaldehyde, or other potentially harmful chemical emissions?
- Does the product contain mineral fibers?
- Is the product an installation hazard for workers?
- Are nontoxic, low-VOC adhesives, finishes, sealants, and maintenance products available for the product?
- Is the product low maintenance?

Resource Recovery

- Is the product or material salvageable?
- Does the manufacturer provide a take-back option for the product?
- Is the product or material recyclable?
- Is the product or material biodegradable?

P|A|I|E|L|O 5.2. Identify issues of particularly high or low priority based on building type and location. For example, use of local materials may be especially important in remote areas, and concerns about indoor air quality will be less important for open-air structures.

P|A|I|E|L|O 5.3. Make a commitment to use HVAC, electrical, lighting, and plumbing fixtures and equipment that are energy and water efficient.

P|A|I|E|L|O 5.4. Make a commitment to use "good wood," which has been certified as sustainably harvested in accordance with Forest Stewardship Council (FSC) guidelines. [$C]

P|A|I|E|L|O 5.5. Make a commitment to use low-VOC paint, adhesives, and finishes.

P|A|I|E|L|O 5.6. Make a commitment to use materials with high recycled content. Consider use of the EPA Comprehensive Procurement Guidelines to establish minimum recycled content requirements, and explore opportunities to improve upon them (see box on next page).

6. Make a commitment to reduce waste and promote recycling; establish and quantify waste reduction goals.

P|A|I| |O 6.1. Set goals for recycling operational waste, including white and mixed paper, glass bottles, aluminum cans, and cardboard, as well as food and yard waste for composting. [$M]

P|A|I| |O 6.2. Consider use of reusable china and tableware for food service areas, and reusable mugs in coffee areas. Provide space for washing apparatus. [$C]

P|A|I| |O 6.3. Consider participation in EPA's WasteWise program.

EPA's WasteWise Program

WasteWise is a free, voluntary EPA program through which organizations design their own solid waste reduction programs tailored to their needs, to reduce, reuse, and recycle solid waste materials. EPA provides partners with access to their publications and resource library, personalized technical assistance, and public recognition through awards, journal articles, and advertising.

Upon joining the program, each new WasteWise partner is assigned a WasteWise representative, who is available to provide individual assistance. WasteWise representatives help partners establish their goals, assist them in completing their annual reporting forms, and provide technical assistance.

WasteWise partners are encouraged to highlight their participation by using the WasteWise logo. The logo is often incorporated into employee education tools such as posters, newsletters, and progress reports. EPA's goal is that the WasteWise logo will be recognized as a symbol of environmental leadership.

Call the toll-free helpline at (800) EPA-WISE.

Source: http://www.epa.gov/wastewise/

EPA Comprehensive Procurement Guidelines

The Comprehensive Procurement Guidelines (CPG) program is part of EPA's continuing effort to promote the use of materials recovered from solid waste. Buying recycled-content products ensures that the materials collected in recycling programs will be used again in the manufacture of new products.

EPA has designated products that are or can be made with recovered materials and has recommended practices for buying these products. Once a product is designated, procuring executive branch agencies are required to purchase it with the highest recovered material content level practicable.

Recommended recycled-content ranges for CPG products are based on current information on commercially available recycled-content products, and the levels are updated as marketplace conditions change. All proposals, designations, and recommendations are published in the *Federal Register*. While directed primarily at executive-branch agencies, this information is helpful to everyone interested in purchasing recycled-content products.

The Web site contains a brief description for each of the designated products, and a listing of current proposed products. You also can view EPA's recommended recycled content range and a list identifying manufacturers, vendors, and suppliers for each item.

Designated Construction Products

- Building insulation products
- Carpet
- Cement and concrete containing:
  —Coal fly ash
  —Ground granulated blast furnace slag
- Consolidated and reprocessed latex paint
- Floor tiles
- Laminated paperboard
- Patio blocks
- Shower and rest room dividers/partitions
- Structural fiberboard

Designated Landscape Products:

- Garden and soaker hoses
- Hydraulic mulch
- Lawn and garden edging
- Yard trimmings compost

Designated Park and Recreation Products

- Plastic fencing
- Playground surfaces
- Running tracks

Also includes an assortment of office products and paper products.

Source: http://www.epa.gov/cpg/

Programming

7. Explore opportunities to reduce building area requirements through consolidation, shared uses, telecommuting, and so on.

`P|A|I|  | |O|` 7.1. Explore opportunities to consolidate program areas through the creation of shared file areas, out-of-office conferencing, and shared resources such as libraries or print rooms. [$C]

`P|A|I|  | |O|` 7.2. Consider co-locating conference areas to allow for more efficient scheduling and use.

`P|A|I|  | |O|` 7.3. Explore the potential use of telecommuting, and consider its impact on space planning and design.

   To realize space efficiencies, telecommuters must share workstations or develop some form of "hoteling," which involves shared use of common unassigned workstations. Hoteling sometimes requires an increase in storage requirements to compensate for the decrease in offices and workstations.

8. Identify the desired life span of buildings and/or building components and the rate of churn in interior spaces.

`P|A|I|  | |O|` 8.1. Gather information on the owner's anticipated need for the building to determine its desired life span. Include expectations for resale of the property at the end of the current owner's occupancy. Organize information on anticipated life spans as specifically as possible.

   By understanding the expected life span of buildings and building elements, the design team can better evaluate the cost and benefit associated with improvements in building durability. If the desired life span is very short, encourage planning for future uses.

`P|A|I|  | |O|` 8.2. Estimate the rate of churn in office areas, that is, the rate at which building occupants move to different offices or workstations within the same office.

`P|A|I|  | |O|` 8.3. Estimate the rate of churn in retail spaces. Some retail areas will change seasonally, whereas others will reorganize and renovate less frequently.

9. Develop space requirements for operational recycling and composting.

   Early research and analysis prior to design will streamline the process of incorporating recycling and composting and may lend valuable information to the design of both the site and the building. For example, recycling chutes or designated area for composting need to be integrated early on in schematic design.

`P|A|I|  | |O|` 9.1. Obtain information from the client on the projected waste stream. Information should include the type and quantity of recyclable materials that building users generate, such as white and mixed paper, glass bottles, aluminum cans, and cardboard, as well as food and yard waste for composting.

`P|A|I|  | | |` 9.2. If information on the building user's waste stream is not available, offer to conduct a waste stream analysis to determine recycling opportunities. [$F]

| P | A | I | | | 9.3. Identify area requirements for recycling containers, compactors, and staging for collection. Consider use of recycling chutes in multistory buildings, and plan accordingly when developing building core areas. [$C]

Recycling chutes can be developed for the transport of one type of recyclable each, or use of a sorting mechanism at the base of the chute can allow for transport of multiple materials through a single chute. Chutes that are used to transport garbage or food waste for composting require wash-down systems within the chute.

Research

10. Identify locally manufactured building materials and products.

| A | I | E | L | 10.1. Identify local manufacturers and suppliers of building materials for the design team. This will streamline the materials research process during the design phase, and will enhance early consideration of locally manufactured types of products.

| A | I | E | L | 10.2. Seek out sources of information on locally available materials and products that have already been developed by other organizations.

11. Research local recycling requirements and local infrastructure to support recycling beyond the mandated minimums.

| A | I | | | 11.1. Identify locally mandated requirements for recycling.

| A | I | | | 11.2. Identify local infrastructure for recycling of operational waste as well as construction and demolition (C&D) waste. Contact local and state Departments of Solid Waste for information, lists of haulers, and associated costs. Inquire about local resource guides to assist designers and contractors with recycling.

| A | I | | | 11.3. Determine whether materials for recycling will be commingled, partially commingled or individually separated. Mixed-paper recycling is becoming increasingly common, as are mixed metals and plastics.

| A | I | | | 11.4. Compare the cost of landfill disposal with recycling. Landfill tipping fees vary nationwide, but when they are approximately $50 per ton or more, it is usually cost-effective to recycle commingled waste rather than landfill it. Also, some materials such as cardboard and metals generate income. [$C]

Optimization

12. Explore opportunities to enhance flexibility and future adaptability.

| A | I | E | | 12.1. Avoid the use of embedded infrastructure for power, data, or HVAC systems, because it limits long-term flexibility. Building systems should isolate structural and building enclosure systems from infrastructure for power, data, or HVAC systems.

| P = Planner | A = Architect | I = Interior designer | E = Engineer | L = Landscape architect | O= Owner consultation |

[T] = Could affect length of construction (+ or –), [$C] = Affects construction costs (+ or –), [$E] Affects energy costs, [$F] = Affects fees (+ or –), [$M] = Affects maintenance costs (+ or –).

The HOK Guidebook to Sustainable Design

|A|I|E| | 12.2. To achieve long-term flexibility, coordinate interior planning modules with building structural systems and MEP distribution.

|A|I|E| | 12.3. Give priority to simple building forms and forms that are articulated as separable parts, to enhance flexibility and adaptability.

|A|I|E| | 12.4. Give priority to the use of building materials and systems of durable and "patchable" construction.

|A|I|E| | 12.5. Design for expansion both within the building and outside the building, where possible.

Interior expansion allows for additional space requirements to be accommodated within the building floorplate through the displacement or consolidation of less critical functions; exterior expansion involves the construction of additional building area.

13. **Evaluate and select building materials and systems that reduce impacts to the environment and the health of building occupants over their full life cycle.**

Review products available in the marketplace and select manufacturers whose products meet performance requirements and also limit environmental and health impacts throughout their life cycle. In many cases, large differences exist between different manufacturers' products.

|A|I|E|L| 13.1. Use life cycle assessment of materials as a tool for decision making. [T]

|A|I|E|L| 13.2. Balance environmental performance goals with traditional performance requirements of all alternatives, including:

Cost	Acoustical performance
Durability	Energy performance
Fire rating, flame spread	Safety requirements
Strength characteristics	Maintenance requirements

|A|I| | | 13.3. Choose products with compatible maintenance requirements to the greatest extent possible. Materials requiring dry maintenance should have adequate separation from materials requiring wet maintenance. [$M]

|A|I|E|L| 13.4. Give preference to locally manufactured materials where cost and performance are equal. [$C, T]

|A|I|E|L| 13.5. Carefully review materials to limit use of those that generate hazardous waste during construction (e.g., solvent-based paints and adhesives, sealants, waterproofing, etc.). Also give consideration to the hazardous waste that will be generated from materials used to clean up after use (e.g., solvent–based thinners, cleaners, paint removers, etc.).

14. **Explore opportunities to use locally available materials and products and salvaged materials.**

|A|I|E|L| 14.1. Develop the design aesthetic to make use of regionally appropriate materials and locally available building materials.

Regionally appropriate materials are ones that are made from locally available renewable resources, such as wood in the Northeast or Northwest, wheat straw in the Midwest, and so on.

| A | I | E | L | 14.2. Look for opportunities to use salvaged materials, such as used bricks or timbers, refurbished office furniture, or refurbished carpet. Contact local salvage yards and resale outlets to check on availability of materials. [$C, T]

15. Design for disassembly of materials and systems.

| A | I | E | L | 15.1. Design for disassembly and reuse of materials where possible, particularly for applications that are likely to change frequently. [$C]

| A | I | E | L | 15.2. Design to accommodate future needs and anticipate future retrofit requirements.

| A | I | | | 15.3. Consider use of movable partition systems. [$C]

| A | I | E | | 15.4. Consider use of raised-floor systems. [$C]

16. For projects that involve demolition, propose salvage, reuse, and recycling of demolition materials.

| A | I | E | | 16.1. Explore opportunities to salvage materials for reuse, such as brick, wood flooring, windows, doors, cabinets, plumbing fixtures, light fixtures, lamps, duct work, framing lumber, hardware, wiring, piping, and so on prior to demolition. Schedule a walk-through with local building salvager(s) to determine what items have value for resale or reuse. [$F, T, $C]

| A | I | | | 16.2. Determine whether the demolition schedule can afford time for manual removal of selected building elements followed by mechanically assisted demolition, or whether the schedule will allow for whole-building disassembly. [T]

| A | I | | | 16.3. Consider requirements for site storage and transportation of materials to salvage company. Consider donation of materials to a nonprofit group or salvage company.

| A | I | | | 16.4. For demolition projects with carpet, consider carpet recycling programs such as the DuPont Carpet Reclamation Program, BASF's 6ix Again, and Monsanto's Partners for Renewal.

| A | I | | | 16.5. For demolition projects with large amounts of ceiling tiles, consider the Armstrong Ceilings Reclamation Program. The program recycles certain types of mineral fiber acoustical ceiling tile.

17. Integrate requirements for materials collection systems for recycling into the building design.

| A | I | | O | 17.1. Locate materials collection containers for recycling near the point of use. For example, collection containers should be located near lunchrooms and vending areas for beverage containers, and containers should be located near printers and copy machines for used paper.

| A | I | | | 17.2. Locate collection containers near vertical transportation in multistory buildings.

| P = Planner | A = Architect | I = Interior designer | E = Engineer | L = Landscape architect | O= Owner consultation |

[T] = Could affect length of construction (+ or –), [$C] = Affects construction costs (+ or –), [$E] Affects energy costs, [$F] = Affects fees (+ or –), [$M] = Affects maintenance costs (+ or –).

`|A|I| | |` 17.3. Provide ample space for containers, compactors, and balers (where applicable), and staging space at the building loading dock. [$C]

`|A|I| | |` 17.4. In areas without residential recycling, consider locating containers for recyclables near parking decks or other building access points.

Documents and Specifications

Construction Documents

18. Develop resource-efficient design detailing based on material modules.

`|A|I|E| |` 18.1. Develop detailing that maximizes the use of standard-sized modules. [$C]

`|A|I|E| |` 18.2. Avoid structural overdesign by optimum-value engineering, advanced framing, and so on. [$C]

`|A|I|E| |` 18.3. Minimize the amount of waste produced by selecting long-lasting, reusable, and/or recyclable materials and equipment.

`|A|I| | |` 18.4. Avoid the use of finish materials where not necessary for performance or aesthetics. For example, maintenance areas generally require no finishes. [$C]

`|A|I|E| |` 18.5. Dimension materials carefully using standard-sized modules to the greatest extent possible, to minimize construction off-cutting waste. [$C]

19. Develop design detailing that minimizes impacts on IAQ.

`|A|I| | |` 19.1. Design interior millwork, handrails, custom metalwork, and the like to be shop-finished and installed to the greatest degree possible, to limit the need for the need for on-site painting and finishing.

`|A|I|E| |` 19.2. Review manufacturer-recommended adhesives, finishes, and sealants carefully, and ask for alternative recommendations where necessary, to ensure that adhesives are free of solvents, contain no toxic materials, and are low in VOCs.

Specifications

20. Document detailed environmental performance criteria for the environmental performance of materials in the specifications.

`|A|I|E|L|` 20.1. Document all environmental requirements in the specifications and require submittals from manufacturers to certify their compliance with the requirements.

`|A|I|E|L|` 20.2. Specify minimum recycled-content requirements for building materials. Consult recycled-content building material information sources for additional information as needed, including the National Recycling Coalition, the Harris Directory, REDI on the Oikos Web site, and others.

| A | I | E | | 20.3. Explore the potential to eliminate use of materials that contain or are manufactured with ozone-depleting substances, including HCFCs and methyl bromide. Production of other ozone-depleting substances—CFCs, halons, carbon tetrachloride, methyl chloroform, and HBFCs—have already been fully banned in the United States. Develop a CFC and halon management and five-year phase-out plan for existing buildings being rehabilitated. [$C]

| A | I | E | L | 20.4. Specify maximum VOC content for all applicable materials and products. VOCs are detrimental to health in the indoor environment; however, they are also an issue for exterior materials, as VOCs contribute to the formation of ground-level smog.

21. Develop construction waste recycling section for specification; include a salvage and reuse plan for demolition of existing construction.

| A | I | | | 21.1. Require construction waste recycling of asphalt, concrete and masonry, wood (dimension wood, not engineered wood), metals, cardboard, and paint at the job site at a minimum. These materials are recycled in most parts of the country and are generally cost-effective to recycle. [T]

| A | I | | | 21.2. Consider the recycling of other materials, such as rigid foam insulation, engineered wood products, glass, gypsum drywall, ceiling tile, carpet, and carpet padding. [$C, T]

| A | I | | | 21.3. Determine the method of recycling. Three possible methods are on-site separation of materials, phase-based separation by hauler, and off-site sorting of mixed waste. [T, $C]

| A | I | | | 21.4. For projects that require on-site separation of materials, require that individual bins be clearly labeled for each kind of waste. Individual bins keep waste "clean," and clean waste always brings a higher price.

| A | I | | | 21.5. Determine whether materials for recycling will be commingled, partially commingled, or individually separated, based on the information gathered from inquiries about local recycling opportunities and associated costs. [T, $C]

| A | I | | | 21.6. Require that the contractor submit a construction waste management plan prior to the outset of demolition and/or construction. The plan should include:

- Types of waste material to be recycled
- Estimated quantities of waste produced
- Estimate of quantities of materials to be recycled
- Cost difference for recycling as opposed to disposal
- On-site storage and separation requirements
- Transportation methods, licensed haulers
- Names of licensed recycling centers that will receive materials

| A | I | | | 21.7. Require recycling of other types of construction-related waste, such as paper, plastic, aluminum cans, and miscellaneous wrappers and packaging.

| P = Planner | A = Architect | I = Interior designer | E = Engineer | L = Landscape architect | O= Owner consultation |

[T] = Could affect length of construction (+ or –), [$C] = Affects construction costs (+ or –), [$E] Affects energy costs, [$F] = Affects fees (+ or –), [$M] = Affects maintenance costs (+ or –).

22. Develop specifications for appropriate handling for hazardous waste materials, such as oil, paint, and lighting.

> |A|I| | | 22.1. Evaluate requirements and plan ahead for applicable hazardous waste handling, such as oils, paints, lighting, and medical waste, which requires licensed contractors.

> |A|I| | | 22.2. Suggest that leftover paint be transported to municipal paint recycling facilities.

> |A|I| | | 22.3. Require proper disposal or recycling of lighting waste. Investigate recycling programs for lamps containing mercury, including fluorescent, mercury vapor, metal halide, high-pressure sodium, and neon. A list of lamp recyclers is included in the EPA brochure "Lighting Waste Disposal."

23. Specify reuse of on-site materials to the greatest extent possible. Shred wood for use as mulch, and crush rock for gravel.

> |A| |E|L| 23.1. Specify reuse of on-site materials to the greatest extent possible. Shred wood for use as mulch and crush rock for gravel if quantities required justify the cost. [T, $C]

> |A| |E|L| 23.2. Stockpile existing topsoil for reuse on site.

> |A| |E|L| 23.3. Assess the suitability of the site for the application of pulverized gypsum waste (from unpainted material only) as a soil amendment. Apply gypsum waste in accordance with the results and the specified landscape treatment. This strategy is particularly valuable in parts of the country where disposal of gypsum waste is restricted. [T]

Bidding, Construction, and Commissioning

24. Include waste management as an agenda item in the pre-start meetings.

> |A|I| | | 24.1. Review construction waste recycling specification with the contractor and subcontractors.

> |A|I| | | 24.2. When the project involves demolition prior to construction, ensure that adequate time has been allocated for salvage of materials and fixtures prior to actual demolition.

25. Enforce special environmental requirements related to use of environmentally preferable materials.

> |A|I|E|L| 25.1. Verify that environmentally preferable building materials are provided as specified before subcontracts are finalized. Review proposed substitutions carefully.

> |A|I|E|L| 25.2. Verify that special installation requirements will be met before subcontracts are finalized. Review proposed substitutions carefully.

> |A|I| | | 25.3. Participate in take-back programs to the maximum extent possible. Some manufacturers of building materials and products (including many carpet manufacturers

and some ceiling tile manufacturers) have initiated programs to take back scrap material after installation is complete, so that they can recycle the material. [T]

[A|I| |] 25.4. Ensure proper handling, storage, and disposal of hazardous and toxic materials.

26. **Encourage vendors to reduce packaging, to employ reusable packaging, and to transport materials to the site efficiently.**

[A|I| |] 26.1. Encourage suppliers to ship materials to the construction site using minimal, recyclable, or reusable crates or packaging systems.

[A|I| |] 26.2. Encourage energy-efficient transportation of materials to the site. For example, materials can be shipped disassembled, dry-mixed, or in bulk.

Operations and Maintenance

27. **Offer to provide a comprehensive operations and maintenance manual with a plan that minimizes indoor air quality hazards from cleaning and maintenance products and minimizes waste from building refurbishment, including lighting waste disposal.**

[A|I|E| |O] 27.1. Consider development of a comprehensive operations and maintenance manual for the building owner that minimizes indoor air quality hazards from cleaning and maintenance products, and that minimizes waste from building refurbishment, including lighting waste disposal. [$F, $M]

[A|I|E| |O] 27.2. Develop a long-term plan for the handling and disposal of hazardous waste, including solvent-based paints and adhesives, sealant, waterproofing, and other materials.

[A|I|E| |O] 27.3. Minimize the use of toxic maintenance and cleaning products, and consider alternatives.

28. **Quantify operational waste. Publicize and reward recycling efforts.**

[A|I| |L|O] 28.1. Consider developing a plan to monitor the waste stream during occupancy, and reward successful recycling efforts. [$F]

| P = Planner | A = Architect | I = Interior designer | E = Engineer | L = Landscape architect | O= Owner consultation |

[T] = Could affect length of construction (+ or –), [$C] = Affects construction costs (+ or –), [$E] Affects energy costs, [$F] = Affects fees (+ or –), [$M] = Affects maintenance costs (+ or –).

SUMMARY OF MATERIAL RECOMMENDATIONS

The following is a summary of recommendations that can be used to guide materials selection and specification.

Division 02—Site Work

02500—Paving

| A | E | L | 1. Specify use of crushed rock or recycled concrete rubble as subbase fill for pavement. [$C]

| A | | L | 2. Choose brick or concrete unit pavers from local sources. Consider use of salvaged materials or products made with oil-contaminated soils, fly ash, or other industrial waste.

| | E | | 3. Consider using rubber modified asphalt (RMA) with a crumb rubber content no greater than 20 percent. (RMA using higher than 20 percent crumb rubber has been reported to have problems.)

| A | E | L | 4. Use pervious paving materials whenever possible to allow water to enter soil, thereby limiting stormwater runoff. Pervious paving is available in two basic types: poured asphalt or concrete with air spaces left by removing fine aggregate, and unit paving systems of plastic or concrete with voids for gravel or grass. [$C]

| A | E | L | 5. Look for pervious paving products with a recycled content. Some porous paving systems are made with 100 percent postconsumer recycled HDPE plastic.

02500—Site Furnishings

| A | | L | 1. Consider specifying furnishings made from recycled plastic, such as trash containers, benches, wheel stops, and deck timbers. [$C]

02810—Irrigation

| | E | L | 1. When irrigation is required, use drip irrigation or bubbler systems to reduce water waste from surface evaporation. [$C, $E]

| | E | L | 2. Equip irrigation systems with rain sensor overrides. [$C, $E]

| | E | L | 3. Avoid high-pressure misting sprinklers, which waste water.

| | E | L | 4. Use soaker hoses made from recycled rubber.

02900—Landscape Work

☐ | | | |L| ☐ 1. Use plants that are native to the region in order to reduce need for soil amendments and irrigation. Research and list specific species. [$C, $M]

☐ | | | |L| ☐ 2. Consider use of biosolids and sludge from wastewater treatment facilities as a soil amendment.

Division 03—Concrete

03300—Cast-in-Place Concrete

☐ |A| |E| | ☐ 1. General: Utilize many of the positive aspects of concrete, such as fire resistance, thermal mass, and longevity. High calculable strength, moldability, and transportability make cast-in-place concrete highly advantageous as a structural material; however, formwork creates much waste.

☐ |A| |E| | ☐ 2. Cement: Specify 20 percent fly ash or 30 percent ground granulated blast furnace slag in cement. Higher percentages may be used, depending on the strength potential that is required. [$C]

☐ |A| |E| | ☐ 3. Reinforcement: Inquire about the use of scrap steel in the manufacture of reinforcing steel. Many sources of reinforcing steel use 100 percent recycled content.

☐ |A| |E| | ☐ 4. Formwork and accessories: Where removable formwork is used, specify a biodegradable form release agent made from rapeseed oil. [$C]
   Where possible, allow reusable formwork or recycle formwork.
   Consider use of permanent formwork made from expanded polystyrene or fiber-cement blocks. Also known as insulating concrete forms (ICFs), these provide improved R-values, and some of these products contain recycled content.

☐ |A| |E| | ☐ 5. Curing compound: Use products that have less than 160 g/l VOCs. The EPA recommends 350 g/l as a maximum, but many products have a far lower VOC content. [$C]

03400—Precast Concrete

☐ |A| |E| | ☐ 1. General: See Cast-in-Place Concrete.

☐ |A| |E| | ☐ 2. Cement: Specify 20 percent fly ash or 30 percent ground granulated blast furnace slag in cement. Larger proportions of fly ash may be used, depending on strength required. [$C]

☐ |A| |E| | ☐ 3. Formwork and accessories: Specify use of biodegradable form release. Some plants use this exclusively. [$C]

P = Planner	A = Architect	I = Interior designer	E = Engineer	L = Landscape architect	O= Owner consultation

[T] = Could affect length of construction (+ or −), [$C] = Affects construction costs (+ or −), [$E] Affects energy costs, [$F] = Affects fees (+ or −), [$M] = Affects maintenance costs (+ or −).

Division 04—Masonry

|A| |E| | | 1. Consider use of industrial waste materials (coal waste, pelletized expanded blast furnace slag, or a combination of pelletized fly ash and coal slurry) as lightweight aggregates to replace sand in mortar.

04200—Masonry Units

|A| | | | 1. Masonry units are typically heavy, and as such have high transportation costs and embodied energy. Choose locally manufactured products wherever possible. [$C]

|A| |E| | 2. When using brick masonry, take advantage of its multifunction capabilities. Modern use of brick is usually confined to a thin veneer. This use of the material overlooks the potential benefits of thermal mass.

|A| | | | 3. Consider using bricks made from oil-contaminated soils. Bricks fired at high temperatures neutralize waste materials.

|A| |E| | 4. Consider using adobe, pressed-soil-cement, or other natural, low-embodied-energy masonry technologies. [$C]

|A| |E| | 5. When using concrete masonry units (CMUs), look for products with high-recycled-content aggregate (including recycled concrete, ground glass, and other waste material) as much as technically feasible in the given application.

|A| |E| | 6. Consider using specially designed polystyrene inserts for CMUs to improve thermal performance. [$C]

|A| | |L| 7. Consider use of interlocking CMUs (requiring no mortar) for landscape retaining walls, particularly when disassembly is likely. [T]

Division 05—Metals

|A|I| | | 1. General: Consider designs that will facilitate recycling of aluminum later. Avoid using mixed-material assemblies.

|A|I|E|L| 2. Metal finishing: Give preference to factory finishing rather than site-finishing wherever possible. The greater control in factory finishing may significantly reduce material waste and environmental hazards. [$C, T]

Consider metal finishing based on physical processes such as abrasive blasting, grinding, buffing, and polishing rather than coatings, where applicable.

Where metal coatings are required, specify powder-coated fabrications. Solvents are not emitted in the powder-coating process, and therefore little if any VOCs are emitted. Powder overspray can also be reclaimed for reuse. [$C]

Avoid plated metals. When plating is necessary, ensure that the process does not use cadmium or chromium as the plating material, or cyanide- or copper/formaldehyde-based electroless copper as the plating solution. Safer alternative processes are currently available.

$\boxed{A|I|E|L}$	3. Aluminum: Consider less-energy-consuming alternative materials in applications where the advantageous characteristics of aluminum (light weight, color, corrosion resistance) are not needed. Aluminum is a finite, nonrenewable resource requiring very high energy use in production (over five times that of steel by weight). [$C] Specify aluminum products fully or partially made from recycled scrap (many alloys cannot be made from 100 percent recycled scrap).
$\boxed{A|I|E|L}$	4. Steel. Inquire about recycled content in steel products. Steel is one of the most recycled building materials. The steel typically used in products whose major characteristic is strength may contain as much as 100 percent recycled steel, of which 75 percent may be postconsumer. Reduce on-site steel waste by ordering prefabricated materials. [$C, T]

Division 06—Wood and Plastics

$\boxed{A|I|E|L}$	1. When using wood, use it efficiently. Choose products made from smaller-sized wood pieces. Wherever possible, specify independently certified sustainably harvested wood. The Scientific Certification Systems (SCS) and the Smartwood Program of the Rainforest Alliance are two certification programs approved by the Forest Stewardship Council (FSC). [$C]
$\boxed{A|I|E|L}$	2. Consider using reclaimed wood products from demolition salvage. Structural timbers and hardwood flooring are commonly salvaged from older buildings and can be remilled and refinished. To find local sources of these and other reclaimed wood products, check the *Good Wood Directory* by the Good Wood Alliance.[$C]
$\boxed{A|\ |L}$	3. Consider wood-plastic composite products, made from recycled content, for exterior applications such as benches, fencing, and decking. [$C, $M]
$\boxed{A|\ |L}$	4. Do not use wood treated with CCA (copper chromium arsenate). Use less toxic preservatives, such as ACQ (ammonium copper quaternium) or CDDC (copper hydroxide sodium dimethyldithiocarbamate) and have treated wood sealed. [$C]

06100—Rough Carpentry

$\boxed{A|I|E|\ }$	1. To relieve pressure on timber supplies, seek alternatives to dimension lumber and other wood products that are made from whole trees. Alternatives include steel studs and plastic lumber, which typically contain a high percentage of recycled content and are recyclable themselves. [$C]
$\boxed{A|I|E|\ }$	2. Minimize use of large timbers by using glue-laminated beams and other prefabricated assemblies. [$C]

P = Planner	A = Architect	I = Interior designer	E = Engineer	L = Landscape architect	O= Owner consultation

[T] = Could affect length of construction (+ or –), [$C] = Affects construction costs (+ or –), [$E] Affects energy costs, [$F] = Affects fees (+ or –), [$M] = Affects maintenance costs (+ or –).

|A|I|E| | | 3. Minimize use of plywood by using composite boards, including paper and wood/paper building boards that use milling by-products, waste woods, recycled paper, and/or agricultural waste.

A wheat-straw fiberboard underlayment product is available from Naturall Fibreboards. When plywood is necessary, look for products made from sustainably harvested wood. [$C]

|A|I|E| | | 4. When using composite boards, look for products that do not use urea-formaldehyde binding resin. [$C]

|A|I|E| | | 5. Specify structural fiberboard with a minimum of 85 percent postconsumer waste material. Homasote paneling, made from postconsumer newspaper, has been on the market since 1909. Its uses include wall sheathing, tackable wall panels, carpet underlayment, floor decking, and roof decking.

06400—Architectural Woodwork

|A|I| | | | 1. Require use of tropical and domestic woods from independently certified sustainable forestry operations. An increasing number of forestry operations are certified by Scientific Certification Systems and by the Smartwood Program of the Rainforest Alliance, two certification programs approved by the Forest Stewardship Council (FSC). [$C]

|A|I| | | | 2. Do not use endangered wood species. Consult the Convention on International Trade in Endangered Species (CITES) current list of internationally restricted endangered timber species.

|A|I| | | | 3. Use lesser-known sustainable species to prevent overexploitation of more popular woods. An excellent tool for identifying alternative wood species with desired characteristics is the Woods of the World database by Tree Talk, Inc. [$C]

|A|I| | | | 4. Consider the following as alternatives to uncertified rainforest woods:

Flooring
- Beech
- Oak
- Hard maple
- Pecan

Veneer
- Alder
- Oak
- Birch
- Red Gum

Casework and Furniture
- Ash
- Oak
- Beech
- Pecan
- Birch
- Sycamore
- Cherry
- Walnut

|A|I| | | | 5. Substitute birch or alder plywood for lauan plywood where hardwood plywood is required. States Industries, in Eugene, Oregon, manufactures Apple-Ply, which is made from certified alder, a domestic hardwood. At this time there are no certified sources of lauan.

|A|I| | | | 6. Use formaldehyde-free products for woodwork substrates, including straw fiberboard, honeycomb cardboard, and medium-density fiberboard (MDF). These products

are available from PrimeBoard, Inc., Gridcore Systems International, and Medite Corporation, respectively. [$C]

|A|I|E| | | 7. Limit use of solvent-based adhesives with high VOC emissions. Use water-based adhesives where allowable.

|A|I| | | 8. Install plastic laminates with low-emissions adhesives to minimize indoor air impacts.

|A|I| | | 9. Plywood should not be used as a substrate for laminate surfaces; however, formaldehyde-free MDF, Gridcore, and wheat-straw board are acceptable alternatives to particleboard or traditional MDF, which contain a formaldehyde binder.

|A|I| | | 10. If millwork substrate contains a formaldehyde binder, require that all edges, ends, and holes or other penetrations in plastic-laminate-covered casework, countertops, and paneling be sealed to encapsulate core material and reduce urea-formaldehyde emissions from the binding agent.

|A|I| | | 11. Wood finishing: See 09930, "Paints and Coatings: Stains and Varnish."
Use stains and transparent finishes having less than the following VOC content:

- Stains: 200 g/l
- Transparent finishes: 250 g/l
- Floor coating: 300 g/l

06500—Structural Plastics

|A| |L|O| 1. Consider using plastic lumber with recycled content for exterior decking, fencing, parking appurtenances, and outdoor site furnishing. Currently there are dozens of manufacturers of plastic lumber and related products. [$C, $M]

Division 07—Thermal and Moisture Protection

07200—Building Insulation

|A| |E| | 1. Specify that insulation materials manufactured using chemical compounds with ozone-depleting potential (ODP), such as CFCs or HCFCs, are not permitted. HCFCs are less damaging to the environment than CFCs (which are now banned internationally), but HCFC-free materials are preferred.

|A| |E| | 2. Plastic Foam Board Insulation: These can contain VOCs and are not biodegradable, a serious problem in landfills. There are better alternatives, but if plastic foam board insulation must be used, look for products with over 10 percent recycled material by weight.
Most extruded polystyrene (XPS) phased out the use of CFCs by 1993 and replaced it with HCFC-142b, which still has some ODP and is scheduled to be restricted by 2010 and fully banned by 2020. Polyisocyanurate insulation is also blown with an HCFC blowing agent.

| P = Planner | A = Architect | I = Interior designer | E = Engineer | L = Landscape architect | O= Owner consultation |

[T] = Could affect length of construction (+ or –), [$C] = Affects construction costs (+ or –), [$E] Affects energy costs, [$F] = Affects fees (+ or –), [$M] = Affects maintenance costs (+ or –).

Consider using expanded polystyrene (EPS), which uses pentane gas as the expanding agent, instead of HCFCs. High-density EPS is reported to have acceptable water impermeability for many below-grade applications. [$C, $E]

|A| |E| | 3. Spray-Applied Foam Insulation: Use spray foams that are not blown with CFCs or HCFCs. In the United States and Canada, at least three polyurethane or modified polyurethane (Icynene) products are blown without CFCs or HCFCs. [$C]

Magnesium silicate foam (Air-Krete) is a unique alternative that is mineral-based and both CFC and HCFC free. Its advantages include fire-stopping ability and benign IAQ impacts; however, it is an expensive alternative at this point in time. [$C]

|A| |E| | 4. Cellulose Insulation: Sprayed cellulose insulation is made from 75–85 percent recycled newsprint. Embodied energy is relatively low, about 150 BTU/lb. It contains 20 percent nontoxic chemical additives to meet the fire retardancy requirements of the Consumer Product Safety Commission (CPSC). It is also biodegradable. There is no significant risk of indoor air quality problems if appropriate installation procedures are followed.

Specify that sprayed cellulose insulation must contain over 85 percent recycled material by weight. [$C, $E]

|A|I|E| | 5. Fibrous Batt and Board Insulation: Consider using fiberglass that does not contain formaldehyde. Fiberglass generally uses a phenol formaldehyde binder, which emits less free formaldehyde than urea formaldehyde. Miraflex, by Owens Corning, is specially fabricated to require no binder, yet is usable only as attic insulation at this time (batts for vertical installations are under development). [$C]

Specify that fiberglass insulation contain over 35 percent recycled material by weight; 20–25 percent is common in the United States and is recommended as a minimum by the EPA. Ottawa Fibre, a Canadian manufacturer, uses 60–80 percent recovered material. Look for mineral wool batt or board that contains at least 50 percent recovered blast furnace slag from steelmaking operations.

Avoid the use of unfaced material that is not encapsulated by other construction in areas where it will come in contact with the airstream (such as plenums and shafts). Do not use unfaced fiberglass or mineral wool batt insulation loosely laid over the top of a suspended ceiling for acoustic control. Fiberglass and mineral fibers are respirable fibers that have been identified as probable carcinogens and are likely to become airborne in return air systems.

Fiberglass and mineral fibers are also fleecy materials that can become sites for microbial growth if exposed to moisture or excess humidity.

|A| |E| | 6. Safing Insulation: Fire-safing insulation and window wall insulation such as the USG Thermafiber products are mineral composition insulations manufactured from blast furnace slag and aluminum potliner, both of which are industrial wastes. See "Fibrous Batt and Board Insulation," above.

07500—Membrane Roofing

|A| |E| | 1. Single-ply membranes: When low-VOC adhesives are used (<250 g/l), single-ply membranes may be less toxic to installers than built-up roofing. They also can be recycled, though this is not widely done today. [$C]

Full adhesion of membrane is recommended by many, and is necessary in some climates, but makes membrane removal and recycling nearly impossible. Ballasting and mechanical fastening are adhesive-free alternatives, though ballasting can only be used in low-wind areas for safety reasons. [$C, $M]

EPDM is the most common single-ply elastomeric membrane. It has a good track record for lasting in excess of twenty-five years. [$M]

PVC is the most common thermoplastic; it typically lasts ten to twenty years. Several manufacturers now offer polyolefinic materials as alternatives to PVC; however, the life span of these new materials remains to be determined. [$C, $M]

Where the building will experience a net cooling load, choose lighter-color membranes. ASTM and Oak Ridge National Laboratory are developing formulas to factor albedo (surface light reflectance) into overall energy performance calculations. [$E]

|A| |E| | 2. Roof Insulation: See 07200, "Building Insulation." Specify a layer of sheathing between membrane and roof insulation to allow for membrane replacement without damage to insulation. [$C, $M, T]

Avoid insulation products manufactured using CFCs or HCFCs, or containing formaldehyde. These include polyisocyanurates and extruded polystyrenes.

Consider using Foamglass, a cellular glass insulation board made by Pittsburgh-Corning. Though formaldehyde free, the product is currently not made with any recycled content. This product is particularly beneficial in applications where its compressive strength justifies its additional cost, such as roof decks and plazas. [$C, $E]

Consider that many of the various fiberboard insulations do not offer enough insulation value to justify their use as an environmentally preferable insulation material. [$E]

07900—Joint Sealants

|A|I|E| | 1. Schedule installation of sealants as early as possible in the sequence of finish installation. All solvent-based curing sealants emit harmful chemicals during the curing period. [T]

Solvent-based silicone sealants used for exterior applications require about 487 hours for solvent evaporation. Water-based silicone sealants should be used only for interior applications.

Acrylic latex sealants used for interior applications cure by evaporation of mineral spirits or ethylene glycol solvents and require a month for complete curing.

|A|I|E| | 2. Specify low-VOC sealants. For acrylic latex and/or silicone sealants, choose products having less than 50 g/l VOCs. For polyurethanes, choose products with less than 100 g/l. California's Bay Area Air Quality Management District prohibits the use of any architectural sealant having more than 250 g/l VOCs.

|A|I|E| | 3. The environmental consequences of manufacturing, using, and disposing of compressible foam joint filler, essentially polyester polyurethane foam impregnated with neoprene rubber or acrylic esterstyrene copolymer, are minor compared to solvent-based curing sealants, and they are free from VOC emissions. Use these in lieu of curing sealants where feasible. Choose products that are not blown with HCFCs.

| P = Planner | A = Architect | I = Interior designer | E = Engineer | L = Landscape architect | O= Owner consultation |

[T] = Could affect length of construction (+ or –), [$C] = Affects construction costs (+ or –), [$E] Affects energy costs, [$F] = Affects fees (+ or –), [$M] = Affects maintenance costs (+ or –).

| |A|I|E| | | 4. Avoid sealants formulated with aromatic solvents (organic solvent with a benzene ring in its molecular structure), halogenated solvents, fibrous talc or asbestos, formaldehyde, mercury, lead, cadmium, hexavalent chromium, or their compounds.

Division 08—Doors and Windows

08100—Steel Doors

| |A| | | | | 1. Where insulated steel doors are used, specify alternatives to insulating cores made with ozone-depleting chemicals, such as fiberglass or expanded polystyrene (EPS). See 07200, "Plastic Foam Board Insulation" section. Though these typically have a lower R-value than extruded polystyrene, lower insulating value in exterior doors can be easily balanced with slightly more insulation in walls. [$C, $E]

08200—Wood Doors

| |A|I| | | | 1. Specify wood doors made with independently certified sustainably harvested solid or veneer wood. Though most commercial wood door manufacturers do not currently use sustainably harvested wood, many will agree to use a certified wood sourced by the architect. [$C]

| |A|I| | | | 2. Look for wood doors with alternative core materials, such as honeycomb cardboard or straw board. Solid-core wood doors typically have particleboard cores, which are made with urea-formaldehyde binders. [$C]

| |A|I| | | | 3. Consider using doors made with waste wood or agricultural waste material.

| |A|I| | | | 4. Specify low-VOC stains and transparent finishes. See 09930, "Stain and Varnish."

08800—Glass and Glazing

| |A| |E| | | 1. Since many buildings are dominated by cooling loads due to the high amount of heat generated internally, study climatic and building program data to determine whether high R-value or low shading coefficient is preferred. High-performance windows generally excel at one or the other. Balance shading coefficient with value for visible light transmittance. Low-E windows have much higher visible light transmittance than reflective windows. [$C, $E]

| |A| |E| | | 2. Provide thermally efficient exterior glazing units throughout the building. Opaque walls normally provide a thermal resistivity of R-19. Compare this with the following thermal resistivities of various kinds of glazing: [$C, $E]

- Clear single-pane glazing: R-1
- Clear double glazing: R-2
- Double glazing with low-E coating: R-3
- Double glazing with two low-E coatings and argon gas between panes: R-4
- Superwindows with a 3¼" overall dimension and two air spaces: R-12

| A | E | | 3. Heat Mirror manufactures windows with R-values ranging from .9 to 9.09. Superwindows have thermal resistivity values as high as R-12. [$C, $E]

| A | E | | 4. Some utility companies offer rebates on window coefficients. Qualifying shading coefficient ranges from .30 to .75. The lower the number, the less energy that is transmitted. [$C, $E]

| A | E | | 5. Consider using Cloud Gel, a new energy-control glazing system. [$C, $E]

| A | E | | 6. Consider using integrated photovoltaic curtain wall assemblies. Kawneer has an off-the-shelf system available called Powerwall. [$C, $E]

Division 09—Finishes

09200—Lath and Plaster

| A | I | | 1. Use plasters with no VOC-emitting additives, such as epoxy or other resins.

| A | I | | 2. Use lathing board made with higher percentages of recycled gypsum from construction waste. See 09250, "Gypsum Drywall Construction."

| A | I | | 3. Inquire about recycled content in steel lath. See Division 05, "Steel."

09250—Gypsum Drywall Construction

| A | I | | 1. Where possible, plan spaces in standard-sized modules to reduce wallboard waste. Avoid designs that result in excessive board waste during installation. [T, $C]

| A | I | | 2. The natural gypsum in drywall is hydrated calcium sulfate, a widely available material. Environmental concerns, other than the strip mining to obtain gypsum, are relatively negligible, yet alternatives to using virgin gypsum exist (see below). Indoor air quality impacts are also extremely low once installed, though unpainted drywall may absorb VOCs from other off-gassing materials.

| A | I | | 3. Specify that drywall facing paper be manufactured from 100 percent recycled newsprint including postconsumer waste. This is what is typically used for drywall faces.

| A | I | | 4. Where locally available, specify 75 percent or greater synthetic gypsum content in drywall. Synthetic gypsum is recovered flue gas from the stack scrubbers of coal-fired power plants. Most major drywall manufacturers produce this material in some of their facilities, based primarily upon proximity to coal-fired power plants. These companies are strategically locating their new facilities adjacent to the power plants to provide plentiful future supplies.

| P = Planner | A = Architect | I = Interior designer | E = Engineer | L = Landscape architect | O= Owner consultation |

[T] = Could affect length of construction (+ or –), [$C] = Affects construction costs (+ or –), [$E] Affects energy costs, [$F] = Affects fees (+ or –), [$M] = Affects maintenance costs (+ or –).

`|A|I| | |` 5. Look for gypsum board manufactured with at least 20 percent recycled gypsum. Unpainted gypsum board, including construction and in-plant scrap, is completely recyclable into new drywall.

`|A|I| | |` 6. Consider paper-faced compressed straw panels as an alternative for interior wall partitions. See 09840, "Acoustical Wall Panels." As solid panels, these have inherent sound-absorbing qualities that eliminate the need for and expense of additional sound-attenuation insulation. [$C, T]

`|A|I| | |` 7. Sound attenuation: When sound attenuation insulation is used in gypsum construction, ensure that it is completely encapsulated within partitions and does not occur where particulate matter can enter return air plenums or other circulation channels.

Specify that glass-fiber sound-attenuation blanket insulation contain over 35 percent recycled glass by weight. See 07200, "Fibrous Batt and Board Insulation."

`|A|I| | |` 8. Installation. Screw-attach multilayer gypsum board applications. Do not laminate with adhesives. In wood framing, use drywall stops or clips to save wood. The Nailer is a drywall stop made from recycled plastic.

Use paper joint tape rather than fiberglass tape. [$C]

Use joint compound that is zero- or low-VOC (<20 g/l). Consider use of joint compound that is free of antifreeze, biocide, and pesticides when freshness of materials can be ensured. Consider using dry-mix joint compound to minimize packaging and transportation waste.

Specify thorough cleaning and removal of all silica/gypsum dust upon completion of gypsum drywall installations, including, but not necessarily limited to, all components in plenum spaces, including tops of pipes and sills, and insides and outsides of ducts. [$C, T]

09510—Acoustic Panel Ceilings

`|A|I| | |` 1. Where possible, use ceiling tiles with a minimum 65 percent recycled content (for mineral composition or cellulose composition ceiling tiles). Mineral fiber products contain slag wool from steel production waste. Cellulosic fiber ceiling panel products are made from recycled newsprint of mostly preconsumer origin.

`|A|I| | |` 2. Choose ceiling tile products that are free of formaldehyde. Fiberglass and some mineral composition products are made with a phenol formaldehyde binder, although emissions are reported to be low. Wood fiber ceiling panels such as Tectum have no added formaldehyde.

`|A|I| | |` 3. Specify that painted finish for mineral composition tiles be of water-based, low-VOC (<10 g/l) interior paint. Very durable ceiling panels and tiles can be reused and repainted.

`|A|I| | |` 4. Instead of vinyl-faced ceiling tiles, consider use of conventional ceiling tiles with scrubbable paints for areas subject to frequent washing.

`|A|I| | |` 5. Use USDA-approved fiber-reinforced plastic panels for food service areas. Inquire about recycled content in these products.

`|A|I| | |` 6. Consider metal pan ceiling systems, which are washable, very durable, and free of particulates. [$C, $M]

`|A|I| | |` 7. Suspension systems: Use steel suspension systems for general use in dry areas. In humid areas or where subject to frequent washing, aluminum systems may be more appropriate. See Division 05: "Metals."

Reuse suspension systems during remodeling wherever possible.

`|A|I| | |` 8. Installation: Install tiles after wet finishes have been installed and solvents have cured. Tiles can act as a sink for VOCs off-gassing from other products. [T]

Do not use unfaced fiberglass batt insulation loosely laid over the top of a suspended ceiling for acoustic control with plenum return air systems. Particulate matter and moisture can work their way into insulation and become a nest for microbial growth.

`|A|I|E| |` 9. Ensure maintenance of proper humidity levels in spaces where acoustic ceiling tiles are employed. Higher humidity levels promote sagging and can lead to microbial growth in the tile material, posing a health risk to occupants.

09640—Wood Flooring

`|A|I| | |` 1. See Division 06, "Wood and Plastics." Specify independently certified sustainably harvested wood species or use salvaged wood flooring. [$C]

`|A|I| | |` 2. Use floor coatings that have less than 300 g/l VOCs. See 09930, "Stain and Varnish."

`|A|I| | |` 3. Consider using bamboo flooring, which is available from several manufacturers, though it is typically imported. Bamboo is a rapidly growing plant (technically a grass) that matures in three years and regenerates without need for replanting, and it requires minimal fertilizers or pesticides. The flooring is very hard, durable, and dimensionally stable. [$C]

`|A|I| | |` 4. Installation: Consider installation techniques that minimize the need for adhesive, such as steel-track, floating, and nail-down systems.

Where flooring adhesive must be used, choose water-based products with less than 100 g/l VOCs.

09650—Resilient Flooring

`|A|I| | |` 1. Use tile rather than sheet flooring to minimize waste in replacing worn or damaged areas. [T, $M]

`|A|I| | |` 2. Consider linoleum made with linseed oil polymer. Linoleum is biodegradable, comes from renewable resources, and emits no dangerous gases. It may last forty years or longer and can be maintained using a dry maintenance system. [$C]

`|A|I| | |` 3. Consider other renewable, low-emission resilient flooring, such as cork and cork composition materials. [$C]

`|A|I| | |` 4. Consider using rubber flooring made with a minimum of 90 percent postconsumer rubber (from scrap tires). Rubber floor tiles are particularly useful for heavy-duty areas, as well as specialty areas such as playgrounds and sports facilities. [$C]

| P = Planner | A = Architect | I = Interior designer | E = Engineer | L = Landscape architect | O= Owner consultation |

[T] = Could affect length of construction (+ or –), [$C] = Affects construction costs (+ or –), [$E] Affects energy costs, [$F] = Affects fees (+ or –), [$M] = Affects maintenance costs (+ or –).

|A|I| | | | 5. Where solid vinyl tile must be specified, choose products made with high recycled content. Vinyl sheet products produce more chemical emissions than vinyl tile due to the addition of plasticizers in the roll product.

|A|I| | | | 6. Consider alternative synthetic products, such as nonvinyl flooring from Amtico. [$C]

|A|I| | | | 7. Installation: Use low-VOC (< 100 g/l) adhesive. Regulations in California prohibit the use of products with more than 150 g/l VOCs. Water-based products have lower VOCs than solvent-based products. Special adhesive is required for linoleum due to its linseed oil content.

09680—Carpet

|A|I| | | | 1. Use carpet tile rather than broadloom to minimize waste in replacing worn or damaged areas. Six-foot rolls offer a hybrid of these two carpet types. [$M]

|A|I| | | | 2. Consider the indoor air quality impacts of textile flooring, since it is more prone to collecting dust and may require more maintenance than other types of flooring. Keep carpet away from entrances where dirt tracked in from outside can collect, and away from water sources that might wet the carpet. Consider area rugs instead of wall-to-wall carpeting. [$M]

|A|I| | | | 3. Look for the Carpet and Rug Institute (CRI) Indoor Air Quality Testing Program "green label" as an indicator of low-emissions carpet, adhesive, and carpet cushion.

|A|I| | | | 4. Seek carpet that is fusion bonded, needle punched, and low pile with tight loop construction for durability. Carpet that is woven does not have as much latex adhesive in the backing as do tufted goods, and is thus a preferred end product. [$C]

|A|I| | | | 5. Seek out alternatives to carpet backing systems made with styrene butadiene (SB) latex, which is a primary emitter of 4-phenylcyclohexene (4-PC). Many carpets that are not labeled "latex-backed" still use a thin precoat of latex in the backing system. [$C]

|A|I| | | | 6. Consider wool fiber carpet with jute backing, both of which are renewable resources that are biodegradable. Specify low-toxicity treatments for stain resistance and soil release. Wool fiber is very durable and naturally fire resistant, which reduces the treatments required to meet performance standards and fire codes. [$C, $M]

|A|I| | | | 7. Consider sea grass, coir, jute, cotton and sisal as alternative carpet raw materials; they are from renewable, biodegradable, natural resources. [$C, $M]

|A|I| | | | 8. When specifying synthetic fiber carpet, such as nylon and polyester, look for products that are solution-dyed rather than piece-dyed, to minimize environmental impacts. Solution-dyed carpet may limit style selection, however, and some manufacturers have developed closed-loop dying systems to recover water and dyes.

|A|I| | | | 9. Look for recycled content in polyester carpet. Polyethylene terephthalate (PET) from plastic soda bottles can be recycled into polyester carpet fiber. Polyester carpet is not recommended in high traffic areas.

|A|I| | | 10. Recommend use of carpet with integral cushion backing of polyurethane, vinyl, or a composite "hardback" for increased durability and water resistance, which will reduce potential IAQ problems. [$C]

|A|I| | | 11. Where nonintegral carpet cushion is used, choose carpet cushion products with high recycled content, such as bonded urethane, rubber, or rubberized jute (from used burlap bags). Beware of potentially high emissions from urethane and rubber carpet cushion.

|A|I| | | 12. Consider carpet recyclability in selecting carpet systems. Carpet made exclusively with nylon fiber from DuPont, BASF, or Monsanto may be reclaimed by the fiber manufacturer. Wool-nylon blends are nearly impossible to recycle, unless fibers are chopped into carpet cushion or stuffing material. Milliken offers a carpet tile refurbishment program, in which worn tiles are cleaned, retextured, and reprinted. Currently, carpet backing recycling is limited to vinyl-backed products.

|A|I| | | 13. Installation: Minimize the indoor air quality impacts of adhesives. Use low-VOC (<50 g/l), water-based adhesives and seam sealers (or look for CRI's green label). For broadloom, use low-VOC premium multipurpose adhesive and seam sealer. In residential applications, tackless strips at room perimeters suffice.

Avoid double glue-down of carpet to cushion and cushion to floor by specifying carpet with integral cushion (see above).

For carpet tile, use pressure-sensitive, releasable, low-VOC water-based adhesive. Specify installation by the frame method, fully adhering a frame of tiles about the same size as the building structural grid, and free-laying infill to minimize use of adhesives. Fully adhere all tile in areas of heavy traffic.

Install carpet after wet finishes have been installed and solvents have cured out. Carpet can act as a sink for VOCs off-gassing from other products. [T]

09720—Wall Coverings

|A|I| | | 1. Consider using natural wall coverings, such as sisal or jute. Cork and cork-linoleum are other alternatives that are tackable, sound absorbing, and naturally fire resistive. [$C]

|A|I| | | 2. Consider polychromatic finish coating as an alternative to wall coverings. It is a durable, scrubbable paint that is available in water-based low-VOC formulations. [$C]

|A|I| | | 3. Installation: Use only water-based adhesive having no more than 50 g/l VOCs.

09840—Acoustical Wall Panels

|A|I| | | 1. Consider use of natural jute or synthetic fabrics instead of vinyl-faced acoustical wall panels.

| P = Planner | A = Architect | I = Interior designer | E = Engineer | L = Landscape architect | O= Owner consultation |

[T] = Could affect length of construction (+ or –), [$C] = Affects construction costs (+ or –), [$E] Affects energy costs, [$F] = Affects fees (+ or –), [$M] = Affects maintenance costs (+ or –).

[A|I| | |] 2. Avoid acoustical wall panels manufactured with formaldehyde. Fiberglass panels usually use phenol formaldehyde as the binder.

[A|I| | |] 3. Look for acoustical wall panels that have high recycled content. Acoustical wall panels often have lower recycled content than ceiling tiles.

[A|I| | |] 4. Consider using fabric- or cork-faced Homasote panels in areas with low acoustical requirements. Though not as sound absorbing as other materials, Homasote is nontoxic, tackable, and made from 100 percent recycled paper.

[A|I| | |] 5. Consider paper-faced compressed straw panels as an integral sound-absorbing interior wall system, eliminating the need for and expense of additional acoustical treatment. These make excellent use of an agricultural by-product, are fully biodegradable, and use only heat and pressure to bind the straw together. [$C, T]

[A|I| | |] 6. Installation: Do not use adhesives to install acoustical wall panels. Many manufacturers include metal frames to attach panels for easy assembly and disassembly.

Install panels after wet finishes have been installed and solvents have cured out. Panels can act as a sink for VOCs off-gassing from other products. [T]

09910—Paint

[A|I| | |] 1. For general interior and exterior applications, use water-based, zero- or low-VOC (<10 g/l for interior paints, <50 for exterior) latex paints and primers. Water-based paints generally contain low levels of solvents such as glycols and alcohols. VOC levels are significantly lower in latex paints than in other paint types. [$C]

[A|I| | |] 2. Specify that water-based paints must not be formulated with aromatic hydrocarbons (organic solvents with a benzene ring in their molecular structure), formaldehyde, halogenated solvents, or mercury or mercury compounds; nor should they be tinted with pigments of lead, cadmium, chromium VI, antimony, and their oxides.

[A|I| | |] 3. Do not use paints formulated with methylene chloride, toluene, ethyl benzene, vinyl chloride, naphthalene, 1,2-dichlorobenzene, phthalates, isophorone, 1,1,1-trichloroethane, methyl ethyl ketone, methyl isobutyl ketone, acrolein, acrylonitrile, and ethylene glycol, all of which pose varying threats to human health.

[A|I| | |] 4. Consider using natural or alternative paints in interior applications where possible, following the manufacturer's instructions for application. This includes casein paints made from milk protein. [$C, $M]

[A|I| | |] 5. Use solvent-based paints (alkyds) only when necessary, such as for high resistance to weathering. Specify VOC levels in solvent-based paint not to exceed 250 g/l. Specify that solvent-based paints not be formulated with more than 1 percent aromatic hydrocarbons by weight.

High-performance acrylic paints are a low-VOC option that generally outperforms alkyd paints in terms of durability and abrasion resistance. A small premium will be paid for the acrylic paint; however, the life cycle cost should be less.

[A|I| | |] 6. Where indoor air quality and color selection are not concerns, consider using paints and primers with 50-100 percent recovered content. [$C]

7. Consider special orders and deliveries of fresh paint to minimize the need for in-can preservatives and freeze-thaw protection.

09930—Stain and Varnish

1. Use water-based stains and transparent finishes wherever possible. Aside from lower toxicity, water-based products have the advantage of faster drying time, which can speed up application. One difference among some transparent finishes is the penetrating rather than barrier coat finish, but a barrier coat may not be necessary for many applications. [$M]

2. Consider using natural stains and varnishes, which are made without the use of petrochemical products. Many of these use natural oils derived from citrus plants. [$C]

3. Where conventional stains and transparent finishes are specified, choose products having less than the following VOC content:

- Stains: 200 g/l
- Transparent finishes: 250 g/l
- Floor coating: 300 g/l

09940—Decorative Finishes

1. Specify water-based multicolor finish that has less than 130 g/l VOCs and that is free of all or most of the hazardous chemicals listed for paints. See 09910 "Paint."

09970—Coatings for Steel

1. Specify rust-inhibiting metal primer that has less than 250 g/l VOCs and that is free of all or most of the hazardous chemicals listed for paints. See 09910, "Paint."

09980—Coatings for Concrete

1. Specify water-based penetrating concrete sealer that has less than 100 g/l VOCs and that is free of all or most of the hazardous chemicals listed for paints. See 09910, "Paint."

Division 10—Specialties

10160—Toilet Compartments

1. Consider solid plastic toilet compartments fabricated from recycled high-density polyethylene (HDPE) from plastic milk jugs. Life cycle cost per ASTM method is less than that of metal-finished products.

| P = Planner | A = Architect | I = Interior designer | E = Engineer | L = Landscape architect | O= Owner consultation |

[T] = Could affect length of construction (+ or –), [$C] = Affects construction costs (+ or –), [$E] Affects energy costs, [$F] = Affects fees (+ or –), [$M] = Affects maintenance costs (+ or –).

`|A|I| | |` 2. Where metal toilet compartments are used, specify powder-coated steel compartments with a honeycomb cardboard core having at least 30 percent recycled content. Stainless steel compartments are also available but are much more expensive than powder-coated steel and may have more complicated maintenance issues. [$C]

10520—Fire Protection Specialties

`|A| |E| | |` 1. Specify multipurpose dry chemical or CO_2 fire extinguishers in lieu of halon extinguishers. Halon is an ozone-depleting chemical that has been banned in the United States.

Division 11—Equipment

11170—Solid-Waste-Handling Equipment

`|A| |E| |O|` 1. To facilitate recycling by multistory building users, consider specifying a recycling system that uses a revolving tray of bins; these save space by requiring only a single chute. [$C, $M, T]

Division 12—Furnishings

12600—Window Treatment

`|A|I|E| |` 1. Consider shading devices for sun control and for thermal control. Shading systems may be automated or manually operated. [$C, $E]

12600—Furniture and Accessories

`|A|I| | |` 1. Consider the environmental impacts of individual material components in furniture. Most furniture companies are secondary manufacturers because they buy manufactured materials and assemble them. Only a few industries, such as all-wood furniture manufacturers and cane and rattan makers, do most of their own processing. The environmental costs related to furniture components include logging, wood products manufacture, metal smelting and refining, and textile dyeing. See specific (wood, aluminum, etc.) CSI section for more detail on furniture raw materials. [$C]

`|A|I| |O|` 2. Consider refurbishing existing systems instead of buying new. Seek furniture distributors that sell refurbished systems. Herman Miller's Action Office and Phoenix lines are examples. [$C]

`|A|I| | |` 3. Choose furniture products that are easily disassembled for recycling. Steelcase's Protege chair and Herman Miller's Avion chair represent environmental initiatives implemented throughout the product's entire life cycle.

`|A|I| | |` 4. Seek wood furniture manufacturers that use wood from a certified sustainable source. For example, Knoll's Gehry collection uses maple veneers grown by the Menominee Tribal Enterprise, certified by Scientific Certification Systems (SCS) as a sustainably managed forest. Bronx 2000 manufactures products from all reclaimed wood, another alternative. Haworth's Crossings system also uses recycled wood.

`|A|I| | |` 5. Avoid metals that are coated with spray-applied, solvent-based paints. Also avoid plated metals, which have high environmental impacts. The best choices for metal furniture parts are painted or powder-coated steel and bare aluminum.

`|A|I| | |` 6. Inquire about the origin of leather products. Selecting leathers processed in a region with substantial environmental regulation of tanneries is a minimum requirement of an environmentally aware choice. For most furniture uses, a leather with a low-maintenance finish will have the least environmental cost over its lifetime.

`|A|I| | |` 7. Look for low-toxicity fabrics, and foam made without CFCs and containing no toluene. Design-Tex fabrics are manufactured without toxic chemicals using a closed-loop water system.

`|A|I| | |` 8. Consider natural-fiber fabrics, which are fully biodegradable and in many cases quite durable. These include cotton, hemp, wool, and jute. When selecting cotton fabrics, look for organically grown cotton. Inquire about what additional stain-resistant and flame-retardant chemicals are added to the fabric. [$C]

`|A|I| | |` 9. Consider synthetic fabrics made with recycled content, such as products from Guilford Textiles.

`|A|I| | |` 10. Inquire about adhesives used in furniture products. Seek more environmentally sensitive types, such as polyvinyl acetates (PVAs), which are waterborne adhesives; hotmelts, which are 100 percent solid thermoplastics (no solvents needed); and water-based adhesives.

`|A|I| | |` 11. Consider alternative surfacing materials, such as Environ biocomposite, Syndecrete recycled lightweight concrete, or linoleum tops instead of plastic laminates or wood veneer. [$C]

Division 13—Special Construction

13600—Solar Equipment

`|A| |E| |` 1. Explore local and/or state rebate programs for solar equipment (including both solar electric and solar water heating) to reduce first costs. [$E, $C]

`|A| |E| |O|` 2. Design solar systems to maximize cost benefits. The advantages of wiring photovoltaic (PV) panels to the utility grid vary. In some cases the savings achieved by avoiding the wiring costs themselves may be substantial. In other cases, particularly where net

P = Planner	A = Architect	I = Interior designer	E = Engineer	L = Landscape architect	O= Owner consultation

[T] = Could affect length of construction (+ or −), [$C] = Affects construction costs (+ or −), [$E] Affects energy costs, [$F] = Affects fees (+ or −), [$M] = Affects maintenance costs (+ or −).

The HOK Guidebook to Sustainable Design

metering is available (the ability to allow the utility meter to run backward for energy produced from the sun), integrating with the existing grid (and, therefore, reducing or eliminating the need for batteries) may be advantageous. [$E, $C, $M]

|A| |E| |O| 3. Consider building integrated photovoltaic (PV) systems as curtain walls and roofing systems. PV panels are generally opaque; however, Pilkington makes a panel called Optisol, which applies the photovoltaic material in a pattern that looks like fritted glass—the result is a translucent panel that can double as a solar shading device. Solarex also has a semitransparent panel, which is made by laser-etching their thin film material. [$E, $C]

Crystalline photovoltaic cells are more expensive than flexible (amorphous or thin film) photovoltaics but operate at considerably higher efficiencies. However, the efficiency of the thin film material is increasing, and the total embodied energy in the thin film panel is less than the embodied energy of the crystalline panel.

Division 14—Conveying Systems

14200—Elevators

|A| |E| |O| 1. Consider using high-speed elevators with AC variable-frequency drives. These drives consume less energy and operate more cleanly than traditional DC elevator drive systems. Since their motor generators do not use carbon brushes, they do not produce carbon dust particles that can infiltrate heating, ventilating, and air-conditioning systems. [$E, $C, $M]

Division 15 —Mechanical

15060—Pipes and Pipe Fittings

|A| |E| | | 1. For nonpressure pipes and fittings for drainage, seek those that have a 40–100 percent recycled content.

15400—Plumbing

|A|I|E| | 1. Specify low-water-consumption toilets, urinals, faucets, and shower heads. The Energy Policy Act of 1992 set maximum water-flow standards for the manufacture of these fixtures in the United States. Many products are available that use even less water. (See page 114 for EPACT water flow standards.) [$E]

|A|I|E| | 2. Specify water-saving appliances. Dishwashers and washing machines are being redesigned to use much less water than earlier models. Front-loading washing machines use less water than top-loading machines. [$C, $E]

|A|I|E| | 3. Consider self-closing, slow-closing, or electronic faucets, particularly in high-use public areas where faucets may be carelessly left running. [$C, $E]

|A|I|E| | 4. Consider new dual-flush toilets that use either a low- or ultra-low-flush setting. [$C, $E]

|A|I|E| | 5. Consider composting toilets and waterless urinals as zero-water-use alternatives. [$E, $C, $M]

|A| |E| |O| 6. For projects where there is a shortage of water or where sewer capacity poses a problem, consider an on-site wastewater treatment system for the reclamation of wastewater. [$E, $C, $M, T]

15880—Air Distribution

|A|I|E| | 1. Avoid the use of exposed internal fiberglass duct liner. Internal duct linings are difficult and expensive to clean, and contamination in the ductwork is difficult to detect. [$C]

Division 16—Electrical

16500—Lighting

|A|I|E|L| 1. Specify the most efficient lighting system appropriate to the given application.

|A|I|E|L| 2. Choose lighting fixtures with high efficacies, greater than 65 percent if possible.

|A|I|E| | 3. Interior lighting: Specify fluorescent rather than incandescent lighting. Compact fluorescent lamps (CFLs) typically use 25 percent as much energy and last ten times longer than incandescent bulbs. CFLs are particularly useful in wallwashers and downlights. [$E, $C, $M]

    When using linear fluorescents, specify a combination of T–5 or T–8 fluorescent lamps and electronic ballasts for higher efficiency and greater performance. [$E, $C, $M]

|A| |E| |O| 4. Exterior lighting: Specify metal halide or high-pressure sodium lamps for general-purpose exterior lighting. Both types of lamps are generally more efficient than fluorescent lighting, although low-temperature fluorescents may be suitable for some applications. [$E, $C, $M]

    Consider solar-powered exterior lighting wherever possible. This can reduce installation costs and long-term utility costs while using a renewable energy source. [$E, $C, $M]

|A|I|E| | 5. Emergency lighting: Specify LED (light-emitting diode) exit signs. These are very energy efficient, often using 1–5 W per illuminated face, and may last from eighty to five hundred years, greatly reducing replacement costs. Energy Star–rated signs use no more than 5 W per illuminated face and have a minimum five-year warranty. [$E, $C, $M]

|A|I|E| |O| 6. Lighting controls: Utilize timers or sensors with lighting systems that operate eight hours per day or longer, such as office lighting. Sensors may respond to movement of

| P = Planner | A = Architect | I = Interior designer | E = Engineer | L = Landscape architect | O= Owner consultation |

[T] = Could affect length of construction (+ or –), [$C] = Affects construction costs (+ or –), [$E] Affects energy costs, [$F] = Affects fees (+ or –), [$M] = Affects maintenance costs (+ or –).

The HOK Guidebook to Sustainable Design

occupants or may respond to overall lighting conditions, which vary with daylight. [$E, $C]

Utilize incremental controls, allowing certain areas of a space to be individually illuminated as needed. Areas close to daylight may not need additional lighting until sundown. [$E, $C]

|A| |E| | 7. Lighting waste disposal and recycling: Choose lamps that are accepted by a recycling program. Venture Lighting, a metal halide lamp manufacturer, has a lamp recycling program for both its own lamps and those made by others.

To reduce the need for disposal of lamps as toxic waste, choose lamps, particularly fluorescent and high-pressure sodium (HPS) products, that pass the Toxic Characteristic Leachate Protocol (TCLP) test for lead and mercury. Philips and GE both manufacture low-mercury fluorescents; Philips also makes low-mercury and lead-free HPS lamps. Lead content in exterior lighting depends upon whether the lamp base uses a lead-based-solder, uses a lead-free (silver) solder, or is welded. [$M]

Case
Studies

Federal Reserve Bank of Minneapolis Headquarters and Operations Center

Minneapolis, Minnesota

Building size:	*625,000 SF (777,000 SF with garage)*
Site:	*8.2 acres*
Completion:	*1997*
Cost: Budget	*$93.5 million ($144/SF without garage, $116/SF with garage)*

The new 625,000 SF headquarters facility for the Federal Reserve Bank of Minneapolis serves all administrative and operations needs of the bank's Ninth District. The project, which was designed by HOK and completed in 1997, consists of an eight-story office tower, a four-story operations center, and 152,000 SF of structured parking.

Environmental Goals

The goals for the new facility were to meet the bank's internal needs, to achieve a quality of architecture sympathetic to the urban environment, to lower the long-term cost of operations, and to create a healthy facility of long-term value. These goals influenced every design decision that would be made.

The design team interpreted their mandate broadly and proposed that all opportunities to improve the environmental performance of the facility be considered.

Design Overview

After evaluating several options, the bank selected a site in downtown Minneapolis next to the Mississippi River, known as the Bridgehead site. The Bridgehead site is the location of the city's original river crossing point, first bridge, and initial settlement.

The 8-acre site is also at the junction of Minneapolis' two major street grids: Nicollet Mall and Hennepin Avenue. To the north is a riverfront park and the West River Parkway. To the south and west is the Historic Warehouse District, dating from the late nineteenth century.

It was extremely important to the bank that all the project goals be achieved without building a "fortress." This site represented one of the last opportunities to provide public pedestrian access from the city to the

The goals for the new facility were to meet the bank's internal needs, to achieve a quality of architecture sympathetic to the urban environment, to lower the long-term cost of operations, and to create a healthy facility of long-term value.

river. The design restores the site to its traditional public use and role as gateway to the river.

The facility includes two separate structures: an eight-story office tower and a four-story operations center. Passages located both above and below the outdoor courtyard link the two buildings.

The eight-story office tower houses the administrative and economic research activities for the Fed's Ninth District. Except for the extremely rigid security requirements, the office tower functions much like any modern office facility.

The four-story operations center houses the bank's check, currency, bond, computer, and financial oversight functions. This part of the bank is nearly industrial in its need for simple material flow and efficient processing.

Economics

The project was built within a standard budget, with no additional funds provided for environmental design. Most of the environmental design features added no cost to the project, and many of them led to reduced first cost. The final construction cost for the building and all site work was $90.4 million, $3 million below the original project budget.

After making the decision to abandon their thirty-year-old facility because of inadequate space as well as structural and environmental problems, the bank resolved that their new headquarters and operations center would have long-term value by being a "100-year asset" for the Federal Reserve Bank System.

Within the available budget, the bank was interested in exploring investments that would enhance the longevity of systems and reduce long-term operating costs. Life cycle cost analysis was used to select equipment and systems; those that produced a ten-year simple payback or less were considered acceptable.

Design Process

Because of the public nature of the project and its prominent site, the design process required extensive public review that reduced the time available for design and documentation. Strong support from the bank and the design team for the environmental design goals, and a design delivery process that included a construction manager (CM) throughout the process, enabled the team to keep nonstandard design solutions intact even given an accelerated schedule.

PUBLIC INVOLVEMENT
A high level of public involvement throughout the design process created the need for a truly collaborative effort among the project's design and construction team.

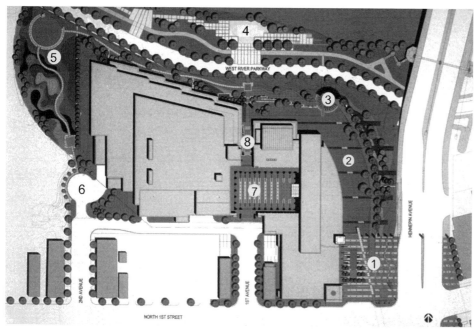

This site represented one of the last opportunities to provide public pedestrian access from the city to the river. The design restores the site to its traditional public use and role as gateway to the river.
Key:
1. Bridgehead Square
2. Bridgehead Park
3. Mississippi Overlook
4. Seven Flag Park
5. West Park
6. Operations Entry
7. Auto Court Main Entrance
8. 1st Avenue River Access

The 8-acre site is also at the junction of Minneapolis' two major street grids: Nicollet Mall and Hennepin Avenue. To the north is a riverfront park and the West River Parkway. To the south and west is the Historic Warehouse District, dating from the late nineteenth century.

As a public, institutional building on a historic, high-profile riverfront site, the bank wanted to maintain an open planning process. A public design advisory group and approximately thirty public and private entities, ranging from neighborhood groups to the State Office for Historic Preservation, all had input into the design.

In addition to these groups, the bank had its own review committee of three outside architects and required several layers of approval both within the Federal Reserve Bank in Minneapolis and in Washington, D.C.

The site's public nature, coupled with the demolition of some existing buildings, created controversy around the project. By the time construction began, the design had survived more than a hundred public meetings, multiple layers of approvals, and several lawsuits.

NO ONGOING ENVIRONMENTAL REVIEW
Outside the core design team, the design process did not include an ongoing review of environmental design issues.

After discussing environmental design goals with senior bank officers early in the programming and design phases, the team was instructed to do whatever it deemed appropriate to enhance environmental performance, so that the bank could focus on the ongoing public debate about the project. The only exceptions requiring bank approval would be actions that would potentially threaten the budget or expose the bank to unusual risk. In the end, all of the design team's recommended systems and materials were included in the final design.

INCLUSIVE TEAM
From the beginning of the project, the design team included the architects, the engineers, the subconsultants, and the construction manager. Three bank staff members devoted all their time to the project, while a senior vice president spent nearly half his time on it. Throughout the project, this core design team met every Wednesday with senior bank executives for half-day meetings. The close communication within this group helped the team balance the project's various goals, including the environmental issues.

Including the construction manager on this team meant that materials could be evaluated and priced early in the process. Because many mate-

The HOK Guidebook to Sustainable Design

rials were relatively new to the market, questions about supply, installation details, or other issues could be raised and answered openly. The construction manager also was instrumental in influencing suppliers to reengineer products to accommodate the bank's needs and to provide improved environmental performance within the project's pricing and scheduling constraints.

Site

The materials for all site paving, structures, and interpretive displays were selected based on an analysis of whether the original source was sustainable, the material's embodied energy, and whether the materials would be recyclable. The result is a durable, low-maintenance palette that comes from local sources.

Energy

The Federal Reserve Bank operates three shifts in an extremely cold climate. Because of the nature of the bank's operations, many of its systems are more energy intensive than those found in a standard office building.

Early energy models revealed that the facility's primary energy loads were related to the internal loads for lights, equipment, and people. The energy required for heating ventilation air in the winter was another significant load. Infiltration and radiant losses at the exterior were a third significant factor in energy consumption and comfort. The design strategy to minimize those loads included a low interior lighting load, energy-efficient equipment, and a tight exterior envelope.

The design strategy to minimize energy loads included efficient interior lighting, energy-efficient equipment, and a tight exterior envelope. The resulting design—which uses less than 45,000 BTU per SF—cut energy consumption while also reducing overall capital costs.

Federal Reserve Bank of Minneapolis, Headquarters and Operations Center

High-Performance Insulating Glass

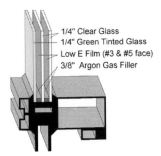

- 1/4" Clear Glass
- 1/4" Green Tinted Glass
- Low E Film (#3 & #5 face)
- 3/8" Argon Gas Filler

The construction manager worked with the design team and glass suppliers to reengineer a conventional glass product that met the design team's goals for energy performance. The final product, which became the building standard, had a U-value of 0.13. It was a triple-glazed unit with two low-E films and with argon gas in both cavities.

The result was a design that cut energy consumption while also reducing overall capital costs. Estimated net annual energy consumption was less than 45,000 BTUs per SF per year. After two years of operations, these estimates have proven accurate.

EXTERIOR ENVELOPE

Based on energy modeling, the team set a target value of 0.035 for the overall U-value of the exterior wall (including glazed areas), in the hopes of limiting heat gain and loss and eliminating the need for perimeter radiation.

The window selection initially presented a problem. While the best commercially available windows in the United States at the time had a U-value of 0.28, the team found a Canadian product that achieved a U-value of 0.13. The team decided, however, that the Canadian product was too risky for the project because it was a relatively new product that required very different framing details.

The construction manager worked with the design team and glass suppliers to reengineer a more conventional glass product that met the design team's goals for energy performance. The final product, which became the building standard, had a U-value of 0.13. It was a triple-glazed unit with two low-E films and with argon gas in both cavities.

While the glass cost more than standard double-pane insulated glass units, the additional cost was offset by the lack of need for most of the perimeter radiation units. The only perimeter radiation in the building is under very high expanses of glass in public areas. The use of the triple-paned glass represented a net reduction in the building's overall capital cost and reduced its long-term energy use.

LIGHT FIXTURES

All lighting fixtures are high-efficiency units, with most controlled by occupancy sensors. Many common-area lights are on time-of-day controls, because daylight is sufficient to provide ambient lighting during daylight hours.

All lighting is controlled and monitored by the central control system. This led to a design of 0.85 W/SF connected and 0.65 W/SF projected actual lighting load, whereas ASHRAE 90.1 permits up to 2.5 W/SF. The reduced lighting load not only helped cut overall energy consumption in lighting and cooling, but also reduced the building's initial capital costs.

COOLING

The cooling was supplied by Minneapolis Energy Center (MEC), which provides year-round district chilled water in the city. To allow the bank to join the system, the central system was extended and a new chilling plant built adjacent to the bank, restoring an existing nineteenth-century commercial structure. Extending and connecting to the central system minimized the environmental impact on the region through the use of this more efficient system.

Chilled water is distributed throughout the facility to air handling units serving office spaces, lobbies, dining areas, kitchen, computer rooms, fitness areas, training space, a pistol range, currency and coin vaults, and various other spaces. Extending the chilled water and steam loop will allow smaller users in this part of the city to access these services, saving additional resources in the process.

When the outside temperature is less than 55 degrees F, cooling is provided by outside air economizers, for a "free cooling" system. This reduces district chilled water use and costs. To accurately control minimum outside air intake quantities, low-leak minimum outside air dampers are provided at air handling units.

HEATING

The Minneapolis Energy Center also provides heat for the facility from district high-pressure steam. Steam is reduced and converted to hot water at the building entry, and then distributed to air handling units and other heating systems. Steam condensate return is routed through a water-to-water heat exchanger, extracting and transferring heat before returning the heating water to MEC. This is an unusual approach to heat recovery; however, the heat that is extracted would otherwise be lost to line loss on the return to the central plant. Instead, the recovered heat is used to preheat incoming ventilation air.

VARIABLE-FREQUENCY DRIVES

Variable-frequency drives (VFDs) are installed on most air handling units and pumping systems, and all systems have high-efficiency motors. The use of fan-powered variable air volume (VAV) boxes reduced static pressure in the system and reduced horsepower requirements for the main air handling units.

TEMPERATURE CONTROL AND ENERGY MANAGEMENT

Temperature control and building energy management are performed through a computer-based, electronic control system. The system is capable of operating the equipment to provide the maximum energy efficiency. It also allows the building operators to monitor and trend the entire system, and to make necessary system changes from a central location. The system has distributed logic that allows the equipment to continue to operate even if the main computer is damaged or disconnected, thus providing increased system reliability.

The parking garage has a carbon monoxide monitoring system to provide ventilation of this area as required. This significantly reduces the overall energy consumption for this part of the building.

WATER HEATING

The water heaters for the kitchen and fitness center are high-efficiency gas-fired units. Areas with smaller hot water demands, such as the rest rooms and galleys on the typical office floors, incorporate small, self-contained electric water heaters.

Federal Office Building at Foley Square

New York City, New York

Building Size:	1,000,000 SF, 30 stories
Site:	70,000 SF
Completion:	December 1994
Cost:	$276/ SF

Highlights of the Design

■ Integration of the architectural and engineering design helped to optimize systems. Energy-efficient measures had immediate payback and resulted in a record $3 million rebate from Consolidated Edison Company, the local utility.

■ The building's main energy source is utility steam, a cogeneration by-product. In addition to providing heating and humidification, this utility steam drives three 1,300-ton high-efficiency steam turbine chillers for air-conditioning.

■ All office fixtures, which are double-lamp T-8 parabolic fixtures with electronic ballasts, are controlled by motion sensors.

Water

All plumbing fixtures are low flow, and water closet flush valves have automatic on–off controls. All shower heads have water restrictors to reduce water use, and triplex domestic water pumps provide the most flexibility for low-flow and full-load conditions.

Indoor Environment

Mechanical systems were designed to ensure that the outside air supply maintains healthy indoor air quality for building occupants. Ventilation air in occupied areas varies from the minimum quantity required based on occupancy, and increases to as much as 100 percent of the total cooling air quantity, as outside conditions permit.

Building materials were selected that have reduced chemical emissions, such as formaldehyde–free wood products and low-VOC paint, adhesives, and finishes. Opportunities to reduce impacts on indoor air quality related to cleaning procedures were also considered. Linoleum flooring, for example, can be damp-mopped with neutral cleansers, as opposed to vinyl flooring, which requires the regular application of finish coatings.

- Foley Square's ventilation and air-conditioning systems are based on the concept of low-temperature air distribution.
- Supply diffusers are small, closely spaced, and limited to 100 CFM each; this provides a consistently fresh, conditioned air supply that prevents hot spots and stale air within the predominantly open-plan offices.
- A specification for all finishes, materials, and adhesives prohibited irritants such as urea formaldehyde. Only materials with low-VOC (volatile organic compound) content were permitted. When possible, adhesives were eliminated; carpet tiles, for example, are loosely laid over raised flooring to eliminate the need for adhesives.
- The Rochester Midland Corporation developed a Green Housekeeping Program that recommended healthy cleaning products and provided training for maintenance personnel. The focus on cleaning practices produced environmental benefits and reduced operating costs while ensuring the health of building occupants. The program has decreased the use of chemical cleaning products by about 50 percent compared to a typical office building, significantly cut packaging waste disposal, and greatly reduced VOC emissions. It won the prestigious White House Closing the Circle Award.
- The design team's energy-saving measures combined to help the building earn a 1999 DOE/EPA Energy Star award—the first such honor bestowed on a federal building.

Material Resources

The team selected building materials based on the sustainability of the original source, the product's recycled content, the recyclability of the product at the end of its useful life, and the product's effect on indoor air quality. The result was a palette of materials that enhances durability, requires less maintenance, and comes primarily from local sources.

EXTERIOR MATERIALS
The exterior building materials reflect the bank's location and the local context. The facility combines local brick, the primary material in the North Warehouse District, and Kasota stone, which is indigenous to Minnesota, with crisp, contemporary detailing in precast concrete. All stone was quarried less than 100 miles from the site, and the brick is from the closest available source.

INTERIOR MATERIALS
Interior materials include low-VOC paints and adhesives, formaldehyde-free wood products, and many high-recycled-content products. All wood used in the building comes from certified sustainable sources.

The facility combines local brick, the primary material in the North Warehouse District, and Kasota stone, which is indigenous to Minnesota, with crisp, contemporary detailing in precast concrete. Interior materials include low-VOC paints and adhesives, formaldehyde-free certified wood products, and many high-recycled-content products.

Linoleum is the material for all raised flooring. Linoleum is made from renewable resources and has performance advantages of improved durability, low-toxicity maintenance, and antistatic properties. Yet because the raised floor suppliers had not previously used linoleum, this initially was a challenge.

The team needed to resolve issues related to supply contracts and installation procedures, and to verify all performance characteristics. In the final cost analysis, the increased cost of the linoleum material was offset by the fact that antistatic clips, which are typically required for vinyl flooring products, were not required.

CONSTRUCTION WASTE RECYCLING

The construction waste recycling program was extremely effective. The construction waste was subcontracted to a local recycling company that used the local recycling industry. Parts of this industry are extremely organized, while some are quite informal. While some site separation of materials took place, the majority of refuse was separated off-site and recycled to produce a recycling rate of about 70 percent and a decrease in overall project construction costs.

Some aspects of the recycling program were informal and improvised. At one point, for example, when the demand from institutional users for recycled wood began to decline, the team created a salvage yard for materials that could be reused and not just recycled; this proved quite popular. Materials that could only be used a certain number of times for a given use, such as sheet plywood for concrete formwork, but which were still useful for other purposes were made available to anyone who wanted them.

Benefits of the Design

The building was one of the first major public buildings to exhibit a concern for environmentally responsible development. Every system and material that the design team selected was successfully incorporated within the original budget and schedule.

In addition to the fact that the building has been extremely well received by the public and its users, the first two years of operations have confirmed a dramatically lower cost of operations for the bank.

Edificio Malecon

Buenos Aires, Argentina

Building Size:	*125,000 GSF*
Site:	*1.5 acres*
Completion:	*September 1999*
Cost:	*U.S. $75/SF gross building and site development*
	U.S. $~100/SF gross building area tower

The development consortium of Newside SA commissioned Edificio Malecon as the first building in a 4 million SF planned commercial development in Puerto Madero, a redevelopment area in the city of Buenos Aires, Argentina. HOK provided site planning, architecture, interior design, and landscape design services for the project.

Environmental Goals

The design team was charged with creating "the most technologically advanced" office building in the city within the context of a traditional speculative building pro forma.

Implicit in this mandate was the need to design a building that functioned at the cutting edge of key technologies within this market. The team would search for highly innovative solutions in terms of the floorplate configuration, building envelope technologies, integration of data and telecommunications, efficient HVAC systems, and improved control technologies.

Design Overview

Edificio Malecon is sited at one of the most prominent and identifiable locations in Puerto Madero. The building site is located at the terminus of a 2,600 m axis created by four former docks called the Diques, which were the original industrial port for the city during the era of the tall ships. The site marks the southernmost point of this precinct in the city and offers the building unparalleled views of the existing city center, the active port, and the Rio de la Plata, the river that empties into the Atlantic at Buenos Aires, creating its port.

The design response was developed as a long, narrow slab to minimize solar gain on the structure. To ensure views to all, the slab ends are pinched at the east and west extremities of the building. The broad northern face, the primary solar exposure in the Southern Hemisphere, is

Edificio Malecon is located within the redevelopment area of Puerto Madero, in the city of Buenos Aires, an area at the southernmost point of the precinct that used to be the original industrial port for the city, during the era of tall ships. The location offers the building unparalleled views of the existing city center, the active port, and the Rio de la Plata.

shaped to track the sun and is fully screened with deep sunshades that virtually eliminate direct solar radiation during peak cooling months. The south face, which reflects the geometry of the northern facade, is equipped with the same high-performance curtain wall system as the other facades, minimizing solar gain from early morning and late evening sun during peak cooling months.

Edificio Malecon's energy-efficient shape also reinforces its prominence on the site and in the city. First, the building presents a broad, powerful face to the axis created by the Diques, ending the axis and closing the southern end of this new urban space. Second, as seen from the east and the west, the tower creates a tall, elegant silhouette on the skyline that marks the southern extremity of Puerto Madero.

The building is constructed on the original basement and foundations of the existing warehouse; a cast-in-place concrete frame is clad with an aluminum and glass curtain wall. Portions of the podium are clad in stone. Interiors are finished with aluminum and indigenous wood ceil-

Edificio Malecon

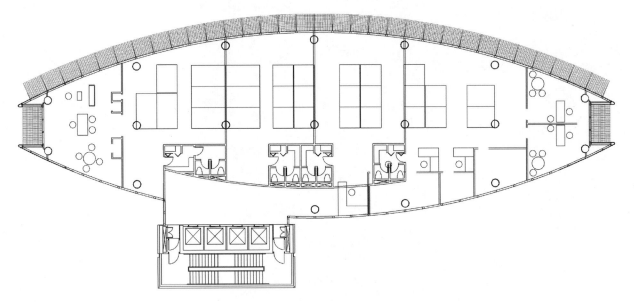

The slab ends are pinched at the east and west extremities of the building, to provide views to all. The broad northern face, the primary solar exposure in the Southern Hemisphere, is fully screened with deep sunshades that virtually eliminate direct solar radiation during peak cooling months.

ings. Raised floors are used throughout. Wall finishes include glass, stone, and plastered gypsum wall panels.

Economics

One of the owner's key goals included minimizing annual energy costs. The opportunity to consider long-term energy utilization as an important design consideration is unique in the speculative building market primarily because financial goals are very short-term for this building type in most parts of the world. In this case, however, because the building was going to be sold by floor, life cycle cost and energy efficiency could be promoted as an important factor in the long-term value of the sale.

Edificio Malecon was built for less than half the cost of competitive international-quality projects under way in the city at the time of its design and construction. This was due in great part to the design team's attitude toward building. Based on the experience of other developers in the city, the design team chose to build, to the extent possible, with indigenous materials and with the best of local technologies. In order to enhance energy efficiency, high-performance, low-E glass was imported from the United States; however, most major building components were produced or manufactured in the city of Buenos Aires or elsewhere in Argentina.

This building was designed for the sophisticated high end of the local and international market for office and commercial space in Buenos Aires. Because the owner understood the marketing value of this approach to the building design, he was willing to take the time and the risk to produce a building that combined a unique approach to both the first cost of the building and its long-term operating cost.

Design Process

In seeking to achieve the goals of the client for a "cutting-edge" building for the city of Buenos Aires, HOK and the owner sought out high-quality local architectural engineering firms as collaborators. In addition, a respected general contractor and a curtain wall consulting group were added to the design team. Before developing initial concepts for the building, the team researched available building technologies to determine the availability of preferred construction systems.

Work sessions including all team members were held in Buenos Aires to review building materials from local suppliers, subcontractors, and city officials. Based on these meetings, a strategy for design and construction was established prior to development of initial concepts. These strategies included the approaches to framing, cladding, conditioning, and technology integration for the building. These work sessions continued through the design of the building in order to challenge and reinforce key concepts and augment thinking on these concepts as the design evolved. The concepts included:

- Establish a strategy to defend against the hot sun of the peak cooling season while taking advantage of the moderate climate for the remainder of the year.
- Maximize views and energy efficiency through the use of high-performance curtain wall systems.
- Harness the breeze coming from the river by providing operable windows in each potential office space.
- Naturally ventilate stairwells.
- Maximize individual control of the mechanical system.
- Utilize local materials within the experience of local trades.
- Include low-maintenance, indigenous plant materials.
- Maximize building flexibility and long-term effectiveness.

These concepts evolved and were realized in the building because the team established a common set of objectives early in the process and worked together to achieve them.

Site

The building is located on a site called the Diques, which was the original industrial port for the city during the era of the tall ships. The building provides a powerful presence at the end of a 2,600 m axis created by the former docks, and marks the southernmost point of this precinct in the city. By building on the site of a demolished warehouse facility, the project revitalizes an important yet underutilized part of the city.

A grass roof has been installed on the roof of the retail podium to provide an attractive landscape element that reduces the stormwater runoff from the site. The grass roof is a low-maintenance design feature that contributes to energy efficiency and extends the life of the roof.

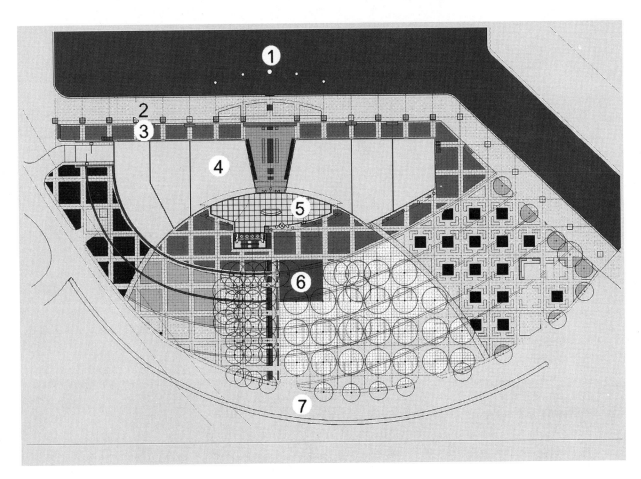

The landscape was designed with low-maintenance, indigenous plant materials. A vegetated roof on the building podium (retail area) is part of the site's stormwater retention system, reducing runoff.
Key: 1. Dique 1; 2. Malecon;
3. Terrace; 4. Retail; 5. Lobby;
6. Entry Court; 7. Calle Brasil

Energy

This goal of providing an energy-efficient design solution, together with the desire of the owner for maximum glass on the building, led to a strategy for energy conservation that was integral to the overall concept for the building. The building's shape and size are a direct response to the action of solar loads on the building and provide the opportunity to maximize natural ventilation in the building. Selection of the cladding and mechanical systems support both the reduction of energy gain on the building and the passive cooling and heating of its interior volumes.

BUILDING PLAN GEOMETRY

The plan geometry of the tower serves to reduce energy consumption in three ways. First, the curved shape of the facade and pinched ends allow sunscreens to effectively shade the glass at these exposures during the peak summer months. The geometry also allows the sun to heat the building during the limited heating season, as the sun angle descends below the sunscreens on the north facade. Second, the shallow dimension of the tower slab, 17.5 m at its greatest dimension, allows the prevailing winds to flow through the building, naturally conditioning the interior spaces. Last, this narrow slab dimension coupled with full-height glass

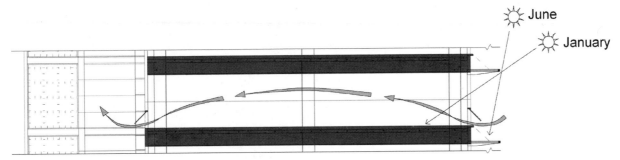

reduces the need for general office illumination for much of the day, significantly reducing energy consumption on the office floors.

BUILDING ENVELOPE

The envelope of the office tower consists of a high-efficiency curtain wall system with integral sunscreens shading the north, east, and west facades. The elevator and stair core, located on the south outside the office slab, is clad in composite aluminum panels and glass block.

Super-low-emissivity glass is utilized throughout the building within the curtain wall system in order to control solar gain during periods of direct solar radiation. Glass block supported by a steel framing system encloses the naturally ventilated stair tower. The glass block tower includes aluminum louvers at each floor, allowing natural convection in the tower as the skin and building mass warm and cool through the day.

The building podium is clad in stone and includes high-performance glass window wall infill. North-facing storefronts are screened with a system of sunscreens similar to those on the tower. Solid walls are backed up with concrete and insulated with rigid insulation. In order to protect the large podium roof area from the sun, its roof is covered with soil and planted with grass. The insulating values of the soil and turf combine to reduce heat gain on the entire building podium.

LIGHTING

Daylighting greatly reduces dependence on lighting systems in the office tower during daylight hours. Only high-efficiency, compact fluorescent fixtures are used for general illumination in the tower. This system is supported by limited amounts of incandescent accent lighting and sufficient power to support task lighting.

MECHANICAL SYSTEM

The design of the mechanical system was intended to satisfy three objectives in order to provide an energy-efficient, comfortable environment for users of the building. First, in order to respond to varied solar loads on the building, the system was intended to be directly responsive to specific loads as they were applied to the building throughout the day and year. Second, the system was intended to provide maximum control by users in the building in order to allow the application of heating and cooling only as needed by specific users within the building. Lastly, the system was

The shallow dimension of the tower allows the prevailing winds to flow through the building, naturally conditioning the interior spaces. The narrow slab dimension coupled with full-height glass provides daylight access, which significantly reduces energy consumption.

Located in the Southern Hemisphere, the office tower is composed of a high-efficiency curtain wall system with integral sunscreens shading the north, east, and west facades.

intended to work effectively with the operable window system in the building to ensure user comfort while conserving energy.

These objectives for this system all required a design that was highly responsive to user demand and directly controlled by the user. The resultant solution met both of these requirements. The system is based upon providing seven zones for each 7,000 SF floor, or one zone per 1,000 SF of usable area. Each zone is supported by a high-efficiency electric heat pump that provides HFC 407 refrigerant to seven evaporator units supplying tempered air to each zone. Each unit is thermostatically controlled and can be programmed or overridden by users, providing optimum user control of the system.

This system, combined with a plan configuration and building envelope designed for optimum passive solar control, ensures an energy-efficient, highly user-friendly office environment in all parts of the building.

Water

Water use for this building is extremely low—no irrigation is required on the site, and water use is not required for the HVAC equipment. All of the plumbing fixtures are water-efficient low-flow products.

Indoor Air Quality

The use of small building floorplates together with integrated design strategies to promote use of daylighting and natural ventilation have created a striking interior office environment that enhances comfort while providing a connection to nature.

The building mechanical system enhances comfort while providing optimum user control of the system. Individual thermostatic control of small 1,000 SF zones can be programmed, and overridden if necessary, by the building occupants.

Materials

Materials have been selected to enhance the building's durability and long-term flexibility, providing value for the building owner and conserving resources over the long term.

DESIGN FLEXIBILITY

The design maximizes building flexibility and long-term effectiveness through the use of highly accessible floors and ceilings. Raised floors are used throughout to enable the building to readily adapt to changes in wire- and fiber-based technologies. An accessible metal ceiling system was selected as a durable solution that provides access for future modifications.

LOCAL MATERIALS

The team explored all opportunities to build within the local economy, utilizing local materials within the experience of local trades. This allowed the building to be extremely economical while minimizing total embodied energy for its fabrication and construction.

The building's concrete frame was constructed of locally mined and manufactured materials, which were mixed close to or on the site. Locally extruded and assembled aluminum was used for the curtain wall and many of the building details. Interior wall, flooring, and paving systems also utilize local materials such as wood, glass, stone, and plastered gypsum wall panels.

Use of local materials, including concrete and aluminum for the outer wall and wood, glass, stone, and plastered gypsum for interior flooring and wall systems, allowed the building to be extremely economical while minimizing total embodied energy for its fabrication and construction.

Benefits of the Design

The Edificio Malecon has achieved a high level of architectural and urban design quality while also addressing the owner's concerns for energy conservation, profit, and long-term operating effectiveness.

The building has been recognized as a "new urban monument" at Puerto Madero; it is highly successful financially and has set a new standard for energy-efficient glass office towers in this part of the world.

National Wildlife Federation New Headquarters Office Building

Reston, Virginia

Building Size:	*95,000 SF*
Site:	*7 acres*
Completion:	*2000*
Cost:	*$9 million for building, interiors, and site ($95/SF)*

The new headquarters for the National Wildlife Federation will be a 95,000 SF office building located in Reston, Virginia, adjacent to the 475-acre Lake Fairfax Park. HOK is providing programming, site planning, architecture, interior design, and landscape design services for the project, which is scheduled for completion in late 2000.

Environmental Goals

While NWF initiated its move to a new facility in order to reduce operating costs, the new headquarters building was also seen as an opportunity to expand its educational outreach mission—in terms of both the work housed in the headquarters and the design. NWF embraced the tension between its ideals and its program funding objectives and described its vision for the building as one that would follow a "common sense and common ground" approach to conservation.

The goal for the new facility was to create an inspiring, healthy workplace with modern communication tools and daily contact with wildlife and their habitats in order to foster continuous learning and advance educational outreach. Additional goals identified by NWF included the desire to enhance quality of life and productivity; to encourage community, teamwork, and collegiality; and to reflect the history and culture of NWF.

The National Wildlife Federation made a commitment that its new headquarters building will demonstrate sensible stewardship of its financial resources through use of rigorous payback analysis to select "state-of-the-shelf" construction technologies and materials. The design team was charged to search for an optimal balance between the following competing objectives:

- Building a unique, specific facility that is identifiable with NWF while maintaining the widest appeal in a future market for sale or lease.

- Minimizing habitat loss and securing a place for wildlife on the site while occupying a large portion of the site for buildings, parking, and roads.
- Creating a model of environmental sensitivity and providing an example for others to follow while exhibiting fiscal responsibility.
- Creating a climate of collaboration while providing for individual privacy and solitude.
- Providing amenities to enhance day-to-day life needs while reducing occupancy costs.
- Respecting tradition while fostering experimentation.

Design Overview

The steeply sloped site for NWF's new headquarters building backs up against a large wooded county park, providing an ideal environment for the study of wildlife in an otherwise conventional suburban office park.

The landscape design accommodates the building and a 285-car surface parking lot while creating a rich variety of native habitat areas. Features include large medians between the bays of parking that provide for bioretention of stormwater and create habitat, a dry pond that fluctuates with the seasons, a water habitat pond at the building entrance, wildflower meadows, undisturbed forest, and reforested areas.

The site plan orients the building so that the long elevations face north and south, capturing many views into the park and providing good solar access. The three-story office building responds to the site topography by stepping down the hill and by introducing a subtle shift in the office floorplates. A vertical fin, which contains a large conference room on each floor, marks the shift in the building form.

The building elevations respond clearly and decisively to the building orientations. Windows on the south-facing entry side of the building are

The goal for the new facility was to follow a "common sense and common ground" approach to conservation—to create an inspiring, healthy workplace with modern communication tools and daily contact with wildlife and their habitats in order to foster continuous learning and advance educational outreach. The south-facing, entry side of the building is protected by a trellis structure that supports deciduous vines, to shade the facade in summer and allow sun to penetrate in winter.

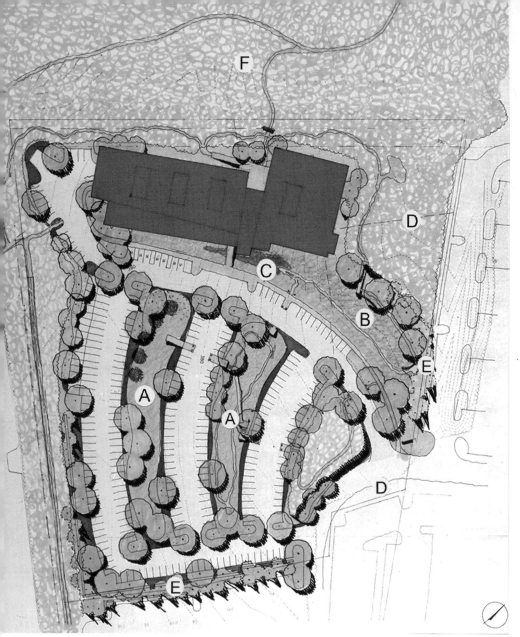

The steeply sloped site for NWF's new headquarters building backs up against a large wooded county park, providing an ideal environment for the study of wildlife in an otherwise conventional suburban office park. Large medians between the bays of parking for bioretention of stormwater, a dry pond that fluctuates with the seasons, a year-round pond at the building entrance, wildflower meadows, and forested areas create a rich variety of native habitat areas on the site.
Key: A. Bioretention area (meadow/forest habitat);
B. Dry pond (meadow habitat);
C. Year-round pond (aquatic habitat);
D. Tree-save area (forest habitat);
E. Evergreen buffer; Lake Fairfax Park

protected by a trellis structure that supports deciduous vines, shading the facade in the summer and allowing sun to penetrate in winter. The northern side of the building, which faces Lake Fairfax Park, has larger windows, nearly floor to ceiling, creating breathtaking views into the park that do not require sun shading. The east and west facades of the building are essentially opaque, to control the seasonal impacts of the sun.

The building will house office space as well as an education and training center dedicated to education outreach. The J. D. Hair Center, which will be located on the ground level, will receive visitors of all ages interested in learning about wildlife and conservation. The office interiors will be predominantly open-plan, to allow for a high degree of flexibility and increased communications between working groups. A communicating stair, open conference areas, a community lunchroom and fitness center, picnic areas, and trails through the site have all been developed to create a positive workplace environment that will enhance collaboration.

The northern side of the building facing Lake Fairfax Park has larger windows, nearly floor to ceiling, creating breathtaking views into the park that do not require sun shading.

Economics

The building will be a class B+ office building; the budget for the base building was originally set at $55'SF with $20/SF for interiors. To fund potential value-added upgrades, NWF set aside a contingency budget representing approximately 5 percent of the overall budget.

The conservative budget presented a challenge to the design team. Their task was to systematically challenge the typical low-cost development formula, providing a better building with lower environmental impacts. By staying within the budget, the team is creating a building that can act as a credible model for others.

EXIT STRATEGY

To protect its investment in the building, NWF feels strongly that the building must be able to be understood and valued by the local real estate market, in case the organization needs to vacate in the future. The concern for "exit strategy" influenced all design decisions and imposed an additional tension on the design process.

Design Process

NWF began its design process with an in-depth goal-setting session with the architectural firm William McDonough + Partners. Once its goals statement was complete, those goals guided site selection and the selection of the architect and provided guidance throughout the design process.

SITE INVENTORY

Prior to the outset of design, NWF staff from several departments formed a Site Inventory Team to prepare an inventory of the natural features and wildlife on the wooded site and adjacent land. During design, the design team kept in regular contact with the Site Inventory Team.

As the site design progressed and plant selections were made, the design team could draw on the results of the site survey to select supplementary plantings that already exist on the site and those that would be complementary. As work progressed on the "backyard habitats," the team knew what wildlife was already resident on-site and so could design to accommodate it.

ENERGY MODELING

Architectural Energy Corporation provided energy modeling using DOE-2, a software program that allows for accurate simulation of architectural design strategies.

Energy modeling was first performed early in schematic design so the team could understand the impact of issues related to building orientation and massing. This early study allowed the team to construct a "base case" code-minimum energy model specific to the site and occupancy, and compare it to a series of "improved" design options.

Parametric analysis was used to establish the range of improvement possible for each design strategy, to help the design team focus their effort.

The team used energy modeling once again during design development to evaluate the cost and benefit associated with the various options. Detailed evaluations of the building design using alternative architectural and HVAC system solutions helped determine the most cost-effective solutions and quantified the relative environmental benefit of each.

ANALYSIS OF PLUG LOADS

New office buildings are typically designed based on assumptions about plug loads that are greatly inflated, which can lead to expensive and unnecessary oversizing of equipment.

To guard against that, NWF metered its existing energy use and determined that its hypothetical peak load—with all computers and printers in use simultaneously—was just 1 W/SF. The lighting load based on the design required less than 1 W/SF.

When that information was balanced against concerns about re-marketability, the team decided to compromise on a design load of 2 W/SF for plug loads and lighting, for a total of 4 W/SF.

CONSTRUCTION PARTNER

NWF engaged its general contractor, the James G. Davis Construction Corp., for preconstruction planning so that cost could be evaluated throughout the process. The construction partner joined the team at the outset of design development and participated in all key meetings.

Cost modeling allowed the team to evaluate the cost associated with different materials, systems, and equipment as decisions were being made. To integrate life cycle costs in the cost analysis, the economic benefit of energy savings from the various design options was built into the cost modeling process.

Site

NWF's site for their new headquarters building is a previously undeveloped land parcel in a conventional suburban office park. One of the reasons the team selected this site was its location next to a 130-acre conservation area within a 475-acre woodland county park.

LAND PURCHASE
NWF's land purchase decision represented a departure from typical development formulas. While NWF's budget constraints meant that structured parking was not an option, purchasing additional land beyond the minimum required for its office facilities enabled it to preserve a modest amount of open space.

SITE DESIGN
The site inventory had determined that much of the site vegetation was low quality because of the dominance of invasive exotic plants (e.g., wisteria); however, the northeastern corner contained a flourishing ecosystem with mature high-value vegetation that will be preserved to the greatest extent possible. A half-acre tree-save area in the property's northeast corner will prevent at least thirty mature trees (over 30-inch caliper) and associated understory vegetation from being removed.

The team carefully located the building to create the best orientation for daylighting and energy conservation while also fitting with the natural topography and preserving the most valuable trees. The building steps with the steeply sloping terrain, nestling into the topography to minimize the need for excavation and fill.

PARKING REDUCTION
The market standard for parking calls for at least four spaces per 1,000 gross square feet (GSF) of a building. After confirming that a future owner could add parking to meet that requirement, NWF opted to develop only 2.6 parking spaces per 1,000 GSF—the minimum required by the county. The reduction in parking greatly reduces impervious surface area and protects open space.

Runoff from the parking lots flows into two large medians that have been designed as bioretention areas. The low areas are planted with seasonal color such as yellow flag iris, spicebush, river birch, and button bush. To address concerns about employee safety and visibility, taller shrubs are concentrated at the bottom of the swales.

BIORETENTION

Stormwater runoff can pose water quality problems from the release of excess nutrients and sediment from landscaped areas, as well as hydrocarbons from roadways and parking areas. County regulations require that new development include measures to retain stormwater on-site and to improve water quality before it is released. Typical dry ponds often do not integrate well with natural environments because of steep grading necessary to fit them into the site and because plantings are not allowed in the embankment areas, which are actually designed to prevent infiltration. The bioretention area at NWF reduces the need for a larger stormwater retention area, or dry pond.

NWF chose to develop a natural stormwater management system that improves water quality, increases groundwater recharge, and nourishes adjacent Colvin Run that is part of the Chesapeake Bay watershed. The natural system will provide a diverse environment rich with habitat for wildlife.

Native trees, shrubs, and ground covers that can handle the ebb and flow of water will be used in combinations found naturally in the region, to create a living water filtration system. The low areas will be augmented with seasonal color such as yellow flag iris *(Iris versicolor)*, spicebush *(Lindera benzoin)*, river birch *(Betula nigra)*, and button bush *(Cephalanthus occidentalis)*. To address concerns about employee safety and visibility, taller shrubs will be concentrated at the bottom of the swales.

The parking areas will be lined with curbs with **V**-shaped cutouts, allowing runoff from the parking lot to flow into two large medians that have been designed as bioretention areas. Runoff from the building roof surfaces will be piped into the bioretention areas. Contaminants suspended in the runoff will be filtered naturally as the water percolates through the soil. In contrast to sand and gravel filtration systems, these living systems will not need periodic replacement.

Native trees, shrubs, and ground covers that can handle the ebb and flow of water will be used in combinations found naturally in the region, to create a living water filtration system. Contaminants suspended in the runoff from parking lots and rooftops will be filtered naturally as the water percolates through the soil. Key: 1. Sheet flow from parking lot; 2. Native trees, shrubs, and ground covers; 3. Planting soil; 4. Sand layer for dewatering; 5. Gravel layer with perforated underdrains; 6. Outlet pipe to dry pond; 7. Overflow inlet

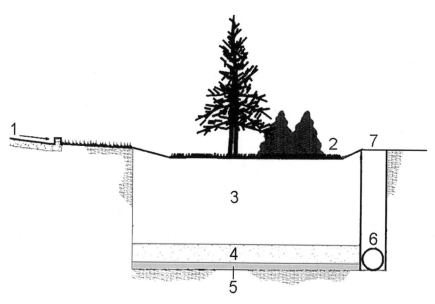

A dry pond at the low end of the site is designed to control water quantities that exceed what the bioretention areas can manage; water will be retained in the pond and released slowly into a nearby stream. Water flows in the bioretention areas that cannot infiltrate fast enough will flow through underground pipes to the dry pond at the site's lower end. The dry pond will fluctuate with the seasons, retaining as much as six feet of water during rainy periods and remaining dry at other times.

BACKYARD HABITATS

Well known for its Backyard Wildlife Habitat program, NWF viewed this headquarters project as an excellent opportunity to showcase habitat demonstration areas. The team developed the site to accommodate a diverse range of meadow, woodland, and aquatic wildlife habitats. NWF's objective is for the entire site, even the building's patios and parking lots, to serve as demonstration wildlife habitats.

Landscape architects paid special attention to providing shelter, food, and water for wildlife in each habitat area. The landscape design includes fruit-bearing plants for food and logs and brush piles for shelter, while the ponds provide water.

The dry pond area and open space in front of the building create meadow habitats, and the park edge on the site's north side is a forest habitat. An aquatic wildlife habitat is planned at the building entry; visitors entering the building will cross over this habitat on a bridge for a close look. The bioretention area will be a habitat that changes over time as in natural succession. It will start as a meadow and, as the plantings mature, develop into a forest habitat.

A variety of deciduous native vines that are popular with wildlife, such as Virginia creeper *(Parthenocissus quinquefolia)*, Dutchman's pipe *(Aristolochia macrophylla)*, and trumpet vine *(Campsis radicans)*, will climb the trellis structure, providing shade in the spring, summer, and fall. The trellis will also promote NWF's Backyard Wildlife Habitat program by providing a "vertical habitat."

The building features a "green trellis" that will form a screen wall six feet in front of the south elevation. A variety of deciduous native vines that are popular with wildlife, such as Virginia creeper, Dutchman's pipe, and trumpet vine, will climb the trellis structure, providing shade in the spring, summer, and fall. The trellis will also promote NWF's Backyard Wildlife Habitat program by providing a "vertical habitat."

LOW-MAINTENANCE LANDSCAPING

The landscaping will minimize the need for irrigation by including only native species and emphasizing those that originally existed on the site. The only water used for irrigation will be a drip irrigation system for the vines on the trellis.

The team selected grasses and ground covers that are about 24 inches high and will be mowed only twice per year. Because of safety concerns, an option has been developed that provides a limited mowing zone along walkways and parking lots.

Energy

Decisions about basic building form and orientation had a considerable impact on energy performance and proved to be a cost-effective way to improve performance.

PASSIVE SOLAR DESIGN

To maximize daylight, the design orients the building with the long sides facing north and south. Building faces oriented toward the east and west, which will experience difficult-to-control low-angle sunlight, are mostly opaque. The opaque west elevation effectively reduced peak loads that occur in the afternoon, after the building has experienced a full day of gradually rising temperatures.

Cost-effective upgrades to the building envelope include infiltration control and thermally broken frames for all windows. The team was surprised to find that improvements to the building insulative values could not be cost-justified. The expense of improving the building envelope from R-11 to R-19 and the roof from R-19 to R-30 had a fifteen-year payback. The team searched unsuccessfully for less expensive design strategies to increase the insulative value.

GREEN TRELLIS

The building features a "green trellis" that will form a screen wall six feet in front of the south elevation.

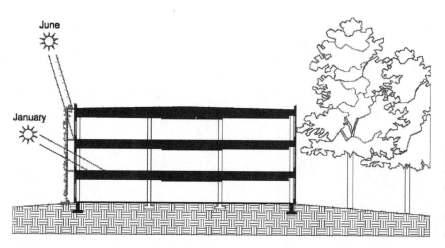

In summer, this green trellis reduces heat gain on the building's south side and filters the intense direct sunlight. In the winter, when the deciduous vines are dormant, the building will benefit from heat gain.

In summer, this green trellis reduces heat gain on the building's south side and filters the intense direct sunlight. In the winter, when the deciduous vines are dormant, the building will benefit from heat gain.

Energy modeling confirmed that this deciduous sunscreen was more effective at improving energy performance than more expensive design options that relied on fixed architectural sunscreens.

In the winter, when the deciduous vines are dormant, the building will benefit from heat gain. Energy modeling confirmed that this deciduous sunscreen was more effective at improving energy performance than more expensive design options that relied on fixed architectural sunscreens.

EFFICIENT COOLING SYSTEMS

While the design will use a standard, low-cost, packaged VAV mechanical system, it will incorporate some significant upgrades.

Improvements to the rooftop units will include the use of a low-temperature air system that reduces energy usage for fans by providing smaller quantities of air for cooling at 50 degrees. An evaporative condenser has been specified instead of the standard air-cooled condenser, boosting efficiency from 1.1 kW/ton to 0.85 kW/ton. The building will also have high-efficiency pumps and motors and variable-frequency drives.

Strategies such as the enthalpy wheel for heat recovery—which might have been cost effective in a building with higher energy requirements—could not be cost-justified for this building.

The most promising alternative system that was studied used hot water for radiant heat combined with a straight VAV system. Because heat naturally flows upward and cooling naturally flows downward, fan-powered units would not be required. Unfortunately, because gas service was not readily available at the site, the first cost of the system was too high.

EFFICIENT LIGHTING

The lighting design will achieve substantial upgrades in both quality and energy efficiency. Occupancy sensors will be used throughout, and daylight switching will be used in perimeter zones.

Lighting will be able to be simply turned off during most daylight hours in the perimeter zones. While it will involve a bit more participation from building occupants, separate switching circuits for the perimeter lighting zone will be much less expensive than daylighting dimming ballasts and sensors, and the energy savings can be even greater.

With the decision to increase ceiling height to just over 9 feet, indirect lighting became possible. Low-cost pendant direct/indirect fixtures will be no more expensive than typical recessed fluorescent fixtures. Single-bulb "next-generation" T-5 fixtures mounted over the workstations will provide an even distribution of ambient light, which will be supplemented by task lighting.

ADVANCED COMMUNICATIONS

NWF's new headquarters will be a high-tech learning center that can link electronically to classrooms and conference centers worldwide. Online distance learning with live, nature-based lessons will be available over the Internet and through videoconferencing.

Network and telecommunication connections for employees are wired throughout the building, as well as to outdoor patios and picnic areas.

Water

Water-conserving plumbing fixtures will be used throughout. Lavatories will use aerators and water-metering faucets, while water closets will use manually operated flush valves.

Rainwater collected on rooftops and condensate from cooling will be routed through the roof drains to the bioretention areas in the parking lots, thereby reducing the quantity of water requiring treatment.

Indoor Environment

The indoor environment will be enhanced by the presence of daylight, improved electric lighting, and measures taken to protect indoor air quality and acoustics.

INDOOR AIR QUALITY

Several enhancements will improve indoor air quality compared to the typical speculative building model. Ventilation rates will exceed ASHRAE Standard 62 for indoor air quality, air filtration will make use of 85 percent instead of 35 percent filters, and the VAV system will use a fan-powered system that improves air mixing and ventilation.

During construction, the building will be continuously ventilated to minimize buildup of contaminants from wet building materials as they cure. The contaminants released during construction will be limited, however, because water-based, low-VOC paints, adhesives, and finishes will be used throughout.

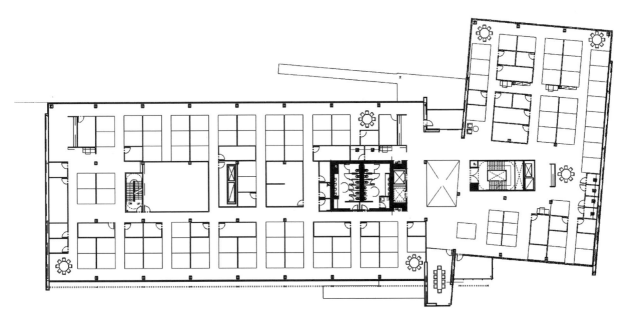

ACCESS TO DAYLIGHT

The building massing will have a large impact on the availability of daylight. Because of the relatively narrow building proportion, the majority of workspace areas will be within 25 feet of a window. The interior space planning will support the use of daylighting through the coordination of panel heights, location of "closed" support spaces in interior zones, and use of light-colored, light-reflective materials.

The majority of workspace areas will be within 25 feet of a window, because of the relatively narrow proportions of the building. Low-cost pendant direct/indirect fixtures will use single-bulb "next-generation" T-5 fixtures mounted over the workstations to provide an even distribution of ambient light.

Material Resources

The team selected building materials that are environmentally preferable and practical. For NWF's headquarters, this means the materials will be durable, low-maintenance, and low cost. While many natural, renewable materials are being considered for use, wood substitutes will be selected in lieu of wood products wherever possible.

SITE MATERIALS

While some decks and stairs will be made with recycled plastic lumber, because it resists rotting, many of the materials used on the site will come from the site itself. The contractor is planning to stockpile topsoil on-site for reuse and to have land-clearing debris shredded for reuse as mulch. Gypsum board scrap will be ground for use as a soil amendment or sold to local landscaping contractors. Some of the plant material from the existing NWF headquarters site will be moved to the new site by volunteers.

EXTERIOR BUILDING MATERIALS

The building envelope will include split-face concrete block for large opaque areas and profiled metal panels for spandrel areas. The contractor is seeking out local sources of concrete block, and sources of metal panels and mullions with recycled content that use a powder-coated finish.

Powder coating is a zero-waste, zero-pollution factory finish that is an environmentally friendly alternative to traditional high-performance finishes.

INTERIOR BUILDING MATERIALS

The palette of interior materials will be a simple one. Linoleum and carpeting will be the primary flooring materials. Ceilings will use a highly light-reflective ceiling tile with high recycled content. Walls will be gypsum board and paint. Doors, millwork, and accent materials will use natural, renewable biofiber materials that offer alternatives to the use of wood or synthetics. For example, compressed agricultural fiber doors and solid-surface biocomposites for built-in millwork are being considered for use.

Systems furniture is being selected based on functional requirements as well as the manufacturer's initiatives to eliminate waste and pollution from the manufacturing process and to reduce chemical emissions from the furniture itself.

RECYCLING

The design will make recycling easy and unobtrusive. Recycling containers will be built into galleys, kitchenettes, and print rooms so that recyclables can be collected at the point of use. Space has been provided at the loading dock for a compactor and baler for paper and cardboard.

Benefits of the Design

NWF's new headquarters will set a standard for commonsense ways to incorporate environmentally sensitive design into commercial office construction.

The design represents a measured departure from conventional low-cost office development. While the economics of the project limited to some extent the range of options considered, many enhancements were made that improve the quality of the interior environment while reducing negative environmental impacts.

The site design is particularly noteworthy because it will be both visually striking and environmentally significant. Because the innovations to the site design are new to the county, they have the potential to impact other projects that will follow. Future approvals should be easier because the procedure will no longer be without precedent.

World Resources Institute Headquarters Office Interiors

Washington, DC

Building Size: *38,000 SF*

Site: *One full floor and one partial floor of an eight-story office building*

Completion: *March 1999*

Cost: *$43/SF*

The World Resource Institute (WRI) headquarters offices were built within two floors of a recently completed office building in Washington DC. The 38,000 SF space includes offices, conference rooms, library, lunchroom, and print room, as well as a large, divisible, multipurpose conference room. HOK provided programming, interior design, and consulting services.

Environmental Goals

Since its founding in 1982, WRI has become one of the world's most respected independent policy and research centers for the study of environmentally, socially, and economically viable development paths. WRI believes a healthy environment and a healthy economy can coexist, and that the future will be shaped by decisions and choices made today.

WRI's move provided an opportunity to create an office environment that would express its mission in tangible terms through environmentally friendly design.

At every step from initial conception to finishing touches, the team's goal was to seek out materials, products, and building systems from around the world that represent promising alternatives to typical unsustainable practices. In particular, the team searched for materials and systems that preserve biological resources and reduce the threat of climate change.

Another design goal was to recognize the individual manufacturers and suppliers that are "leaders in industry" based on their proactive efforts to improve the environmental performance of their products.

Design Overview

Contrary to current trends toward open office planning, WRI chose to develop a plan that would meet their needs for solitary focused work interspersed with both spontaneous and scheduled collaborations.

WRI's move provided an opportunity to create an office environment that would express its mission in tangible terms through environmentally friendly design. The bright and welcoming reception area contains a screen wall with built-in planter to support climbing vines, and cork flooring in the elevator lobby; the door to the main conference room is made from reclaimed wood.

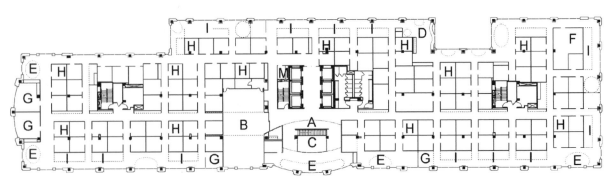

Eighth Floor

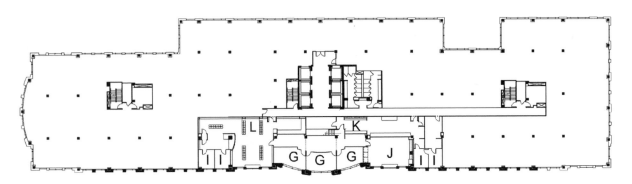

Seventh Floor

Small, private offices accommodate focused work, and light-filled meeting areas encourage creative interaction. A coffee bar and built-in window seats are located along the perimeter.

Key: A. Reception; B. Main conference room; C. Stairs down/open to floor below; D. Coffee bar; E. Open conference; F. G.I.S. lab; G. Small conference; H. Closed office; I. Open office; J. Lunchroom; K. Copy/mail room; L. Library

Small, private offices accommodate focused work, and light-filled meeting areas encourage creative interaction. Open workstations and open conferencing, a coffee bar, and support spaces with printers and fax machines are located along the perimeter, while the offices are located "inboard." This encourages people to move around the space and enables them to share the daylight and views.

The central conference room, located off the reception area, accommodates larger gatherings and takes advantage of new technology, including videoconferencing, to facilitate communication among staff, visitors, and collaborators. A new open staircase connects the reception area to common spaces on the seventh floor, including conference rooms, the library, the lunchroom, and a supply room and mailroom.

Economics

The new environmentally conscious space was built within a typical leased office space and within a standard budget.

Additional funds were provided by the landlord to accommodate the cost of cutting an opening and adding a communicating stair between the seventh and eighth floors.

Design Process

The project began with a series of presentations to educate WRI staff about environmental issues and opportunities related to buildings and construction. While WRI is a prominent research organization well versed in the issues under discussion, the sessions focused on the range of design strategies that would be relevant to their particular design challenge and helped to establish a common vocabulary for discussing them.

Visioning sessions during the programming phase focused on defining the organizational values of WRI for the design team and clarifying the goals and concepts that would guide the design. The time spent together to define a common vision for the project was essential to the success of the project.

Those sessions were followed by interviews to determine space requirements and a survey to explore the staff's priorities for the green design. The entire staff ranked lists of issues related to energy and resource conservation, building materials, and indoor environmental quality. The responses indicated a high degree of interest in all of the areas.

During design, a consensus process was used for decision making. A design committee representing a cross section of the office handled day-to-day decisions, and periodic meetings were held to review progress and solicit feedback from staff.

SITE SELECTION

During the site selection process, the team tested each potential lease space not just to see if WRI would fit in the space, but to ensure that the building could accommodate the goal of creating a green office. The sites were

A new open staircase behind a "living" wall connects the reception area with common spaces on the seventh floor. Climbing vines will progressively cover the stainless steel trellis over time. All wood paneling and millwork is from certified sustainably managed forests.

evaluated for daylight access, access to mass transit, the building recycling program, and support for bicyclists. The building systems were evaluated for their energy efficiency and the ability to provide sufficient fresh air. Because fresh air requirements in buildings have changed many times over the past twenty years, this can be an important consideration.

The building WRI ultimately selected was a freestanding building of narrow proportion providing excellent daylight access with above-average HVAC systems in terms of efficiency and fresh air supply. Additional benefits included access to transit, a fitness center that could be used by cyclists, low-flow plumbing fixtures, and an effectively functioning recycling program.

Site

The building that WRI chose to occupy is located just one block from Union Station, providing easy access to both train and metro, and within easy walking distance of Capitol Hill. Cyclists have access to the building fitness center and a secure bike room. These measures were important, as a full 90 percent of WRI's staff bicycle, walk, or take public transit to work.

Energy

Though WRI's new office space was an interior fit-out of an existing building, they found many opportunities to enhance energy efficiency. In fact, the innovations in WRI's offices have caught the attention of the building management, who are considering replicating some of the efficiency measures on other floors of the building as well.

DAYLIGHTING
Conference rooms, informal team spaces, open office areas, and support spaces such as the coffee bar, lunchroom, and library are filled with natural daylight. Closed offices have access to "shared" daylight through clerestory windows set six feet high. The design was developed so that daylight and views to the outside are available at the end of nearly every corridor, as well as through the clerestory windows, to create an open feeling in an office space densely populated with closed offices. Indirect lighting in the closed offices bounces additional light off the ceiling to enhance the open feeling.

LIGHTING
Energy-efficient lighting provides better, more comfortable lighting with personally controlled dimming options. Sensors and smart controls enhance energy savings by cutting off or reducing the power supply when products are not in use.

WRI's project marked the introduction of Ledalite's revolutionary new Ergolight fixture to the marketplace. The pendant fixtures hold three Philips low-mercury fluorescent lamps; two lamps are aimed downward

Closed offices have access to some daylight through clerestory windows set six feet high. Indirect pendant light fixtures provide better, more energy-efficient lighting with personally controlled dimming options. Work surfaces of wood fiberboard are finished with a zero-emissions, zero-waste process that allows for soft curves, eased edges, and a natural appearance.

onto work surfaces, while one lamp is directed upward to reflect light from the ceiling panels, creating a balanced light atmosphere, reducing glare and shadows.

These fixtures, which are used in all offices, have integral occupancy and daylight dimming sensors. Sensors in the light fixtures automatically dim the lights when the office is empty, leaving 10 percent of the light to illuminate the ceiling so the office does not seem dark or "empty." The daylight dimmer maintains constant workplace brightness throughout the day and night.

The Ergolight fixtures are linked to the computer in each office to give occupants individual control of the lighting level and dimming intervals, through Windows-based software.

Because only one fixture is required in each office, and because it has been designed to be extremely easy to install, the total installed cost of this fixture is slightly less than the building standard, which would have used two typical 2 ft × 2 ft recessed fluorescent fixtures. This fixture also has the environmental and economic benefit of eliminating the need for wall switches. When electricity expenses, lighting-related cooling, and relamping are considered, the life cycle cost of the fixture is less than half the building standard.

The installed full load is 0.76 W/SF; when the automated controls are factored in, the figure drops to about 0.40 W/SF. The installation represents savings of 77 percent compared to the building standard, with electricity savings of over 64,000 kWh annually. In terms of CO_2 reduction, the annual lighting savings are equivalent to planting more than 12 acres of forest.

The main corridors and public spaces such as the library, lunchroom, and some of the conference rooms use Ledalite's Minuet fixture, another direct/indirect fixture that is distinctive for its narrow proportions as well as its energy-efficient operation.

Miscellaneous downlights and accent lighting are compact fluorescent, with some metal halide lighting in display areas where a sharper light source was desired. These fixtures are between four and ten times

Turner Feature Animation Office and Production Facility

Glendale, California

Building Size: 64,000 SF

Site: N/A (Interiors project)

Completion: 1998

Cost: $40/SF (including furniture)

Highlights of the Design

■ The focus was on energy-efficient lighting, minimal use of materials, and selection of materials that are from renewable, nonendangered resources that are nontoxic in production, installation, and use.

more efficient than incandescent or halogen fixtures, which are still commonly used in office environments.

LAMPS

Although fluorescent lamps substantially reduce environmental pollution compared to less efficient light sources, ordinary spent fluorescent lamps have been classified by the U.S. EPA as hazardous waste because of the mercury content, which dissolves in the environment and contaminates fish and water resources. Philips Lighting has launched an exemplary worldwide effort to pass EPA's standard for mercury content at every phase of lamp life. WRI used their Alto lamp, which contains nearly 70 percent less mercury than the industry average.

EXIT SIGNS

All exit signs utilize an LED light source, with a maximum of 5 W per illuminated face and an expected life span of eighty to five hundred years. Typical incandescent exit signs using a "long life" 40 W bulb must be replaced every eight months.

APPLIANCES

Efficient "Energy Star" appliances and office equipment further reduce the use of fossil fuels.

Appliances in WRI's new facility have the EPA Energy Star rating, as do computer monitors, copiers, and printers. The American Council for an Energy Efficient Economy has recognized the Asko dishwasher as the most efficient model available.

- Use of energy-efficient zoned lighting, with a mix of direct and indirect fixtures, supports "pace" changes, providing relief for employees working long hours.

- Materials include linoleum flooring, linoleum tackable wall panels, and rubber floor tiles made from recycled automobile tires.

- Fine casework is made from American white birch, a nonendangered species native to the United States. Reception desk surfaces, executive board tables, and teaming tables are made of biocomposite from soy-based resin and recycled newsprint.

- Ceilings were left open in many areas, eliminating the need for ceiling tile, and tackable wall panels of Homasote, a material made from 100 percent recycled paperboard, were left exposed and painted, eliminating the need for fabric wall covering and glue.

TECHNOLOGY

Videoconferencing technologies reduce the need for staff and collaborators to travel, which reduces energy demands and carbon dioxide emissions.

Water

WRI uses reusable coffee mugs. In addition to the fact that dishwashers are much more water efficient than washing by hand, the Asko dishwashers installed by WRI are exemplary for their water efficiency.

Chilled, filtered water is dispensed through the refrigerator in the lunchroom, which will significantly reduce the use of bottled drinking water.

Indoor Environment

The indoor environment is enhanced by the presence of daylight, good indoor air quality, and the fact that staff members are able to customize their workspace. Personal dimming allows staff to control the settings on their lighting and to automate it as they see fit.

Because building materials, adhesives, sealants, and finishes were selected with careful attention to avoiding toxins and eliminating VOCs, indoor air quality within the office space is exceptionally good.

Personal controls for airflow were considered carefully during design of the project, to solve the common problem of people in office buildings being either too hot or too cold. Because the project is a tenant fit-out, opportunities to offset the first cost of an underfloor air supply system, which would have offered excellent individual control, were extremely limited. As a compromise solution, diffusers were selected for the offices with an adjustable damper that could be controlled by portable electronic "zappers"; however, the additional cost of approximately a dollar and a half per SF proved to be prohibitive.

Material Resources

The materials selection process, which took advantage of HOK's Healthy and Sustainable Building Materials Database, considered the full life cycle of each product, from raw materials acquisition and manufacturing practices that reduce waste and pollution to use and ultimate reuse or recycling.

WALLS

Wall partitions are made of gypsum board with high recycled content. The facings are covered with 100 percent recycled paper and finished with a low-VOC joint compound. Acoustic insulation within the walls is made from mineral fiber, an industrial by-product.

Compressed straw panels were considered for the partitions and showed promise as a flexible, low-cost solution that would provide good acoustical performance. While several plants are under development in the United States to produce the panels, at the time the WRI offices were being constructed no U.S. production facilities were yet operational. Unfortunately, the time and cost required to ship panels from Europe was prohibitive.

PAINT

Walls, ceilings, and miscellaneous metal are treated with ICI paint that is water-based and completely free of petroleum-based solvents and VOCs. ICI Paints (previously known as Glidden) pioneered the formulation of "odor-free," zero-VOC paint in the United States. Accents in the lunchroom are done with milk paint made from milk protein, lime, earth pigments, and clay fillers, created by the Old Fashioned Milk Paint Company.

CEILINGS

To take full advantage of the natural light, the new facility uses Hi-LR Ultima RH90 ceiling tiles by Armstrong World Industries. These tiles, which are highly reflective, returning up to 89 percent of ambient light to occupants, are created with 79 percent recycled content. Approximately 60 percent of the recycled paper is postconsumer.

FLOORING

The elevator lobby has flooring made of cork, a natural, renewable, and sustainably harvested material, from the Natural Cork Ltd. Co. When taken in small, infrequent extractions, the cork tree can continue to produce replacement bark. The natural resilience and acoustical performance

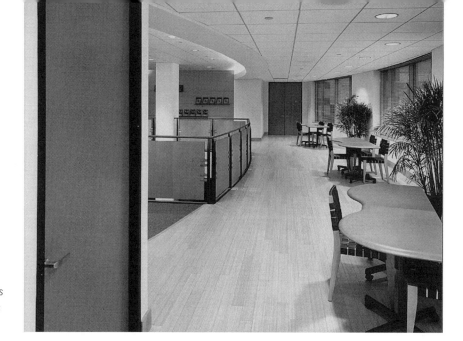

The bamboo flooring in the reception area is warm and attractive—it also is a naturally renewable material that is durable and easy to maintain.

of cork create an attractive, long-lasting, and comfortable surface. The cork tiles, prefinished with a UV-cured acrylic coating that is durable, formaldehyde free, and zero-VOC, are low maintenance, requiring only sweeping and mopping.

The flooring in the reception waiting area is bamboo from Mintec Corp. Grown in Southeast Asia, bamboo is a fast-growing grass that requires no pesticides or fertilizers. It regenerates without replanting, so it is a low-energy, naturally renewable material. Bamboo is also strong, stable, and versatile as a building material. The water-based polyurethane finish is highly durable and easy to maintain.

Kitchen and workroom floors are covered with linoleum from Forbo Industries and DLW. An environmentally friendly alternative to vinyl, linoleum is made from wood flour, cork flour, natural rosins, linseed oil, and limestone, with a backing of biodegradable jute fiber. Available in a wide variety of colors, this product has a life expectancy of forty to sixty years.

CARPETING

Offices and hallways are tiled with 100 percent solution-dyed carpet manufactured by Interface Flooring Systems. Individual tiles, which are installed with a water-based, zero-VOC releasable adhesive, can be replaced when and where needed, thus minimizing waste. The carpet tiles have an integral cushion backing that improves comfort while increasing the durability of the product. Unlike standard latex-backed carpet, the backing is water impermeable, which means the flooring is easier to clean, and because it cannot retain moisture, there is no possibility for molds or mildew to grow.

Interface offers a unique carpet leasing program in support of its company's commitment to preserving the environment and reducing waste in landfills. Instead of buying the carpet outright and disposing of it in a few years, at the end of the lease period Interface removes the carpet and recycles it into new carpet.

DOORS

All office doors in WRI's new facility are made by Architectural Forest Enterprises from compressed wheat straw fiberboard. Wheat straw is an agricultural waste product that is normally burned, emitting harmful gases and particles into the atmosphere. WRI's new facility was the first application of this material for commercial doors

The wheatboard is compressed with formaldehyde-free binders and finished with water-based dyes and zero-emissions UV-cured acrylic coatings in a variety of colors. Staff members chose the color of their individual office doors. The door core material is kraft paper honeycomb, a strong formaldehyde-free material made with recycled content (traditionally wood doors are made with particleboard cores that do contain formaldehyde). Rails and stiles are made of lumber from forests certified by the Forest Stewardship Council.

Sliding doors in the main conference room use the same wheat straw material, with maple veneer that originated from forests certified by the Forest Stewardship Council.

Some doors to nonoffice spaces were salvaged from the construction site. To prevent them from going to the landfill, WRI repainted and used them in its new space. Doors to the main conference room are custom made from salvaged lumber.

SUSTAINABLY HARVESTED WOOD

Wood paneling in the reception area, handrails, the wood base, and the reception desk are constructed of certified sustainably harvested wood from EcoTimber International and Architectural Forestry Enterprises. The handrail and guardrails on the stairs and the reception desk top are made from wood that originated in a project called Plan Forestal Estatal (PFE), a community-based forestry program located in the state of Quintana Roo, on Mexico's eastern Yucatán Peninsula.

The maple woodwork in the reception area and main conference room is of U.S. origin, also from independently certified sustainable sources. The maple selected is "character grade" wood, which further conserves resources because sub-premium-grade wood is commonly disposed of as an inferior material of limited commercial value.

RECLAIMED WOOD

The design uses reclaimed wood in the reception area. Reclaimed wood makes use of a beautiful and increasingly rare material that would otherwise be destined for the landfill.

In turn-of-the-century Virginia, the abundant local heart pine was rapidly depleted to meet a growing need for construction lumber. Today, the Virginia pine is near extinction, and most remaining stands are second- or third-growth forests. As older structures are replaced with modern facilities, salvage companies have begun to carefully disassemble old factories, houses, and stores to recover the pine. Lumber is then remilled and used to create hardwood floors, railings, and, in WRI's case, beautiful and unique doors to its main conference room.

CABINETS AND WORK SURFACES

Cabinets found in WRI's kitchens and workrooms are made from two types of biofiber materials. These formaldehyde-free fiberboards are being used in lieu of the more conventional plastic laminate on particleboard. With a clear finish, the material does not require laminating, eliminating the use of plastic as well as adhesives. The Eco-colors wheatboard is similar to that used for the office doors; the Dakota Burl is made from compressed sunflower seed hulls.

Kitchen countertops are made of linoleum on a wheatboard substrate, while dry areas use linoleum "desktop." Some work surfaces use Environ, a solid, formaldehyde-free biocomposite made from soybeans and recycled newspaper. All millwork surfaces are sealed with Tried and True zero-VOC clear finishes made of polymerized linseed oil.

Kitchen cabinets and workroom surfaces are made from a variety of solid-surface biofiber materials, in lieu of conventional plastic laminate on particleboard. The copy/fax areas use a biocomposite made from soybeans and recycled newspaper, with cabinets made from clear-finished wheat straw; kitchen cabinets made from compressed sunflower seed hulls use a linoleum top and wood edge trim.

FURNITURE

The selected office furniture manufacturer, Haworth Inc., is known for reducing processing waste and emissions. For this project, the designers configured all offices and workstations to allow for the maximum amount of workspace and the best integration of technology. Soft curves, eased edges, natural finishes, and mobile pedestals enhance comfort and flexibility. As an alternative to plastic laminate, the work surfaces are made of a durable wood fiberboard finished with a zero-emissions, zero-waste UV-cured process. All metal components in the workstations are electrostatically powder-coated, which is also a zero-emissions, zero-waste process.

Workstation panels, which are used in the open office areas, are covered with fabric made from 100 percent recycled PET plastic.

For lounge seating, WRI selected an attractive, resource-efficient chair by Danko, a division of Persing Enterprises, Inc. The chairs are made of just 11 pounds of laminated maple each. The woven seat and back are made of surplus automotive seatbelt material. The easy-to-clean woven seatbelts provide a comfortable seat without the need for foam, which produces poisonous gas when burned and degrades over time.

MOVING BOXES, NOT WALLS

One goal was to maximize flexibility so future needs could be accommodated with little cost by "moving boxes, not walls." All the offices, including that of WRI president Jonathan Lash, are the same size and have the same access to daylight. The result is an equitable distribution of space that allows staff to move easily from one location to another within the office without costly reconfigurations.

WASTE REDUCTION

Many design decisions reduced waste being sent to landfills, and the office itself is fitted out to support an effective recycling program. WRI installed recycling bins in all copy/fax areas and coffee/lunchroom areas; the bins are made out of ductwork left over from the construction of the air circulation system.

Improvements in WRI's Internet-based communications technology enable people worldwide to have access to more of its information electronically, reducing the demand for paper and other forest products.

Benefits of the Design

The space is a real-life example of strategic environmental and business management—using smart design to create sustainable environments that are better for people. WRI hopes it provides inspiration for other organizations to do the same.

This case study was adapted from text published in *Mission Design: WRI's Office Environment* (Washington, DC: World Resources Institute, 1999).

The Nature Conservancy
New Headquarters Building

Arlington, Virginia

Building Size:	*172,000 SF*
Site:	*1.6 acres*
Completion:	*1999*
Cost:	*$16.25 million ($94/SF)*

The Nature Conservancy's new headquarters is an eight-story 172,000 SF office building in the Ballston area of Arlington, Virginia. The Conservancy occupies six floors and leases two floors, which provide room for growth. Parking is accommodated in a garage below the building; the remainder of the site has been transformed into a half-acre landscaped park. HOK provided programming, architecture, interior design, and landscape design for this build-to-suit project.

Environmental Goals

The Nature Conservancy wanted their new headquarters to reflect both their commitment to protecting the environment and their conservative use of donated funds.

As a private, nonprofit group that relies on donor support, the Conservancy is proud of the fact that most of its operating budget goes toward land conservation. Their goal for their new headquarters was to develop an environmentally responsible building design based on proven materials and technologies that would not increase the first cost of the building or compromise future re-marketability.

Design Overview

The Nature Conservancy's new headquarters building occupies a full block in downtown Ballston. The principal exit of the Ballston Metro station is located on the southeastern corner of the site, with the Metro entrance and terminal diagonally across the street.

The building design is essentially a simple rectangle in plan, with a regular grid of deeply set windows in a precast concrete facade. The exceptions are the corner that faces the Metro, and the main conference room, which extends into the park on the north side of the building. On the corner facing the Metro, a three-story block marks the front entry, and the upper floors are pulled back 12 feet from the street line.

The Nature Conservancy wanted their new headquarters in the Metro-accessible Ballston area of Arlington, Virginia, to reflect both their commitment to protecting the environment and their conservative use of donated funds.

The interior office layout is more than 90 percent open plan, a strong departure from their old building's traditional planning, with closed offices along the building perimeter that isolated interior spaces from daylight and views. In this design, the closed offices were relocated to the building core and outfitted with full-length glass partitions, leaving the perimeter zone entirely open for daylight access and flexible planning.

The use of additional small conference rooms, shared teaming spaces, and "touchdown" stations for visitors and employees from field offices were features that helped make the open office planning work. The new offices also provide a ground-level conference center and lunchroom that offers direct access to the park for staff and visitors.

Economics

The Conservancy's new headquarters was built within a standard speculative office building budget. No extra funds were allocated for green design. The cost of the building, exclusive of the parking garage, was about $64 per square foot. The cost of the interior fit-out for the Conservancy space was about $21 per square foot.

Typically, a build-to-suit headquarters project would have a slightly higher budget; however, the Conservancy was eager to keep its costs within market rates.

CONSTRUCTION PARTNER

To help control costs, the Conservancy entered into a negotiated contract with Foulger-Pratt Construction. The contractor, who was also serving as the developer for the site, participated as a member of the design team throughout the design process to provide cost estimating of design options.

220

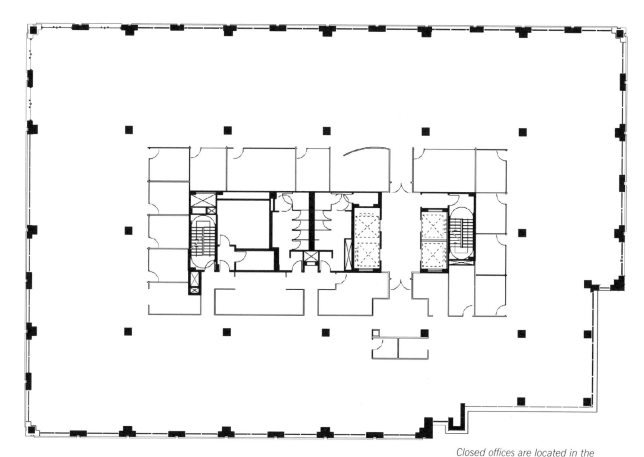

CREATIVE TRADE-OFFS

Because the Conservancy built their own building, they were able to make creative trade-offs with their budgeted dollars. Instead of using expensive finishes in the entry lobby or a complex building form, for example, they were able to invest in an integrated daylighting solution that includes larger windows, perimeter light shelves, improved light fixtures, and daylight dimming controls.

INTERIOR DESIGN PRICING

The interior fit-out phase of the project used the more conventional design-bid-build delivery method. To help control costs, the team benchmarked potential fit-out costs using historical construction cost data, and also developed an interim pricing package during design development. The combined effort helped ensure that construction bids would conform to the budget once contract documents were complete, and that the project would be delivered on time.

Design Process

STRATEGIC PLANNING

Prior to selecting a site for their new facility, HOK worked with the Staubach Company to develop a strategic plan. The plan evaluated whether the Conservancy should renovate its existing headquarters, renovate a different building, or build a new facility. The economics associ-

Closed offices are located in the building core area and outfitted with full-length glass partitions, leaving the perimeter zone entirely open for daylight access and flexible planning. On the ground level, a conference center and lunchroom offer direct access to the park for staff and visitors.

ated with each scenario were considered together with an assessment of the environmental impacts and opportunities of each.

While their existing building had excellent Metro access, it had poor energy performance and a limited fresh air supply. Reuse of their existing 1960s-vintage building would have required extensive renovation. Architecturally, the building also posed limitations because of low floor-to-floor heights and small floorplates.

A criteria document was developed to communicate to prospective developers and building owners the level of design quality and environmental performance that the Conservancy wanted to achieve. Broad environmental performance goals were translated into building specifications to the greatest extent possible, so various site options could be reasonably compared. Topics included connection to public transit, daylight access, HVAC systems efficiency, water conservation, indoor air quality, green building materials, and infrastructure to support recycling.

LEED GREEN BUILDING RATING SYSTEM

The Leadership in Energy and Environmental Design (LEED) Green Building Rating System, developed by the U.S. Green Building Council, was used as a design guidance tool throughout the design process. The rating system was still under development at the time; however, the framework of issues had been established and released.

GREEN CLEANING REVIEW

During design development, specialists from Rochester Midland Corporation conducted a "green cleaning review" with members of the future building maintenance crew. The review generated a fairly long list of suggested revisions that would reduce maintenance requirements and limit environmental impacts.

Site

Ballston is a rapidly growing inner-ring suburban community. Convenient Metro access, an evolving street life, and considerable mixed-use development are transforming this bedroom community into an urban locale.

GOOD NEIGHBOR

The Conservancy's new headquarters building acts as a "good neighbor" to the community.

The brownfield site, once home to a gasoline station and most recently a surface parking lot, now contributes to Ballston's urban fabric.

The site plan placed the compact building along the street line, preserving a half-acre behind the facility for a neighborhood park, with ample seating for informal use and formal gatherings.

REDUCED PARKING REQUIREMENTS

Though surface parking was permitted, the Conservancy built a below-grade parking structure. Because many employees take the subway or

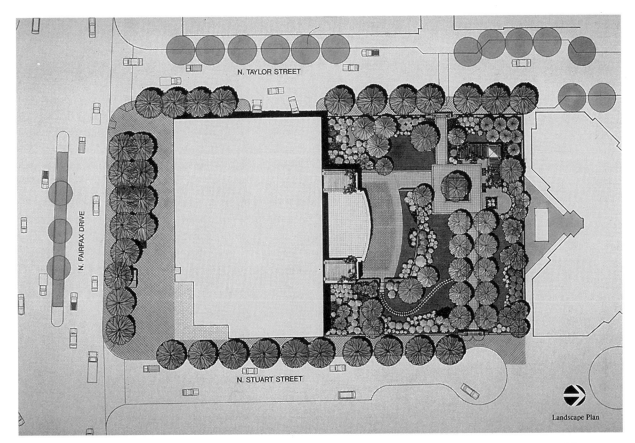

N. TAYLOR STREET

N. FAIRFAX DRIVE

N. STUART STREET

Landscape Plan

The new headquarters building occupies a full block in downtown Ballston. The site plan placed the compact building along the street line, preserving a half acre behind the facility for a native plant garden that has already become an attraction for this urban community, drawn to it by its beauty and educational opportunities.

ride bicycles to work, the Conservancy's requests to decrease the size of the garage were approved by the county. Use of "buddy parking," in which cars are parked behind each other, also helped to reduce the size and cost of the garage.

The facility provides locked storage and shower areas for bicycle commuters and an on-site recharge station for electric vehicles.

NATIVE PLANT GARDEN
The site plan includes a half-acre native plant garden behind the building. The garden courtyard will serve as a gathering place for employees and as an outdoor reception area for Conservancy events.

Planting areas were developed to illustrate the four stages of secondary succession in the coastal Piedmont region. Secondary succession is nature's process of reclaiming cleared areas. In the first stage a wildflower meadow is formed; seedlings of trees and shrubs emerge in the second stage. The third stage is marked by the gradual forming of layers of forest canopy. The fourth phase, which takes over two hundred years to establish, is a mature forest, which in this garden is symbolized by a mature oak tree. The large oak is especially appropriate in the garden because its leaf is the symbol used for the Nature Conservancy.

The garden presents a spectacular collection of native plants, both from the region and from parts of the United States with similar climates. Besides familiar natives such as black-eyed Susans, rhododendrons, azaleas, and native roses, the Conservancy chose rare and endangered species such as box huckleberry, buffalo clover, and barber's button.

One incredible survival story is "told" by the franklinia trees. Once native to the Altamaha River region in the southern Appalachians of Georgia, this species had not been seen in the wild since 1800; however, the species was revived by two botanists who propagated the tree from cuttings.

Because no irrigation system is required, use of native plants provides both beauty and economic benefits. The mix of wildflowers and grasses creates an alternative ground cover that is drought tolerant and also limits the need for frequent mowing.

Proving that nature conservation can become part of the urban setting, this native plant park already has become an attraction for the entire community. Lured by its beauty and educational opportunities, the garden's visitors include everyone from schoolchildren to office workers, parents with strollers, hobby gardeners, and neighbors out for a walk.

Energy

Extensive energy modeling was done during design to seek out cost-effective energy-efficient solutions. While significant savings were realized based on the use of daylighting and efficient electric lighting, the relatively small size of the building and modest energy requirements made it difficult to economically justify many energy-efficient upgrades to the HVAC equipment.

DAYLIGHTING
The architecture and interiors were developed to create bright, daylit office areas. Large floor-to-ceiling windows with high-performance glazing draw in daylight while minimizing heat gain. The deep precast concrete facade and light shelves on the south, east, and west facades provide sun shading to further reduce heat gain.

The deep precast concrete facade and light shelves on the south, east, and west facades provide sun shading to further reduce heat gain.

The HOK Guidebook to Sustainable Design

Architectural light shelves direct daylight onto the 9-foot-high ceiling, which is finished with special high-reflectivity ceiling tiles to create a spacious, airy feeling.

Along the building perimeter, Mecho Shades made of translucent shade cloth are mounted to the underside of the light shelf to control brightness. Above the light shelf, fixed louvers control glare from low-angle sun.

Inside the office floors, systems furniture partitions surround the open-office workstations to enhance privacy. The bright ceilings and views of buildings and sky above the light shelf are important for maintaining an open feeling on the floor, given that many of the partitions are 6 feet high.

To optimize the selection of the window glazing, Lumen Micro was used for daylighting analysis, while energy modeling monitored the impacts of the options on overall energy performance. The glass above the light shelf is clear with no low-E coating, to maximize daylighting, whereas the glass below the light shelf has a spectrally selective green tint with an advanced low-E coating on the south, east, and west facades and a standard low-E coating on the north facade.

ELECTRIC LIGHTING

The office areas use high-efficiency, low-brightness lighting with automated daylight dimming and occupancy sensors to maximize energy efficiency while creating an exceptionally comfortable work environment.

The open-office lighting consists of 2 ft × 2 ft sixteen-cell deep louver fluorescent parabolic light fixtures that conceal T-5 compact fluorescent lamps. The lights are connected to a daylight dimming system that adjusts lighting levels based on changes in daylight availability. Lighting in the inner perimeter offices and support spaces is connected to occupancy sensors.

To differentiate the circulation space along the core from the open-office areas, recessed 2 ft × 2 ft uplighting fixtures provide brightness that compensates for diminished daylight levels.

MECHANICAL SYSTEMS

The mechanical systems developed for the building are fairly conventional for the building type, with a few noteworthy upgrades.

During operating hours, heating and cooling are controlled by VAV systems that maximize individual control. Small, modular chillers on each floor, which allow for one quarter of a floor to be operated at a time, provide a high degree of operational flexibility for after-hours operation.

During the heating season, building systems use an efficient gas-fired boiler for the morning warm-up cycle. The gas-fired boiler was a highly cost-effective upgrade for the building, accommodating almost all the heating load. Once the building has been started up in the morning, the heat generated by people and equipment is nearly enough to maintain temperatures throughout the rest of the day.

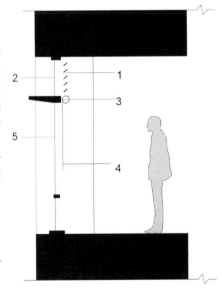

Along the building perimeter, Mecho Shades made of translucent shade cloth are mounted to the underside of the light shelf to control brightness. Above the light shelf, fixed louvers control glare from low-angle sun. Key: 1. Fixed louvers; 2. Clear insulated glazing; 3. Light shelf; 4. Mecho Shade; 5. Tinted glazing with high-performance low-E coating

The concern for re-marketability made it difficult to realize savings from downsizing the HVAC systems. Because of the conventional expectations of the real estate market, the building was designed to 5 W/SF for lighting and plug loads even though the anticipated use is less than 2 W/SF.

OPTIONS CONSIDERED

If the building used a central chilled water plant with the floor-by-floor VAV system, instead of the self-contained VAV system, the efficiency of the chillers would have increased from 0.80/ton to 0.65/ton or 0.58/ton. Even more important, the self-contained units lose efficiency at part load and the central chiller gains efficiency at part load.

Given the size of the building, however, the central chilled water plant, with its thirty-year payback, could not be cost-justified. The options that combined the central chilled water plant with either ice storage or gas absorption units (which would receive a utility rebate) had more favorable but still inadequate payback periods of eleven years and ten years, respectively.

Operable windows were considered carefully but eventually not included in the design, because of concerns about how to accommodate those who may not agree on whether windows should be open or closed.

HUMIDIFICATION

The ASHRAE 55 guideline for thermal comfort can be difficult to comply with in borderline climates like the mid-Atlantic, where humidity drops below recommended levels only a few days a year. While the Conservancy was concerned with providing a comfortable workspace for its employees, the cost of a full humidification system was prohibitive. As a compromise solution, central humidification is provided at the outside air intake rather than on each floor, a much lower-cost solution that was sufficient to produce comfortable humidity levels throughout the winter months.

PHOTOVOLTAICS

Pending support from the Virginia Alliance for Solar Energy and other donors, the Conservancy is currently considering installation of a photovoltaic array on the roof of the building. The array was not part of the original construction effort because it could not be accommodated within the budget.

The solar array, designed by Solar Design Associates, uses thin film photovoltaics mounted to simple ballasted frames on the roof. Rooftop photovoltaic applications are not difficult to install as a retrofit because no penetration through the roof membrane is required.

Water

Office buildings in northern Virginia, where summer water shortages are common, typically have in-ground irrigation systems. Because native plantings were used on the site, no irrigation system was required. This reduced construction and operational costs while also conserving water.

All plumbing fixtures meet the water conservation requirements of the U.S. Energy Policy Act.

A central water purification system distributes purified water to the pantry sinks and coffeemakers. This low-cost feature reduces reliance on bottled water and its associated costs and wasteful packaging.

Indoor Environment

The use of daylight in the building has a strong impact on the indoor environment. Office areas retain an open feeling because of the floor-to-ceiling windows with light shelves. On the entry level, a double-height space spills light into the lobby outside the main conference room, bringing natural daylight into that large floorplate.

INDOOR AIR QUALITY

The building was designed to comply with ASHRAE 62, the industry standard for indoor air quality, and ASHRAE 55, the industry standard for thermal comfort.

Building materials were carefully selected to promote good indoor air quality. All interior materials—from the carpeting to the adhesives, paints, coatings, and sealant—have been screened to limit VOCs and other chemical content.

To reduce contamination during construction, the design team provided a suggested sequence of finish installation for the contractor. The

On the entry level, a double-height space spills light from above into the lobby outside the main conference room. The main conference room beyond has large floor-to-ceiling windows; the lower panels of the windows are operable, and doors open directly into the garden.

sequencing is based on installation of wet materials that off-gas as they cure prior to installation of dry, fleecy materials, because the latter can adsorb contaminants and reemit them over time.

Material Resources

The team specified building materials that limit environmental impacts, waste, and pollution throughout their life cycles. This included natural materials, local materials, and materials made from renewable resources and/or materials with recycled content.

LOCAL MATERIALS
The building lobby uses granite flooring from local quarries in Virginia.

HEALTHY MATERIALS
All paints, stains, and adhesives have low VOC content. All solder for basic piping materials, underground utilities, and pipe fittings is lead free. The team specified low-VOC joint and seam sealers for all mechanical joints and seams, as well as low-VOC gypsum board joint compound.

RENEWABLE MATERIALS
Cork flooring is used in typical office floor elevator lobbies, and linoleum is used instead of sheet vinyl for pantry and copy room floors.

All wood material came from sustainably managed forests, as certified by a Forest Stewardship Council-accredited certification agency. The ash wood veneer doors use a "character-grade" wood, which makes use of wood that would otherwise be considered waste.

RECYCLED CONTENT MATERIALS
Site furnishings are made entirely of recycled plastic. Tectum, a formaldehyde-free, 100 percent recycled cellulose fiberboard product, serves as the backing for fabric panels in conference centers. Other materials with recycled content include ceiling tiles, insulation, steel, aluminum, and gypsum board.

RECYCLING
Each office floor contains a pantry and copy/fax/printer area with recycling and trash bins incorporated into the millwork base cabinets. The ground-floor loading dock accommodates the storage and staging of recyclables.

A chute system was considered for recyclables, but was not included in the final design because it had a negligible effect on maintenance costs and no real effect on recycling rates. It was determined that recycling rates would depend on the provision of convenient collection areas and the commitment of the staff, not the method used to convey materials to the ground floor.

CONSTRUCTION WASTE RECYCLING
Cost-effective recycling of construction waste was a priority for the Conservancy. Prior to the start of construction, the general contractor evalu-

ated options to determine whether waste should be separated on-site or off-site. The decision was made to have waste materials separated off-site for recycling instead of separating on-site because of space limitations on the site and the cost associated with using multiple containers.

The lobby uses granite flooring from local quarries, white walls for displays, and accents of wood, which is used sparingly as a precious material. All wood is from certified sustainably managed forests that meet the Forest Stewardship Council guidelines.

Benefits of the Design

The Conservancy's new headquarters offers an alternative to the typical suburban development model that has improved energy efficiency and reduced environmental impacts as well as a bright and airy office environment at no additional first cost. The project demonstrates that environmental improvements are possible even within a limited budget and the market constraints typical of speculative office development.

The site, previously a surface parking lot with some contaminated soils, is now a positive amenity at the center of town. In fact, the property values of three bordering residential high-rise buildings went up substantially with the creation of the native plant garden.

The Metropolitan Washington and Virginia Chapters of Associated Builders and Contractors has also recognized the project with an Excellence in Construction Award in the category for interiors under $25/SF.

Monsanto Company
A-3 Leadership Team Offices

St. Louis, Missouri

Building Size: *35,000 SF office floor renovation; site design/parking lot*
Site: *One floor of a building on Monsanto's 210-acre corporate campus*
Completion: *March 1998*
Cost: *Confidential*

The new offices for Monsanto's Leadership Team are a 35,000 SF renovation of an existing executive office floor in a 1950s-era building at Monsanto's suburban St. Louis headquarters campus. Monsanto wanted the renovation to create a new kind of office environment that would promote cultural changes within the company. HOK collaborated with Holey Associates and Rocky Mountain Institute's Green Development Services on this interior design project that included some improvements to the base building.

Environmental Goals

Monsanto has made a commitment to move toward more environmentally friendly design and construction for all of its facilities projects.

Design Overview

The existing 1950s-era building was typical of many others on the campus. A number of changes over the years—including a dark film placed over the original clear glass—had blocked interior spaces from the building perimeter, creating many dark, uninviting spaces.

Monsanto asked the design team to create space that encouraged dynamic new work styles based on communication, collaboration, and creativity. To do this, the new offices—including those of senior executives—contain 100 percent open workstations. The space also provides several dens for private work, "parlors" for meetings, nonterritorial drop-in space for visitors, a coffee bar and cafes, and several collaborative team spaces.

Special spaces include a retreatlike library, a media center for videoconferencing, and meeting rooms dubbed "Greenhouse" and "Silo." The entire design is deliberately noncorporate and casual.

Monsanto wanted the renovation to create a new kind of office environment that would promote cultural changes within the company. In terms of both creative design and commitment to the environment, the project has served as a prototype for subsequent Monsanto office renovations around the world.

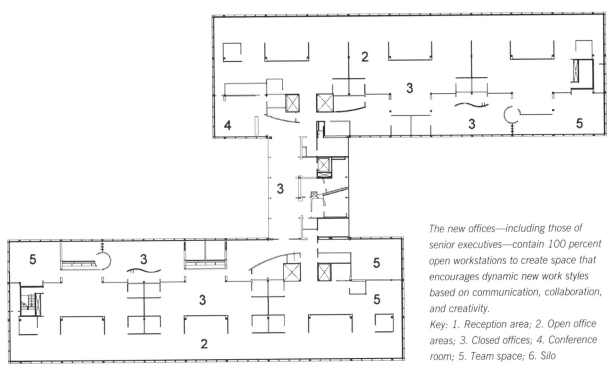

The new offices—including those of senior executives—contain 100 percent open workstations to create space that encourages dynamic new work styles based on communication, collaboration, and creativity.
Key: 1. Reception area; 2. Open office areas; 3. Closed offices; 4. Conference room; 5. Team space; 6. Silo

Monsanto Company, A-3 Leadership Team Offices

Special spaces include a retreatlike library, a media center for videoconferencing, and large meeting rooms dubbed "Greenhouse" and "Silo." The entire design is deliberately noncorporate and casual.

Upgrades were also made to the building envelope to improve comfort and reduce energy consumption. The existing steel frame structure had been reclad with granite panel over the existing metal panel construction in the 1980s; however, the exterior wall had not been insulated, there was little roof insulation, and the single-pane glass was not replaced.

The renovation design includes installation of a secondary wall—dubbed the "climate wall"—that was built inside the existing wall, to form a relatively inexpensive double envelope that cut heat loss and infiltration dramatically.

Design Process

FAST-TRACK SCHEDULE

The project was fast-tracked, with a total design and construction period of six months. Despite the many user reviews and stringent environmental requirements—some of which required extensive product research—the project was completed on time. The early purchasing of materials helped keep construction moving.

INTEGRATED DESIGN PROCESS

The project began with a two-day meeting in which the design team and Monsanto facilities staff developed a common understanding of sustainable design issues and opportunities that would influence the design.

This session was followed by a series of four parallel charrettes: one for basic programming, one for conceptual design, one for mechanical and system decisions, and another for construction sequencing and procurement. Sustainable design issues were implicit in each.

The design team was scattered across several cities—potentially a problem for meeting the quick schedule. But biweekly conference calls kept the team together and the information flowing throughout the process. In most calls, environmental issues merited their own dedicated area on the meeting agenda. This ensured that the team remained focused on these goals along with the schedule and budget.

ENERGY MODELING

Energy modeling began along with programming, enabling the team to evaluate strategies prior to developing the final design. Early energy models indicated that loss through the exterior envelope and high air infiltration were problems in the existing facility.

Because the buildings had not been submetered, the team could not calculate the specific energy consumption of the A3 building. The base case energy model thus was based on overall consumption throughout the campus, modified to reflect the specific geometry, orientation, and characteristics of A3. As the design progressed, the energy model was updated and refined.

Site

HOK also designed a parking lot to provide secure parking for Monsanto executives, which provides an important pedestrian link from the research campus to the cafeteria.

The fifteen-car parking lot is located in a gardenlike setting, in an expanse of tall native Missouri grasses that obscures many of the cars from pedestrian view. Plantings were chosen for their hardiness and their low water and maintenance requirements.

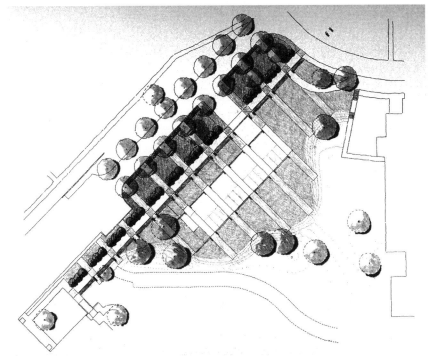

The parking lot, which occurs along an important pedestrian link from the research campus to the cafeteria, has been integrated into the overall landscape design that is taking shape on the campus. Hardy, low-maintenance grasses and native Missouri wildflowers, which bloom throughout the growing season, are transforming the corporate campus into a gardenlike setting while creating habitat for wildlife.

Monsanto Company
Nidus Center for Scientific Enterprise

St. Louis, Missouri

Building Size: 41,770 SF

Site: Northeast corner of Monsanto's 210-acre corporate campus

Completion: Fall 1999

Cost: $9.7 million for building, interiors, and site work ($232/SF)

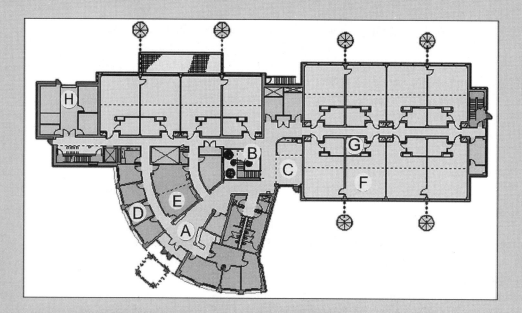

Highlights of the Design

■ The landscape design introduces native plantings rich in color and texture, including native river birch, cinnamon fern, flowering dogwood, and Moonbeam coreopsis. No in-ground irrigation system is needed. Instead of the standard turf grass, buffalo sod is being planted.

Red maples, little bluestem grass, granite chat pathways, and limestone columns line both sides of the pathway and focus the pedestrian movement along this line toward the cafeteria. Mixed in with the grasses are native Missouri wildflowers, which bloom throughout the growing season. Once established, the grasses will require only periodic mowing or burning.

Energy

The team hoped to reduce A3's overall energy consumption by 75 percent. Primary energy conservation strategies included control of infiltration, a high insulating value for the walls and roof, strict control of electric light-

- A single HVAC system serves both lab and non-lab spaces, resulting in greater fresh air flows and better air quality for the office and conferencing areas. The air that passes through the office spaces is then recirculated in the laboratory zones. Use of a combined system decreased initial cost, simplified operations, and reduced future maintenance requirements.

- An "extract air" system separates the general lab exhaust from the fume hood exhaust. Separation of the airstreams allows the exhaust air to be run through thermal wheels, to reclaim heating and cooling, and to preheat incoming fresh air. The system uses enthalpy wheels, which recover more than 50 percent of the waste heat.

- Two galvanized, aboveground cisterns collect rainwater from the roof and store it for site irrigation. This system saves water and associated pumping energy while reducing the load on site drainage and storm sewer systems.

- Indoor air quality will be enhanced by a "living wall" of indoor plants in the atrium, which provides for natural air filtration. Air supply diffusers located at the base of the wall promote airflow through the plant material. A Monsanto plant scientist who specializes in plants for indoor air quality is providing guidance on plant selection.

- The design team specified locally manufactured brick and metal roofing. Earth fill, concrete, CMU block, steel, drywall, doors, and window blinds were also available locally. Overall, more than 60 percent of the materials used to construct the building have been acquired from within a 300-mile radius, and more than 50 percent of the materials contain significant recycled content.

- All of the interior materials, including paint, adhesives, and finishes, are low-VOC. The waste management subcontractor provided separation of materials for recycling off-site. Asphalt, concrete, metals, cardboard, and plastics were all recycled.

- The Nidus Center has been accepted as one of the pilot projects for the initial launch of the LEED Green Building Rating System. As a participant in the pilot stage of the rating system, the Nidus Center has contributed to the refinement of this important market incentive program for green buildings. The team expects to receive a silver rating.

ing, maximum use of daylight, and the incorporation of high-efficiency (Energy Star) equipment.

Several potential strategies simply were not feasible for the renovation of just one floor. These included heat recovery, a raised floor for distribution of air and cable management, and making the main mechanical spaces more efficient. These ideas will be reconsidered when the entire building is renovated.

CLIMATE WALL

One challenge was improving the poor performance of the existing forty-year-old curtain wall, which had recently gone through a cosmetic

Red maples, little bluestem grass, granite chat pathways, and limestone columns line both sides of the pathway and focus the pedestrian movement along this line toward the cafeteria.

upgrade. The wall's single glazing and excessive infiltration rates resulted in high energy consumption for space conditioning systems and poor thermal comfort for occupants.

The team considered replacing the single-pane glass with insulated glass in the existing frames, but energy models showed less-than-desirable returns—mainly because of the inability to thermally break the existing aluminum frame.

After evaluating several retrofit options, the team chose to build a secondary wall—dubbed the "climate wall"—inside the existing wall.

The climate wall consists of an inner glazed surface (installed during the renovation) and an outer weatherproof envelope (the existing wall) that together form an inexpensive, efficient double envelope. The existing exterior wall was insulated with foam from the inside and the drywall portion was insulated with mineral fiber batts.

This solution creates an air circulation path between the two walls. As air leaves the room at room temperature and passes though this outer chamber, or cavity, it is drawn into the return air system. The air movement through the climate wall neutralizes thermal conduction losses of the exterior glass, during both heating and cooling seasons, and does not allow this load to transfer into the space.

Blinds are located within the double wall cavity to intercept the solar load before it passes into the space. The transfer air passes through the cavity, washing across the blinds and removing the solar energy, which would otherwise be converted into heat and reradiated into the room. The neutral-temperature room air in the air cavity keeps the surface temperature of the inner glass at nearly the same temperature as the room. This improves comfort at the window wall by eliminating mean radiant temperature differences from the envelope and its negative comfort impacts.

The envelope enhancements allowed the perimeter finned tube radiators to be removed, eliminating simultaneous heating and cooling.

The size of the glass within the new wall matches that of the existing glass. The existing dark film simply was removed from the exterior glass. Frameless clear glass panels in the climate wall slide in a track, providing access to the space between the interior and exterior glass for maintenance.

The double envelope concept has been used on several U.S. buildings and in Europe. Though typically employed for new construction, it was attractive for the A3 renovation because it did not require removing the existing curtain wall and allowed individual floors to be renovated in phases. This approach also avoided waste generation and disposal costs that would have been associated with removal of the exterior wall.

DAYLIGHTING

To bring daylight into the center of the floorplate, the ceiling slopes from a high point at the building's exterior wall down toward the interior. Skylights were added to the interior to draw in additional daylight.

LIGHTING

Energy-efficient indirect lighting fixtures with occupancy and daylight sensors were used throughout the space to optimize the lighting design.

Personal lighting controls allow users to dim lighting above individual workstations—handheld remote units "memorize" individual preferred light levels and automatically restore light levels when the workstation is occupied.

Desktop occupancy sensors automatically dim lighting to 10 percent of the full power setting when workstations are not occupied. Programmable time-clock controls turn off all lighting after office hours.

Water

All on-site fixtures were replaced with equipment that exceeds the requirements of the U.S. Energy Policy Act of 1992.

Material Resources

Materials were selected based on overall environmental performance and their ability to showcase the wide range of environmentally preferable materials readily available from commercial suppliers.

MATERIALS SELECTION

The team required manufacturers and suppliers to describe the overall life cycle impact of their raw material, including source, production, installation, use, and subsequent disposal. Key issues included use of recycled materials, emissions from manufacturing techniques, dyes, and impact on indoor air quality.

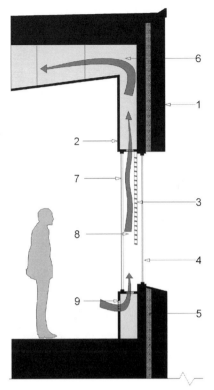

The climate wall consists of an inner glazed surface, which was installed during the renovation, and the existing wall, which forms an outer weatherproof envelope. Together the walls form an inexpensive, efficient double envelope. The existing exterior wall was insulated with foam from the inside and the drywall portion was insulated with mineral fiber batts.
Key: 1. Existing wall; 2. New interior wall; 3. Adjustable louver blinds; 4. Existing window system; 5. New rigid insulation; 6. Plenum space; 7. Sliding temperature glass panel; 8. Return air

Energy-efficient indirect lighting fixtures with daylight sensors were used throughout the space to optimize the lighting design. Desktop occupancy sensors automatically dim the lighting to 10 percent of full power when workstations are not occupied.

Materials were selected based on overall environmental performance and their ability to showcase the wide range of environmentally preferable materials readily available from commercial suppliers. Here, the "Greenhouse" uses sustainably harvested wood for doors and paneling.

The materials used in the A3 renovation included cork, composite veneers, wheatboard, water-based paints, recyclable carpet, recycled plastic made into fabrics, cork, terrazzo, and linoleum.

The design team explained the logic behind each material selection to users so they can pass on this information to visitors.

REUSE AND RECYCLING

The team identified several components from the existing space for salvage and reuse in the office renovation. Monsanto was able to save 50 percent of the ceiling grid; the tile was taken apart during demolition, cleaned, and reused. Demountable partitions and high-efficiency light fixtures were reused elsewhere on the campus.

To promote recycling by staff and visitors, recycling collection bins were built into the millwork at all coffee bars and copy/business centers.

Benefits of the Design

The leadership group's new workplace has reaffirmed to all Monsanto employees the company's commitment to innovation, change, and a sustainable future.

Both in terms of creative design and commitment to the environment, the project has served as a prototype for subsequent Monsanto office renovations around the world.

The design team has made regular visits to the new space to monitor its performance over time. These visits have confirmed that virtually all the energy-efficient materials and systems have performed well. The only "problem" seems to be the constant stream of visitors who want to tour the space.

The team has used these informal postoccupancy evaluations to guide subsequent campus renovation and new building projects.

Nortel Networks, Brampton Centre

Brampton, Ontario, Canada

Building Size:	*855,000 SF*
Site:	*56 acres*
Completion:	*Original consolidation, 1996; Westside expansion, 1998*
Cost:	*U.S. $77/SF for buildings, interiors, and site work*

Brampton Centre is a renovation project that has transformed a 680,000 SF, 1963-vintage switching manufacturing complex into Nortel Networks' new world headquarters. The first phase was completed in 1996, and an additional 100,000 square feet of space was converted in 1998, after the last of the manufacturing operations had moved out. HOK provided programming, architectural and interior design, and planning for these renovation projects; the Canadian firm B&H was architect of record.

Environmental Goals

With the shift from manufacturing to a service-based economy, high-tech companies can end up with an overabundance of industrial real estate. When companies abandon large-scale industrial facilities—whether in a mature suburb such as Brampton or in an inner city—the result can be devastating for area businesses and residents.

In addition to benefiting the community, Nortel Networks' decision to recycle this industrial facility instead of building on a greenfield site conserved the land, energy, and natural resources that would have been required to manufacture a new headquarters.

The goal for the facility was to strategically satisfy Nortel Networks' asset management and business evolution needs while reinforcing its companywide commitment to environmental responsibility.

Design Overview

The project has transformed a single-story high-bay manufacturing space into a quality office environment for about 3,500 employees.

Brampton Centre was conceived of as a virtual city with a tremendous variety of public spaces, private work areas, and team neighborhoods that are organized using city planning concepts, complete with boulevards, plazas, side streets, and shortcuts. Skylights and light courts enliven the space and provide a sense of orientation for the "residents."

A curvilinear glass wall marks the entry to the recycled factory that has become Nortel's new world headquarters. The glass facade encloses a welcoming, light-filled, two-story atrium space that provides a glimpse of the work environment beyond.

Brampton Centre was conceived of as a virtual city with a tremendous variety of public spaces and private work areas that are organized using city planning concepts, complete with boulevards, plazas, side streets, and shortcuts. Skylights and light courts enliven the space and provide a sense of orientation for the "residents."

Nortel Networks, Brampton Centre

The office interiors have been developed as "next wave" offices, with each of the office work groups creating its own environment based on a defined "kit of parts." The result includes a diverse range of solutions from traditional cubicles and closed offices to more chaotic, process-driven, team-based space. The space has also been adapted to accommodate employees who telecommute, hotel, or use one of the many "touchdown stations" scattered across the city.

Economics

At \$77/SF for architecture, interiors, and landscaping, the savings Nortel realized based on its decision to renovate an existing structure were significant. The renovated building shell, which turned out to be a very exciting space to inhabit, cost about half as much as constructing a new building.

Many design enhancements were included within the renovation budget, based on the high value Nortel Networks places on its employees. Skylights, courtyards, and gardens built within the building floor area were "extra" expenses in terms of added cost and increased gross floor area; however, they were also seen as essential to the overall success of the project and the productivity and creativity of the workforce.

Design Process

In 1994, convinced that Nortel Networks' space in three Class A, high-rise towers in the Toronto area could no longer support its burgeoning space requirements, the company's corporate real estate group began to explore new options for housing its workforce. Financial, work process, and growth models suggested that reusing the company's outdated digital switching factory in the Toronto suburb of Brampton was a viable solution.

An indoor courtyard in the "city" invites social gatherings and get-togethers as well as intellectual activities such as playing chess.

Nortel Networks
New Technology Building

Harlow, England, U.K.

Building Size: 103,000 SF
Site: 43 acres
Completion: February 1998
Cost: £100/SF ($162/SF)

The team used the British Research Establishment Environmental Assessment Method (BREEAM), an environmental scoring system that awards points to facilities based on a comprehensive list of environmental criteria, as a tool during the design process. The New Technology Building design score of 39 was 13 points more than the 26 required to achieve a rating of "excellent." After completion of the building, the facility received an official BREEAM certification of "excellent" from an independent field assessor.

INTEGRATED DESIGN PROCESS

Intensive work sessions with the full design team—architects, interior designers, engineers, contractors, facilities management, building engineers, and future users—produced a highly inclusive, collaborative design effort that condensed the overall design and construction schedule. Because the design for their new facility was actually created on-site, in sessions that ran continuously for a week at a time, a large cross section of the future building users were able to participate in the process.

The first session was dedicated to goal setting and concept design. Together the team identified important concepts such as the metaphor of the city, the focus on daylight in the workplace, reuse of materials, and others. Next, a full inventory of the existing building was presented as well as a preliminary analysis of the mechanical system options. By the end of the first session the design concept was complete. The following sessions were used to collaboratively develop and refine every detail.

Renovations of older buildings can be uncertain, leading to delays and unexpected costs. By the time the contractor began selectively deconstructing and rebuilding, he had participated in every design decision and was intimately familiar with the building and its contents.

Site

To "re-green" the site, existing fences were replaced with native landscape materials and numerous trees and shrubs were planted. Additional open green space was reclaimed from land that had previously been used for surface parking.

Energy

To "re-green" the site, existing fences were replaced with native landscape materials, and numerous trees and shrubs were planted. Additional open green space was reclaimed from land that had previously been used for surface parking.

The building envelope was upgraded to conserve energy. Measures included replacing the existing factory windows with double-pane, low-E windows and insulating the previously uninsulated exterior concrete block walls.

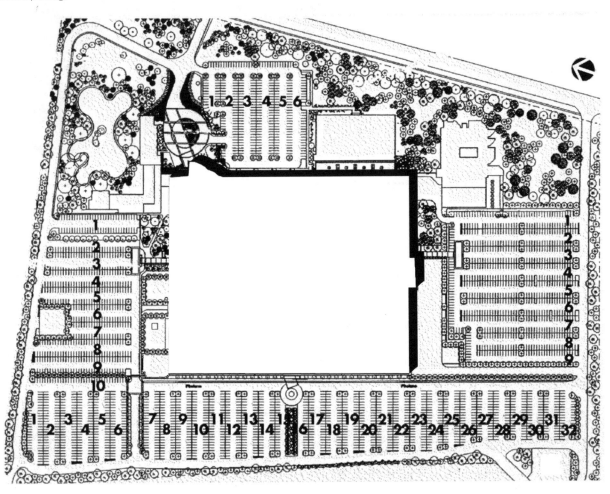

High-efficiency HCFC-free and CFC-free chillers replaced the facility's old chillers. A new DDC energy management system was installed, which greatly conserves lighting and energy required to heat and cool.

DAYLIGHTING

The key to the lighting strategy was to use natural daylight from windows, skylights, and outdoor plazas to create a pleasant work environment and to conserve energy. To take best advantage of natural light, Brampton Centre created zoning bylaws that require construction of high partitions to occur along an east-west axis.

At the building's entry, the designers replaced an existing brick facade with an east-facing, curvilinear glass wall that offers a glimpse into the work environment and creates a transparent, daylit circulation spine. Using this glass facade to enclose space between the recycled factory and an adjacent building also created a light-filled, two-story atrium to welcome employees and visitors.

Inside the office floorplate, light monitors with clerestory windows illuminate circulation routes, and nineteen skylights were punched into the 23-foot-high sky-blue ceilings to draw in additional natural light to help orient people in the space. Seven indoor public parks were cut into the floorplate. One of the parks, a 60-by-30-foot open-roof Zen garden, surprises visitors and provides a reflective space for employees.

EFFICIENT LIGHTING

Artificial lighting supplements the daylight. The existing metal halide shop floor fixtures were dismantled and reballasted to provide energy-

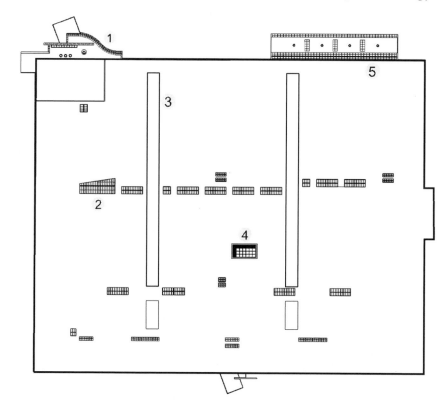

Roof plan shows all skylights, including existing roof monitors with clerestory windows, and skylights over the Zen garden and the cafeteria.
Key: 1. Building entry; 2. New skylights; 3. Refurbished roof monitors; 4. Zen garden; 5. Cafeteria

Seven indoor public parks were cut into the floorplate. One of the parks, a 60-by-30-foot open-roof Zen Garden, surprises visitors and provides a reflective space for employees.

efficient lighting without disposing of the existing fixtures. Where mezzanine space was installed, high-efficiency fluorescent fixtures, recessed into the intermediate ceilings, supplement general lighting for offices. Occupancy sensors conserve lighting energy in closed offices and conference rooms.

Water

The design team improved the water quality of an existing pond, where sediment had built up over time, by introducing a new filtration and circulation system to increase the water's oxygen levels. Today the rejuvenated pond provides a haven for flora and fauna, including water lilies and a flock of Canadian geese.

Indoor Environment

The use of natural daylight from skylights, indoor plazas, and gardens creates a pleasant work environment and provides office workers with a connection to nature. The team removed doors, loading docks, and portions of the building facade to increase daylight and provide views. Varied wall heights, from low near the windows to high near the back of the space, allow natural light to pass through the office space.

Material Resources

The mandate for Brampton Centre's design team was to reuse and recycle as much as possible, to keep costs down while also conserving resources. The decision to renovate had preserved the embodied energy and resources already invested in the factory's frame, roof deck, floor slabs, steel, concrete, windows, and other materials. Finishes that were added during the renovation were used sparingly.

Instead of installing new light fixtures, the design team wrapped existing shop floor fixtures in decorative shrouds and added louvers to help fit them into a modern office environment.

The HOK Guidebook to Sustainable Design

An abundance of natural light entering the office floor through skylights and light monitors enables employees to work creatively. One of the touchdown stations where everyone can take advantage of natural light is the cafeteria, which is an infill space between the manufacturing plant and an adjacent office building.

Rather than spending time and money hiding functional elements such as wiring and cabling, the design team presented "technology in action." Electrical and communications raceways, which were mounted on the building's structural support columns, became known as "utility trees," and were even painted green. In addition to salvaging existing cabling and cabling trays, the team reused ducts, distribution panels, electrical transformers, and portions of firewalls.

RECYCLING WASTE MATERIALS

Brampton Centre was designed to promote extensive recycling of waste by the building occupants. Nortel Networks estimates that more than half of Brampton Centre's waste materials will be recycled. Annual estimates for this recycling stream are shown below.

Recycle Category	Annual Tons
Mixed paper	172
Cardboard	93
Scrap metal	32
Food organics	30
Confidential paper	23
Beverage containers (cans/bottles)	15
Polystyrene	3
Estimated Annual Total	368 tons

Benefits of the Design

Headquarters buildings offer companies a rare opportunity to make a public statement about their values and culture. Brampton Centre makes an eloquent statement of what is most important to Nortel Networks: its customers, its employees, and the environment.

The industrial makeover at Brampton Centre has been so well received—both within and outside Nortel Networks—that the company's real estate group believes it has established a new benchmark for Nortel Networks' facilities.

Instead of spending time and money hiding functional elements such as wiring and cabling, the design team presented "technology in action." The building's structural columns became "utility trees," to support electrical and communications raceways.

ECONOMIC BENEFITS

Nortel Networks expects that the U.S.$50 million renovation will save the company nearly a quarter of a billion dollars over the next decade. That figure is based on a reduced lease cost of $29 per square foot, versus $30 to $50 per square foot for their previous leases, $100 million in capital costs savings for not building a new building, and reduced costs for maintenance, support, and interbuilding travel.

Because of the greatly enhanced workplace that has been created, Nortel also expects to see a substantial increase in productivity and creativity of its workforce.

BUSINESS WEEK/ARCHITECTURAL RECORD AWARD

In 1997 the facility won the prestigious *Business Week/Architectural Record* Award, which is sponsored by the American Institute of Architects. The award—which was developed to recognize architecture's ability to solve corporate problems, increase the productivity of workers, and boost the bottom line—is a testament to the use of creative, environmentally responsible architecture to support business goals.

S. C. Johnson Wax
Commercial Products Headquarters

Racine, Wisconsin

Building Size:	*250,000 SF*
Site:	*52 acres*
Completion:	*Summer 1997*
Cost:	*$34.75 million for building, interiors, and site ($139/SF)*

S. C. Johnson Wax's new Commercial Products Headquarters is a 250,000 SF office and laboratory facility that includes a cafeteria, conference center, and fitness center. HOK was the design and sustainable design consultant; Zimmerman Design Group was the architect of record for architecture and interiors.

Environmental Goals

The project mandate, to be a model of environmental responsibility, came directly from Mr. Samuel C. Johnson, then chairman of S. C. Johnson and a member of the President's Council for Sustainable Development. Mr. Johnson, who wanted the building to serve as a benchmark for environmentally responsible design and construction, believed the building could do this only if built within conventional cost parameters. His charge to the team was to create the most advanced, environmentally responsible building possible without adding to the overall cost.

Design Overview

S. C. Johnson expected that the design of its new world headquarters and R&D facility would help the company meet its goals for increased productivity. The building design supports S. C. Johnson's business objectives by consolidating business and research units in a way that enhances communications.

The compact, almost square-shaped building and floor plan is based on an L-shaped block of labs and supporting offices along two sides of the building and an L-shaped block of offices on the other two sides. Bridges spanning a daylit atrium link the labs and offices. Within the center of the atrium are common support spaces for interaction such as conference rooms, lounge areas, stairs, and elevators.

The charge to the team was to create the most advanced, environmentally responsible building possible without adding to the overall cost.

The floor plan is based on an L-shaped block of labs and supporting offices and an L-shaped block of offices on the other two sides. Bridges span the daylit atrium to link the labs and offices. Spaces for interaction such as conference rooms, lounge areas, stairs, and elevators are located within the atrium.
Key: 1. Open offices; 2. Conference area; 3. Coffee area; 4. Lab offices; 5. Labs; 6. Specialty labs; 7. Mechanical; 8. Terrace; 9. Toilets

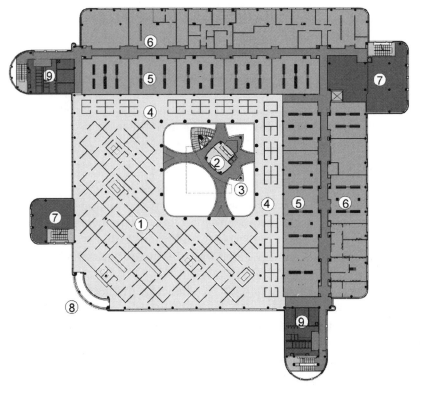

The design moves S. C. Johnson's people out of private offices and into 100 percent open office space to encourage communication and collaboration. Researchers and their laboratories are grouped a short distance from the corporate business groups supporting their efforts, making it easy for development teams to work together.

The team designed generic laboratories that will serve a variety of research needs over time as the company refines and develops new products. Assigned research laboratories are on the inside of the lab sectors; the offices just outside their labs are adjacent to the atrium and common functions. Walls between labs and lab office areas are glass, allowing researchers to remain in close contact with their labs and each other while maintaining a separation of lab and office functions.

Economics

The team's goal was to make the project a model of sustainable design within conventional cost parameters.

At approximately $130 per square foot for the building and $9 per square foot for the site, the facility was built well within S. C. Johnson's budget and 10–15 percent below the U.S. average for comparable office and lab buildings.

The close, collaborative process that was utilized to design the facility helped keep pricing down. Because the bidding climate was so noncompetitive when the project went to bid, it was sometimes difficult for the construction manager to find subcontractors. Looking back, the team believes that the integrated design process not only supported the focus on environmental design issues, but also familiarized the entire team (including contractors and subcontractors) with the project from its early stages.

Design Process

The unique design process was critical to the team's success in meeting the ambitious organizational and environmental goals. The same outcome could not have been achieved within a traditional design-bid-and-build process.

The team was also challenged by a tight schedule. Programming was completed in June 1995, the design concept was accepted in July, and construction began in late August. Initial move-in started in late March 1997, with final move-in and site work completed in early summer of 1997. This meant that the team made decisions quickly and had little opportunity for backtracking.

TEAM BUILDING

The creation of an inclusive, integrated design team was key to the success of the project. The architects, interior designers, laboratory designers, structural engineers, MEP engineers, daylighting consultants, construction manager, major subcontractors, key suppliers, and the eventual

3M Company, Austin Center

Austin, Texas

Building Size: 1,750,000 GSF
Site: 162 acres
Completion: June 1989
Cost: $101/SF

building manager worked together with S. C. Johnson's project manager, user representatives, and chief financial officer throughout the design process.

Because only a few team members had experience with sustainable design, the project began with a series of educational events. Outside speakers were brought in to talk to the entire team about environmental issues. These discussions were followed by a series of goal-setting sessions in which the team defined issues and opportunities. Spending time up front discussing what they wanted to achieve environmentally—and why—helped guide the team throughout the process. As a result, the team developed an "eco-efficient project statement" that read:

> The facility promotes sustainable development by adding value to the business and the environment. The following principles will be used as key decision criteria: energy efficiency, pollution prevention, risk reduction, waste minimization (approach zero waste), communication of environmental actions, and biodiversity.

This statement was developed into a decision matrix that included detailed subcriteria supporting the six criteria identified in the mission statement.

The design features regional architectural concepts, including courtyards and punched window openings, and the use of local materials. The "paseo," or atrium street, brings diffuse natural light through skylights deep into the building interior. CRS (now HOK) provided architecture, engineering, and interior design and landscape design services.

Highlights of the Design

- The xeriscaped landscape design features a native plant palette, including Texas wildflowers. The site was revegetated with native long-stem blackland prairie grasses that had been overgrazed and lost during the previous hundred years.

- The design protects nesting habitat for the golden-cheeked warbler, an endangered species with an extremely restricted breeding range. In addition, an adjacent 200-acre site was designated as a permanent habitat preserve.

- The atrium skylight is equipped with 3M's passive daylight management system to bring daylight deep into the interior atrium.

- Each of two 20-cylinder (greater than 8,000 hp) natural gas engines generates 6 MW of power, and a steam turbine generates an additional 1.5 MW of electricity.

- Four stormwater detention and filtration ponds capture runoff from parking areas to protect the ground and aquifer beneath from contaminants.

- Native limestone found on the site was recovered during excavations and reused for foundations and site work.

The decision matrix was then used to evaluate the impact of every material, system, and process in terms of the environment, budget, schedule, and risk.

WHOLE TEAM WORK SESSIONS

The entire team met in all-day work sessions once a week for much of the project. This allowed every team member to stay in contact not just with the standard issues of a fast-track project, but with the evolution of the project's environmental design strategies. Members of the design team remained together from the beginning of the design process through completion of construction.

The early effort relied heavily on developing a "positive tension" among the multidisciplinary team. To align theory with what was actually practical, the team worked together to determine which solutions were feasible and cost-effective. The group reduced risk by using readily available, proven design systems and materials. The focus was on "thinking smarter" and incorporating state-of-the-market—rather than state-of-the-art—solutions.

COMPUTER MODELING AND LARGE-SCALE MOCK-UPS

As the design progressed, the team questioned each component and process to achieve the most with the least amount of resources. Energy modeling guided the team as they searched for optimized design solutions that integrated internal equipment loads, lighting systems, exterior form and massing, window and skylight detailing, and landscaping with mechanical and electrical systems.

Daylight modeling relied on two parallel paths. LAM Lighting Design used its own software to test daylighting levels, using large-scale models equipped with daylighting sensors. At the same time, a University of Wisconsin team used Lumen Micro v. 6 software to analyze each proposed design. The physical models were compared to the computer modeling, and when the results from the two methods were inconsistent, the team would meet to determine why and then make the appropriate modifications. Only after the two working groups achieved the same results from the software-based model and the physical model would the team move forward.

CONSTRUCTION PROCESS

The number of people involved in a project swells substantially as suppliers and subcontractors begin work on their portions of the building. That is why construction is such a key phase in the delivery of an environmentally responsible facility.

The most important aspect of the construction process was the early participation of general contractors M. A. Mortenson and Riley Construction. These contractors were included in early discussions about sustainability, beginning with the initial team-building and conceptual design phases and continuing through move-in.

To educate subcontractors about the environmental goals, the contractor conducted periodic reviews of environmental issues for the foremen of various trades. This on-site education, modeled after their traditional approach for stressing job safety issues, helped the team keep its focus on the critical environmental issues during the rapid construction process.

This clear definition of environmental issues and goals also freed the construction team to discover its own solutions. Many innovative construction waste management accomplishments, for example, came from the job site team during the project buyout.

LEED GREEN BUILDING RATING SYSTEM

S. C. Johnson's project was evaluated during construction using a just-released draft of the LEED Green Building Rating System developed by the U.S. Green Building Council. This evaluation helped shape some late decisions and provided feedback to the council on the draft rating system.

Site

The 52-acre site, which is contiguous to the company's main worldwide production facility in Racine, was once a farmer's field and had virtually no trees when S. C. Johnson began to develop the project.

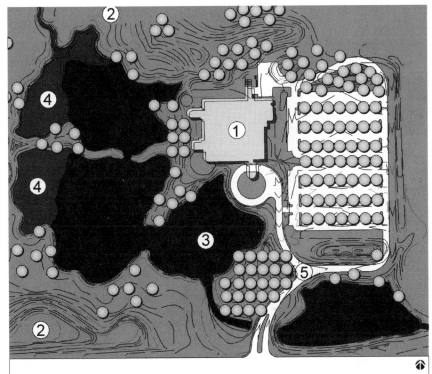

The site was restored with drought-tolerant plants, including prairie grass, wildflowers, and other native species. A portion of the site was set aside for orchards; vegetable and herb gardens produce food for use on-site. Manicured landscaping is limited to the area surrounding the main entry and cafeteria.

Key:
1. World Professional Headquarters building
2. Native grassland planting
3. Holding ponds
4. Wetlands
5. Fruit orchards

Early in the site analysis, the team discovered a major regional drainage system beneath the site. The water flowing onto the site was fairly polluted from upstream agricultural fields and a series of parking lots. Finding a solution to both the volume and quality of the water became a priority.

To clean contaminated upstream runoff before it would be released downstream into the river, the team designed a series of holding ponds and constructed wetlands. Water leaving the site is now much cleaner than when it enters the site.

LANDSCAPING

Most of the site was restored with drought-tolerant plants, including prairie grass, wildflowers, and other native species. A portion of the site was set aside for orchards, along with vegetable and herb gardens that produce food for use on-site. The only manicured landscaping is a small part of the site around the main entry and cafeteria.

The reliance on indigenous, low-maintenance plants instead of turf grass limits the need for fertilization, pesticides, and irrigation, saving S. C. Johnson as much as $3,000 per acre in annual maintenance costs. However, early plantings on the site and in the ponds have not performed as well as expected. The team believes that latent weed killers used when the site was a farm have hindered the growth of these plants.

Energy

Energy studies projected that the building's gross annual energy consumption would be approximately 73,000 BTU/SF—about 60 percent

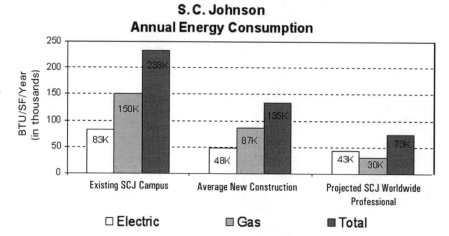

less than the average for similar buildings operating 40 hours per week. Based on the International Facility Management's Association (IFMA)'s statistics for average new construction in Wisconsin, this reduced energy consumption will save S. C. Johnson nearly $100,000 per year. To date, actual energy savings have been greater than predicted, with heating less expected and electric use higher than expected. This energy performance was the result of an integrated design process that included all team members.

DAYLIGHTING

An important element influencing the building design was the desire to maximize daylight. Daylight provides the majority of ambient lighting in the open office areas, reducing the electrical and cooling loads generated by light fixtures. Daylighting was also important from a humanistic standpoint, to create a pleasant working environment.

On the building's south and west faces, large windows with light shelves draw daylight into the building. The 14-foot floor-to-ceiling height was a result of the need for a 17-foot-high slab-to-slab dimension that was required in laboratory areas to accommodate piping and ducting. Light shelves bounce daylight into the building interior of the building while cutting off most direct radiation into the space. Automated translucent roller shades provide additional sun control for low-angle sun during morning and early evening hours.

In its first few years of operations, the team determined that the window shades in the south and west walls were incorrectly placed at the window head above the light shelf, rather than at the bottom of the light shelf. As a result, when light sensors lowered the shades to reduce glare on the bottom half of the windows, the shades also blocked the upper portion of the windows—cutting off the daylight to the interior. This meant that the interior lights were on more than expected, adding to the building's electricity use for lighting and cooling load. S. C. Johnson now plans to correct the position of the blinds.

Daylight provides the majority of ambient lighting in the open office areas. Light shelves bounce daylight into the building interior of the building while cutting off most direct radiation into the space.

Daylight also is introduced into the building through a central atrium. Light scoops at the edges of the atrium direct daylight down to the floors below. With daylight coming from both sides of the 88-foot-deep floorplate, the brightness contrast from one side to the other is minimized. Glass in the partitions between lab offices and the labs allows the daylight from the central atrium to extend into the labs.

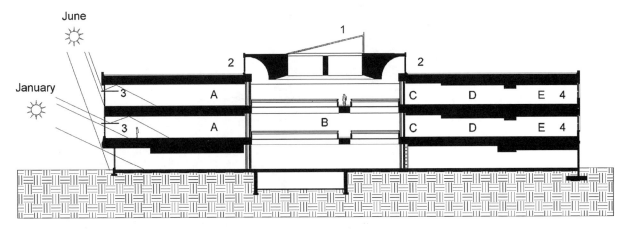

Daylight is also introduced into the building through a central atrium. Light scoops at the edges of the atrium direct daylight down to the floors below.

S. C. Johnson Wax, Commercial Products Headquarters

ELECTRIC LIGHTING

The typical office lighting, except a few special display areas, is by indirect pendant-mounted high-efficiency fluorescent fixtures, with photoelectric dimming controls and occupancy sensors.

Labs have high-efficiency fluorescent direct/indirect pendant fixtures. The direct lighting component aids sample inspections at the lab bench, while the indirect component provides high-quality overall lighting that reduces shadowing.

PERSONAL ENVIRONMENTAL CONTROLS

The building's office area has a raised-floor system that accommodates cable management and serves as the primary air supply. This raised floor acts as a charged air plenum to deliver conditioned air to any location on the floor.

Air is distributed to each individual workstation through a Johnson Controls Personal Environmental Module (PEM), which brings air from the floor plenum to the desktop. PEM controls include air diffusers, which are mounted on the desktop to allow each individual to control temperature, air movement, lighting, and white noise levels in his or her workstation. Occupancy sensors shut off the system when the individual leaves the space.

Because this PEM system reduced the requirements for installed HVAC capacity, it offered considerable first cost savings. And by providing conditioning at each workstation, the supply air temperature can be higher than typically possible in office buildings of this type. This reduces energy consumption for operations.

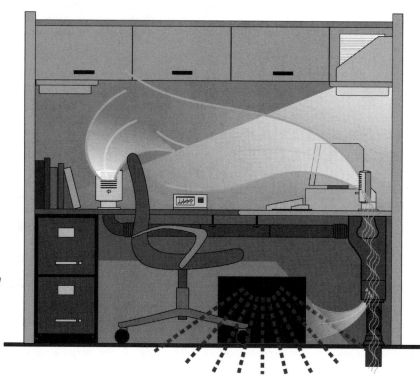

Air is distributed to each individual workstation through a Johnson Controls Personal Environmental Module (PEM), which brings air from the floor plenum to the desktop. PEM controls include air diffusers, which are mounted on the desktop to allow each individual to control temperature, air movement, lighting, and white noise levels in his or her workstation. (Image courtesy of Johnson Controls, Inc.)

This modified displacement ventilation system decreases the quantity of air that needs to be conditioned, because it allows air temperatures to stratify in the space. Conditioned air is supplied low, where people and equipment in the space heat the air, which then naturally rises to the ceiling to be exhausted. Ventilation effectiveness is increased with this system while fan energy requirements are reduced, further reducing overall energy consumption.

HEAT RECOVERY

Even though laboratories require frequent air changes, making them high energy users, S. C. Johnson's 72,000 SF of labs conserve energy through the use of a heat recovery wheel.

The heat recovery wheel recovers both sensible (temperature) and latent (moisture) energy, with four levels of protection against cross-contamination, including a 3 Å molecular sieve desiccant coating. Because it allows for transfer of moisture as well as heat, greater quantities of outside air can be provided without sacrificing efficiency. The system is reliable, low maintenance, and low in operational cost, and it provides good humidity control.

CONTROLS

A microprocessor-based facility management system (FMS) controls all air handling units, chillers, boilers, terminal units, and so on. Manually operated fume hood sashes conserve energy, by enabling occupants to reduce the volume of air changed in labs when the fume hood is not in use.

Water

High-efficiency plumbing fixtures with low-flow flushments, aerators, flow-restricting nozzles, and automated shutoffs are used throughout the building to conserve water use.

Outside, the reliance on indigenous plantings means that little water is required for irrigation. Parking lot runoff passes through on-site below-grade filters before flowing back into the lake system.

The team considered, but did not install, a gray water system. Much of the facility's water is generated within the labs and thus is not recyclable.

Indoor Environment

The indoor environment contributes to S. C. Johnson's goal of increasing productivity by creating a facility that is bright and airy and enhances the comfort of building occupants. The integrated use of daylighting, together with the PEM system, creates an enhanced environment that offers occupants control of their own temperature, airflow, lighting, and acoustics within an open office environment.

INDOOR AIR QUALITY

Good indoor air quality begins with source control, or limiting the amount of potential contaminants introduced into the building. The team specified

The indoor environment contributes to S. C. Johnson's goal of increasing productivity by creating a facility that is bright and airy and enhances the comfort of building occupants.

low-emissions, nontoxic materials, finishes, and furnishings throughout the facility. S. C. Johnson also prohibits smoking in the facility.

Laboratory, copy center, and food preparation areas—which have potential for high concentrations of air contaminants—are isolated with separate exhaust systems.

Ventilation, another critical aspect of air quality, exceeds ASHRAE 62-89 guidelines for acceptable indoor air quality. All supply and return ducts are carefully located to optimize airflow.

CONSTRUCTION PROCEDURES

Dry, fleecy materials, such as carpeting and ceiling tile, can adsorb contaminants from materials curing during construction and then rerelease chemicals over time. Specifications required that the construction be sequenced so that wet materials would be installed first to provide time for them to cure, and for any chemical off-gassing to occur, before the dry materials were installed.

After construction and before employees occupied the building, the building was flushed out with 100 percent outside air.

Material Resources

Because this was a fast-track project, there was little time for materials research and selections had to be made quickly. Most of the building materials came from HOK's Healthy and Sustainable Building Materials

Database, which rates the relative environmental impact of material choices and provides product-specific environmental information.

The team specified materials that, within budget and performance limits, were deemed the right choice for the environment over their entire life cycle. Life cycle cost was considered together with environmental criteria such as recyclability and reusability, impact on indoor air quality, and whether the raw material sources were sustainable. To fill gaps in existing information, additional research was done by the team and by the University of Wisconsin, Milwaukee.

The business of S. C. Johnson Worldwide Professional is to provide products and services that help maintain buildings. This means the company has many business alliances with material suppliers. It was important to S. C. Johnson that the building include an array of these materials for demonstration purposes. This was achieved while maintaining the overall environmental criteria.

EXTERIOR MATERIALS

The predominant exterior material is brick veneer on a precast concrete unit (CMU) backup—both are durable, low-cost materials that are manufactured locally. Expanded polystyrene insulation was used instead of the more commonly used extruded polystyrene, because it is made without HCFC blowing agents.

INTERIOR MATERIALS

Low-VOC paints and adhesives, and formaldehyde-free medium density fiberboard (MDF) substrates for millwork, were selected to reduce impacts on indoor air quality. Mineral fiber ceiling tiles that were selected are high in recycled content. Wood used in the facility is birch and maple from local sources.

Metalwork is either stainless steel or powder-coated metal; powder coating is a finishing process that eliminates waste and pollution.

Flooring materials include solution-dyed carpet, which has improved color retention and reduces water use for manufacturing; linoleum, which is made from natural, renewable materials; rubber flooring, which is made from 100 percent recycled rubber; concrete and terrazzo, which are highly durable.

The construction manager checked initial material selections for price and schedule implications. In many cases, materials were selected without competitive bids but secured through negotiation by the construction manager.

CONSTRUCTION WASTE

The construction team recycled 86 tons of construction material waste, including metal, glass, wood, cardboard, concrete, and drywall. The team also required materials suppliers to remove pallets and packaging, and made scrap wood available to local residents. Additionally, the construction manager arranged to have many products delivered to the site without packaging by wrapping materials in reusable blankets instead.

ONGOING WASTE MANAGEMENT

The team designed the building to accommodate recycling of paper, glass, aluminum, plastic, and cardboard. All employees received information about S. C. Johnson's recycling goals in move-in information packets.

Today, an employee-led task force is attempting to move the company away from paper and toward electronic communication.

Benefits of the Design

The team proved that it is possible to develop a design that satisfies a large organization's critical functional needs while using proven, cost-effective methods to set a new standard for environmentally responsible building. To date, the building has proven extremely popular with users and visitors.

S. C. Johnson's willingness to share its unique project process, costs, successes, and even problems has equipped other organizations with practical information for developing their own sustainable facilities.

U.S. Environmental Protection Agency Environmental Research Center

Research Triangle Park, North Carolina

Building Size: *1.1 million SF*

Site: *133 acres*

Completion: *2001*

Cost: *$225 million for building, interiors, and site (including central plant and garages)*

The new EPA campus in Research Triangle Park, North Carolina, is a 1.1 million SF research and administrative facility that will house one of the largest multidisciplinary groups of environmental scientists in the world. This campus of laboratory and office buildings is under construction, with completion expected early in 2001. HOK provided programming, site planning, architecture, interior design, lab design, and landscape design services for the project.

Environmental Goals

The U.S. Environmental Protection Agency (EPA) exists to protect the environment. Designing and building this massive new environmental research center presented the agency with an extraordinary opportunity to demonstrate its environmental ethics.

EPA's goal was to balance concerns related to cost, function, and the environment as every decision was made, to improve building performance and limit environmental impacts within their fixed design and construction budget. If done right, the agency believed, its facility could become a real model for the greening of other public and private sector facilities, helping advance sustainable design and construction as an industrywide practice.

Design Overview

The EPA's new research center is located on a 133-acre site within a 500-acre federal parcel dedicated to environmental and public health research. Laboratory facilities for the National Institute of Environmental Health Sciences (NIEHS) are located across the lake.

The site, which had once been farmland, was densely covered with second-growth hardwoods and conifers. At the high point of the site, a wooded knoll is home to the site's oldest trees; at the low point, a series of

Designing and building a research center for one of the largest multidisciplinary groups of scientists in the world presented the EPA with an extraordinary opportunity to demonstrate its environmental ethics. The design embeds the new campus into the rolling terrain, allowing large portions of the landscape to remain intact. Parking garages built into the hillside reduce the need for surface parking.

small wetlands fronts a 23-acre man-made lake. Distinct ridges and valleys mark the 60-foot drop to the lake's edge.

The design embeds the new campus into the rolling terrain, allowing large portions of the landscape to remain intact. Parking garages built into the hillside reduce the need for surface parking. The campus buildings—four five-story laboratory blocks, three office blocks of three stories, and a six-story office block—are linked by a series of enclosed atrium spaces that provide a main street of circulation for the complex.

The new campus will house over two thousand people and six hundred lab modules. Laboratory types include wet labs, materials testing labs, destructive testing labs, automobile testing labs, animal labs, and special high-bay labs.

Economics

The project was built within a fixed first cost budget. Life cycle cost analysis was used to evaluate options; however, all upgrades that required a first cost investment had to be offset with reductions in other areas.

GREEN VALUE ENGINEERING

Throughout the design process, the issue of cost, and particularly the cost of green design strategies, was under careful scrutiny. In addition to ongoing analysis of options by the cost consultant, who was a member of the design team, EPA chose to engage in focused value engineering (VE) reviews.

In aggregate, the VE cost reduction exercises produced a greener building. One reason the VE sessions were so successful was that the inclusive process, which involved the design team, allowed for informed, interdisciplinary brainstorming to occur. Also, the team recognized the importance of looking at the project and the budget as a whole, not simply line by line.

Design Process

First and foremost EPA made a commitment to design and build a green building. From there, they proceeded to inject sustainability goals into each stage of the project planning, design, and construction process.

PROJECT PLANNING

The program of requirements (POR) contained broad-based environmental design considerations that were supported by detailed descriptions of features to be considered during the design process.

In addition to the requirements detailed in the POR, the architect/engineer (A/E) contract contained specific deliverables for indoor air quality, energy analysis and reports, site surveys, specimen tree studies, and an environmental assessment. In anticipation of construction and operations of the facility, the contract required an indoor air quality facilities operation manual and a building acceptance test manual, to support improvements in energy performance, indoor air quality, and construction quality overall.

GOAL SETTING

EPA held a two-day-long kickoff session for all key team members at the outset of the project, for goal setting and team building. When the entire team agreed that environmental design and functionality were the two most important goals for the facility, environmental performance expectations expanded beyond the collection of contract requirements for specific studies and reports to become a core issue for the design team.

PERFORMANCE BENCHMARKS

When the project began, in 1991, the sustainable design movement was still in its infancy, and consensus had not yet emerged on what issues should be considered or how success would be measured. Performance benchmarks, which compare building performance against established norms, were actively sought out to help the entire team identify typical and improved performance.

MATERIALS RESEARCH

Fairly early in the design process, the team determined that they needed in-depth information about products from specific manufacturers, to enable side-by-side comparisons of available options. HOK initiated an independent effort, using a product questionnaire that was sent to every manufacturer considered for use in the project, to systematically gather life cycle environmental impact information about products.

COMPUTER MODELING

As the design team evaluated options, models and evaluation tools that simulate future performance became essential aids to decision making. The team used Trace for energy modeling, Lumen Micro and physical models for daylighting evaluation, and Exposure for indoor air quality modeling. Computer and physical models were also used for water quality calculations and airflow modeling in the labs.

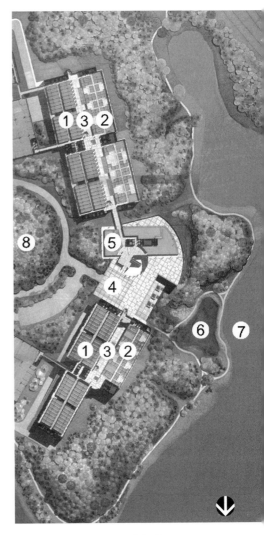

The campus buildings are linked by a series of enclosed atrium spaces that improve energy efficiency while providing a main street of circulation for the complex.
Key: 1. Laboratory building;
2. Office building; 3. Atrium;
4. Entry plaza with conference center below; 5. Office tower with cafeteria below; 6. Wetland pond;
7. Pond; 8. Wooded knoll

EMISSIONS TESTING

An emissions testing program was developed to evaluate the potential impact of building materials on indoor air quality. To make the program manageable, materials were targeted for testing that are used in large quantities in the office buildings only—testing of materials for the laboratories was deemed less important because of the high airflow in those spaces.

A set of threshold values was established to determine the concentration of contaminants that would be permitted in the indoor air, based on what experts determined to be both acceptable and achievable. When emissions are measured in terms of indoor air concentrations, the design team has an indication of what air quality will ultimately be like in the building prior to occupancy.

GREEN SPECIFICATIONS

To diminish the possibility that either contractors or subcontractors could claim to have misunderstood requirements that are not typical in the industry, division one of the specifications was used to highlight environmental requirements.

At the very beginning of division one, a new section entitled "Environmental Requirements" succinctly stated EPA's environmental goals for the project, whereas "Environmental Certification of Materials" was created to provide a preview of all the individual environmental performance requirements that would appear in the detailed specification sections that followed. Other unique division one sections included "Baseline Indoor Air Quality Testing," "IAQ Testing of Materials," "Site Protection," and "Construction Waste Materials Management and Recycling."

GREENING THE TEAM

Recognizing that optimal sustainable design strategies rely on synergy, the team collaborated across disciplines to find the best solutions. Even though that collaboration required the team to spend more time in meetings, the design process as a whole turned out to be more efficient. EPA and HOK each designated an environmental advocate to guide the design from within the team, while also reaching out to the local sustainability network for additional support.

EPA also organized a voluntary committee from within its own ranks, called the Pollution Prevention Committee, to support the design effort. The committee developed an extensive list of specific green design strategies to be considered during the design process. Some of the members of that group remained involved as advisors to EPA to assist during design reviews.

Site

The site design accommodates the building, site work, and infrastructure in a coordinated plan to maintain existing open space and habitat areas, increase groundwater recharge, and make use of natural filtration strategies.

MINIMIZE SITE DISRUPTION

To reduce site disturbance, the team challenged the master plan, which required a four-lane road with a median on a campus that receives only local traffic. Instead, a two-lane road was built that required 40 percent less paving, saved acres of trees, and provided a much more appropriate appearance to the entry for the facility. Site utilities were routed under the roadways or within areas already disrupted by construction.

Structured parking further decreased the overall size of the development footprint, and incentives for carpooling and alternative means of transportation were developed so the parking requirement could be reduced by more than 30 percent.

STORMWATER

Grassy swales instead of curb and gutter were used at the edge of roadways to the greatest extent possible to encourage water to "sheet-flow" over vegetated areas, naturally filtering contaminants as the water percolates through the soil.

Stormwater runoff from roadways and parking areas will be treated naturally using a water quality pond in combination with ten smaller "pocket wetlands" tucked into the woodland environment. A water quality pond at the south end of the site will retain as much as 0.5 acre-feet of water (160,000 gallons) in a constructed retention area filled with wetland plantings to filter and cleanse the water. The "pocket wetlands" for bioretention are filled with subsurface compost and plant material to enhance filtration, retention, and infiltration of stormwater.

While bioretention was new in North Carolina prior its use by EPA, it has recently been identified by the North Carolina Department of Environmental Management as a Best Management Practice for others to follow, largely because of their positive experience with the EPA campus project.

By challenging the originally planned four-lane road and instead building only a two-lane road, the team was able to minimize site disturbance and maintain existing open space and habitat areas. Stormwater runoff from parking areas will be treated naturally using a water quality pond in combination with ten smaller "pocket wetlands" tucked into the woodland environment.

WILDFLOWER PLANTINGS

Natural woodlands and wildflower plantings have been used in place of turf grass. This minimizes the need for irrigation, fertilizer, and pesticides—and brings down maintenance costs. The woodlands and wildflowers, meanwhile, are beautiful and more appropriate to the natural setting.

WETLAND GARDEN

To replace a small wetland lost due to roadway construction, an existing quarter-acre wetland near the building cafeteria was enlarged and planted with native species to create a wetland garden. The other wetland areas—which cover over nine acres of land where the site's drainage swales meet the lake—were protected by a 100-foot-wide buffer that supports only mulch pathways for walking and jogging.

PLANT RESCUE

"Plant rescues" were held to physically remove plant material from within the site clearing limits before they were destroyed. Volunteers

Natural woodlands and wildflower plantings have been used in place of turf grass. A small wetland, lost due to roadway construction, was replaced by enlarging an existing quarter-acre wetland near the building cafeteria, which was planted with native species to create a wetland garden.

were invited to remove thousands of native plants from areas slated to be cleared and replant them elsewhere on the site, on the NIEHS campus across the lake, or at their own homes. Staff from the North Carolina Botanical Gardens took ferns and other native plants back to the gardens in Chapel Hill.

Energy

The team used simple, low-maintenance upgrades to the architecture, lighting, and HVAC systems to generate considerable energy savings.

IMPROVED ENVELOPE DESIGN

Heat gain is reduced through the building envelope because roof and exterior wall surfaces are light-colored, with high albedo ratings. The typical precast concrete facades also provide some sun shading because of the depth of the cladding. To shade large glass areas on the cafeteria and conference center, a horizontal trellis was introduced that supports deciduous vines.

Infiltration is controlled with air barriers and positive pressurization. Air locks are provided at all building entries. All-aluminum window frames are thermally broken, which improves comfort and eliminates condensation that could lead to the growth of mold and mildew.

Because of the mild climate, insulation use is moderate. High-performance, low-E coated insulating glass screens out unwanted heat; the atrium skylight and elevations with direct southern or western exposure were upgraded to use an improved low-E glass with an even higher shading coefficient.

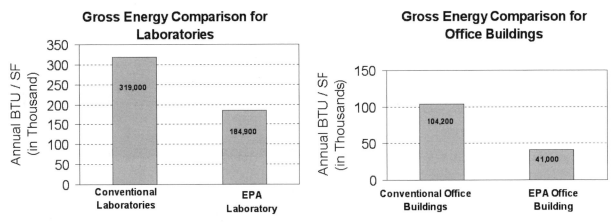

Gross Energy Comparison for Laboratories

Annual BTU / SF (in Thousand)

- Conventional Laboratories: 319,000
- EPA Laboratory: 184,900

Gross Energy Comparison for Office Buildings

Annual BTU / SF (in Thousands)

- Conventional Office Buildings: 104,200
- EPA Office Building: 41,000

Use of energy-efficient systems and passive solar architectural design strategies reduces the facility's energy use by 40 percent compared to U.S. Department of Energy statistics for comparable lab and office buildings. Based on energy modeling, the EPA lab buildings will consume about 185,000 BTU/SF/yr, and the office buildings will consume about 41,000 BTU/SF/yr.

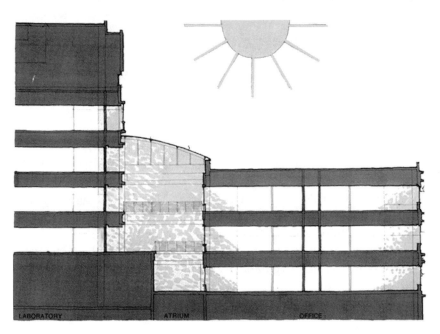

The atrium reduces heat gain and loss through the building envelope while bringing natural light into the building. Computer modeling determined that the skylight provides ample daylight for office areas while cutting peak energy use in the atrium by two-thirds compared to an all-glass skylight with high-performance glazing.

ATRIUM SKYLIGHT

The atrium reduces heat gain and loss through the building envelope, while bringing natural light into the building. Only 26 percent of the skylight is covered with high-performance glass; the rest is covered with translucent and opaque polymer panels. Computer modeling determined that the skylight provides ample daylight for office areas while cutting peak energy use in the atrium by two-thirds compared to an all-glass skylight with high-performance glazing.

LIGHTING

Office space planning supports daylighting through the use of light-colored finishes, low partition heights, and a planning concept in which almost 50 percent of the perimeter is dedicated to open-office workstations so that light can penetrate into interior office areas. The

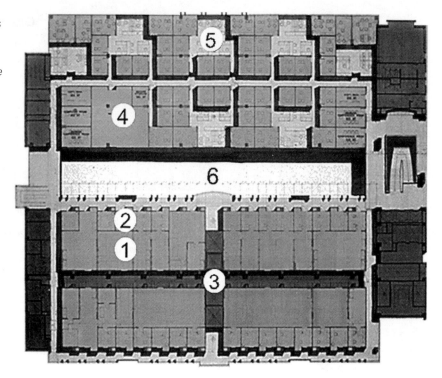

connected load for office lighting is 1.1 W/SF; with the occupancy sensors and daylight dimming, the actual load will be about half that.

Laboratories use direct/indirect pendant fixtures complemented with task lighting, to increase efficiency and provide better-quality lighting that minimizes shadows on the work surface. The indirect/direct lighting scheme has a connected load of 1.38 W/SF, compared with 1.85 W/SF, for a direct lighting scheme using high-efficiency fixtures.

LED exit signs and efficient accent lighting are used throughout the facility, which saves energy and also reduces maintenance requirements for relamping.

EFFICIENT LABORATORY DESIGN

The laboratories use low-maintenance solutions that do not require expensive operator training. The laboratories use two-position airflow control for night setback, which is linked to occupancy sensors to ensure safe operations. To further conserve energy, the fume hoods were designed to operate at an 80 percent sash height; 100 percent sash openings will be used only in setup mode.

MEP SYSTEMS

High-efficiency building systems include VAV systems with efficient fans and motors and variable-speed drives. A simple "straight" VAV system is used, which reduces fan energy requirements, with a minimum of three air changes per hour to maintain airflow. Air handling units monitor pressure drop across filters and alert maintenance staff when they need to be changed, to improve the efficiency of fans.

High-efficiency chillers and boilers were used in the central utility plant, and part load efficiencies were carefully considered. To optimize operating efficiency, multiple chillers are used in operation and an additional redundant chiller has been provided, so full or very slight loading can be avoided.

Outside air economizer cycle operation, also known as "free cooling," allows the air handling units to operate at up to 100 percent outdoor air mode when the temperature and humidity outdoors allow. Enthalpy controllers sense relative humidity and protect the building from overly humid air.

DDC central control systems will control all of the HVAC systems and many of the electrical components. Full systems commissioning, which includes a separate testing and start-up procedure for the DDC controls, will enable future operators and maintenance personnel to enhance their understanding of the systems.

HEAT RECLAIM

Because of the low government rate for electricity and the moderate climate in North Carolina, use of a heat reclaim system was not cost-justified. The final design was developed with space reserved for a future system, based on the strong likelihood that heat reclaim will become cost-effective in the future.

Water

Use of indigenous landscape materials and wildflowers contributed to water conservation of about 250,000 gallons of water per month (summer) while providing first cost savings because no irrigation system was required.

Efficient plumbing fixtures with low-flow flushments, aerators, flow-restricting nozzles, and automated shutoffs reduce water use in the facility.

WATER-EFFICIENT COOLING TOWERS

The cooling towers utilize a dynamic water analysis system that allows blowdown to be minimized, reducing water and chemical use. By increasing the cycles of concentration from the industry standard of 6–8 to 12–14, approximately 4 million gallons of water are saved per year.

Indoor Environment

The design team had the unique opportunity to develop an IAQ program together with the same EPA researchers who had provided indoor air criteria for the landmark State of Washington program. Together they worked to minimize potential sources of contamination during design and construction and to develop an integrated IAQ management plan for the operations and maintenance phase.

SOURCE CONTROL

In contrast to traditional methods for ensuring good indoor air quality, which rely almost exclusively on ventilation strategies, source control strategies attempt to completely eliminate potential sources of contamination. Strategies included carefully locating intake and exhaust air sites, limiting fibrous materials, and avoiding sites of microbial growth. By carefully selecting building materials, finishes and adhesives, emissions of volatile organic compounds, and other toxic and irritating substances were reduced.

Internal duct lining was prohibited as a preventative measure, to avoid possible contamination of the ductwork over time. Buildings built without internal duct lining require larger ducts and careful planning of mechanical room layouts so that sound can be attenuated.

SOURCE ISOLATION

Source isolation strategies were used to control contamination in the building that could not be completely eliminated. For example, desktop copiers were moved out of office areas into copy rooms. Laboratories and chemical storage areas, copy areas, food prep areas, loading docks, and toilet rooms each have dedicated outside exhaust; negative-pressure relationships are maintained to further discourage unwanted air flows.

SOURCE DILUTION

Source dilution refers to ventilation and filtration of building air to dilute airborne contaminants. Filtration has been enhanced to 85 percent efficiency, and ventilation standards were developed so that the building could operate with ventilation rates 20 percent greater than those required by ASHRAE 62-89, to accommodate potential unforeseen circumstances. Ductwork in the office areas was designed with flexible connectors for easy relocating, so adjustments can be made over time to improve ventilation effectiveness.

EMISSIONS TESTING

To predict the off-gassing of various materials during construction and occupancy, the team reviewed MSDSs and emission testing results. As a further precaution, the contractor was required to engage in emissions testing of the actual assemblies of materials, including adhesives and finishes, which were proposed for use in office areas.

Materials were tested using ASTM Standard D5116-90, "Standard Guide for Small-Scale Environmental Chamber Determinations of Organic Emissions from Indoor Materials/Products." Any material assemblies that contributed more than one-third of the allowable indoor air concentration for the specified contaminants would undergo further analysis prior to acceptance.

IAQ CONSTRUCTION PROCEDURES

To protect IAQ and lower overall construction costs, the team proposed an alternative to the extended postconstruction flush-out period that was required by the state of Washington program. Instead, the specifications for the EPA campus include construction sequencing and continuous ventilation during construction, together with baseline indoor air quality testing.

Prior to construction the contractor was required to submit a schedule describing the sequence of finish installation, to verify that wet materials, which can off-gas as they cure, would be installed before dry, fleecy materials, which can adsorb contaminants and rerelease them over time. To provide further protection from contaminants, temporary ventilation with 100 percent outside air is required from the time the building is significantly enclosed until occupancy.

After construction is complete and prior to occupancy, baseline indoor air quality testing is required to verify that indoor air concentrations of contaminants fall below maximum allowable limits. Based on predictive modeling using EXPOSURE, a program developed by EPA researcher Les Sparks, the team was able to demonstrate that use of low-solvent, low-emissions materials as specified, combined with ventilation during construction, would meet the prescribed thresholds. As an

TABLE 1

SUGGESTED MAXIMUM INDOOR AIR CONCENTRATION STANDARDS TO ENSURE GOOD INDOOR AIR QUALITY IN REGULARLY OCCUPIED BUILDINGS

A set of threshold values was established to determine the concentration of contaminants that would be permitted in the indoor air, based on what EPA experts determined to be both acceptable and achievable. After construction is complete and prior to occupancy, baseline indoor air quality testing is required to verify that indoor air concentrations of contaminants fall below maximum allowable limits.

Indoor Contaminants	Allowable Air Concentration Levels*
Carbon monoxide (CO)	<9 ppm
Carbon dioxide (CO_2)	<800 ppm
Airborne mold and mildew	Simultaneous indoor and outdoor readings
Formaldehyde	<20 $\mu g/m^3$ **
Total volatile organic compounds (TVOC)	<200 $\mu g/m^3$ **
4 phenyl cyclohexene (4-PC)***	<3 $\mu g/m^3$
Total particulates (PM)	<20 $\mu g/m^3$
Regulated pollutants	<NAAQS
Other pollutants	<5% of TLV-TWA

*All levels must be achieved prior to acceptance of building. The levels do not account for contributions from office furniture, occupants, and occupant activity.

**Above outside air concentrations.

***4-PC is an odorous contaminant constituent in carpets with styrene-butadiene-latex rubber (SBR).

TLV-TWA: Threshold Limit Value–Time Weighted Average.

Source: Facilities Operation Manual for EPA campus in Research Triangle Park, NC

enforcement measure, the contractor is required to ventilate the building until it meets the established limits, and repeat the testing if the initial air quality testing results are not successful.

IAQ MANUAL

The *Indoor Air Quality Facilities Operation Manual* was both an end product and a method for tracking issues throughout the design process. Interim IAQ reports were produced at each major design milestone to document the design and to advance work on the manual itself. The manual includes procedures for monitoring IAQ during occupancy, and it documents design decisions for building operators so that future building renovations will not inadvertently undermine air quality.

Material Resources

MATERIALS SELECTION

The team selected building materials that minimized environmental impacts over their full life cycle and that were durable, low maintenance, and locally manufactured to the greatest extent possible. The team engaged in extensive research to identify preferred interior, exterior, and site materials and then to develop performance-based specifications mandating specific improvements that could be met by a competitive range of manufacturers.

Material selections include local brick, local recycled-content concrete, and CMU; wood from certified sustainable sources; low-VOC water-based paints, adhesives, caulks, and sealant; and recycled-content products such as asphalt paving, cast-in-place concrete, steel studs, insulation, wood fiberboard, gypsum board, ceiling tile, and rubber floor tile.

Carpeting uses solution-dyed fibers, has a water-impermeable backing that improves durability, and is recyclable. Solution-dyed carpeting is recommended for better color retention and because, generally, less water is used in its manufacture, although some manufacturers have begun to use closed-loop systems for fiber dying.

Detailed specifications ensure compliance with environmental requirements for recycled content, limits on chemical emissions, and prohibitions against the use of hazardous materials.

FLEXIBLE DESIGN

Design flexibility conserves resources by minimizing the impact of future changes. Modular lab and office designs ensure that lights, ceilings, sensors, sprinklers, and building services remain intact when changes are made, reducing renovation expenses and limiting material disposal.

The campus will accommodate recycling of paper, glass, aluminum, plastic, and cardboard. A lower-level service tunnel links collection points at elevator cores to a staging area with compactors at the loading dock.

REUSE OF SITE MATERIALS

The contractor for the EPA campus salvaged all cleared timber for either sawlogs or pulpwood and ground the remaining debris into mulch with

The contractor used a portable rock crusher to process excavated material from site excavations. The crushed rock was reused as structural fill and backfill throughout the site. After construction completion approximately 75 percent of all construction waste will have been recycled, including concrete, brick, metals, glass, carpet, wood, gypsum board, cardboard, and paper.

portable tub grinders. The contractor used a portable rock crusher to process excavated material from site excavations. The crushed rock was reused as structural fill and backfill throughout the site.

ON-SITE BATCH PLANT

A portable concrete batch plant was erected on-site, at the contractor's option. Environmental benefits included reduced truck traffic to and from the site and establishment of a zero-waste operation on-site. A roto-reclaimer was installed to eliminate concrete delivery truck waste by reclaiming the sediment. Fine and coarse aggregates are separated out, and the remaining cement settles in a series of holding tanks. When settling is complete, the concrete is reclaimed and reused, and the clean water is recovered and returned to the system to wash the next truck.

CONSTRUCTION WASTE MANAGEMENT

When construction is complete, approximately 75 percent of all construction waste will have been recycled, including concrete, brick, metals, glass, carpet, wood, gypsum board, cardboard, and paper.

Separation of materials for recycling occurs on the floors, with debris going into special waste-handling carts instead of chutes. Local businesses are using the drywall scrape for soil additives for landscaping, scrap metal is being recycled into metal reinforcing bars, and concrete waste is crushed and reused as aggregate. By the time construction is complete, an estimated 1,500 tons of material will have been diverted from local landfills.

Benefits of the Design

The EPA's new campus illustrates the potential to limit environmental and health impacts while developing an attractive, productive, and cost-effective workplace. The EPA hopes it will contribute to the ongoing dialogue on sustainable design and encourage others to do the same.

Specifically, this project gave momentum to professionals defining improved standards for indoor air quality and environmentally preferable materials. The EPA has distributed the *Indoor Air Quality Facilities Operation Manual* to many interested professionals, as the procedures documented in it describe a proactive approach to protecting indoor air quality. The research on materials has also reached many professionals, as it formed the basis of an ongoing research project at HOK to develop its Healthy and Sustainable Building Materials Database, which is available to the public on-line.

As an additional benefit, significant reductions in long-term operating costs will result from the conservation of energy, water, and materials; waste recycling; and the use of low-maintenance landscaping. Energy-efficient measures alone are expected to save the EPA more than $1 million per year.

GREEN OPERATIONS AND MANAGEMENT
The EPA is planning to carry its focus on the environment into the operations of the new facility as well. Procurement of recycled content paper and supplies, two-sided copying, transportation alternatives, and aggressive waste recycling are just some of the initiatives under development. To recycle valuable organic materials, a composting area is being set up for landscaping debris, and a large vermiculture system is planned to handle food waste from the cafeteria. The EPA's goal is to raise awareness among its research staff, while reducing wasteful practices in their day-to-day routines.

This case study was adapted from an EPA publication entitled *The Greening Curve: Lessons Learned in the Design of the New EPA Campus*, which was produced with EPA funding under order number 7D-2124-NTLX. For more information on the EPA campus, see http://www.epa.gov/rtp.

Smithsonian Institution National Air and Space Museum, Dulles Center

Fairfax County, Virginia

Building Site:	*700,000 SF*
Site Area:	*176.5 acres*
Completion:	*2003*
Cost:	*$160 million for architecture, interiors, furniture, and site work*

The Smithsonian Institution's new National Air and Space Museum (NASM) Dulles Center, scheduled for completion in 2003, is located at Washington Dulles International Airport in northern Virginia. The center will display more than 180 aircraft and 100 spacecraft, including the space shuttle *Enterprise*, the B-29 Superfortress the *Enola Gay*, and an SR-71. HOK provided master planning, architecture, engineering, interior, and landscape design for the project.

Environmental Goals

By limiting environmental impacts related to construction and operation of the facility itself, the design goals support the mandate of NASM to "memorialize aviation and space flight...while also using the history of flight and its technology to illuminate the impact of human activity on the environment."

Because photovoltaic technology was developed by researchers involved with the U.S. space program, the Smithsonian identified the installation of building integrated photovoltaics on the new facility as a goal with particular educational value.

NASM and the Smithsonian were also influenced by the recently published executive orders mandating that federal facilities consider sustainable design opportunities. The requirement to utilize all life cycle cost-effective energy-efficient building technologies fit with their need to closely control operational costs associated with the facility.

By limiting environmental impacts related to construction and operation of the facility itself, the design goals support the mandate of NASM to "memorialize aviation and space flight . . . while also using the history of flight and its technology to illuminate the impact of human activity on the environment."

Design Overview

Dulles Center is being built on the southern end of Dulles property, to provide easy access to an active runway for transporting aircraft. The facility will include a 215,000 SF main exhibit hangar, several other exhibition areas, an archival resource center, a restoration hangar with public observation areas, educational facilities, a large-format theater, an auditorium, restaurants, museum shops, and an observation deck for visitors to watch Dulles air traffic.

The building massing consists of three parts: the curved transparent "landside" building, housing public amenities and office space; a large aircraft hangar serving as the main exhibit space; and a rectangular "airside" building for the space hangar, restoration, and storage. A strong cross axis connects the pedestrian walkway from the parking areas, through the main entrance hall, to the overlook for the main exhibition hangar. The main entrance hall creates a daylit circulation spine that draws visitors into the main exhibition hangar.

Economics

The $160 million required to build the new Dulles Center ($130 million for the building and $30 million for site work) is being generated through donations from individuals, corporations, and foundations. The current National Air and Space museum on the Mall in Washington, D.C., is the world's most frequented museum, and the Smithsonian and Virginia officials project that the Dulles Center will attract two to three million visitors per year.

Because operating expenses must be appropriated from public funds, the Smithsonian is strongly in favor of design strategies that would reduce those costs.

A strong cross axis connects the pedestrian walkway from the parking areas, through the main entrance hall, to the overlook for the main exhibition hangar. The main entrance hall creates a daylit circulation spine that draws visitors into the main exhibition hangar.

LIFE CYCLE COSTING

Life cycle costing was used throughout the process to guide decision making. Because the project budget was fixed, however, increased investment in one area had to be offset with reductions in another. The iterative design process and detailed analysis were employed so that more expensive design options could be offset by other economies, such as downsizing equipment.

OFF-BUDGET FEATURES

Because their use could not be justified based on conventional life cycle economics, a separate fund-raising effort was initiated to support the use of photovoltaics. BP Solarex has donated photovoltaic cells and inverters for the building, and the Virginia Initiative for Solar Energy, a partnership between state utilities and photovoltaic manufacturers located in the state, will provide for some additional cost sharing.

Design Process

Throughout the ten years that have elapsed from the beginning of master planning to the end of construction documents, the same project management guided the design team. This enabled decision making to be made based on a full understanding of the project history.

The design team worked with a number of outside and in-house specialists who were called on to guide the design toward environmentally preferable options. The National Renewable Energy Lab and the Lawrence Berkeley National Lab contributed to the design effort, and HOK assigned a sustainable design advocate to track progress toward meeting environmental goals.

Located in close proximity to Dulles International Airport for easy access to an active runway for transporting aircraft; the landscape design is simple and natural, with extensive use of tall grasses and wildflowers, which reduces maintenance requirements. The facility will include a 215,000 SF main exhibit hangar, several other exhibition areas, an archival resource center, a restoration hangar with public observation areas, educational facilities, a large-format theater, an auditorium, restaurants, museum shops, and an observation deck for visitors to watch Dulles air traffic.

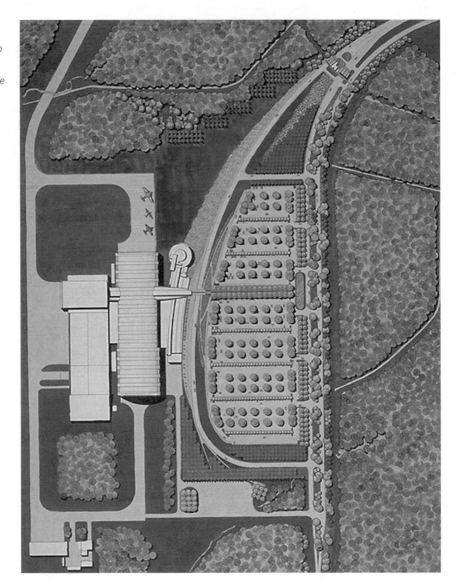

Site

The site design was strongly influenced by airport requirements. Within those constraints, the team worked to minimize disruption of the site and to develop a naturally sustainable landscape using predominantly native plant species.

ALTERNATIVE TRANSPORTATION
Initially, bus service will be provided from the most accessible Metro station and perhaps the Mall. When Metro service to Dulles Airport is completed, shuttles will transport visitors from the new Dulles station. If the long-range proposal to create a light-rail link succeeds, the entrance to Dulles Center will be modified to accept that transit link. A bicycle lock area has also been provided to accommodate staff and visitors who ride to the center.

The HOK Guidebook to Sustainable Design

LANDSCAPE DESIGN

Because Dulles Center's main access road is close to the end of a runway, no trees can be planted, and this area will be maintained as grasslands. The landscape leading to the entrance is simple and natural, with extensive use of tall grasses and wildflowers, which reduces maintenance requirements. No irrigation is required, and mowing requirements are minimal.

Areas immediately north of the main building, which will be used for temporary displays, will be maintained as mowed grass. Areas south of the main building, which will be for future expansion, will remain tree-covered for now. A setback area along the edge of the grassland area will also be mowed grass because of concerns about possible fires that might result from pedestrians smoking cigarettes.

STORMWATER AND EROSION CONTROL

All stormwater is accommodated on-site through a series of water retention features. Installing multiple stormwater drainage systems reduced the amount of site grading required. Erosion control devices required during construction were coordinated carefully with stormwater retention areas to minimize disruption of wetlands and forested areas.

PHOTOVOLTAIC SITE LIGHTING

Photovoltaic site lighting is a design option, depending on the success of the fund-raising effort. Photovoltaic panels mounted to the light poles would charge batteries to power fluorescent lights during dusk and evening hours. This option would require more light poles, with the light sources mounted closer to the ground; however, the quality of lighting would be less harsh, and light spill to the night sky would be reduced.

Energy

The need to provide strict environmental controls to preserve the artifacts while also accommodating visitors created a unique challenge for the design team. Unlike more conventional museums, where artifacts are located close to floor level, this museum has large hanging artifacts occupying the entire space. Strict temperature controls and a requirement for 40 percent relative humidity (±5 percent) throughout the space had a

The building design reduced energy requirements through use of a highly insulated shell—the average insulating value for the walls and hangar doors is R-19, and the minimum insulating value for the roof is R-30. An innovative approach is being used to control outside air ventilation rates—the building automation system will monitor the population of visitors and adjust the proportion of fresh air accordingly.

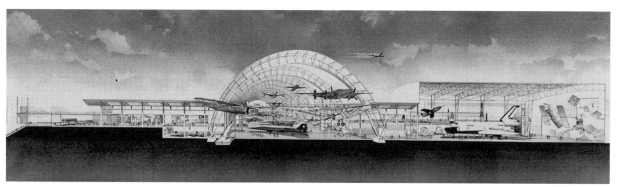

Missouri Historical Society Museum Expansion and Renovation

St. Louis, Missouri

Building Size: 129,000 SF
Site: 3.5 acres
Completion: January 2000
Cost: $147/SF

Highlights of the Design

- Based on energy modeling, the design is projected to use 50 percent less energy than a comparable facility built according to ASHRAE 90.1 standards. The team achieved this through basic energy conservation methods that proved to be good investments when evaluated in terms of life cycle cost. Strategies included natural lighting using high-performance low-E glazing, improved insulation, exterior as well as interior motorized sun shading, high-efficiency chillers with waterside economizers, reduced fan power for the VAV system, and efficient cooling towers, motors, and boilers.

large impact on the design. Design strategies that would reduce energy loads were particularly valuable.

BUILDING ENVELOPE

The building envelope in the artifact areas was designed to neutralize the impact of external temperature swings. The building design utilizes a highly insulated shell—the average insulating value for the walls (which have very few windows) is R-19, including the massive insulated hangar doors, and the roof has a minimum value of R-30.

Construction detailing includes air barriers and vapor retarders to control air and moisture flow from the exterior. The specially designed insulated main hangar canopy-type doors also allow very little air infiltration.

To reduce solar heat gain during the summer and decrease heat loss during the winter, all glazing is insulated glass, and much of it has a low-E coating. The light gray Hypalon roof membranes and the light, reflective wall material also reduce heat gain.

LIGHTING

Daylight was not initially permitted in artifact areas, and extensive analysis was required to demonstrate that the small proportion of indirect daylight ultimately permitted in the space would have no adverse impact on the artifacts. All daylight in the display hangar is indirect and passes

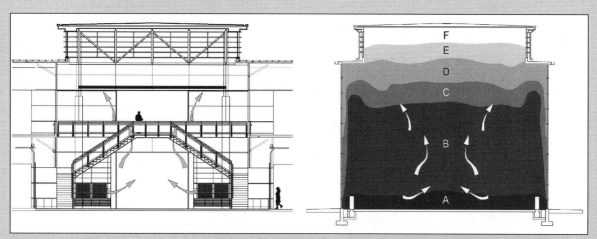

Instead of conditioning all the air at the top of the space, only the air in the occupied zone—up to an 8-foot level—is conditioned. The temperature then stratifies through the upper portions of the space.

■ **The design calls for air distribution by displacement in large public spaces. Because less air is being conditioned than in a conventional system, displacement ventilation significantly reduces energy use. Instead of conditioning all the air at the top of the space, only the air in the occupied zone—up to an 8-foot level—is conditioned. The temperature then stratifies through the upper portions of the space.**

through insulated laminated glass to eliminate UV damage. The team used Radiance, a powerful daylight modeling tool developed by the Lawrence Berkeley National Lab, to study the contribution of daylight within the exhibit hangar.

Throughout the artifact areas, the team used indirect lighting to meet Smithsonian criteria of 20 foot-candles. HID (high-intensity discharge) lamps and daylight from clerestory windows illuminate the large curved hangar roof. The light shelf, which is used to bounce daylight onto the ceiling, serves the dual purpose of providing a walkway for maintenance staff to service indirect light fixtures.

In other areas, outside of the artifact areas, daylighting is used to the greatest extent possible. Floor-to-ceiling glazing provides natural light in office and public amenity areas.

The electric lighting system uses high-efficiency fluorescent and HID lamps together with preprogrammed timed event controls, occupancy sensors, and daylight dimming systems to control the unnecessary use of lighting. Incandescent lamps, which provide high heat output and are much more energy intensive to use, are rarely used.

LOW-TEMPERATURE CHILLED WATER WITH ICE STORAGE
The need for extensive dehumidification of outside air in addition to space conditioning requirements could have led to an extremely energy-

intensive solution. When desiccant dehumidification was compared to a range of chilled water options, the team discovered that the low-temperature chilled water system would use much less energy.

Because the colder the chilled water is, the more moisture it removes from the air, systems that use colder water tend to be more efficient. The challenges are to avoid excessive energy use for reheating and to avoid moisture problems from condensation. The final scheme utilizes low-temperature water in combination with an ice storage system. The ice storage system provides the double benefit of peak load shaving, to help the local utility control future power plant growth, and chilled water at 32 degrees.

CONDITIONING THE SPACE HANGAR

The space hangar was studied extensively to develop an energy-efficient conditioning strategy. Standard office buildings typically require five to six air changes per hour (ACH) to meet their conditioning requirements, which ensures air mixing. Because of the relatively low conditioning requirements within the hangar, which has building population as the primary variable, a constant-volume system could be used at a fixed rate of 2 ACH. Computer modeling using computational fluid dynamics was used extensively to fine-tune the placement of air distribution systems, so adequate air mixing could be achieved with the low air change rate.

OCCUPANCY-CONTROLLED VENTILATION

An innovative approach is being taken to control outside air ventilation quantities. Because the population of visitors in the building will vary dramatically during the day and throughout the year, the ideal ventilation rate will also vary widely. The quantity of air moving in the display areas remains constant; however, the proportion of outside air will vary based on need. The building automation system will monitor the population of visitors and adjusts the proportion of fresh air accordingly.

ENERGY-EFFICIENT HVAC

Energy-conserving HVAC strategies included use of high-efficiency pumps and motors and the selection of chillers that accurately match the loads. Oversizing units for redundancy or extra capacity, a common approach, would have compromised efficiency. Hydronic heating is used throughout.

OZONE-FRIENDLY REFRIGERANTS

The specification allows for use of either R-123 or R-134A refrigerant for the HVAC equipment, both of which have low ozone-depleting potential.

HOT WATER HEATING

The building uses efficient, localized hot water systems. Localized water heaters in toilet rooms are on specific seven-day time clocks.

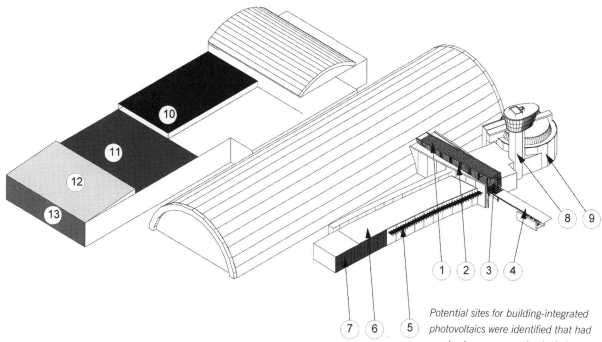

BUILDING-INTEGRATED PHOTOVOLTAICS

Kiss + Cathcart Architects worked with the team to identify potential sites for building-integrated photovoltaics and to estimate the energy that could be generated from each proposed material in those locations. Electrical energy generated from photovoltaics varies depending on the orientation of the surface it is applied to, as well as the type of material used and the hours of sunlight and intensity of sunlight specific to the region.

To further enhance the educational value of the array for visitors, an assortment of applications was selected that placed much of the material in highly visible locations on the building.

The options that have been proposed include use of semitransparent photovoltaic material on glass, which would be glazed into insulated glazing units; opaque material on glass, which would be glazed into spandrel units and also mounted on tilted frames and ballasted on the roof; and opaque material on metal roofing substrates. Two types of semitransparent material on glass have been proposed. One makes use of thin film material that has been laser etched to remove portions of the film, and the other uses crystalline or polycrystalline material mounted with spaces in between the cells to achieve transparency.

Water

The design specifies use of tempered, low-consumption water faucets with automatic on-off sensors in all public areas. Urinals also have automatic on-off sensors. The use of waterless urinals was considered for the facility; however, they were dropped because of concern about public reaction to the unfamiliar fixtures.

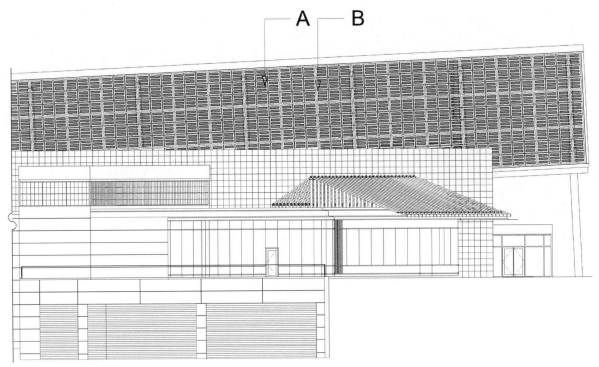

A — B

The roof and the south facade of the entry hall have been designed for building-integrated photovoltaics. Crystalline material will be mounted on the glass with spaces in between the cells to achieve transparency. The photovoltaic material provides beneficial sun shading that filters the light in this public space while also generating electricity.
Key: A. Photovoltaic material; B. Clear glass in between photovoltaic cells

A sand filtration system is being used to recirculate cooling tower water, thereby reducing blowdown requirements. Use of the filtration system reduces both water consumption and chemical use.

Indoor Environment

Indirect lighting, which is reflected off the large curved roof of the exhibit hangar, and clerestory windows, which admit daylight along the edge of the pedestrian mezzanines, provide soft, naturalistic lighting in the exhibit hangar.

Indoor air quality in the center complies with ASHRAE 62-89, the industry's voluntary standard for indoor air quality, and additional design considerations have been addressed to further improve air quality.

VENTILATION

Building setbacks and landscape buffers protect fresh air intakes from pollution by cars and buses. Careful location of building exhaust grilles, especially those from the restoration areas, further protects indoor air quality.

Potential air contaminants are isolated from habitable areas and separately ventilated. No smoking is permitted in the facility, and copy machines and print rooms have separate exhaust systems. All storage space for janitorial supplies operates under negative pressure and ventilates directly to the outside. Loading docks have a cold storage room for food waste and separate truck exhaust systems.

FILTRATION

The entire HVAC system has 85 percent efficient particle filtration for all spaces. Activated carbon filters in exhibit spaces reduce gaseous contamination of outside and recirculated air.

An innovative system is being used to control dirt and particulates at the building entry. All visitors enter through one main entry, which is equipped with walk-off grating and an underfoot air exhaust system.

LOW-EMISSIONS MATERIALS

Interior building materials and finishes were screened for low particulate emissions, total VOC, and toxic components. Guardrails were designed for disassembly so that painting maintenance could be done off-site.

The design reduces the potential for microbial contamination by limiting the use of fibrous materials. Carpet, for example, is used sparingly—mostly in office areas.

Material Resources

The building was designed to be highly durable and low maintenance, and to make use of materials that would not off-gas contaminants following installation and periodic maintenance.

MINIMAL, DURABLE MATERIALS

The design team avoided the use of finish materials whenever possible. Hangar ceilings are unfinished, concrete floors are sealed with a water-based low-VOC sealer, and walls use low-VOC paints and sealers. Throughout the facility, the design specifies use of durable materials such as terrazzo flooring, ground-face concrete masonry units, sealed concrete, ceramic wall and floor tile, and stainless steel trim.

ENVIRONMENTALLY PREFERABLE MATERIALS

Steel, the primary structural material, has a high recycled content. The same is true for the extensive mezzanine flooring, which is made of 100 percent recycled rubber. Likewise, carpet, acoustic ceiling tiles, and plastic toilet compartments have high recycled content.

Painted medium-density fiberboard (MDF) panels are used as an alternative to wood paneling, and the MDF material that has been selected is formaldehyde free.

EFFICIENT USE OF MATERIALS

Building and material modules were chosen to minimize cutting waste. The dimensions of metal liner panels, for example, which come only in imperial units, are used despite the fact that this is a metric project. Metric door heights work with either imperial or metric concrete masonry units.

Materials have also been conserved simply because the extensive use of compact warehouse and document storage reduced the overall size of the facility.

Throughout the facility, the design specifies the minimal use of highly durable materials. The main display hangar has unfinished ceilings, concrete floors are sealed with a water-based low-VOC sealant, and mezzanine flooring is made of 100 percent recycled rubber.

WASTE MANAGEMENT AND RECYCLING

The building design includes a recycling room to collect waste materials for recycling. Built-in containers are used for collecting recyclables in the cafeteria; freestanding containers will be used in the office areas.

The design protects against possible contamination from hazardous materials by providing containment of hazardous waste from the aircraft restoration process, using dust collectors for all appropriate restoration shop equipment; and using recessed spill containers for chemical shop vats.

CONSTRUCTION WASTE RECYCLING

The contractor is required to submit a construction waste management plan. At a minimum, the contractor must recycle untreated lumber, gypsum wallboard, paper products and cardboard, plastics, metals, glass, and other salvageable materials. Gypsum scrap may also be used on-site as a soil amendment.

Benefit of Design

Because the building was designed with a long-term perspective, maintenance and operating costs will be significantly reduced. Savings will come from reduced repair and maintenance, simplified cleaning requirements, reduced landscaping costs, and reduced waste hauling fees, as well as reduced energy and water costs. These savings represent good steward-ship of public funds.

The new Dulles Center ensures that the Smithsonian can preserve artifacts that describe the history of aviation and space flight for future generations. Because the building design is mindful of limited resources and is proactively supporting the development of sustainable technologies, Dulles Center will also present a model of responsible development for future generations.

Future exhibits will include materials describing the history of photovoltaics, including real-time exhibits measuring the electricity generated from the building's photovoltaic arrays.

University of Wisconsin, Green Bay New Academic Building

Green Bay, Wisconsin

Building Size:	*120,000 SF*
Site:	*6 acres*
Completion:	*Fall 2001*
Cost:	*$14 million for building, site improvements, and interiors ($116/SF)*

The new two-story academic building at the University of Wisconsin, Green Bay, will serve as a new campus center, housing twenty classrooms, which will represent about half of all classroom space on campus when the project is complete. HOK provided programming, architectural design, lighting design, and environmental consulting; Somerville Architects, of Green Bay, is the architect of record.

Environmental Goals

In accordance with its strong environmental studies program, the university wanted a building that would help strengthen its focus on environmental issues. The state's goal is to make the project a model for energy conservation by reducing energy consumption for heating, cooling, and lighting by at least 50 percent compared to similar buildings. The state also wanted to promote the potential environmental and economic benefits of using renewable energy resources.

Design Overview

One of the design goals for this new building is to provide a physical and metaphorical campus "front door" to the campus.

This new building has been sited carefully so that it will help form a quadrangle space between this new building and the existing library and student union. The quadrangle will serve as an entry point to the campus and a trailhead to the path that leads to the main arboretum.

Designed in the 1960s, the University of Wisconsin's original campus at Green Bay has a windowless below-grade tunnel system connecting all the buildings. The new facility will create a new circulation system for the campus that is daylit and visually connected to the campus green spaces.

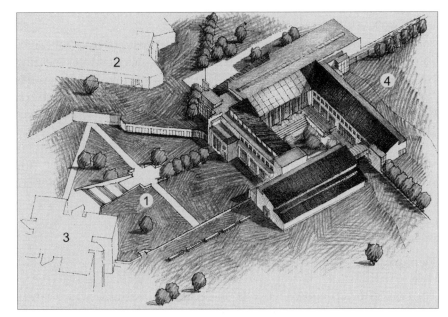

The new classroom building has been sited carefully, to form a quadrangle space between this new building and the existing library and student union. The quadrangle will serve as an entry point to the campus and a trailhead to the path that leads to the main arboretum.

Key:

1. Campus quadrangle

2. Student union

3. Library

4. Building courtyard

New connecting tunnels between the buildings are inset into the landscape, with the entire length of the tunnels glazed and open to a newly defined central quadrangle on one side. By completing the final side of the quadrangle with a building, a gathering space has been created that is sheltered from the wind.

The first floor contains most of the classrooms and special program offices. The rest of the classrooms are located off the building's lower tunnel level, which opens to the central quadrangle. Many of the classrooms have interior windows that provide an opportunity to "look in on learning."

The second floor houses faculty offices along a double-loaded corridor, with daylighting from the roof monitors above.

Special collections areas that require completely controlled environments with no daylight are located in the only true basement space.

Economics

With a tight budget and a difficult site, the design team's first priority was to satisfy the university's space needs. Even so, most of the sustainable design features were achieved within the base budget.

The team evaluated each energy conservation feature on a life cycle basis and implemented many. For example, the energy model predicted that extensive daylighting could create energy savings in excess of $18,000 per year. The proposed daylighting strategies thus will pay for themselves in approximately five years.

The payback analysis was complicated, however, by the fact that the state of Wisconsin pays all utility bills directly, so the university had no direct financial incentive to include energy conservation measures. As a result, the university has recommended that the state change this administrative procedure to give users financial incentives to conserve energy.

DEMONSTRATION TECHNOLOGIES

Some sustainable design features that are not yet cost-effective but can be funded separately will be included in the design to demonstrate emerging technologies. For example, the local utility, Wisconsin Public Service, has funded building-integrated photovoltaic panels for the project, to research this technology and to investigate the effectiveness of distributed power generation in this northern climate.

Additional design features awaiting private funding include demonstration gardens, constructed wetlands or "living machines" for wastewater treatment, and an interior "living wall" made up of plant life that acts as a natural biofilter to clean the air.

Design Process

The university's proposed move-in date combined with the state's extensive review process created a fast-track design schedule.

DESIGN CHARRETTE

The design process began with a four-day charrette in April 1998. During this brainstorming meeting the team met with university faculty, students, and staff to discuss design goals, tour the site, and develop initial concepts. The team then refined the design options, based in part on a series of public meetings, energy model evaluations, systems development studies, and site analyses. The university selected a final scheme in late June 1998.

EARLY ENERGY STUDIES

As part of the design workshop, the team created a DOE-2 energy model and discussed energy conservation ideas. These early studies were an important part of the conceptual design. The model was also updated regularly as the design progressed.

Led by the team's energy and daylighting consultant—Architectural Energy Corporation (AEC) of Boulder, Colorado—the team created a hypothetical "reference" building design based on the architectural program and current practice levels of energy efficiency as defined by the Wisconsin Commercial Building Energy Code.

After acquiring Green Bay climatological data and information about local utility rates, the team used DOE-2 building energy analysis software to simulate energy use. AEC created a series of elimination parametrics to evaluate the overall impact of each individual building component, including lighting, people, equipment loads, ventilation, and skin. This data provided the first set of energy conservation targets.

As the initial high-energy components were lowered, other areas became more important in the overall energy use of the building. The team then initiated additional sets of elimination parametrics and conservation strategies until no more energy-conserving strategies could be identified.

292

LEED SYSTEM

The team used the U.S. Green Building Council's LEED (Leadership in Energy and Environmental Design) Green Building Rating System as a design guidance and decision-making tool. Because the project currently is out to bid, it is too early to make a final judgment; however, as designed, the project would earn a gold award from the LEED rating system.

DAYLIGHTING STUDIES

AEC built two daylighting models with changeable parts so that different strategies could be studied as the building design developed, to test and refine the concepts. One model featured one of the building's large lecture halls with a skylight and integrated daylight deflector. The other model included a circulation corridor with a daylight monitor, and adjacent office areas using a clerestory daylighting system.

OPERATIONS AND MAINTENANCE ISSUES

The university's director of buildings and grounds, along with key staff members, were involved in all aspects of the programming and design. This will familiarize the owner's team with operations and help them understand the best, healthiest maintenance systems for the building they will inherit.

Daylighting models were built with changeable parts so different strategies could be studied as the building design developed, to test and refine the concepts. This model included a circulation corridor with a daylight monitor, and adjacent office areas using a clerestory daylighting system.

Site

The site for the building was chosen, in part, because of the opportunity to create a campus quadrangle. Enclosure of the quadrangle with buildings as well as the single-story-high revealed building tunnels will create a wind-protected area for outdoor gatherings during the times of year with mild temperatures.

LANDSCAPE DESIGN
The building courtyard will be developed as a demonstration area for native plants, extending the existing arboretum into the campus core.

The entire building site, including the new campus quadrangle, will be replanted with low-maintenance native plant materials to replace the existing high-maintenance, non-native landscape of turf grass and ornamentals.

Energy

DOE-2 energy models indicate that the building's energy consumption will be 60 percent less than a base case building designed to be minimally compliant with the Wisconsin Commercial Building Energy Code.

Early energy modeling indicated that heating energy required for ventilation air in the classrooms represented the single largest component of the baseline building's annual energy performance. The next-largest component was lighting energy. The design team thus focused on ventilation and electric lighting as the two biggest opportunities for energy savings in the initial approach to energy conservation.

CONTROLLED VENTILATION
Ventilating the classrooms requires a great deal of energy. To reduce this load, the building automation system will be reprogrammed each semester to reflect the new class schedules. Ventilation will be supplied to a classroom only when class is in session there. A manual override equipped with a timer will accommodate unscheduled gatherings.

The building courtyard will be developed as a demonstration area for native plants, and the rest of the site will be replanted with low-maintenance native plant materials. The building roof design draws daylight into second-level corridors through roof monitors, and the south-sloped glazing illustrated here contains semitransparent photovoltaic glazing.

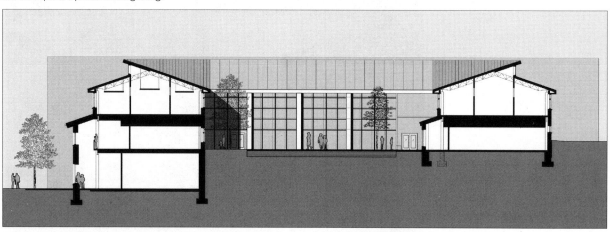

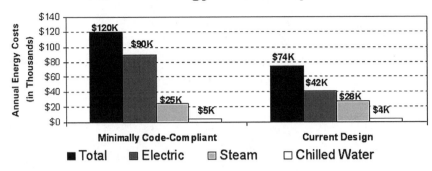

University of Wisconsin, Green Bay
Annual Energy Cost Comparison

DOE-2 energy models indicate that the building's energy consumption will be 60 percent less than a base case building designed to be minimally compliant with the Wisconsin Commercial Building Energy Code.

BUILDING ENVELOPE

The team designed the exterior building envelope with a high R-value for walls and windows. To reflect the different orientations, the windows on all four sides have different transmission characteristics. All glass is gas-filled and has a low-E coating. The building exterior walls will be approximately R-35 and the roof will be approximately R-50.

High-performance low-E glazings that are "tuned" to respond to their orientations reduce solar heat gain during summer months and heat loss during winter months. The glazing also plays an important role in ensuring visual comfort throughout the building's daylit spaces.

DAYLIGHTING

Because both the architectural program and the preliminary energy modeling identified daylighting as a significant energy conservation opportunity, daylighting strategies had a considerable impact on the building's shape and configuration of spaces. The design was developed to maximize the combined impact of windows, rooftop skylights, and light monitors on the interior spaces.

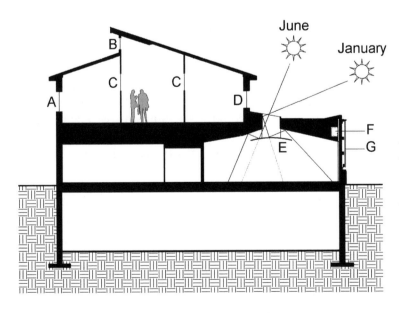

Daylight supplies most of the building's ambient lighting. The design was developed to maximize the combined impact of windows, rooftop skylights, and light monitors on the interior spaces.
Key: A. Window; B. Light monitor; C. Clerestory window; D. Window; E. Skylight with daylight deflector; F. Air intake for transpired solar collector; G. Transpired solar collector

Daylight supplies most of the building's ambient lighting. To provide even, diffuse light in the large lecture halls, skylights channel daylight through light shafts with suspended perforated daylight deflectors that diffuse light and redirect it across the ceiling plane. The result is an illuminated ceiling that provides sufficient general lighting without using the electric fixtures. Motorized blackout shade panels are available for times in which classes need to use audiovisual equipment.

All major circulation spaces are daylit, ensuring that users rarely lose sight of the outside. The second-floor faculty offices are daylit from clerestory windows that bring borrowed light from the main circulation corridor into each office.

The partially below-grade concourse connections to other campus buildings will be glazed to provide light and a visual connection to the lower-level central quadrangle, a substantial improvement over the university's current use of windowless tunnels.

ELECTRIC LIGHTING

To maintain classroom lighting levels, the design incorporates a combination of daylighting and electric lighting with dimmable electronic ballasts. Photocells measure daylight from the daylight sources. On a bright day, the clerestory windows will enable the system to turn off unnecessary lights. On overcast days or evenings, the system will adjust the fluorescent fixtures to the required light level.

Ninety percent of all lighting fixtures are fluorescent, which provides efficiency, easy maintenance, and a long life span. Indirect/direct fluorescent pendants provide an illuminated ceiling of ambient light and direct tabletop light. These lamps have a life span of twenty thousand hours, which means they will need replacing only once every three years. To control lighting during unoccupied hours, most of the building's electric lighting is controlled by occupancy sensors.

MECHANICAL SYSTEMS

An outside air economizer cycle will supply outside air for cooling and ventilation during summer months or when outside temperatures permit. While operable windows were considered and rejected, the outside air economizer provides "free cooling" in much the same way, by delivering 100 percent outside air when temperature and humidity permit.

TRANSPIRED SOLAR COLLECTOR AND PREHEATING SYSTEM

Green Bay, located on the shores of Lake Superior, experiences air temperatures as low as 40 degrees below zero during winter months, which results in a considerable requirement for heating outside air during winter. In response, the team explored opportunities to reduce energy consumption by using solar energy to preheat ventilation air. The team chose to integrate a low-cost solar preheating system developed by Conserval Systems of Buffalo, New York, and the National Renewable Energy Laboratory.

Known as a transpired air solar collector, the system is a perforated metal collector painted black to absorb solar radiation. Convection draws the intake air through the perforations into the cavity behind. There, the solar-heated metal panels preheat the air, so it enters the building many degrees warmer than the outside air. These panels make up the finished portion of several sections of the building's south exterior wall.

RENEWABLE ENERGY

The building design incorporates two types of building-integrated photovoltaic panels, designed by Massachusetts-based Solar Design Associates.

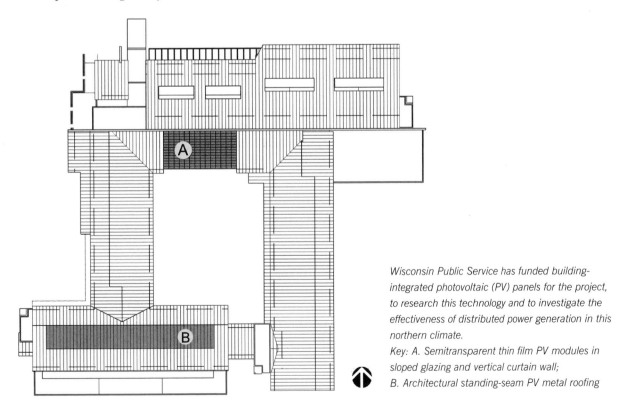

Wisconsin Public Service has funded building-integrated photovoltaic (PV) panels for the project, to research this technology and to investigate the effectiveness of distributed power generation in this northern climate.
Key: A. Semitransparent thin film PV modules in sloped glazing and vertical curtain wall;
B. Architectural standing-seam PV metal roofing

One system comprises thin film technology integrated with the standing-seam metal roof that makes up the building's major roofing system.

The second type is a translucent film-on-glass panel that forms the primary roof element over the winter garden as well as part of the vertical south-facing glass. This represents the first commercial use of this thin film technology in the United States. These panels will be directly connected to the building's electric power grid.

EFFICIENT EQUIPMENT

Many of the computers and office equipment that will be used in the new building are older models with a wide range of energy efficiency ratings. The design team has recommended that all future equipment purchases carry an Energy Star label.

Water

A rainwater harvesting system has been proposed for the courtyard. If incorporated, this system will collect rainwater from the roof structures and store it in pools and/or cisterns in the building courtyard, for irrigation and other nonpotable uses.

Water-conserving plumbing fixtures and appliances have been selected that exceed the requirements of the U.S. Energy Policy Act of 1992.

Indoor Environment

The use of natural light and views to the outside will create a positive learning environment. The extensive use of daylight together with design strategies that limit glare and direct sunlight will improve visual comfort.

To ensure good indoor air quality, the building's mechanical systems and ventilation rates have been designed to meet ASHRAE Standard 62, the industry's voluntary standard for indoor air quality.

SOURCE CONTROL

To reduce potential sources of contamination, the team carefully reviewed materials to minimize chemical off-gassing from the material itself, as well as from chemicals used for cleaning and maintenance. Detailing was developed to minimize potential sites for microbial growth. For example, no fibrous building insulation will be located where it can come into contact with the airstream.

To expel contaminants that may accumulate in the building as wet materials cure during construction, the design team will work with the contractor to develop a detailed construction sequencing plan and establish minimum ventilation rates during construction.

The building design also decreases the introduction of contaminants into the building by providing separate storage areas for cleaning chemicals. Building vestibules with recessed entry gratings will reduce the introduction of dirt and particulates in the building.

Material Resources

The design team sought out materials and products for the building that would provide improved performance while reducing environmental impacts related to the raw materials, the production process, installation and use, and resource recovery.

AAC CONCRETE
Hebel Block, an aerated autoclaved cellular concrete (AAC) building unit, was proposed for exterior walls as a load-bearing material. The AAC concrete blocks have a high R-value, are easy to work with, and use significantly less concrete than standard concrete masonry units.

CARPET
The specifications call for the carpet to have a high percentage of recycled content and to come from manufacturers with reclamation and recycling programs.

RENEWABLE MATERIALS
Linoleum flooring, a biodegradable, renewable material made from linseed oil, rosins, cork, and wood flour, is used in classrooms. Bamboo flooring, a hard, durable material made from the rapidly renewable bamboo plant, is used as a demonstration product in place of typical wood flooring in conference rooms and gathering spaces.

RECYCLED-CONTENT MATERIALS
Gypsum wallboard material uses recycled-content gypsum and kraft paper. Acoustic ceiling tile is made of recycled cellulose and mineral slag. Panel fabric and upholstery fabric is specified to be 100 percent postconsumer recycled polyester from soda bottles.

The specified ceramic tile has more than 60 percent recycled-content, postindustrial feldspar waste as its primary raw material. The manufacturing process is a closed system for solid waste accumulation and reuse.

LOW-VOC MATERIALS
All paint, adhesives, and finishes are water-based and low in VOCs.

NON-OZONE-DEPLETING MATERIALS
No ozone-depleting CFCs, HCFCs, or halons are used in the mechanical systems. Building materials have been selected to reduce or eliminate CFCs and HCFCs from the manufacturing process.

CONSTRUCTION WASTE RECYCLING
The team hopes to reduce construction waste by 90 percent compared to standard practices.

Working with the state waste reduction office—which will be one of the building occupants—the team prepared a detailed construction waste specification. A list of local firms that accept various construction materials for recycling was provided to each construction firm bidding on the project. Before construction begins, the team will work with the contractor to develop a detailed construction waste management plan.

USER RECYCLING

The University of Wisconsin, Green Bay already has an extensive recycling program. The new building will join these existing programs and provide built-in areas for user recycling.

Benefits of the Design

The design provides users with a light-filled facility in which learning and working should be a pleasure. Yet these same characteristics also contribute to exceptionally efficient building operations and reduce long-term operating costs.

In addition to serving as a statewide model for energy conservation, the building will showcase various methods of achieving environmentally responsible design. By demonstrating various sustainable design technologies, the building becomes part of the pedagogical mission of the university's environmental studies program.

INTERNET SITE AND MULTIMEDIA KIOSK

The project team has approached the entire building as a tool for enhancing the university's educational mission.

The main building entry provides a museumlike orientation and demonstration area to teach building users and visitors about the building's environmental mission. Electronic kiosks and other displays will provide real-time and historical reports showing the current and accumulated contribution of solar power through daylighting and photovoltaics.

One proposed feature is an Internet site that will present multilayered, multitracked information about the building and its programs. The site would employ a live Web camera to "broadcast" construction images, emphasizing images of the building-integrated photovoltaics, daylighting, and solar wall features.

U.S. Federal Courthouse Expansion

Denver, Colorado

Building Size:	*370,000 GSF*
Site:	*2.5 acres*
Completion:	*2002*
Cost:	*N/A*

The U.S. General Services Administration (GSA) is managing the design and construction of the 370,000 SF expansion of the U.S. Federal Courthouse in downtown Denver's Federal District, which is scheduled for completion in 2002. HOK is design architect; Anderson Mason Dale P.C. is architect of record.

Environmental Goals

GSA set a goal for the project to "use the latest available proven technologies for environmentally sensitive design, construction, and operation. It should set a standard and be a model of sustainable design."

Another goal, which is central to sustainable design, was to create a building that would remain effective for a hundred-year life span.

Design Overview

The design reflects the city's rich architectural heritage. Recalling a traditional town square courthouse, the two-story pavilion acts as the frontispiece to the entire composition. An open peristyle colonnade supports the roof and transparently encloses the entrance lobby and drum-shaped secured lobby within.

As a series of vertically oriented rectangular planes, the tower celebrates its top with an open framework and a floating horizontal roof of photovoltaic panels.

The eleven-story structure houses six floors of district courts, two floors of magistrate courts, offices for the U.S. marshal and clerk of the courts, a jury assembly area, and a special-proceedings courtroom.

Economics

In planning for the courthouse expansion, the GSA made a conscious decision to challenge its conventional thinking about building economics. This included developing a project budget that allowed for additional investment for sustainable design opportunities.

GSA set a goal for the project to "use the latest available proven technologies for environmentally sensitive design, construction, and operation. It should set a standard and be a model of sustainable design."

The GSA's careful approach to determining the proper level of investment for sustainable design measures included commissioning international construction consultant Hanscomb, Inc., to analyze the projected costs and viability of various green design strategies.

As the design progressed, the design team evaluated all expenditures for upgrades to the design that would improve the environmental performance of the building relative to a sustainable design budget. This ensured that decisions could be justified in terms of life cycle economics, enabling the GSA to recoup its initial investment.

The design team compared initial costs with life cycle paybacks for features such as a daylight dimming system, displacement ventilation, energy-efficient HVAC systems, raised-access flooring, and high-performance curtain wall glazing.

In terms of both conventional and environmental performance, this investment in sustainable design will make the courthouse a better building. While not every green design feature provides a payback, in aggregate the green design measures produce life cycle cost savings that pay back the initial investment within twenty-five years of operation.

Design Process

In late 1996 the GSA sponsored a Green Buildings Workshop to evaluate sustainable design strategies for the Denver courthouse expansion, including systems, materials, and delivery techniques. A twenty-member advisory committee of leading architects, engineers, environmentalists, planners, and scientists met in Washington, D.C., to recommend green building techniques for the GSA's multibillion-dollar national courthouse construction program.

In July 1997 GSA published the results of this study in its Green Courthouse Design Concepts Report. HOK's final design incorporates suggestions from this study while also presenting several new ones.

LEED GREEN BUILDING RATING SYSTEM

The team worked with the U.S. Green Building Council's LEED Green Building Rating System throughout the design process. The rating system helped the team measure environmental performance of the project as a whole as the design evolved, passing through numerous design reviews and value engineering sessions.

The building as designed earns the gold rating, and it is only three points away from earning the platinum rating. The performance will continue to be tracked through construction to ensure that the rating is maintained and to seek opportunities where possible to improve the rating.

PROJECTING ENERGY PERFORMANCE

The design team worked with Architectural Energy Corporation (AEC), in Denver, Colorado, to evaluate the energy consumption of various courthouse design options. Using DOE-2.1E building energy simulation software, the team developed an energy model based on the Denver climate and commercial electric and gas rates supplied by the Public Service Company of Colorado (PSCo).

The team established a baseline energy model simulating a minimally code-compliant building according to ASHRAE 90.1 design criteria. Design options under consideration were then evaluated against the baseline to compare energy savings.

DAYLIGHT MODELS

AEC also produced detailed computer modeling of electric and daylighting systems using Lumen Micro v. 7.5 software, to create a series of simulations that would evaluate design options under a range of times of day and sky conditions throughout the year.

Establishing interior daylighting levels helped the team select compatible energy-efficient glazing and electric lighting systems. The daylighting studies also influenced the selection of office partitions, light shelves, ceiling heights, and shading devices such as fritted glass and roller shades.

Site

The site design reinforces the GSA's sustainable design goals while creating a base worthy of the building's landmark status within Denver's Federal District.

In developing the site design, the team considered four essential concepts integral to expressing the Western landscape: the land surface patterning, the contrast between mountain and plain, the textures and colors of indigenous materials, and the precious nature of water in the region.

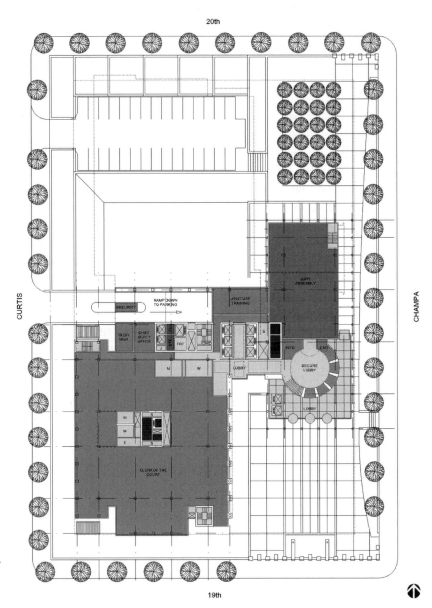

In developing the site design, the team considered four essential concepts integral to expressing the Western landscape: the land surface patterning, the contrast between mountain and plain, the textures and colors of indigenous materials, and the precious nature of water.

LANDSCAPE MATERIALS

The landscape functions as a reasonably self-contained ecosystem that does not require much care or irrigation.

The team selected plant materials that will thrive in the Denver microclimate and urban environment. This includes indigenous and xeriscape (low-water) plants such as drought-tolerant buffalo grass.

To minimize water loss to evaporation, a drip irrigation system provides water for ground cover, perennials, and trees during establishment and as a supplement during drought conditions.

PERMEABLE SITE PAVING

The site's hardscape areas use a variety of materials in sand setting beds instead of concrete. This increases the site's water absorption capacity and reduces stormwater runoff. Interlocking concrete pavers, flagstone pavers, and sandstone, which is used for the plaza surrounding the special proceedings pavilion, will be installed in sand setting beds.

Low-traffic perimeter areas use grass-block paving and crushed stone surfaces that provide even greater permeability and hold up well under freeze-thaw conditions.

PEDESTRIAN ACCESS AND MASS TRANSIT
Public spaces are located near public transportation stops. Good lighting between the courthouse entrances and the public transportation waiting areas encourages people to use Denver's mass transit system.

Energy

The design team worked with Ove Arup, the RMH Group in Denver, and AEC to develop the building's energy-efficient design strategies. The design systematically reduces building energy loads and then satisfies the reduced loads with state-of-the-art, high-efficiency systems and renewable energy sources. The design takes into account Denver's sunny skies and low humidity, to significantly decrease energy requirements.

Based on an improved building envelope, substantial reductions in energy use for lighting, ventilation, and cooling, and energy generated from building-integrated photovoltaics, the new courthouse will consume about 50 percent less energy than a building designed according to the U.S. Department of Energy standards for energy efficiency (ASHRAE 90.1-1989).

BUILDING ENVELOPE
Improvements to the building envelope greatly reduce overall HVAC loads. Building insulation values average R-16 for the walls and R-30 for the roof. Most of the glass on the tower portion of the courthouse is 1-inch insulated, high-performance, low-E glass in nonoperable aluminum frames. The tower will have a high-performance triple-glazed curtain wall system along the public corridor from levels four through eleven.

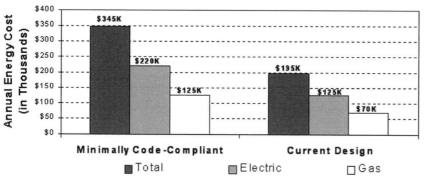

Denver Courthouse
Annual Energy Cost Comparison

Based on an improved building envelope, substantial reductions in energy use for lighting, ventilation, and cooling, and energy generated from building-integrated photovoltaics, the new courthouse will consume about 50 percent less energy than a building designed according to the U.S. Department of Energy standards for energy efficiency (ASHRAE 90.1-1989).

Sam M. Gibbons United States Courthouse

Tampa, Florida

Building Size:	438,000 SF
Site Area:	88,000 SF
Completion:	1998
Cost:	$146/SF, including site, parking, and interior fit-out

Highlights of the Design

■ Back in 1992, when GSA began planning for its new courthouse in downtown Tampa, sustainable design was not yet on its agenda. With HOK's initiative and GSA's management support, green design opportunities for the courthouse were discussed and adopted as project goals at the end of conceptual design.

■ The courthouse was built for approximately $64 million, which was within the original construction and contingency budget. With a project cost of just $146/GSF, the building remains one of the most cost-effective U.S. courthouses built in recent years—even while incorporating state-of-the-art technological and security features.

■ The design team was able to free up funds for building design enhancements by reducing cost in other areas. Savings came from the use of locally available and cost-effective precast concrete, efficient damp-proofing and insulation systems, and downsizing the mechanical systems. For example, sun shading and low-E glazing reduced the peak load for cooling by 180 tons, enabling the team to reduce the size of the mechanical plant.

The triple-glazed system has a low thermal conductance, minimizing heat loss and maintaining thermal comfort in the public corridor area. The triple-glazed system allows for perimeter radiant heating to be eliminated in the public corridors.

A combination of tinted glass and low-emissivity coatings controls solar heat gain while preserving the glazing system's transparency. Glazing tint and frit patterns in the public corridor reduce the visible light transmission of the glazing, eliminating glare and excessive brightness.

DAYLIGHTING

Daylighting reduces dependence on electric lighting, decreasing energy consumption while reducing heat gain from electric lighting. Natural light provides better-quality, full-spectrum light and creates a more stimulating work environment by exposing occupants to the rhythms of the day.

- Daylight sensors in offices and public areas control automated dimming. Occupancy sensors were installed in all office areas to control the lighting. Interior emergency lighting was designed to contribute to night accent lighting, keeping exterior building lighting to a minimum.

- Light-colored building and paving materials reduce the urban heat island effect. In-ground planters collect stormwater for infiltration and groundwater recharge.

- The light color of the precast concrete skin, together with enhancements to the building envelope, reduces heating and cooling loads.

- An emergency generator was designed to participate in the Tampa Electric Company's peak load shaving program.

- Building materials, such as paint, adhesives, and sealants, were selected that are low in VOCs. Before occupancy, the building was ventilated to remove contaminants related to curing of wet materials during construction. Internal duct lining was eliminated as a preventative measure to avoid a possible breeding ground for microbes. Also, a comprehensive HVAC commissioning plan was developed.

- All veneer wood is from certified sustainably harvested sources.

- To allow for separation of construction waste on-site, five recycling containers were required on the site at all times. Recycling logs indicated that a total of 1,800 tons of waste was recycled.

- Based on its energy efficiency accomplishments, the Sam E. Gibbons U.S. Courthouse earned a 1998 National Department of Energy Award—the first such honor bestowed on a GSA Region IV building. For GSA, the courthouse stands as an example of environmentally responsible design that has improved performance and lowered operating costs without adding cost to the project.

Daylight will provide required ambient light levels during most daytime hours within the judges' chambers, perimeter office and conference spaces, and public corridors on the court floors.

In the high-rise portion of the building, perimeter light shelves separate the view and daylight glazing areas. These light shelves diffuse daylight onto the ceiling plane and adjacent surfaces, minimizing direct solar penetration for all spaces except public corridors outside courtrooms. Glazing between the public corridor and the courtrooms allows the public seating area at the rear of the courtroom to be naturally lit as well.

ENERGY-EFFICIENT ELECTRIC LIGHTING

Supplementing the extensive use of daylight will be integrated lighting systems that meet or exceed all EPA Energy Star requirements.

Energy-efficient fluorescent lighting with electronic ballasts and T-5 lamps will be provided throughout the facility. To save energy in daylit

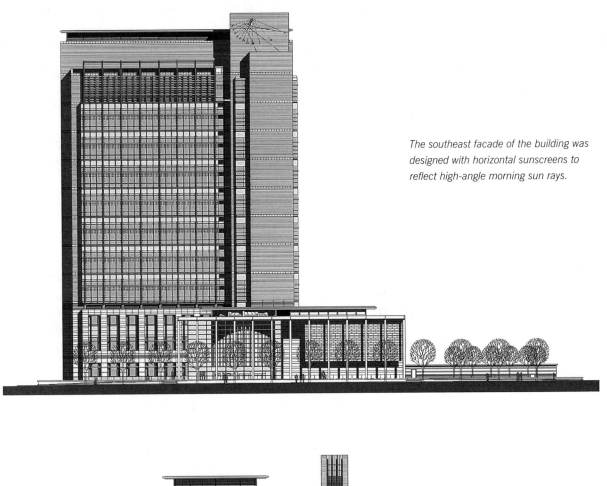

The southeast facade of the building was designed with horizontal sunscreens to reflect high-angle morning sun rays.

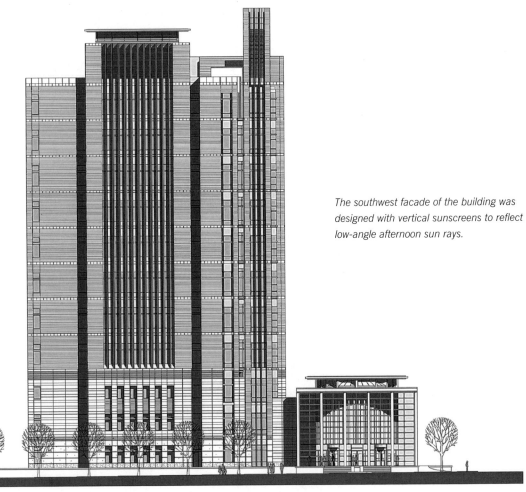

The southwest facade of the building was designed with vertical sunscreens to reflect low-angle afternoon sun rays.

areas, photocells will control the electronic dimming ballasts, which will be capable of dimming to 10 percent of full light output.

Use of incandescent lighting (halogen infrared sources) is limited to areas with special requirements, such as the courtroom well.

Lighting in private offices uses low-level ambient lighting enhanced with occupant-controlled task lighting and occupancy sensors.

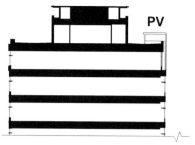

The building is crowned by a series of polycrystalline photovoltaic cells integrated into the top horizontal roof louver of the tower and the skylight above the secure lobby.

INTEGRATED PHOTOVOLTAICS

The building is crowned by a series of polycrystalline photovoltaic cells integrated into the top horizontal roof louver of the tower and the skylight above the secure lobby.

The photovoltaic panels provide electricity during sunlight hours, reducing the building's peak electricity requirements. Direct current from the photovoltaic system feeds into the building electrical system via a series of DC-to-AC inverters. Since the output of the system is much less than the building demand, battery storage is not necessary.

Estimated energy production from the photovoltaic system is 71,000 kWh/year, or about 4 percent of the total annual consumption.

MECHANICAL

The energy-efficient HVAC system includes these energy-saving features:

- Displacement ventilation
- Direct and indirect evaporative cooling system
- Space heating and hot water heating from district steam
- Variable-frequency drives for the air handler and pump motors
- VAV air distribution
- Outside air economizers on all air handlers
- Premium-efficiency motors
- A direct digital controls (DDC) building automation system to optimize operation of air handlers, chilled water, and heating systems

DISPLACEMENT VENTILATION

Displacement ventilation relies on principles of buoyancy and thermal stratification to condition and ventilate. In this project, it is used for air distribution in courtrooms, some offices, and public corridors.

The system uses low-velocity conditioned air introduced at the floor level to ventilate the occupied zone of space (the lower 2 m). Fresh air displaces warm, contaminated air surrounding people and equipment, which rises to return grilles located near the ceiling.

The HVAC system uses low-velocity conditioned air introduced at the floor level to ventilate the occupied zone of space (the lower 2 m). Fresh air displaces warm, contaminated air surrounding people and equipment, which rises to return grilles located near the ceiling.

Key: 1. Judge's chambers; 2. Judge's corridor; 3. Courtroom; 4. Attorney/ client conference room; 5. Public hallway; A. Indirect daylighting; B. Traditional ventilation; C. Displacement ventilation; D. Borrowed light through daylighting glass; E. Daylighting glass; F. Insulated view glass with shade control

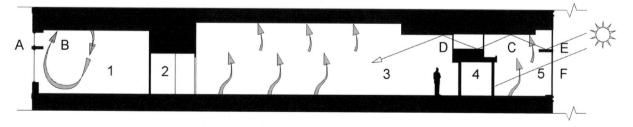

To achieve mixing, a conventional air supply system requires a minimum volume of air typically exceeding the volume required to meet the space cooling/heating load. The displacement system requires only enough air volume to meet the thermal loads in occupied zones. While the average air temperature in the displacement space is higher than that in a fully mixed space, the occupied space temperature is comparable to a fully mixed system. Because the displacement system is only fully conditioning the occupied zone, the total cooling load is reduced. Also, because the air is supplied low and naturally rises as it warms, this system requires much less fan power.

When in heating mode, the displacement system supplies slightly warmer air, and envelope heating loads are met with perimeter radiators in the office areas. The triple glazing together with slightly less critical comfort requirements in the public corridors eliminate the need for radiant heating.

EVAPORATIVE COOLING SYSTEM

An indirect/direct evaporative cooling system satisfies a substantial portion of the building's cooling and humidification loads. The system provides a cooling effect through water evaporation, greatly reducing the need to run an electric-powered chiller.

The low humidity of the Denver climate makes this evaporative cooling system usable for much of the cooling season. In fact, computer simulations predict fewer than 100 equivalent full-load hours of chiller operation per year.

In the winter, the system improves occupant comfort by adding humidity.

BUILDING AUTOMATION SYSTEM

A full DDC system is used to control the HVAC and lighting systems. The system shuts down the HVAC and lighting systems in unoccupied spaces. Combined with the VAV air-handling and pumping systems, this provides efficient operations during times of partial occupancy.

Water

Plumbing fixtures will minimize water use. Water closets and urinals will be low-flush or ultra-low-flush type; lavatory faucets will incorporate flow restrictors and infrared on-off sensors. These "no-touch" faucets reduce water consumption and help prevent transmission of disease.

Indoor Environment

The new courthouse design will create a bright, airy indoor environment that increases the comfort of building occupants. The improved building envelope together with the displacement air system and perimeter heating will eliminate cold drafts in the building. The building design has also been developed to ensure safe, healthy indoor air quality.

United States Courthouse

Miami, Florida

Building Size: 546,000 SF

Site: 302,300 SF

Completion: 2004

Budget: $186/SF, including site, parking, and interior fit-out

The new United States Courthouse, located on a two-block site in downtown Miami directly adjacent to the existing federal complex and Bureau of Prisons, will complete the existing federal complex. Arquitectonica (ARQ) and HOK are collaborating on the design of the facility, providing architecture, interior design, and landscape design services.

Highlights of the Design

- The team achieved a significant reduction in the amount of impermeable surface area. Increased landscaping means less contaminated runoff into the ecosystem.

- Native and drought-tolerant plantings will conserve water and reduce maintenance. An efficient drip irrigation system will deliver water to plants with minimal evaporation.

- The design goal is to provide 50 percent shading of glazed areas, which provides significant reductions in the cooling load.

- The building envelope uses $\frac{9}{16}$-inch laminated glazing for the curtain wall system and punched windows, which removes over 99 percent of ultraviolet (UV) radiation. Low-E glazing proved to be less effective; energy modeling showed that it trapped solar heat gain in the building.

- Since microbial growth is the leading indoor contaminant, no internal insulation will be utilized for HVAC ductwork or sound attenuators. Commissioning before occupancy will also reduce the risk of microbe-related indoor air quality problems.

- Materials include locally manufactured precast concrete; low-VOC paints, adhesives, and finishes; linoleum flooring; low-toxicity waterproofing and damp-proofing compounds; and nonendangered wood species.

- Specifications require construction waste recycling during demolition of the existing television station on the site and during construction of the new facility.

INDOOR AIR QUALITY

The building design complies with ASHRAE Standard 62-1989, the industry standard for indoor air quality. When required, humidity control will be provided by the air handler's direct evaporative system.

Outside air controls maintain the minimum design ventilation rates at all operating conditions. To improve indoor air quality requirements, outside air intakes are at least 50 feet above grade. These intakes are located to avoid reintroducing building exhaust air, vehicle exhaust, or contamination by equipment such as cooling towers.

Before specifying construction and finish materials, the team analyzed their chemical composition to eliminate products and materials with potentially harmful chemical emissions. All paints, adhesives, and finishes will be water-based and low-VOC.

During construction, mechanical systems will be isolated to avoid contamination. Closing off ducts and mechanical equipment will keep them clean, providing a healthier interior environment and prolonging the equipment's life.

Material Resources

The courthouse's exterior cladding system and interior finishes incorporate durable, regionally manufactured materials where possible, such as light buff-colored brick. Exterior paving includes Colorado sandstone.

Interior finishes with high recycled content include acoustic ceiling tile, aluminum ceiling panels and grid systems, steel framing, carpeting, and wood substrates. Renewable resources will be featured in the cork flooring, which is used throughout all courtroom floors.

While the bidding process is open and the specification is performance-based, as required by law for a government project, manufacturers that demonstrate the use of sustainable practices will be included in the specifications as acceptable sources. The team is evaluating companies based on their initiatives to reduce both embodied energy and the pollutants generated during the manufacturing and installation process.

FLEXIBLE PLAN

A flexible space planning system allows interior spaces to adapt to changing requirements over time. A raised-access flooring system for wire management enables easy reconfiguration of the building's communication, data, HVAC, and lighting systems.

MINIMIZING CONSTRUCTION WASTE

The team will reduce construction waste by being efficient about the materials purchased, reusing scrap materials, requesting that manufacturers use minimal packaging, and establishing a construction waste recycling program. Encouraging manufacturers to prefabricate building components in the factory will also help control construction waste.

Benefits of the Design

The new U.S. Federal Courthouse expansion will present an optimistic, forward-looking image to the city of Denver while making a strong case for sustainable design. Inside the courthouse, the design will project a bright, airy appearance. Green design features will also improve the work environment, which can lead to increases in employee productivity and satisfaction.

By investing in improved materials and systems and using an integrated, environmentally conscious design approach, GSA will reduce environmental impacts while reducing long-term operating costs. Because the courthouse expansion has been designated a demonstration project by GSA, lessons from this project will be used to influence future courthouse design projects.

Stadium Australia
2000 Olympic Summer Games

Homebush Bay, Sydney, Australia

Building size: 1,076,391 SF
Site: 39.52 acres
Completion: March 1999
Cost: $A 430/SF (U.S. $279/SF)

The 110,000-seat Stadium Australia is the main venue for the Sydney 2000 Olympics. The stadium will host the Summer Games' opening and closing ceremonies along with the track and field programs for the Olympics and Paralympics. After the Olympics, it will be transformed into Sydney's premier open-air stadium. The project was designed by LOBB, which has since merged with HOK to form HOK + LOBB, and a local Australian firm, Bligh Voller Nield

Environmental Goals

The International Olympic Committee (IOC) decided that the Olympic Games in Australia should be developed as the "Green Games."

The IOC requested that all new facilities for the Games be designed to high environmental standards. Within the established budget, the design team was charged to explore all opportunities to conserve energy and water resources and to develop aggressive waste reuse and recycling strategies.

Design Overview

The stadium was conceived of as an amenity that would bring the surrounding area to life 24 hours a day, attracting people to the stadium's entertainment precincts, as well as its restaurants, offices, and a banquet hall under the seating tiers.

The facility is an impressive structure. Distinctive white steel trusses are 295 m long each, half the span of the Harbour Bridge. The hyperbolic paraboloid roof is buttressed by the seating structure at the back, offering protection to many more spectators than is possible with a cantilevered roof.

After the Olympics, the stadium's upper-end tiers will be removed and end roofs will be added to convert it to an 80,000-seat venue. Placing movable seating tiers on rails allows it to be easily configured to provide optimum spectator sightlines for any event.

Economics

The design team incorporated several principles of ecologically sustainable development within the pre-Olympic building budget of $A 463 million (U.S.$300 million).

Design Process

The design team's energy modeling was among the most comprehensive ever undertaken for a stadium project. It laid the foundation for incorporating passive ventilation and natural daylighting and for selecting building systems and materials based on life cycle assessment to optimize energy use.

Additional environmental measures that were developed as an integral part of the design are cogeneration, water conservation, and advanced waste management techniques.

Site

The stadium's 16-hectare (39.5-acre) site is a former cattle-holding yard in Homebush Bay, a western suburb of Sydney. One of the planning

The stadium is supported by distinctive white steel trusses that each are 295 m long—half the span of the Harbour Bridge. The hyperbolic paraboloid roof is buttressed by the seating structure at the back, offering protection to many more spectators than possible with a cantilevered roof. After the Olympics, the stadium's upper-end tiers will be removed and end roofs will be added to convert it to an 80,000-seat venue.

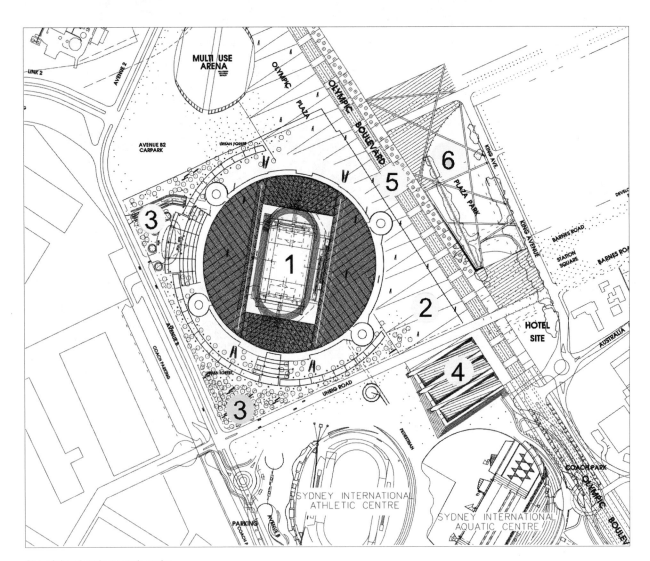

One of the planning team's major challenges was determining how to sensitively integrate such a large-scale venue into the site's suburban context. An "urban forest" highlights the landscape characteristics significant to Australia and to this specific site.
Key: 1. Stadium; 2. Olympic Plaza;
3. Urban forest; 4. Fig grove;
5. Olympic Boulevard; 6. Plaza Park.

team's major challenges was determining how to sensitively integrate such a large-scale venue into the suburban context.

An adjacent "urban forest," designed by Hargreaves Associates, highlights the landscape characteristics significant to Australia and to this specific site.

The site design took into account a nearby rail station for convenient mass transit and stadium access.

Energy

The team designed Stadium Australia to be much more energy efficient than a typical stadium. Strategies include providing passive ventilation to minimize air-conditioning, daylighting to reduce the need for artificial lighting, ample insulation to decrease energy demand, gas cogeneration generators, and gas for cooking.

Openings in the roof and walls will promote ventilation, while the roof itself will help reduce solar heat gain to the seating areas. Architectural sunshades protect the glazed wall of the banquet hall to complement the daylighting system while decreasing solar heat gain in this prominent space.

LIGHTING

The lighting strategy allows daylight to penetrate the building through large glazed walls. Research supplied by the University of Technology, Sydney, included a three-dimensional computer model illustrating how to best balance daylighting and electric lighting.

Microprocessor-based lighting controls—including passive infrared occupancy sensor and photoelectric cell daylight sensors—ensure that lighting energy is not wasted in unoccupied spaces and during daylight hours. The electric lighting system uses energy-efficient, high-lumen-per-watt light sources.

GAS-FIRED COGENERATION

To reduce demand for off-grid electricity, Stadium Australia has a gas-fired cogeneration plant consisting of two 500-kV gas-fired generators. These on-site generators work in conjunction with the main grid supply from 7:00 A.M. to 11:00 P.M., cutting energy demand on the supply authority's network.

FLEXIBLE HVAC

Environmental control systems make maximum use of passive heating and cooling, natural ventilation, and natural lighting.

HVAC services are designed to current best-practice standards, with flexibility for upgrades as technology progresses. Because the stadium's layout is modular and zoned, each sector has easy access for servicing and for making temporary adjustments to accommodate different loads.

Water

The stadium uses water conservation techniques such as a dual water supply, in which toilets and urinals are connected to a nonpotable water supply that comes from the Olympic Coordination Authority (OCA) treatment plant.

RECLAIMING RAINWATER

The most notable water reclamation measure involves collecting rainwater that falls on the stadium roof. Roof water is collected by a siphonic drainage system that passes along the main arch and down the thrust blocks into four large basement tanks with a total capacity of 3,200 m³. This capacity should satisfy the irrigation needs of the stadium's grass field.

Stormwater not collected from the roof will go into the local OCA collection system for downstream treatment and recycling. From there, the water will return to the stadium and other venues as part of a nonpotable water supply. Use of recycled and on-site collected water reduced the potable water demand by 56 percent compared to conventional designs.

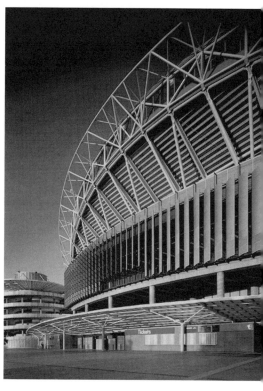

Sun shading protects the front entrance and ticketing area, and the stadium's banquet rooms above, to provide a visible statement of the environmentally sensitive design. The ramp tower beyond is part of the passive ventilation system, drawing hot air out of the stadium and reducing the air-conditioning load.

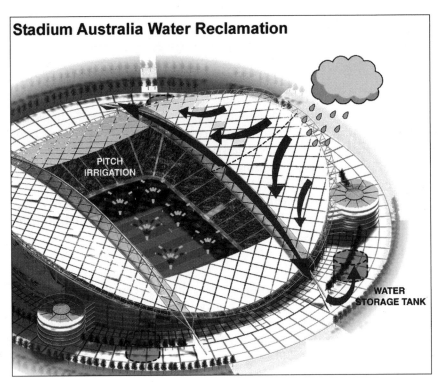

Stadium Australia Water Reclamation

PITCH IRRIGATION

WATER STORAGE TANK

Rainwater that falls on the stadium roof is collected and stored for reuse. The rainwater is collected by a siphonic drainage system that passes along the main arch and down the thrust blocks into four large basement tanks with a total capacity of 3,200 m³, which should satisfy the irrigation needs of the stadium's grass field.

Indoor Environment

Stadium Australia's ventilation system utilizes a combination of naturally driven cross ventilation, passive ventilation and cooling, mechanical ventilation, and air-conditioning. Incorporating a passive ventilation system for natural cooling has reduced the amount of interior areas that need to be air-conditioned.

PASSIVE VENTILATION SYSTEM
The integrated ventilation strategy responds to the IOC's ecologically sustainable design criteria and Multiplex's desire to ensure that patrons will be as comfortable as possible.

A natural ventilation system, using simple window openings, would not have been effective for a building this size. Instead, Stadium Australia's passive ventilation system relies on central shafts, motorized louvers, a central escalator void, and four ramp towers to draw hot air out of the stadium.

Modeling showed that the two-way flow venting via shafts would provide a robust, functional solution. Glazed screens and doors placed around the escalator shaft prevent the "dumping" of hot air from lower levels. Backdraft dampers and radiators at air inlets preheat incoming supply air, and passive night ventilation in hot weather reduces the residual cooling load.

The research, design, and application of the stadium's passive ventilation system were undertaken in England by Short-Ford and Associates

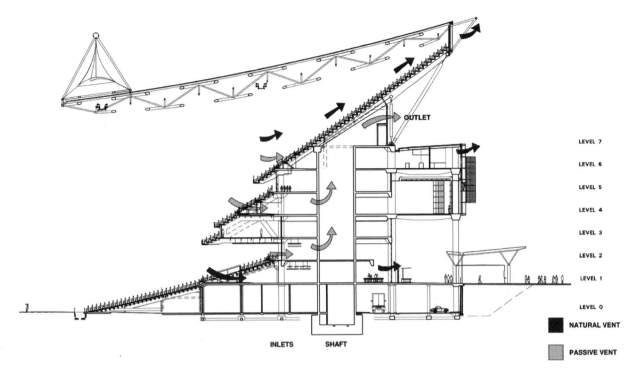

LEVEL 7
LEVEL 6
LEVEL 5
LEVEL 4
LEVEL 3
LEVEL 2
LEVEL 1
LEVEL 0

NATURAL VENT

PASSIVE VENT

OUTLET

INLETS   SHAFT

Section through stadium showing the truncated vent shaft for passive and natural ventilation. The passive ventilation system relies on central shafts, motorized louvers, a central escalator void, and four ramp towers to draw hot air out of the stadium. Backdraft dampers and radiators at air inlets preheat incoming supply air, and night ventilation in hot weather reduces the residual cooling load.

and the Cambridge Architectural Research Institute. These organizations used salt bath and other computer techniques to predict natural air flows.

Material Resources

Materials that were less energy intensive to manufacture—such as steel, concrete, and concrete blocks—were used whenever possible. Steel and concrete make up the stadium's principal structural elements. The building facade consists mostly of shaded glass, concrete blocks, and insulated steel panels.

Timber was obtained from sustainably managed sources, and wood was used sparingly.

Other guiding principles for environmentally preferable material selection included use of local source materials, minimizing use of PVC, avoiding materials that include toxic products or that produce toxins in manufacture and use, and avoiding the use of CFC as a refrigerant.

WASTE REDUCTION

Most waste generated during the stadium's operations comes from food and beverages. The three waste streams include recyclables, compostibles, and landfill waste, which are collected in the stadium's public bins.

For waste separation, the stadium has twenty-four large waste collection rooms (four on each of the six main levels) and two basement compactor rooms. Waste is transferred from concourses and back-of-house areas to these waste collection rooms. From there, compostible waste moves by chute to the basement compactors, while the rest is transferred down by vehicle.

Construction waste recycling helped meet the project goals for reuse and recycling.

Benefit of the Design

When the Games end, Stadium Australia will take its place alongside Harbour Bridge and the Sydney Opera House as a major city icon. Well into the twenty-first century, the stadium will serve as a model of ecologically smart design and act as a valuable part of Sydney's sporting and cultural life.

Use of innovative, ecological design strategies that save energy and water and recycle waste streams will reduce operating cost as well—the stadium's energy use will be reduced by over 30 percent and potable water use by over 50 percent. Based on these initiatives and others, Stadium Australia Trust will be able to realize significant economic benefits for years to come.

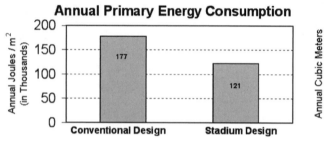

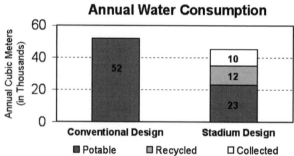

Use of on-site water collection and recycling reduced the potable water demand by 56 percent; annual energy use will be reduced by about 32 percent compared to conventional designs.

Villa Erques Eco-Resort

Tenerife, Canary Islands

Building Size:	*45,400 m² (488,685 SF)*
Site:	*255,348 m² (63 acres)*
Completion:	*2002*
Cost:	*£1,100/m² (£100/SF or U.S. $162/SF)*

Tenerife is one of the seven large Canary Islands just off Africa's western coast. It enjoys a temperate year-round climate and breathtaking natural beauty, and has become a thriving tourist destination. Villa Erques, on the island of Tenerife, will be a prestigious, five-star eco-resort village overlooking the Atlantic Ocean.

Environmental Goals

Villa Erques is an ecologically conscious hotel venture on an island where tourism has surpassed agriculture as the island's most important industry. The Canary Islands have thrived economically from industries such as shipbuilding and agriculture, which have deteriorated the island's natural resources with abusive land, building, and civil practices. The current tourism strategy in the islands seeks to combine growth and concern for the environment through the use of renewable energy sources, low-impact development, and improvement of public transportation.

Villa Erques will be a prestigious, five-star eco-resort village overlooking the Atlantic Ocean. The challenge to the design team was to develop an environmentally responsible tourist destination in an authentic village setting that would respond to Tenerife's climate, culture, history, and natural landscape. A long-term goal for Villa Erques is to receive an internationally recognized certification acknowledging the environmentally responsible design and management of the resort..

The challenge to the design team was to develop an environmentally responsible tourist destination in an authentic village setting that would respond to Tenerife's climate, culture, history, and natural landscape. A long-term goal for Villa Erques is to receive an internationally recognized certification acknowledging the environmentally responsible design and management of the resort.

Design Overview

The Villa Erques site is located midway along the southwest coast of Tenerife, between the inland villages of Adeje and Guia de Isora. Bounding the site are a banana plantation to the north, a deep barranco (dry riverbed) to the south, steep cliffs facing the Atlantic to the west, and a coastal road with a mountain backdrop to the east.

The spectacular setting includes a terraced landscape of bluffs and valleys, streams leading down to pools and a cliff edge, and a small cove at the bottom of the barranco. The site hosts natural vegetation of cacti and local succulents.

The resort layout takes the shape of a "hill village," with traditional housing following the natural contours as it radiates from a central plaza, with a chapel as the focal point.

The resort layout takes the shape of a "hill village," with traditional housing following natural contours as it radiates from a central plaza, with a chapel as the focal point. Narrow streets, open courtyards, gardens, and ocean vistas encourage guests to travel by foot.

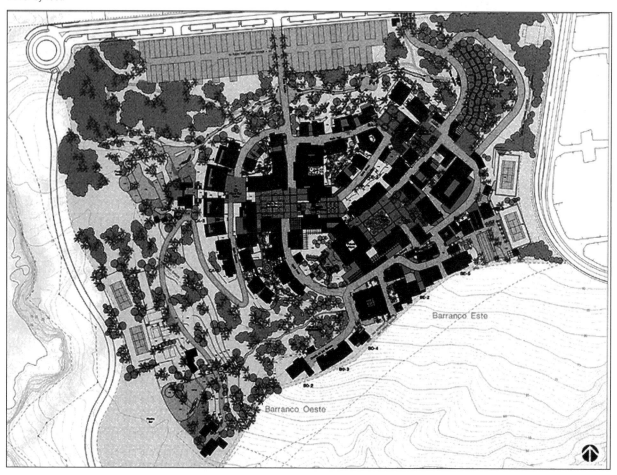

The resort village will consist of a 460-room hotel, seven restaurants, bars, recreation facilities and pools, a Congress Hall to host conferences, and community-related buildings such as a chapel, a museum, and a library.

The eco-resort's guest activities will include nature treks and visits to an organic farm, which provides fruits and vegetables for the resort.

The spectacular setting includes a terraced landscape of bluffs and valleys, streams leading down to pools and a cliff edge, and a small cove at the bottom of the barranco. The resort village, which is terraced into the hillside, will consist of a 460-room hotel, seven restaurants, bars, recreation facilities and pools, a Congress Hall to host conferences, and community-related buildings such as a chapel, a museum, and a library.

Economics

Finca Erques, the developer, understands the value of taking a long-term approach rather than seeking short-term investment returns. Sustainable design strategies are to be comprehensively incorporated throughout the project to create an economically profitable and ecologically viable development.

Local grants will help subsidize some of the features, such as the resort's solar water heating system.

Design Process

The design team performed an in-depth review of eco-tourism labeling programs to determine which one should be used to guide the design effort and ultimately to validate the environmental success of the project. The British Research Establishment Environmental Assessment Method 98 (BREEAM), Ecotel, and Green Globe were identified as the three most appropriate evaluation programs. The BREEAM system has the most detailed, specific guidance for the building and the immediate site design; however, the Green Globe and Ecotel rating systems provide better guidance for resort operations and for land and community issues. Because each of them has distinct strengths, they are all being consulted during design, and a decision has not yet been made regarding ultimate certification.

ECO-TOURISM LABELING PROGRAMS
The BREEAM system is an assessment and certification program for new buildings developed by the Building Research Establishment in England, and is the earliest and best developed of the building assessment programs. BREEAM 98, the most recent release, has a number of relatively sophisticated yet simple-to-use criteria that are weighted by environmental priorities and significance of impact. Because it is not specifically designed for hotels and resorts, however, BREEAM does not directly address many of the hotel operations, community, and social issues.

The Ecotel Certification system evaluates five categories of performance separately: solid waste management; energy efficiency; water conservation; environmental legislation compliance and native land preservation; and employee environmental education and community involvement. It was developed specifically for resorts and hotels and requires the development of a resort management plan as well as inspection of the finished facility.

Green Globe, which is modeled after the ISO 9000 and ISO 14000 systems, evaluates rating applicants in terms of relative improvement from their current state of performance, as opposed to Ecotel and BREEAM, which identify specific performance thresholds. In addition to criteria relating to the building and the site, the system evaluates social and cultural development; involvement of staff, customers, and communities in environmental issues; and environmentally sensitive purchasing.

Site

The resort design is a compact, pedestrian-friendly development that was designed to fit with the natural contours of the site. Valet parking at the perimeter of the site will mean that guests' cars are away from the village; narrow streets, open courtyards, gardens, and ocean vistas encourage guests to travel by foot.

The site's natural resources, including soil type and buildup, were studied prior to development of the site plan. The design has been developed to minimize waste—cut and fill have been balanced, topsoil will be preserved, and rock material from site excavation will be reused on-site.

The resort design is a compact pedestrian-friendly development of traditionally paved, narrow streets, designed to fit with the natural contours of the site. Landscaped buffers between streets and buildings collect and infiltrate runoff where it originates.

LANDSCAPING

The team audited the site's existing plant life to identify species that will be incorporated in the landscape design. The landscaped areas have been zoned to reduce water requirements for irrigation. Large areas will be landscaped with native plantings that do not require irrigation, and garden areas that do require irrigation will be maintained with recycled water sources.

STORMWATER RUNOFF

The master plan offers an ecological solution to stormwater management. Rain gardens and vegetated buffers will be used to collect and infiltrate runoff where it originates. Rain gardens are an attractive landscape strategy that limits the need to build channels, perforated pipes, or trenches to redirect stormwater, which also reduces the cost of construction. Native, drought-resistant vegetated buffers along shorelines and recreational areas increase the total pervious area, providing groundwater recharge.

A lagoon at the resort entrance provides storage for rainwater and runoff, as well as a water source for firefighting.

Energy

The project makes use of passive solar design, efficient lighting, integrated control systems, and renewable energy to reduce energy requirements.

Based on energy modeling, gas consumption, which is for space heating, water heating, and kitchen uses, will be reduced by 60 percent compared to standard design practices. Electricity consumption, which is for lighting, power, and air-conditioning, will be reduced by 40 percent compared to standard design practices.

CLIMATE STUDY

Ove Arup and Partners, MEP engineers for the project, completed a detailed study of the Tenerife climate. The study included analysis of weather data from several local weather stations and collection of rainfall data from the country's Ministry of Agriculture. The analysis of this temperature, humidity, wind, solar, and rainfall data informed the thermal calculations for buildings and helped guide many of the team's decisions.

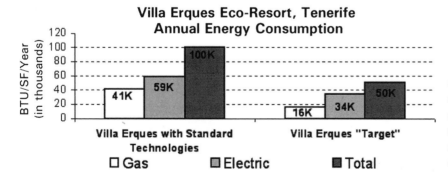

Passive solar design, efficient lighting, and integrated control systems yield an estimated 60 percent reduction in gas consumption and a 40 percent reduction in electricity consumption compared to standard design practices.

PASSIVE SOLAR FEATURES

Passive solar design features will greatly reduce overall energy use requirements. The choice of building materials, the orientation of the buildings, the placement of windows and doors, and their treatments all impact temperatures within the buildings. The building layout and facades have also been designed to promote the use of natural ventilation.

It is intended that the buildings will have thick, well-insulated walls with high thermal mass. Thermal mass, which slows the transmission of heat, creates a thermal flywheel effect in the buildings. Heat from the day slowly penetrates the massive walls, reaching the interior of buildings in the evening, when temperatures are cool; cool evening air infiltrates the building mass overnight to moderate indoor temperatures during the day.

To further minimize unwanted heat gain, windows and doors will be protected from direct sunlight by exterior shutters, interior blinds, and/or overhangs, depending on the orientation.

HVAC SYSTEMS

The passive solar design combined with energy-efficient lighting and appliances will greatly reduce cooling requirements. While buildings will have a cooling system, it is anticipated that mechanical air-conditioning will rarely be necessary. Heating requirements will also be greatly reduced due to the passive solar design and the proposed solar heating system.

Control systems that switch off lighting and air-conditioning when guests are not in their rooms further reduce energy consumption.

ALTERNATIVE ENERGY USE

Tenerife is located on latitude 28°N and benefits from high sun angles year-round. General information about solar radiation for the island indicates an average of 2,800 hours of sunshine per year—about 70 percent of the total hours possible, boosting efficiency of solar energy systems.

A large installation of solar photovoltaics is proposed for the parking areas at the outskirts of the site. The solar energy would be used to charge the batteries for the fleet of electric vehicles, which will be used to service the resort and for guest transportation.

Solar hot water heating is also under consideration. Water piping would be located under the clay tile roofing or beneath the parking lot paving.

Water

The island of Tenerife has a hot, dry climate that receives very little rainfall. Fresh water is a scarce resource that must be wisely managed.

Water conservation strategies include installation of low-water-use appliances, such as low-flush toilets and water-efficient dishwashers and washing machines, along with push-button or sensor taps throughout the resort to minimize water use.

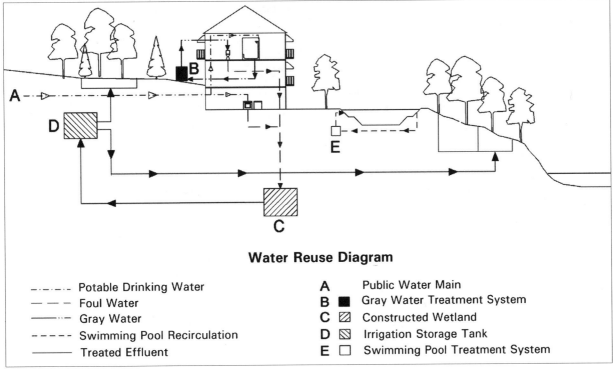

Water Reuse Diagram

–·–·–	Potable Drinking Water	**A**	Public Water Main
– – –	Foul Water	**B** ■	Gray Water Treatment System
–––·–	Gray Water	**C** ▨	Constructed Wetland
– – – –	Swimming Pool Recirculation	**D** ▧	Irrigation Storage Tank
–––––	Treated Effluent	**E** ☐	Swimming Pool Treatment System

GRAY WATER SYSTEM

Gray water from showers, sinks, washing machines, and dishwashers will be treated and then reused to meet some nonpotable water demands such as toilet flushing or irrigation.

As toilet flushing represents approximately 35 percent of the total water use in residential buildings, the reuse of gray water will reduce the total potable water demand significantly. Use of low-flow fixtures together with the gray water system will save over 120 m³/day (30,000 gal/day) of potable water.

SWIMMING POOLS

The resort master plan includes two recreational swimming pools. To conserve fresh water, the pools will be operated as low-salinity pools, using seawater combined with potable water.

Operation of the pools is planned to be entirely sustainable. Heat reclaimed from the resort's cooling system will heat the water for the pools, and solar-generated energy will operate the pumps.

Based on concern over the tremendous amount of water that may be lost from the pools—calculations show over 13,000 gal/day evaporating from 24,000 SF of pool surface—the team is exploring use of vine-covered trellises or canopies to reduce direct sun exposure and evaporation.

CONSTRUCTED WETLANDS FOR WASTEWATER TREATMENT

The setting of Villa Erques adds to the challenge of selecting an efficient and cost-effective on-site wastewater treatment technology. The rudimentary island character, the arid climate, and the focus on ecologically

Gray water from showers, sinks, washing machines, and dishwashers will be treated and then reused to meet nonpotable water demands such as toilet flushing or irrigation. To further conserve potable water, the swimming pools will be operated as low-salinity pools, using recirculating seawater combined with potable water. Treated effluent from the constructed wetland wastewater treatment system would be used for irrigation.

Villa Erques Eco-Resort

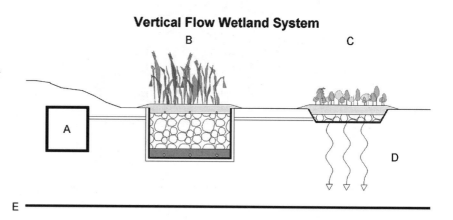

Vertical Flow Wetland System

sound alternatives strongly support the application of biological wastewater treatment. The biological wastewater treatment system also promises to be considerably less expensive than chemically based alternatives.

A vertical flow constructed wetland (also called attached growth or recirculating filter) is under consideration to provide advanced treatment of the wastewater at Villa Erques. Attractive wetland plants planted into a gravel bed purify the wastewater as it comes into contact with the plant roots and bacteria growing in the gravel matrix. Treatment of wastewater occurs subsurface, so there would be no open water surface and no mosquitoes or other nuisance organisms. A mulch layer on top of the gravel bed acts as a biofilter to control odors.

TREATED EFFLUENT FOR IRRIGATION

Treated effluent from the constructed wetland would be used for irrigation. Water pumped from the treatment works to a storage tank in the northeastern corner of the site would be distributed under gravity and pumped to the vegetated areas. Drip irrigation microtargets the root systems of landscaped areas and to keeps water loss through evaporation to a minimum.

Treated effluent that exceeds irrigation demands would infiltrate into the soils to recharge the aquifer, offsetting groundwater withdrawals from the island and preventing seawater intrusion into the aquifer.

Indoor Environment

The resort has been developed to promote an easy open-air environment. The buildings have been designed to provide shelter from the hot midday sun without requiring air-conditioning, and natural ventilation increases the movement of fresh air through the buildings.

INDOOR AIR QUALITY

When doors and windows are closed, the air quality inside will remain comfortable and healthy. Construction materials have been selected that do not off-gas chemicals, and the typical wall system proposed is one that

Typical construction in Tenerife uses a structural concrete frame with concrete block or hollow clay tile infill, which is covered with a limed finish inside and out. Roofs are clay tile, and windows and doors are traditionally made from wood timbers. One alternative solution under consideration that can be locally manufactured and contributes to better energy performance is insulating concrete forms (ICFs). If used, they would bring a new low-tech industry to the island.

"breathes." Both the wall construction and the lime finish are permeable, so that the walls can act as moisture sinks, helping to stabilize the humidity levels in the guest suites. Also, because the materials are alkaline, they will not support mold or mildew growth.

Material Resources

LOCAL MATERIALS

By using materials that are manufactured locally from resources available on the island of Tenerife, the project will conserve energy use and limit costs associated with transportation. Use of materials that originate in Tenerife helps to connect the project to the community and to support the local economy.

TYPICAL WALL CONSTRUCTION

Typical construction in Tenerife uses a structural concrete frame with concrete block or hollow clay tile infill, which is covered with a limed finish inside and out. The materials are abundantly available and low in embodied energy; however, the clay tiles provide an R-value of only 2–4, approximately the same as double-glazed window glass.

The design team searched for a locally manufactured alternative that would contribute to better energy performance. One solution under consideration, insulating concrete forms (ICFs), would bring a new low-tech industry to the island. ICFs use hollow blocks or panels, which are stacked and then filled with reinforced concrete to create a concrete "sandwich." When the thermal mass of the concrete is factored in, 30 cm thick blocks with insulation inserts produce an R-value of 29.

The preferred system is a grid block made of a mixture of cement (15 percent) and mineralized waste wood fiber (85 percent). The material is highly durable, holds nails or screws well, and can be erected without a lot of skilled labor. The blocks are laid up without mortar, rebar is inserted as needed, and the cores are poured with concrete in 1.2 m lifts.

A production facility could be set up on Tenerife to produce the blocks using locally available concrete and waste wood. While wood is not plentiful on the island, waste disposal is an ever-present problem. The feedstock for the ICFs would be waste wood material, including shipping pallets, demolition debris, land clearing debris, and the like. Agricultural waste materials are also eligible for use.

CONCRETE

Procedures are being developed to minimize environmental impacts related to concrete work. By establishing a zero-waste batch plant on-site, waste from washout can be reclaimed and reused, and concrete truck traffic can be reduced.

Only low-VOC biodegradable-form release agents or no-oil panels will be used for all in-situ concrete work. The traditionally used form release oils can impact water and soils. One common yet highly discouraged alternative to form release oil is used engine oil, which may contain heavy metals and PCBs.

TYPICAL ROOFING

The typical roofing material will be unglazed clay tile, a material that is low in embodied energy and is biodegradable at the end of its useful life. Rigid insulation and a reflective membrane will reduce heat transmission.

INTERIOR FINISHES

Interior finishes will be simple, durable, and low maintenance. Floors in the guest suites will be wood or ceramic. Walls will have a natural limed finish and no paint. All wood will be from independently certified sustainable sources. Only the conference center ballroom will be carpeted. Wood, cork, or ceramic flooring will be used for all other public areas.

REFUSE MANAGEMENT

It is estimated that the Villa Erques resort will produce approximately 1,800 kg—about 4,000 pounds—(or 16 m^3) of refuse per week. The majority of this refuse will consist of paper and organic materials.

To reduce waste, packaging will be replaced with containers that can be washed and reused to the greatest extent possible, and shampoo dispensers will be installed in bathrooms to replace individual shampoo sachets.

A compost heap is planned on-site to receive degradable organic wastes from the food service and landscaping operations, and compost will be used as a soil amenity in landscaped areas.

Benefits of the Design

Visitors and staff at the resort will represent a significant proportion of the total island population; however, per capita resource use will be impressively low. By choosing to support sustainable design strategies, the developer is reducing long-term operating costs while also contributing to the long-term health of the island ecosystem and enhancing its natural beauty.

Villa Erques will expose its many guests and the local residents to the principles of sustainability and set an example for other resort developers to move toward environmentally responsible development.

Daewoo Tower Design Competition

Inchon, Korea

Building Size:	*3,300,000 SF (355,000 m²)*
Site:	*21 acres (8.6 hectares)*
Completion:	*N/A*
Budgeted Cost:	*Confidential*

A design competition sponsored by the Song Do Daewoo, held in early 1999, provided an opportunity to define a twenty-first-century city center for the Korean market. The competition brief called for a signature tower, two hotels, a research institute, and an exhibition center in a parklike setting. HOK provided planning, architecture, and landscape design for the competition entry.

Environmental Goals

Daewoo's corporate vision—"challenge, creation, and sacrifice"—guided the teams, as they were asked to integrate intelligent building technologies and to consider sustainable design opportunities.

Design Overview

The Daewoo town site, which is located in the southern part of Inchon with excellent access to the new international airport, will become the gateway to Seoul; a monumental 102-story signature office tower creates a landmark for the new town.

The master plan develops clear pedestrian zones along the waterfront, with a direct link to transit stations and a footbridge to a wooded island preserve area at the water's edge. A raised plaza for pedestrians and local traffic frees the site from the congestion of a six-lane highway and its associated parking and services.

Because the buildings and infrastructure will be designed together, the design team was able to consider architectural design opportunities as well as enhancements to transportation, water, and waste treatment infrastructure.

Economics

The design strategies were evaluated from a life cycle cost perspective. Because energy is more expensive, some strategies that would not be cost-effective in the United States have good payback in Korea.

The Daewoo town site, which is located in the southern part of Inchon with excellent access to the new international airport, will become the gateway to Seoul. A monumental 102-story signature office tower creates a landmark for the new town, with "intelligent" facades that are particularly well suited to their Korean context.

Design Process

The design competition team included all design disciplines. Beyond Space Group and Minwoo Architects participated as Korean partners in the design. The mechanical engineers from the New York office of Flack & Kurtz had previous experience designing highly energy-efficient buildings in Korea and so were familiar with the climate, building codes, and economics associated with building in Korea.

Site

The master plan includes generous amounts of open space as well as public park areas. Two proposed metro stations at the base of the tower will encourage employees and visitors to commute by public transportation, relieving traffic congestion and reducing the need for automobiles.

STORMWATER
The site design reduces concentrated stormwater flows. Where roadways and other impervious surfaces are built up on grade, rather than on parking decks, grassy swales and bioretention zones encourage on-site stormwater retention and groundwater recharge. Given the project's environmentally sensitive site adjacent to the bay, it was important to consider pretreatment of water prior to discharge.

WASTEWATER TREATMENT
Because of the scale of the project, some kind of wastewater infrastructure will need to be developed for the project. HOK recommended that the feasibility of constructed wetlands for on-site wastewater treatment be evaluated as an alternative to conventional sewage systems. Ample availability of parkland and open space around the site promises that the use of biological wastewater treatment—which relies on plant roots and gravel filtration—would be practical and cost-effective.

LANDSCAPING
The landscaping has been designed to minimize maintenance requirements. The large majority of plantings will be native plants tolerant of the site's soils, climate, and water availability. Wherever possible, permanent, low-maintenance ground covers will be used in place of turf grasses.

Energy

The integrated architectural and engineering design solutions achieve significant energy efficiencies. The triangle-shaped office tower was designed with an innovative double-skin climate wall that will dramatically reduce energy loads related to heating and cooling. Energy savings will come from the climate wall, efficient lighting systems, integrated use of daylight, and energy-efficient technologies such as economizer cycles, heat recovery, and cogeneration.

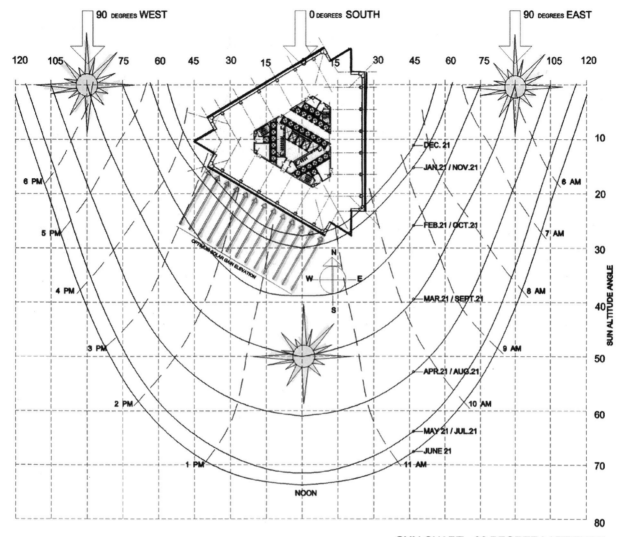

SUN CHART - 38 DEGREE LATTITUDE

Displacement ventilation was studied carefully and dismissed because of the high costs associated with adapting the underfloor ventilation to a high-rise building.

CLIMATE WALL

The double-glazed exterior skin, or "climate wall," which improves energy efficiency, is particularly well suited to Korean conditions. Summer in Korea can be a time of discomfort and reduced productivity for office workers, with local energy codes that do not allow for the use of air-conditioning until indoor temperatures reach as high as 80 degrees Fahrenheit. The climate wall dissipates summer heat gain through an exterior venting channel between the glazing layers, increasing comfort and reducing reliance on mechanical cooling.

Computer-controlled vents installed in the outer curtain wall at two-story intervals regulate ventilation based on varying environmental conditions up and down the tower. Hot air in the exterior wall is vented out of the top of each two-level cavity when thermosensors and dampers

The integrated architectural and engineering design solutions achieve significant energy efficiencies. The triangle-shaped office tower was designed with an innovative climate wall and positioned with an optimized solar orientation. One side faces east and one side faces northwest, with only one side exposed to the south.

The climate wall dissipates summer heat gain by moving air through the space between the glazing layers, increasing comfort and reducing reliance on mechanical cooling. In winter, the climate wall provides an insulating layer of warm air to protect the building interior from heat loss.

Key: 1. Computer-controlled vents are open to the exterior in summer; 2. As warm air rises in the airspace it creates a convective current; 3. The interior curtain wall remains closed; 4. Interior air is circulated through the airspace to heat the building; 5. Computer-controlled dampers open under the raised-access floor; 6. The exterior vents remain closed; 7. Warmed air is drawn out of the air space through ducts that deliver heated air to the cold sides of the tower.

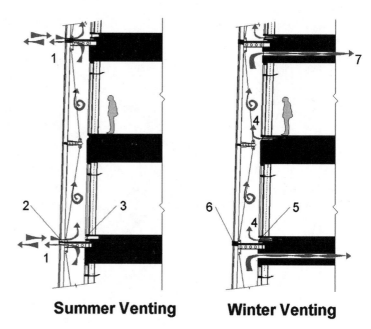

Summer Venting **Winter Venting**

determine that external conditions are within the parameters for venting to occur.

In winter, the climate wall provides an insulating layer of warm air to protect the building interior from heat loss. Vents to the exterior close in winter, so the air space between the glazing layers can be warmed by the sun. Fans will redistribute warmed air from the south side of the building to the air spaces on the colder sides of the building, further reducing the heating load.

Water

Anticipated reductions in potable water consumption are based on use of water-efficient plumbing fixtures and a gray water system. The proposed gray water system will reclaim stormwater, condensate from the chilled water plant, and wash water from lavatories, and reuse the water for toilet flushing. Use of gray water systems is not uncommon in Korea.

Waterless urinals have been proposed to reduce water consumption while also minimizing maintenance costs.

Cooling towers will use an automated blowdown system that allows for increased cycles of concentration, creating savings in water consumption and in chemical use for water treatment.

Indoor Environment

The design creates a high-quality indoor environment in terms of temperature control, fresh air supply, indoor air quality, and lighting quality.

The climate wall design buffers the interior from solar heat gain and temperature extremes. The building will stay cooler in summer than conventional buildings, and will have fewer temperature variations.

INDOOR AIR QUALITY

Indoor air quality will be improved through the use of a minimum of 20 CFM of fresh air per person, an outside air economizer system that will provide increased quantities of outside air when weather permits, and an air filtration system with 30 percent prefilters and 80 percent final filters. Demand-controlled ventilation systems linked to occupancy and CO_2 sensors will allow for decreases in ventilation air quantities only when spaces are unoccupied or partially occupied.

Because smoking is still common in Korea, designated smoking areas will be provided on each floor that will operate under negative pressure, with 100 percent of the air exhausted through dedicated risers.

LIGHTING

Perimeter light shelves project daylight up onto the ceiling and deeper into the interior. Pendant direct/indirect lighting illuminates the ceiling, giving the interior a more spacious feeling. Anticipating the use of a task-ambient lighting approach, the team specified that general ambient lighting levels be reduced to 30–40 foot-candles, with task lighting on the work surfaces. In addition to being more energy efficient, this type of lighting decreases glare and shadowing.

CONNECTION WITH NATURE

Among the features making the building desirable for future occupants is the connection with nature. This includes many natural plantings and generous development of gardens and parks. The design also includes an atrium space, a landscaped plaza over roadways and parking structures, and many views of the water.

LESS MAINTENANCE

Design decisions can minimize future cleaning requirements. Airlock vestibules with removable walk-off mats capture a large proportion of dirt before it is tracked into the building. The air filtration system also reduces airborne particulates. These features can translate into longer intervals between vacuuming and cleaning of flooring surfaces.

Material Resources

A project of this magnitude can significantly affect future markets for materials and can stimulate the market for construction waste recycling. During design development, the design team plans to closely examine all material specifications to select the most environmentally friendly products.

FLEXIBLE DESIGN

The design of flexible office interiors also reduces future waste while increasing the building's market appeal to future tenants. Raised-access flooring for electrical and communications distribution and expansive,

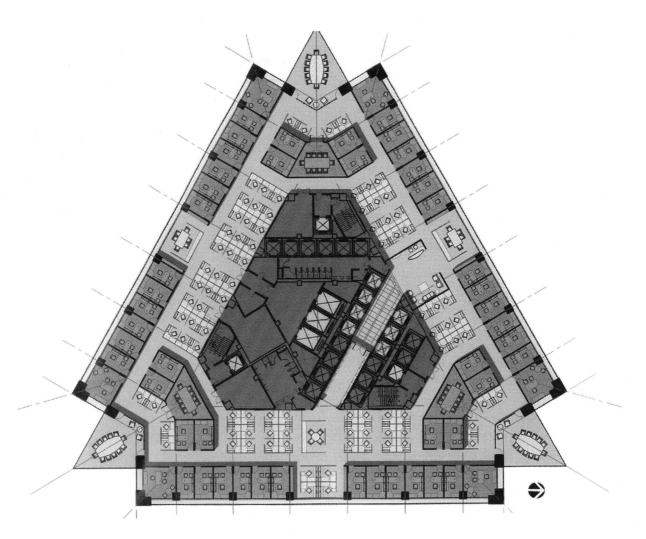

Raised-access flooring for electrical and communications distribution and expansive, column-free interior spaces allow tenants to accommodate future changes with minimal waste and disruption. The building core contains recycling chutes that vertically transport common recyclables and organic waste for composting.

column-free interior spaces allow tenants to accommodate future changes with minimal waste and disruption.

RECYCLING

The tower design facilitates recycling by occupants. The building core contains recycling chutes that vertically transport both common recyclables and organic waste for composting. The chutes conveniently transport materials from the office floors to central recycling collection areas.

Benefits of the Design

As a twenty-first-century "smart building" and potentially one of the tallest buildings in the world, the Daewoo Tower would command a compelling image organic waste for composting within both the city and Korea.

Based on its use of advanced building systems and environmentally friendly design, the Daewoo complex would provide an excellent model of environmentally responsible and economically smart design.

The proposed green design would benefit the developer as well, with tangible reductions in operating and maintenance costs. The largest savings come from reductions in energy consumption due to daylighting and the passive solar double-skin exterior glazing. Savings will also be realized from less consumption of potable water, on-site stormwater and wastewater treatment, low-maintenance landscaping, reduced cleaning requirements, and revenue from recycling.

Fort Bonifacio
New City Master Plan

Manila, Philippines

Building Size: N/A
Site: 1,100 acres (440 hectares)
Completion: 1996 (master plan)
Cost: N/A

Fort Bonifacio is a master plan for a completely new world-class city in metropolitan Manila, on a 440-hectare site that once housed a Philippine military base. HOK created planning, urban design, and landscape guidelines for the city, which has been planned to accommodate a daytime population of more than 1 million people and 250,000 full-time residents.

Environmental Goals

The Fort Bonifacio Development Corporation—a joint venture between a developer and the Philippine government—is concerned not only with its investment, but also with the land and its people. The group believes that "land is not inherited from our forefathers, rather it is borrowed from our children."

The design goal was to create an environmentally sensitive metropolis for the twenty-first century and to reduce sprawl, traffic congestion, and reliance on the automobile. The city has been envisioned as one that is pedestrian friendly and provides ample space for tree-lined boulevards, parks, and open space.

Design Overview

The master plan calls for five phases of development during the next twenty-five to thirty years that will contain 9.3 million m² of public, residential, commercial, and mixed-use space, integrated into a diverse collection of neighborhoods, each with its own distinct character.

At the heart of the northern section of Fort Bonifacio is Central Commons, an open green space, surrounded by the City Center District, an entertainment district that forms the area's inner ring. This city center also contains an extensive underground transit hub for the city.

Fort Bonifacio is a master plan for a completely new world-class city in metropolitan Manila, on a 440-hectare site that once housed a Philippine military base. While Asian cities do not traditionally have much open green space, each of Fort Bonifacio's five districts will have its own unique public parks, plazas, and greenways, making Fort Bonifacio a pedestrian-friendly city.

To the northeast is an institutional district planned to accommodate a university campus, a hospital, a management institute, a civic center, and the new National Cathedral. The quieter residential areas, in which density gradually decreases away from the city center, are to the south and west.

Economics

Investments were made to develop spacious pedestrian-friendly streets and boulevards, convenient public transportation, open space, and parkland. These amenities added cost to the project; however, they were seen as worthwhile investments that would produce a city of lasting value.

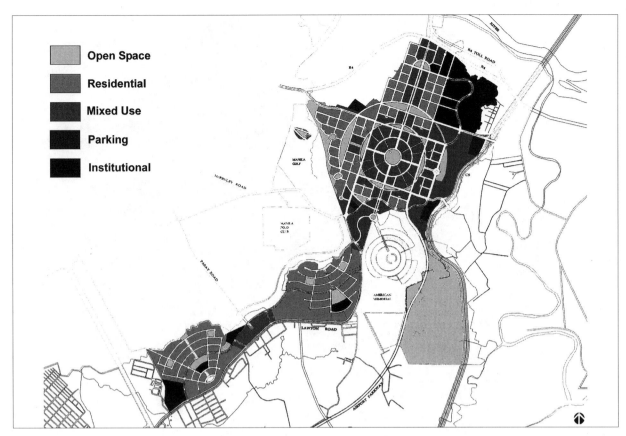

Open Space
Residential
Mixed Use
Parking
Institutional

The master plan contains 9.3 million m² of public, residential, commercial, and mixed-use space that is integrated into a diverse collection of neighborhoods, each with its own distinct character.

Design Process

Before beginning to plan the city, project executives toured thirteen cities in Europe and the United States to spark ideas about the kind of city they wanted to develop.

The design team then worked to plan an urban environment with the density of Manhattan while synthesizing the most desirable characteristics of several cities worldwide. The plan borrows from the formal geometry of New York's street grid, the broad radial avenues of Paris, the skywalks of Hong Kong, transit systems of Frankfurt and London, parking systems in Barcelona and Minneapolis, and the organic lines of Frederick Law Olmsted's picturesque American towns.

Site

The Fort Bonifacio plan is markedly different from the auto-oriented planning approaches prevalent in many parts of the United States and Asia, because it encourages people to walk and use public transportation instead of driving.

TRANSIT
The transit system designed for Fort Bonifacio provides an integrated network of buses, shuttles, taxis, subways, heavy and light rail systems, and

Bonifacio Blvd. (City Center): 4 Lanes - 2 Way - 30 Meter R.O.W.

Bonifacio Blvd. (North & South): 4 Lanes with Dedicated Trolley R.O.W. - 2 Way - 42 Meter R.O.W.

a trolley line. Local and regional transit systems come together in a 15-hectare underground multimodal station near the City Center District.

The future development of these transit systems is ensured through transit route protection of both the above- and below-grade transit systems. These routes are identified both in the master plan and in subsequent specific plans and guidelines for each project phase.

PEDESTRIAN NETWORK

The memorable street framework ranges from grand ceremonial axes such as Bonifacio Boulevard to winding parkways and pedestrian-scaled streets. The ceremonial axes are pedestrian- and transit-oriented, with broad sidewalks and a streetcar line along Bonifacio Boulevard.

Networks of linked building arcades, canopy trees to shade sidewalks, and carefully positioned water features create an appealing pedestrian environment that provides shelter from Manila's hot, humid climate. Throughout much of the development, pedestrians also will have the choice of avoiding street traffic by traveling through a network of second-level skywalks.

The transit system designed for Fort Bonifacio provides an integrated network of buses, shuttles, taxis, subways, heavy and light rail systems, and a trolley line. The ceremonial axes are pedestrian- and transit-oriented, with broad sidewalks and a trolley along Bonifacio Boulevard. The future development of these transit systems is ensured through transit route protection of both the above- and below-grade transit systems.

Networks of linked building arcades, canopy trees to shade sidewalks, and carefully positioned water features create an appealing pedestrian environment that provides shelter from Manila's hot, humid climate.

PARKING

Public parking is distributed between perimeter parking facilities (similar to Minneapolis) and underground garages beneath open spaces (as in Barcelona). These parking facilities are located near transit systems.

Those who park within the City Center District will encounter streets that minimize on-street parking. High garage fees within individual buildings will discourage traffic on local streets.

OPEN GREEN SPACE

While Asian cities do not traditionally have much open green space, each of Fort Bonifacio's five districts—Bonifacio North, Crescent West, City Center, Station Square, and University Park—will have its own unique public parks, plazas, and greenways. These pleasant green spaces help make Fort Bonifacio a pedestrian-friendly city. They also provide gathering places, landmarks, and a sense of place for each neighborhood.

MIXED-USE DEVELOPMENT

The integration of dense office, retail, and residential space within city blocks creates vibrant urban neighborhoods and further reduces the need for automobiles. Shops, offices, and places of entertainment can be reached on foot or through public transportation. While this is common in cities such as New York and Paris, it is rare in a new city. The goal is to create a critical mass of interactions that reduces sprawl and creates true neighborhoods.

Energy

Efficient district cooling is being incorporated on a district-by-district basis, and design guidelines set standards for energy-efficient design criteria such as the use of high-performance glazing.

Water

The development of a gray water system for irrigation is being studied. Plantings requiring high water use, such as grass, are discouraged.

Indoor Environment

Not applicable.

Material Resources

The design guidelines developed for Fort Bonifacio encourage the use of environmentally friendly materials and local materials whenever possible.

Benefits of the Design

The rapid development of Manila in the past ten years has outstripped the capacity of its infrastructure, resulting in a crowded, traffic-congested environment. The development of Fort Bonifacio will help meet the needs of the region's growing population while providing a positive model for future development.

The creation of public parks, plazas, and greenways will create inviting green spaces, making Fort Bonifacio a truly pedestrian-friendly city.

The integration of dense office, retail, and residential space within city blocks creates vibrant urban neighborhoods— shops, offices, and places of entertainment can be reached on foot or through public transportation. The goal is to create a critical mass of interactions that reduces sprawl and creates true neighborhoods.

Glossary

1,1,1-trichloroethane Nonflammable liquid, insoluble in water, soluble in alcohols and organic solvents. Classified as a volatile organic compound and a chlorinated aliphatic hydrocarbon. May cause headache, lassitude, central nervous system depression, poor equilibrium, irritation of eyes, dermatitis, cardiac arrhythmia. Used in rubber floor and wall coverings, paint and paint thinners, synthetic resin and rubber adhesives, and solvent-thinned stains and finishes. Also known as methyl chloroform. *See* 33/50 Program. Identified by EPA as a persistent, bioaccumulative, toxic pollutant. *See* PBT.

1,1,2-trichloroethane Nonflammable liquid with pleasant odor. Insoluble in water, miscible with alcohol and other organic liquids. Classified as a volatile organic compound and a chlorinated aliphatic hydrocarbon. May cause irritation of nose and eyes, central nervous system depression, liver and kidney damage. Carcinogen. Used as solvent for fats, waxes, natural resins, and alkaloids.

2-ethoxylethanol Practically odorless liquid. May cause reproductive and teratogenic effects, blood changes. Used as solvent for lacquers, in varnish removers, cleansing solutions, dye baths. Also known as ethylene glycol monoethyl ether and cellosolve.

33/50 Program One of EPA's initiatives to encourage source reduction, or pollution prevention. This voluntary program had targeted 17 high-priority chemicals for reduction. The program name came from EPA's national goal of reducing production-related chemical releases by 33 percent in 1992 and by 50 percent in 1995, using 1988 quantities as a baseline. The 17 priority chemicals, which should still be avoided where feasible, include benzene, cadmium and compounds, carbon tetrachloride, chloroform, chromium and compounds, cyanide compounds, dichloromethane, lead and compounds, mercury and compounds, methyl ethyl ketone, methyl isobutyl ketone, nickel and compounds, tetrachloroethylene, toluene, 1,1,1-trichloroethane, trichloroethylene, and xylenes. This successful program ended in 1995.

4-phenylcyclohexene (4-PC) Organic chemical formed by reaction of butadiene and styrene. This chemical has a characteristic "new carpet" odor. Classified as a volatile organic compound. Carpet backing containing the synthetic compound styrene butadiene (known as SB) latex, a common secondary backing to broadloom carpets, may contain 4-PC. The results of several tests have indicated that 4-PC and SB latex are not significant toxins at the levels typically present in carpeting. EPA has called 4-PC "unremarkable" in regard to indoor air toxicity. However, the odor from 4-PC may produce discomfort in sensitive individuals, and, in response, the carpet industry has reduced the average concentration of 4-PC in SB latex by 80 percent since 1988. The Carpet and Rug Institute's indoor air quality testing program has set 4-PC limits in carpet and carpet cushion at 0.05 mg/m^2-hr for those products participating in their Green Label program. *See* Carpet backing.

Absorptance The ratio of the radiation absorbed by a surface to the total energy falling on that surface.

Absorption Process whereby a porous material extracts one or more substances from an atmosphere, a mixture of gases, or a mixture of liquids.

Acetate Generic term for man-made fibers composed of cellulose acetate, a substance derived from cellulose by action of acetic anhydride and other chemicals. Used in adhesives. *See* Cellulosic and polyvinyl acetate.

Acetone A volatile, extremely flammable liquid, with a pungent odor. Classified as a volatile organic compound and ketone. Miscible with water, used as a solvent and reagent. May cause irritation of eyes, nose, and throat, headache, dizziness, defatting dermatitis. Used as solvent in waxes, resins, rubber, plastics, lacquers, paints, varnish, varnish remover, rubber cement.

ACH Air changes per hour. Ventilation or infiltration rate that denotes the number of complete changes of the air within the volume of a given space each hour.

Acid rain Precipitation that has a pH below 5.6. Main contributors are sulfur dioxide from industrial burning of fossil fuel, and nitrogen oxide from automobile emissions, which is transformed into nitrogen dioxide.

Acrylic impregnated flooring Prefinished sheet flooring system that has had liquid acrylic forced under pressure into its porous structure. The acrylic hardens, forming an extremely abrasion-resistant finish throughout the entire thickness. Dyes and fire retardants may be added.

Acrylic polymers A family of plastic materials used for rigid plastic sheets (Plexiglas), liquid coatings (floor and wax sealers), paints, and many other products. Acrylics are made from acrylic acids, methacrylate, or acrylonitrile, all derived from petroleum. Acrylonitrile is a known carcinogen. Acrylic plastics are relatively stable and low in toxicity.

Acrylonitrile butadiene styrene (ABS) Rubber and thermoplastic composites made by blending acrylonitrile-styrene copolymer with a butadiene-acrylonitrile rubber, to combine the hardness and strength of the vinyl resin with the toughness and impact resistence of the rubbery component. Use in pipes. *See also* Acrylonitrile.

Acrylonitrile Explosive, flammable, and toxic liquid. May polymerize spontaneously. Miscible with most organic solvents. May cause asphyxia, irritation of eyes, headache, sneezing, nausea, vomiting, weakness, light-headedness, scaling dermatitis. Carcinogen. Used in manufacture of acrylic rubber and fibers, in plastics, surface coatings and adhesive industries. Also known as vinyl cyanide.

Adaptive controllers Controls in which one or more features are sensed and used to adjust feedback control signals to satisfy performance criteria.

Additive A substance added to facilitate processing, strengthen, stabilize, or otherwise improve the performance of a product. The most widely used additives to plastics are plasticizers (mainly phthalates and phosphates), which both improve the processing of plastics and increase their flexibility; antioxidants (phenols and amines); metal scavengers (amides, hydrazones, and hydrazides); light stabilizers (2,4-dihydroxybenzophenone); lubricants (fatty acids), which expedite processing during manufacture; fillers, extenders, or reinforcements (talc, wood flour, sand, nut shells, glass, graphite); flame retardants (polyhalogen compounds, phosphorus compounds, antimony trioxide). Also may include antistatic agents, pigments, whitening agents, blowing agents, accelerators, impact modifiers, biostabilizers (pesticides).

Adhered backing A secondary carpet backing that is applied to the primary backing with adhesives (latex adhesives are the most common). Cushion backings usually fall into this category.

Adhesive Material that bonds surfaces of different materials. Adhesives may be liquid or tacky semisolids, natural or synthetic, organic or inorganic, waterborne, solvent-borne, or solventless. Examples of natural adhesives include water solutions of starch, dextrin, or casein glues (for sizing of textiles), bituminous adhesives from petroleum asphalt, coal and pitch (for roofing), rubber and latex (in pressure-adhesive tapes), sodium silicate (for ceramics). Synthetic adhesives include acrylics, cyanoacrylates, epoxies, synthetic rubbers, phenolic resins, polyolefins, polyamides, polyesters, styrene-butadiene polymers, silicones, urethanes, and vinyl polymers and copolymers (for metals, wood, plastic, glass, and ceramics). Solvent-based adhesives can be sources of VOC emissions (including aliphatic hydrocarbons, aromatic hydrocarbons, chlorinated hydrocarbons, ketones, and/or esters) during and after application. Alternatives to adhesives to eliminate VOC emissions include use of mechanical connectors and other products, e.g., cementitious grout compounds. VOC limits in adhesives have been set by regulatory entities such as California's South Coast Air Quality Management District to prevent smog formation.

Admixture A material, other than aggregate, cement, or water, added in small amounts to a cement base mixture (e.g., concrete or plaster) to change its properties, such as improved workability, faster setting time, increased strength, greater watertightness. Examples include accelerators, air entraining agents, plasticizers, waterproofing agents, water reducing agents, coloring agents.

Aerobic digestion Treatment of sludge or other thickened slurries that is typically used to decrease the solids content of a sludge or to remove pathogenic organisms. In concentrated slurries, aerobic digestion can generate considerable quantities of heat. Examples include extended aeration and ATAD (auto thermal aerobic digestion). Composting can be thought of as an aerobic digestion process using a relatively small water content.

Aerobic treatment Removal of organic pollutants in wastewater by bacteria, requiring oxygen with water and carbon dioxide as the end results of the treatment process. Processes include trickling filtration, activated sludge, and rotating biological contactors.

AFUE Annual fuel utilization efficiency of a combustion heating appliance. AFUE differs from steady-state efficiency since it employs an empirical equation to deduct all operational losses, which include vent losses, cyclic effects, part-load operation, and continuously burning pilot lights (now rare).

Aggregate Natural sands, gravels, and crushed stone used for mixing with cementing materials in making mortars and concretes. Also can be added to paint for texture or nonslip flooring surface.

Agricultural by-product Ancillary product of farming, several of which may be used in building materials, e.g., straw used to make wall panels, or as bales in a technique called straw bale construction.

Air changes *See* ACH.

Air economizer A ducting arrangement and automatic control system that allows a cooling supply fan system to supply outside air to reduce or eliminate the need for mechanical refrigeration during mild or cold weather.

Air infiltration barrier (AIB) An AIB consists of one or more air-impermeable components, sealed at all seams and penetrations to form a continuous wrap around building walls. Air infiltration barriers can dramatically reduce the air infiltration rates through a building envelope.

Air-to-air heat exchanger *See* Heat recovery ventilator. A heat recovery ventilator (also known as an air-to-air heat exchanger) transfers heat directly from one airstream to another through either side of a metal transfer surface. This surface can be convoluted plates (for low-temperature use in HVAC systems) or tubes (for boiler flue gas heat transfer). The heat exchangers are available as packaged units or custom made. Efficiencies tend to be lower than 50 percent, but these exchangers are relatively inexpensive, have low resistance to airflow, need no power input, and are durable.

Alcohol Organic compound having one or more –OH (hydroxyl) group; lower alcohols are water soluble. Used as solvents and organic intermediates. Common building-related alcohols include methanol, ethanol, isopropanol, butanol, glycol, butanediol, amyl alcohol, glycerol, and ethylene glycol.

Aldehyde Organic compound (e.g., acetaldehyde, acrolein, benzaldehyde, formaldehyde, or ketene). May cause irritation and sensitization. Acrolein is a suspected carcinogen, and formaldehyde is a recognized carcinogen. Used in plastics, resins, sealants, wood preservatives, and biocides.

Aliphatic hydrocarbon Organic compound characterized by straight-chain, branched, or cyclic carbon chain. Lower-molecular-weight aliphatic hydrocarbons are classified as volatile organic compounds. Aliphatic hydrocarbons differ from aromatic hydrocarbons by the absence of benzene or fused-ring systems.

Alkyd resins A class of transparent, flexible, and tough adhesive resins made from unsaturated acids and glycerol. Properties depend on starting material. Used in coatings, adhesives, plasticizers, paints, binders, enamels.

Allergen Chemical or biological antigenic agent that is capable of causing allergic reactions in susceptible individuals, which may be evidenced by skin rashes, breathing difficulties, malaise or hay fever. *See* Antigen.

Alloyed metal A metal consisting of a combination of two or more elements. Alloys have different properties than the pure metals, e.g., strength, corrosion resistance, or hardness. Examples include brass, bronze, steel.

Ambient air Surrounding atmosphere.

Ambient lighting Lighting throughout an area that produces general illumination.

Ambient temperature Dry bulb temperature of the medium (air, water, or earth) surrounding people, objects, or equipment.

Amine Organic compounds that can be considered to be derived from ammonia by replacing one or more hydrogens by functional groups. The simplest aromatic amine is aniline. 4,4'-methylene dianiline (MDA) is used to manufacture methylene diparaphenylene diisocyanate (MDI), which is used in formaldehyde-free medium-density fiberboard. Other common amines include butylamine, dimethylamine, ethylamine, hexylamine, and methylamine. May cause irritation and sensitization.

Ammonia fumigation A process using ammonia gas to neutralize formaldehyde emissions from such materials as particleboard and adhesives. *See also* Hexamethylene tetramine *and* Formaldehyde scavengers.

Ammonia   Corrosive, alkaline, nonflammable gas that is very soluble in water, has a characteristic pungent odor, is lighter than air. Manufactured from natural gas. May cause eye, nose and throat irritation, dyspnea, bronchiospasm and chest pain, pulmonary edema, pink frothy sputum, skin burns, vesiculation. Used to manufacture melamine, urea formaldehyde, nylons, acrylonitrile. Used in the rubber industry for production of polyurethanes and blowing agents for foam rubber. Household ammonia concentrations are typically 5–10 percent in strength, and when mixed with bleach form a toxic gas (ammonium chloride).

Ammonium sulfide   Used to apply patina to bronze and brass and in textile manufacture.

Angle of incidence   The angle direct light (such as the sun's rays) make with a line perpendicular to a surface. The angle of incidence is a key determinant of the percentage of direct light intercepted by a surface. The sun's rays that are perpendicular are said to be "normal" to that surface.

Aniline dye   Oily, combustible, poisonous liquid, with a characteristic odor and burning taste. Intoxication may occur from inhalation, ingestion, or skin contact. Acute effects may include cyanosis, methemoglobinemia, vertigo, headache, mental confusion. Aniline is a carcinogen. Used in manufacture of dyes, resins, varnishes, vulcanizing rubber, and as a solvent.

Annual fuel utilization efficiency   *See* AFUE.

Annual heating degree days (HDD)   The sum of all heating degree days over a calendar year. *See also* Degree days heating.

Annual cooling degree days (CDD)   The sum of all cooling degree days over a calendar year. *See also* Degree days cooling.

Antibacterial agent   A synthetic or natural compound that inhibits the growth and division of bacteria. Differs from bacteriocide, which is used to kill bacteria.

Antigen   Any substance that stimulates the production of antibody and/or activated immune cells.

Antimicrobial agent   Chemical formulations incorporated into or applied onto a material to suppress or retard vegetative bacterial and fungal growth (also known as bacteriostatic or fungistatic agent). Antimicrobial agents may be added to textiles, carpet, hard-surface flooring, roofing products, concrete reinforcements, protective coatings, paints, and wallpaper to retard growth and resulting odors. Many of these products are bound to fibers or material agents and will be limited in effectiveness if a layer of dirt intervenes. Use of antimicrobial agents does not substitute for moisture control and regular cleaning and maintenance.

Antimony and compounds   Silver-white, lustrous, hard, brittle metal, which tarnishes only slowly. Antimony and compounds may cause dermatitis, keratitis, conjunctivitis, and nasal septal ulceration by contact, fumes, or dust. An extremely toxic chemical, stibine, can be formed when free hydrogen (e.g., from storage batteries) reacts with antimony. Antimony is used in metal coating and in the manufacture of alloys. Antimony compounds are suspected of being carcinogenic. Identified by EPA as a persistent, bioaccumulative, toxic pollutant. *See* PBT.

Aromatic hydrocarbon   Unsaturated cyclic organic compound; benzene is the parent compound. Lower-molecular-weight aromatic hydrocarbons are classified as volatile organic compounds. Common examples are benzene, toluene, xylene, and ethylbenzene, derived from coal and naphthas. Used as feedstock for organic chemicals (e.g., nylon, styrene, detergents, plasticizers, alkyd resins).

Arsenic   Poisonous metal. Soft element with metallic luster. Obtained as by-product in flue gases from smelting copper, lead, cobalt, and gold ores. May cause acute and chronic toxicity either by inhalation or ingestion, e.g., skin, liver, bladder, kidney, or lung cancer. Direct contact can cause local irritation and dermatitis. Used as wood preservative, herbicide, pesticide, and in the manufacture of low-melting-point glass. Identified by EPA as a persistent, bioaccumulative, toxic pollutant. *See* PBT.

Arsenical   Biocide containing arsenic (e.g., arsenic acid) used in outdoor decking and other wood products to protect them from insect damage.

Asbestos   The only natural mineral fiber. Asbestos is composed of fibrous silicates of magnesium and calcium, also iron and aluminum. Most asbestos comes from Canada (Quebec), South Africa, and Russia (Ural Mountains). Includes both serpentine (e.g., chrysotile) and amphibole (e.g., anthophyllite, tremolite, amosite, and crocidolite) forms. In the amphibole series, crocidolite is considered most hazardous. Most asbestos used in the United States is chrysotile. Most dangerous route of exposure is through inhalation. Significant exposure may result in a diffuse interstitial fibrosis of the lung tissue termed asbestosis. Carcinogenic. Industrial exposures have resulted in higher rates of lung cancer and mesothelioma. Asbestos is heat-resistant and chemically inert and is used as filler in tile, reinforced cement, gaskets, brake linings, textiles, and insulation.

ASHRAE American Society of Heating, Refrigerating, and Air Conditioning Engineers.

Asphalt Black, semisoft mixture of hydrocarbons from animal origins. Also, residue left after removing tar tailings from petroleum distillation. Asphalt fumes are carcinogenic. Used in adhesives, coatings (roofs, floors, wood), sealants, rubber, and paint.

Asphalt treated paper A paper that is coated or impregnated with a bituminous material known as asphalt. Used to provide a barrier to moisture as a facing on batt insulation.

ASTM American Society for Testing and Materials. Organization chartered to develop standards on characteristics and performance of materials, products, systems, and services.

Atactic polypropylene (APP) One of three primary modified bitumen membrane types used for roofing. Modified bitumen made with atactic polypropylene is heat weldable and has thermoplastic properties. *See also* Modified Bitumen.

Azimuth The angle between true south and the point on the horizon directly below the sun.

Backed vinyl Vinyl product consisting of a surface wear layer of vinyl and a backing layer, usually of fabric, paper, or plastic foam. Also known as laminated vinyl.

Ballast A device used to obtain the necessary circuit conditions (voltage, current, and wave form) for starting and operating an electric-discharge lamp.

Ballast factor (BF) The ratio of light output of fluorescent lamp(s) operated on a ballast to the light output of the lamp(s) operated on a reference ballast.

Ballasted roofing membrane A method by which roofing membranes are held in place by rounded gravel spread on the surface of the roofing material. Ballast protects the roofing material from wind and excessive ultraviolet exposure. With this technique, materials are easily separated at the end of their life for reuse, recycling, or disposal.

Barium sulfate Naturally occurring mineral, practically insoluble in water. Used as filler for rubber, linoleum, oil cloth, polymeric fibers, and resins. Ingredient of the pigment lithopone.

Barrier cloth A special synthetic or cotton fabric that does not allow dust to penetrate. It has a very high thread count (300 per inch) and is tightly woven.

Batt insulation Glass or mineral wool, which may be faced with paper, aluminum, or other vapor retarder. Used in walls and ceiling cavities.

Bentonite A colloidal clay, expansible when wet, forming a highly viscous suspension or gel. Biologically inert when ingested. Used as a base for plasters and as an emulsifier for oils.

Benzene Very flammable, volatile liquid; simplest aromatic hydrocarbon. Long-term exposure has been associated with bone marrow depression and leukemia. Direct contact may cause irritation of eyes, nose, respiratory system and skin, narcotic effects; dermatitis may develop due to defatting action. Carcinogen. Widely used in the manufacture of polymers, detergents, pesticides, plastics, resins, dyes, and as a solvent in waxes, resins, oils, and natural rubber. Major derivatives include aniline, hexachlorobenzene, ethylbenzene, cumene, phenols, cyclohexane, sulfonates.

BIFMA Business and Institutional Furniture Manufacturer's Association. An international association of office furniture manufacturers that works with the EPA to develop chemical emissions testing for office furniture.

Binder Material that holds solid particles together. The resinous constituents of paint coatings are binders, and these are produced from natural drying oils or from synthetics such as acrylics, alkyds, cellulosics, epoxies, melamines, phenolics, polyvinyl acetates, polyurethanes, silicones, ureas, or vinyls. Asphalt and bitumen are binders in paving systems.

Biocide Toxic chemical or physical agent capable of killing or inactivating one or more groups of microorganisms, e.g., vegetative bacteria, mycobacteria, or bacterial spores, vegetative fungi or fungal spores, parasites, or viruses. Includes alcohols (ethyl, isopropyl), aldehydes (formaldehyde, glutaraldehyde), halogens (chlorine, iodine, and bromine compounds), hydrogen peroxide, phenolic compounds, quaternary ammonium compounds (cationic detergents). Chlorine compounds (hypochlorites such as sodium hypochlorite or household bleach, and chlorine dioxide) are commonly used because they are inexpensive, effective against bacteria and fungi, and function as deodorizers. Biocides vary in stability, reactivity, and hazard, and biocide labeling must include precautionary statements and a listing of active ingredients. Biocide manufacturers must obtain EPA approval for specific applications (see National Antimicrobial Information Network, http://www.ace.orst.edu/info/nain). Used in antifoulants, preservatives, paint, polymer and rubber formulations, sizings for textiles.

Biodegradable plastic Material subject to decomposition by microorganisms, includes copolymers of natural and synthetic polymers that are produced by polymerization of starch or cellulose with polystyrene.

Biodegradable Capable of decomposing into elements found in nature within a reasonably short period of time after customary disposal (*see* Federal Trade Commission Guides for the Use of Environmental Marketing Claims).

Biodegradation Decomposition of material due to action of living organisms.

Biological oxygen demand Amount of dissolved oxygen used by microorganisms in the biochemical oxidation process to break down organic matter.

BIPV *See* Building integrated photovoltaics.

Biphenyl Used as heat transfer medium.

Bisphenol A Brown crystals, mild phenol odor. Practically insoluble in water, soluble in some alcohols, ketones, organic solvents. Used as a precursor for thermoplastics, in production of phenolic and epoxy resins and polycarbonates, and as a fungicide.

Bisphenol B Used in the manufacture of phenolic resins.

Bitumen Semisolid or solid carbonaceous mixture occurring naturally or as residue after petroleum distillation, consisting almost entirely of carbon and hydrogen, with little oxygen, nitrogen, or sulfur. Used as tackifier in rubber compounding, asphalt, and tar. Used for road surfacing and waterproofing.

Bituminous Containing carbonaceous material in form of tarry hydrocarbons (bitumen).

Blanket wrapped A form of packaging for shipping furniture, using returnable blankets. This method leaves no packaging materials that require disposal.

Block filler Surface coating used over concrete or CMU substrates that can be thickly applied to reduce or eliminate small holes or other surface imperfections. Block filler smooths out the rough texture associated with CMUs, thus requiring less paint for the finish coating, and increasing cleanability.

Blowing agent Chemical agent added to plastics and rubbers that generates inert gases on heating, imparting cellular structure to resin. Most blowing agents are organic nitrogen compounds. One example, dinitrosodimethyl terephthalamide (NTA), is used with plasticized PVC. Traditionally, chlorofluorocarbons (CFCs) were used as blowing agents, thus contributing to the degradation of the protective ozone layer. Very few, if any, carpet foam cushion manufacturers still use CFCs; however, some have substituted methylene chloride, a gas that also damages the upper ozone layer. Also known as foaming agent.

Bonded urethane cushion Carpet cushion made predominantly of scrap polyurethane foam. A laminating film is applied to facilitate installation. Bonded urethane cushion is made of 90 percent scrap polyurethane.

Borate Salt or ester of boric acid. Wood has been treated with borates in New Zealand and Australia for many years for insect and moisture protection. Commercial applicability is being researched in the United States with a major effort geared toward preventing the borates from leaching out in the presence of moisture. Borates are also commonly used to treat cellulose insulation.

Borax Chemical designation is sodium borate. Borax can cause severe vomiting, diarrhea, shock, and death in children if ingested. Used in soldering metals, the manufacture of glazes and enamels, cleaning compounds, wood preservative, and fireproofing for fabrics.

Boric acid Relatively weak acid produced by treating borax with sulfuric acid. Available as odorless, transparent crystals or white granules or powder. May cause nausea, vomiting, diarrhea, abdominal cramps, lesions on skin and mucous membranes, circulatory collapse, tachycardia, cyanosis, delirium, convulsions. Commonly available in dilute form as eyewash or mild antiseptic. Used for weatherproofing wood and fireproofing fabrics, as a preservative, in the manufacture of cements and carpets, in printing and dyeing, and as an insecticide for cockroaches.

Bottom ash The remaining noncombustible material collected on grates or in other locations during the combustion process. *See also* Fly ash.

Breathability Property indicating permeability to gas.

British thermal unit (BTU) The energy needed to raise the temperature of 1 pound of water 1 degree F. Approximately the amount of energy contained in a wooden kitchen match.

Broad-spectrum biostat A biocide effective on a wide range of microorganisms (including unintended targets). *See also* biocide.

Broadloom carpet Broadloom is defined as a tufted, woven, or knitted rug or carpet in continuous rolls in a variety of widths.

Brownfields Abandoned, idled, or underused industrial and commercial facilities/sites where expansion or redevelopment is complicated by real or perceived environmental contamination.

Building envelope The elements of a building that enclose conditioned spaces through which thermal energy may be transferred to or from the exterior or to or from unconditioned spaces.

Building integrated photovoltaics (BIPV) Portions of a building envelope (walls, roofs, and fenestrations) that not only provide enclosure but also incorporate photovoltaic materials that create useful electricity.

Building-related illness (BRI) Diagnosable infectious, immunologic, or allergic illness whose cause and symptoms can be directly attributed to a specific pollutant source within a building (e.g., Legionnaire's disease, hypersensitivity pneumonitis, tuberculosis, humidifier fever).

Built-up roofing Seamless, flexible, waterproofed roofing material, traditionally of plies of felt mopped with asphalt or pitch.

Cadmium Soft, easily molded heavy metal, accumulates in the environment. Overexposure to cadmium and compounds from acute poisoning due to inhalation may result in headache, chest pains, cough, metal fume fever, weakness. Chronic inhalation may cause pulmonary emphysema and chronic bronchitis. Anemia, kidney damage, and osteoporosis may result from chronic overexposure. A progressive bone demineralization disease, known as itai-itai, occurred in Japan and was associated with a cadmium-induced kidney disorder resulting from high intake of cadmium in food and water. Carcinogen. Principal use is in plating of iron and steel to protect them from corrosion and improve solderability and surface conductivity. Cadmium is used in batteries, pigments, plastic stabilizers, alloys, soft solder, and catalysts. *See* 33/50 program. Identified by EPA as a persistent, bioaccumulative toxic pollutant. *See* PBT.

Calcination Prolonged heating at a high temperature to remove moisture and increase hardness, e.g., gypsum is calcinated to produce plaster.

Calcium carbonate White powder practically insoluble in water, soluble in dilute acids. Commercially available as an antacid and calcium supplement. Very low toxicity. Used in manufacture of paint, rubber, plastics, putty, polishes, insecticides, as a filler in production of adhesives, and in linoleum. *See also* Dolomitic.

Calendering Passing between rollers or places to produce smooth, uniform glossy sheeting, or to impregnate or coat fabrics. Calender machine has two counterrotating heated rollers between which materials are processed. Doughlike emulsions of vinyl are passed through heated rollers, forming flat sheets of flooring.

Caliche Also known as hardpan. Used in unfired bricks, and as a roadbed.

Calorimeter test Use of an apparatus for measuring heat quantities generated in or emitted by materials, called a calorimeter, to determine thermal properties such as heat of combustion.

Caprolactam Used in manufacture of nylon 6. May cause irritation and burning of eyes, nose, and throat. Used in plasticizers, paint, cross-linking of polyurethanes.

Carbon dioxide Colorless, odorless gas. Contributor to global warming, formed by combustion processes. Significant overexposure may cause headache, dizziness, restlessness, increased heart rate and pulse pressure, and elevated blood pressure. Used in manufacture of carbonates and as propellant in aerosols.

Carbon monoxide Poisonous, colorless, odorless gas formed by incomplete fossil fuel combustion. Combines with hemoglobin in blood to form carboxyhemoglobin, which will not release oxygen to the tissues. Overexposure may result in headache, mental dullness, dizziness, weakness, nausea, vomiting, loss of muscular control, increased then decreased pulse and respiratory rate, collapse. Used in organic synthesis.

Carbon tetrachloride Dense, slightly water-soluble, nonflammable, heavy liquid used as a dry cleaning agent. Poisoning may occur by inhalation, ingestion, or skin absorption. Effects may include central nervous system depression, manifesting as loss of consciousness, dizziness, vertigo, headache, depression, incoordination. Skin contact can lead to dermatitis. Inhalation may result in pulmonary edema. Carcinogen. Formerly used in production of CFCs. Its ozone depletion potential is 1.1. *See* 33/50 Program.

Carboxylic acids Organic acids, including acetic acid, acrylic acid, and crotonic acid. May cause irritation. Used in production of acrylic esters for coatings and adhesives.

Carcinogen Cancer-causing agent, may be physical (e.g., radiation, asbestos fibers), viral, or chemical. Cancers arise from aberrations in cellular DNA.

Carnauba Hard natural wax, exuded from carnauba palm leaves. Sparingly soluble in fat solvents. Very low toxicity. Used in waxes, varnishes where a hard, high-polish wax is needed. Also known as Brazil wax.

Carpet backing Backing is the supporting structure for carpet, providing a durable surface to bond the face fibers to each other and to the flooring system. Backing enhances dimensional stability, resilience, and comfort. The backing may be a source of VOC emissions.

Casein Milk protein. Sparingly soluble in water. One of the most nutritive milk proteins; it contains all of the common amino acids and is rich in the essential ones. Forms a hard, insoluble plastic with formaldehyde. Used in manufacture of molded plastics, adhesives, paints, textile finishes, paper coatings, and man-made fibers.

Catalyst Substance that accelerates the velocity or increases the yield of a chemical reaction and which may be recovered at the end of the reaction essentially unchanged.

Catalyzed epoxy Produced by combining an epoxy resin (commonly bisphenol A) with a curing agent. Solvent evaporation causes the surface to dry while chemical cross-linking, copolymerization, is the curing mechanism. The mixture has limited workability time, "pot life," which varies depending on the formulation. When properly cured, catalyzed epoxy coatings have excellent solvent and chemical resistance. Many epoxy coatings can be used on floors in high-traffic areas. Most epoxies develop a nonprogressive chalk face on exterior exposure but otherwise have good durability. Water-based acrylic epoxies approach the durability and performance of their solvent-based counterpart. They offer the added advantage of low odor and can be used over conventional paints on interior applications.

Caulking Heavy paste incapable of significant expansion or contraction, used to make a seam airtight, watertight, or steamtight. Vary from heavy paste, such as synthetic polysulfide rubber and lead peroxide curing agent, to a natural product such as oakum. Caulks fabricated with butyl rubber or polyurethane can be sources of VOC emissions indoors. VOC limits for caulks have been established by specific regulatory entities, such as California's Bay Area Air Quality Management District, to protect against smog formation outdoors. *See* Sealant.

Cellulose insulation Thermal insulation manufactured from recycled newspaper, typically treated with borates to provide fire and vermin protection. The fire retardants and fungicides used in this material may be problematic for sensitive individuals.

Cellulose Main polysaccharide in living plants. Produced from wood by removal of lignin during pulping process. Used in paper and textiles.

Cellulosic Plastics and fibers based on cellulose. Acetate, rayon, and viscose are cellulosic fibers.

Cementitious Includes cements, limes, and mortar, which may be mixed with water or another liquid to form a plastic paste, and to which an aggregate may be added.

Cementitious foam insulation A magnesium oxide–based material blown with air to create an inert,

effective insulation. It may be especially helpful for people with chemical sensitivities. It requires certified installers.

Check metering Measurement instrumentation for the supplementary monitoring of energy consumption (electric, gas, oil, etc.) to isolate the various categories of energy use to permit conservation and control, in addition to the revenue metering furnished by the utility.

Chemical weld A method of joining the surface of two substrates (e.g., edges of vinyl flooring) by applying a solvent or adhesive and joining them together with a chemical and/or physical reaction. *See also* Heat welding.

Chemical or environmental sensitivity Chronic multisystem disorder, usually involving symptoms of the central nervous system and at least one other system. However, no objective test is available to diagnose this condition. Affected persons are frequently intolerant to some foods, and they react adversely to some chemical and environmental agents, singly or in combination, at levels generally tolerated by most people. Reactions may range from mild discomfort to total disability, and improvement may occur by avoiding suspected agents. *See* Multiple chemical sensitivity.

Chemically stable material Material that will not readily break down, release chemicals, or change into other (potentially toxic) chemicals with age, heat, or light.

Chimney effect Tendency of air or gas in a vertical passage to rise when it is heated because it becomes lighter (less dense) than the surrounding air or gas. Useful in promoting cooling through enhanced natural ventilation.

Chipboard or particleboard Low-density paper board made from mixed waste paper, wood chips, or fibers, using a synthetic resin as a bonding agent. *See* Formaldehyde.

Chlorinated hydrocarbons Chemicals containing only chlorine, carbon, and hydrogen. These include chlorinated solvents (e.g., methylene chloride, trichloroethylene, chloroform) and a class of environmentally persistent, broad-spectrum pesticides (e.g., aldrin, chlordane, DDT, dieldrin, endrin, hexachloride, lindane, Mirex, toxaphene). Many of these pesticides have been identified by EPA as persistent, bioaccumulative, toxic pollutants. *See* PBT.

Chlorinated polyvinyl chloride (CPVC) A plastic made from a polymer of the chlorinated polyvinyl monomer that contains 67 percent chlorine. Vinyl chloride monomer is a known carcinogen and its manufacture sometimes results in release of hazardous chemicals with adverse human and environment impacts. *See also* Polyvinyl Chloride.

Chlorinated solvent Organic compound containing chlorine (e.g., methylene chloride, 1,1,1-trichloroethane, tetrachloroethylene, vinyl chloride).

Chlorofluorocarbon (CFC) Class of volatile, nonreactive, noncorrosive, nonflammable and easily liquefied gases. Group of substances derivative of methane or ethane with all or some hydrogen atoms replaced by chlorine and fluorine. Use discontinued because CFCs are believed to be responsible for destruction of stratospheric ozone. Formerly used as refrigerants, as propellants, and in blown Styrofoam. Related compounds also containing bromine, e.g., halons, are used as fire retardants. *See* Ozone *and* Class 1 and Class II substances.

Chloroform Sweet-smelling, nonflammable liquid once used as anaesthetic. May cause dizziness, mental dullness, nausea and disorientation, headache, fatigue. Direct contact may cause irritation to eyes and skin. Banned from use in foods, drugs,and cosmetics by the FDA. Carcinogen. Used as solvent for rubber, waxes, resins, in fire extinguishers to lower the freezing temperature of carbon tetrachloride, and in the rubber industry. Also known as trichloromethane. *See* 33/50 Program. Identified by EPA as a persistent, bioaccumulative toxic pollutant. *See* PBT.

Chlorosulfonated polyethylene A unique elastomeric roofing type that acts as a thermoplastic when installed, giving it heat weldable properties. Over time, it cures into a themoset material.

Chromates Chemical compounds containing chromium. Often refers to potassium dichromate, used in dyes. Many are carcinogenic.

Chromium Steel-gray, lustrous metal. Toxic effects may include dermatitis, skin ulcers, nasal inflammation, perforation of nasal septum, cancer of the lungs, nasal cavity, or paranasal sinus. Chromium and certain chromium compounds have been listed as carcinogens. Used to improve strength and hardness of alloys, and in plating to increase resistance of metals to abrasion, corrosion, and oxidation. Also used as a wood preservative. *See* 33/50 Program. Identified by EPA as a persistent, bioaccumulative toxic pollutant. *See* PBT.

CITES Convention on International Trade in Endangered Species of Wild Fauna and Flora (U.S. Fish and Wildlife Service). Provides lists of endangered species of timber and other natural products.

Class I substance One of several groups of chemicals with an ozone depletion potential (ODP) of 0.2 or higher, including CFCs, halons, carbon tetrachloride and methyl chloroform, and HBFCs and ethyl bromide, as defined by EPA and the Clean Air Act. *See* Ozone depletion potential.

Class II substance A substance with an ozone depletion potential of less than 0.2. All HCFCs are currently included in this classification. *See* Ozone depletion potential.

Clay body A mixture of clays, or clays and other mineral substances, blended to achieve a specific ceramic purpose.

Cleaner Technologies Substitutes Assessment A report that systematically evaluates the relative risk, performance, and cost trade-offs of technological alternatives as part of a pollution prevention initiative (*see* EPA's Designing for the Environment Web site).

Clear cut Harvesting all the trees in an area; can result in accelerated runoff, erosion, sedimentation of streams and lakes, flooding, and destruction of vital habitat.

Closed-loop recycling Reclaiming or reusing wastewater or process chemicals in an enclosed process in manufacturing.

CMU Concrete masonry unit.

Coalescing solvent Chemical that causes droplets of suspended liquid to combine.

Coefficient of performance (COP) The ratio of the rate of heat delivery or removal to the energy input of the machine (in consistent units such as BTU per pound of refrigerant). COP = energy output / energy input.

Coir Coarse, brown fiber from coconut husk. Used in rope, matting, and carpet backing.

Collector efficiency Collector efficiency is a measure of the percentage of available solar energy that the collector will transmit to the heat transport fluid. The calorimetric method uses a closed system consisting of collector and small storage tank and provides a good method for determining the day-long efficiency of a collector. The instantaneous method uses an open system, an isolated collector, and is performed at solar noon under steady-state conditions.

Compact fluorescent Fluorescent lamps used as much more efficient alternatives to incandescent lighting. Also known as PL, CFL, twin-tube, or BIAX lamps.

Compost system Controlled biological decomposition of organic refuse in which such materials are mechanically mixed, ground, or shredded, then decomposed to humus in windrow piles, or in aerated enclosures such as mechanical digesters or drums.

Compost Relatively stable humus material produced for biodegradation of organic refuse.

Composting The controlled degradation by aerobic microorganisms of organic materials in solid waste to produce humus, a soil conditioner and fertilizer.

Composting toilet Toilets that compost human waste, require little or no water, and do not create a health or odor problem when properly installed.

Conditioned air Air treated to control its temperature, relative humidity, purity, pressure, movement, or other characteristics to obtain a desired environment.

Conditioned space Portion of a building where the air is conditioned to provide comfort to the occupants.

Conductive energy transfer Conduction is the process by which heat travels within one substance or from one substance to another by direct molecular interaction.

Conductivity (k) The quantity of heat (BTUs) that will flow through 1 square foot of material, 1 inch thick, in one hour, when there is a temperature difference of 1 degree F between its surfaces.

Connected lighting power (CLP) The power required to energize luminaires and lamps connected to the building electrical service, in watts.

Constructed wetland Engineered wetlands that simulate natural wetlands and utilize natural and biological processes for wastewater treatment. Includes surface and subsurface flow constructed wetlands. Subsurface flow wetlands are further divided into horizontal flow and vertical wetland treatment systems. For more information call North American Wetland Engineering, (888) 433-2115.

Contaminant Foreign and unwanted physical, chemical, biological, or radiological material in a product or in the environment.

Continuous dyeing Coloring textiles by impregnating the cloth with dye and passing it progressively through a series of developing, washing, and drying zones.

Conversion A form of recycling in which a waste material is turned into a useful material of substantially lower quality. An example is the use of crushed concrete and bricks as a granular base for roads and sidewalks. Also known as downcycling.

Conversion efficiency The ratio of raw materials going into a process to the product coming out.

Cooling degree day A unit based upon temperature difference and time, used in estimating cooling energy consumption. For any one day, when the mean temperature is more than a reference temperature (typically 65 degrees F), there are as many degree days cooling as degrees Fahrenheit temperature difference between the mean temperature for the day and the reference temperature. The sum of all degree days over a calendar year is annual cooling degree days (CDD).

Coolness index The visible light transmittance of a glazing divided by its shading coefficient. Glazings with high coolness indices let more light and less heat into a building, which generally improves energy-efficient performance of buildings. *See* Spectrally selective.

Copolymer The product of polymerization of two or more different monomers.

Coproducts Materials that are incidentally or intentionally produced when making another material.

Corrosive Destructive or protective chemical reaction. In metals, electrochemical oxidation. Rusting of iron (corrosion) is destructive. Formation of transparent oxide on aluminum or chromium is protective, and oxidation of copper is considered decorative. Irreversible alteration (damage) to human tissue, e.g., skin, eyes, etc.

"Cradle-to-cradle" A term used in life cycle analysis to describe a material or product that is recycled into a new product at the end of its defined life.

"Cradle to grave" A term used to describe life cycle of materials, e.g., the management of hazardous waste, from their point of generation to their final treatment and/or disposal.

Crumb rubber Rubber fragments ground to the size of sand or silt, used in rubber or plastic products or processed further for use in paving and other asphalt applications. Workers applying crumb-rubber-modified asphalt paving have been reported to experience acute eye, nose, throat, and skin irritation.

Cullet Crushed glass.

Cumene Oily hydrocarbon. Overexposure may include irritation of eyes and mucous membranes, headache, dermatitis, narcosis. Used as additive in motor fuel, insoluble in water, soluble in alcohol and many other organic solvents. Used in manufacture of phenol and acetone.

Curing Conversion of raw products to finished material. In rubber technology, vulcanization. In thermosetting resins, the final cross-linking procedure. In concrete, the process of bringing freshly placed concrete to required strength and quality by maintaining humidity and temperature at specified levels for a given length of time. In textile manufacture, heat treatment with chemicals or resins to impart water or crease resistance.

Cushion The optional cushion that is often applied beneath the carpet. Present varieties include bonded urethane, prime urethane, sponge rubber, synthetic fiber, and rubberized jute. Bonded urethane is the most common, a waste product of the automobile and furniture industries.

Cyanide Inorganic, white solid with a faint almond-like odor, used in plating solutions to produce a hard surface. Cyanide and its compounds are highly toxic. May cause adverse effects on the cardiovascular and central nervous systems, liver, kidneys, and skin. *See* 33/50 Program. Identified by EPA as a persistent, bioaccumulative, toxic pollutant. *See* PBT.

Dammar Hard resin obtained from evergreen trees of genus *Agathis*, or soft, clear to yellow East Indian resin from Dipterocarpaceae trees. Low toxicity. Used in varnishes, lacquers, adhesives, and coatings.

Damp-proofing A treatment, such as a sealer or asphalt coating, that inhibits the transfer of moisture. Used in locations where higher-quality waterproofing is not needed.

Daylight factor Under totally overcast sky conditions, the percentage of light (in foot-candles) that arrives on a horizontal surface within a building compared to the amount of light (in foot-candles) arriving on an unshielded horizontal surface outside.

Daylight sensing control (DS) A device that automatically regulates the power input to electric lighting near fenestration to maintain the desired workplace illumination. This system takes maximum advantage of direct or indirect sunlight.

Daylighted zone (under a skylight) The area under each skylight whose horizontal dimension in each direction equals the skylight dimension in that direction plus either the floor-to-ceiling height, or the dimension to an opaque partition, or one-half the distance to an adjacent skylight or vertical glazing, whichever is the least.

Daylighted zone (at vertical glazing) The area adjacent to vertical glazing that receives daylighting. The daylighting zone depth is assumed to extend into the space 15 feet or to the nearest opaque barrier, whichever is less. The daylighting zone width is assumed to be the width of the window plus either 2 feet on each side or one-half the distance to an adjacent skylight or vertical glazing, whichever is the least. The daylighting zone can be increased by using high glazing strategies or light shelves.

Daylighting strategies Methods that use natural light to minimize the need for artificial lighting during the day. For example, a clerestory allows natural light into the building interior through a raised section of roof with vertical glass; shading the glass allows light in while reducing heat gain.

Dead air space A confined space of air with no airflow. Dead air space tends to reduce both conduction and convection of heat. This attribute is utilized in virtually all insulating materials and systems, such as double-glazed windows, fiberglass batt insulation, rigid foam panels, and loose-fill insulations such as pumice, vermiculite, rock wool, and goose down.

Deciduous Trees that lose their leaves seasonally, differing from coniferous.

Defoliant Toxic chemical sprayed on plants that causes leaves to fall off prematurely.

Degree day heating *See* Heating degree day.

Degree day cooling *See* Cooling degree day.

Demand, electric The rate at which electric energy is delivered to or by a system, part of a system, or a piece of equipment. *See* Peak electrical demand.

Depolymerization Return of polymer to its monomers or to a polymer of lower molecular weight.

Desiccant Drying agent, having great affinity for water, including calcium chloride, glycerol, bauxite, silica gel.

Design energy consumption (DECON) The computed annual energy usage of a proposed building design. Terminology used in ASHRAE 90.1-1989.

Design energy cost (DECOS) The computed annual energy expenditure of a proposed building design. Terminology used in ASHRAE 90.1-1989.

Design for the Environment (DfE) EPA has developed this program to spur new technologies that reduce environmental and human health risks and promote continuous environmental improvement. EPA has entered into partnerships with several industries, including foam furniture (adhesives), wall paints, garment çare. Example initiative is the Garment and Textile Care Program, to reduce exposure to tetrachloroethylene (or "perc") in dry cleaners by developing safer, cleaner substitutes.

Detergent Surface active agent, surfactant. Detergent formulations may contain alcohols, anionic and nonionic surfactants, antiredeposition agents, bleaches, builders, cellulose derivatives, colorants, corrosion inhibitors, emollients, enzymes, foam inhibitors, fluorescent whitening agents (optical brighteners), fragrances, opacifiers, phosphates, sodium sulfate, water, and/or zeolite. Biodegradable and low-phosphate detergents have been developed primarily to avoid polluting waterways.

Dichlorobenzene Includes three isomers, of which 1,2-dichlorobenzene (ortho- or o-dichlorobenzene) and 1,4-dichlorobenzene (para- or p-dichlorobenzene) are used commercially. 1,2-dichlorobenzene is used as solvent and chemical intermediate. 1,4-dichlorobenzene is soluble in organic solvents, used as germicide, insecticide, and chemical intermediate; most common use is in mothballs. 1,4-dichlorobenzene is a carcinogen. Overexposure may result in headache, eye irritation, rhinitis, nausea, vomiting, irritation of nose and eyes, liver and kidney damage, skin blisters. All three isomers have been identified by EPA as persistent, bioaccumulative toxic pollutants. *See* PBT.

Diffuse radiation Radiation that has traveled an indirect path from the sun because it has been scattered by particles in the atmosphere such as dust and water vapor. *See also* Direct radiation.

Dimethyl ether Flammable organic compound, soluble in water and alcohol, used as solvent and refrigerant. Also known as methyl ether or wood ether.

Dimming System that automatically turns down the output of artificial lighting. Dimming is sometimes used in areas of buildings that receive sunlight during the daylight hours to save electricity and reduce the building's cooling load.

Direct expansion (DX) cooling Mechanical cooling where the air of the space being cooled passes directly over the cooling coil (evaporator).

Dioxane Flammable water-soluble liquid, cyclic ether of ethylene glycol. Faint pleasant odor, vapor harmful. Overexposure may cause drowsiness, headache, nausea, vomiting, irritation of eyes, nose and throat, liver damage, kidney failure, and skin irritation. Carcinogen. Used as a solvent. Also known as 1,4-dioxane.

Dioxin Any of a family of chlorinated aromatic hydrocarbons also known as polychlorinated dibenzo-*p*-dioxins (PCDDs). In common terminology, may also refer to the potent 2,3,7,8-tetrachloro-*p*-dioxin, 2,3,7,8-TCDD. Animal testing indicates that 2,3,7,8-TCDD is one of the most toxic anthropogenic chemicals known. The compound is toxic to liver and kidney function and has been shown to induce a variety of tumors in animal models. Adverse effects on the immune system of mammals have also been noted. 2,3,7,8-TCDD is a contaminant of many chemical products and a by-product in herbicide manufacture, and was implicated as a contaminant of the herbicide mixture known as Agent Orange used as a defoliant during the Vietnam War. PCDDs are carcinogens. Released during PVC manufacturer.

Identified by EPA as persistent, bioaccumulative, toxic pollutants. *See* PBT.

Direct gain system Uses vertical and generally south-faced glazing and materials inside to absorb heat (thermal mass). The most widely used passive solar design approach. With direct gain, the occupants are in direct contact with all five elements of the passive solar system collector, absorber, storage, distribution, and controls.

Direct radiation Light that has traveled a straight path from the sun, as opposed to diffuse sky radiation.

Direct dye Commercial dyes, applied directly to fibers in a neutral or alkaline bath. They may have poor wash quality and are used primarily for natural fibers. Includes coal tar dyes that act without a mordant (or agent that fixes the dye to the material, such as alum, phenol, or aniline). Example of direct dye is benzidine dye.

Dispersion Distribution of finely divided particles in a medium.

Direct glue-down Method where the flooring is glued directly to the substrate surface, rendering that material unusable upon removal.

Direct cooling Direct cooling has four major components: keeping heat out, providing ventilation, underground construction, and evaporative cooling. Most of the strategies for keeping the heat out of a building involve avoiding direct solar gain. They include orienting the building away from intense solar exposure; using indirect daylighting instead of artificial lighting; shading roofs, walls, and windows with overhangs, wing walls, and vegetation; adjusting surface-area-to-volume ratios.

Dolomitic Containing dolomite, a carbonate mineral. Very low toxicity.

Domestic hardwood Deciduous trees that grow in the United States. This is the only type of wood in the United States where the regeneration (production of new trees) exceeds the removal rate.

Downstream impact Impact to the environment from an upstream activity. In the case of construction, downstream impacts include those resulting from site preparation, demolition of existing structures and/or materials, and general construction waste materials.

Drip irrigation Aboveground low-pressure watering system with flexible tubing that releases small, steady amounts of water through emitters placed near individual plants.

Dry fog coating Any spray coating formulated so that overspray droplets dry before reaching floors and other unintended surfaces.

Dry joint A joint without mortar between stones or tiles.

Dry-pressed A method of forming individual tiles by compressing dry clay under pressure, then firing it.

Drying oil Linseed, cottonseed, or soybean oil, or other oil which is highly unsaturated, that is readily oxidized and polymerized to form a hard, dry film on exposure to air, in paints and varnishes.

DX *See* Direct expansion cooling.

Dynamic energy models Dynamic energy models take into account the ability of thermal mass to modify and delay heating and cooling loads.

Earth-sheltered design Design of buildings that are partially or totally below ground, either as a result of digging into existing topography or filling over parts of the structure. Earth-sheltered design uses the constant temperature of the deep earth in a location to improve energy efficiency, and can be beneficial for use of contoured sites by decreasing maintenance and environmental impact.

Earth's temperature Earth maintains a mostly constant temperature below about twenty feet. The deep earth temperature in a location is approximately equal to the average outdoor air temperature for that location. This can be used advantageously by certain heating and cooling systems. The higher temperatures found in the earth are also used for producing electricity in some areas.

Ecological integrity A natural system exhibits integrity if, when subject to a disturbance, it has a self-correcting ability to recover to an end state that is normal for that system, not necessarily one that is pristine or naturally whole.

Ecosystem The interaction of organisms from the natural community to one another and their environment.

Ecotone A habitat created by the juxtaposition of distinctly different habitats. An ecological zone or boundary between two or more ecosystems. Also known as edge habitat.

EER *See* Energy efficiency ratio.

Efflorescence A salt crust that forms on the surface of stone, brick, plaster, or mortar when free alkalies from adjoining concrete or mortar leach out.

Elastomer Cross-linked (vulcanized) or thermoplastic high molecular weight polymer that at room temperature can be stretched to twice its length and upon release return to its original size. Includes natural rubber, butyl rubber (BR), nitrile rubber (NBR), neoprene, styrene-butadiene copolymers (SBR). Used in seals, adhesives, tough molded parts, wire and cable insulation.

Electrical demand *See* Demand, electric *and* Peak electrical demand.

Electrochromic Electrochromic materials change their optical properties due to the action of an electric field, and change back upon field reversal. This works through insertion and removal of ions in the electrochromic layer. Electrochromic windows transition from transparent to fully darkened heat-absorbing, and can be maintained at any grade of tint in between.

Electrostatic spraying Application of atomized paint to a conductive object by producing an electrostatic potential between the nozzle and the surface to be painted. Conserves paint and reduces worker exposure to emissions. Useful for painting irregular surfaces.

Embodied energy Embodied energy accounts for all energy expended for production and transportation plus inherent energy at a specific point in the life cycle of a product.

Emission Pollutant gas, particle, or liquid released into the environment.

Emission control Any measure that reduces emissions into air, water, or soil. The most effective emissions control involves redesign of the process so less waste is produced at the source. Common emissions controls are dust collectors, wastewater treatment plants, and in-plant solid and toxic waste reduction programs. *See also* Stack scrubbers. *See* Pollution prevention.

Emissivity *or* Emittance The property of emitting heat radiation. The numerical value of this property is expressed as a decimal fraction. "Normal emittance" is the value measured at 90 degrees to the plane of the sample; "hemispherical emittance" (more commonly used) is the total amount emitted in all directions. Values range from 0.05 for brightly polished metals to 0.96 for flat black surfaces. Most non-metals have high values of emittance.

Emulsion Dispersion of one liquid phase in another. Paints are emulsions.

End-of-pipe Technologies that reduce pollutant emissions after they have been formed. Examples include scrubbers on smokestacks and catalytic convertors on automobile tailpipes. *See* Pollution prevention *for antonym.*

Energy management system A control system capable of monitoring environmental and system loads to adjust HVAC output in order to conserve energy while maintaining comfort.

Energy cost budget (ECB) The maximum allowable computed annual energy expenditure for a proposed building. Terminology used in ASHRAE 90-1989.

Energy cost The cost of energy by unit and type of energy as proposed to be supplied to the building, including variations such as time of day, season, and rate of usage.

Energy The capacity for doing work. Energy exists in several forms, which may be transformed from one to another, such as thermal, mechanical, electrical, or chemical.

Energy efficiency ratio (EER) The ratio of cooling capacity in BTU per hour divided by the electrical power input in watts at any given set of rating conditions.

Energy management system A control system designed to monitor the environment and the use of energy in a facility, and to adjust the parameters of local control loops, in order to conserve energy while maintaining a suitable environment.

Energy recovery ventilator (ERV) Draws stale air from the building and transfers the heat or coolness in that air to the outside air being pulled into the building. This can help reduce energy costs while improving indoor air quality.

Enthalpy The total heat (both sensible and latent) present in an air-moisture mixture.

Environmental cost A quantitative assessment of impacts such as resource depletion, air, water, and solid waste pollution, and disturbance of habitats.

Environmental equity/justice Equal protection from environmental hazards regardless of race, ethnicity, or economic status. In interior design, is associated with the right of building occupants to have a view to the outdoors.

Environmental Protection Agency An independent executive agency of the federal government, established in 1970, responsible for the formulation and enforcement of regulations governing the release of pollutants, to protect public health and the environment.

Environmental restoration The act of repairing damage to a site caused by human activity, industry, or natural disaster. The ideal is to leave a site in a state that is as close as possible to its natural condition before it was disturbed. Examples are replanting forests, stabilizing soils, and filling in and replanting mine pits.

Environmental sustainability Cross-generational maintenance of ecosystem components and functions.

Environmentally preferable Products or services that have a lesser or reduced effect on human health and the environment when compared with competing products or services that serve the same purpose. The comparison may consider raw materials acquisition, production, manufacturing, packaging, distribution, reuse, operation, maintenance, and/or disposal of the product or service.

Environmentally Preferable Purchasing (EPP) EPA program that promotes federal government use of products and services that pose reduced impacts to human health and the environment.

EPA *See* Environmental Protection Agency

EPA Weight-of-Evidence Classification In assessing the carcinogenic potential of a chemical, EPA classifies the chemical into one of the following groups, according to the weight-of-evidence from epidemiologic and animal studies: Group A (human carcinogen); Group B (probable human carcinogen—B1, limited evidence of carcinogenicity in humans; B2, sufficient evidence of carcinogenicity in animals with inadequate or lack of evidence in humans); Group C (possible human carcinogen); Group D (not classifiable as to human carcinogenicity); Group E (evidence of noncarcinogenicity for humans).

EPA 33/50 Program *See* 33/50 Program.

Epichlorohydrin Unstable water-insoluble liquid. Due to chlorine content, epichlorohydrin rubber is nonflammable and resistant to oil and ozone. Epichlorohydrin may cause nausea, vomiting, abdominal pain, respiratory distress, coughing, cyanosis, irritation of eyes and skin with deep pain. Carcinogen. Solvent for natural and synthetic resins, gums, cellulose esters and ethers, paints, varnishes, lacquers, and used to produce epoxy resins.

Epoxy- Prefix indicating presence of epoxide group in molecule.

Epoxy adhesive Glue made of epoxy resin.

Epoxy paint Term applied to pigments held by epoxy binders that can be oil-modified to dry by oxidation, or epoxy resin that is mixed with amine or polyamide to harden and cure. Used in outdoor environments due to abrasion and corrosion resistance, adhesion, hardness, and flexibility.

Epoxy resin Polyether resin that may be formed by polymerization of bisphenol A and epichlorohydrin. Excellent wetting and adhesion properties and resistant to heat, water, and corrosion. High strength and low shrinkage during curing. Used as coating, adhesive, casting, or foam. Used as bonding agent for concrete blocks, epoxy pipes, and floors. Liquid epoxies are used for coatings and adhesives and are cured (cross-linked) with amines. Solid resins can be modified with epoxidized phenol formaldehyde resins.

Equiviscous temperature Measure of viscosity used in tar industry. Temperature in degrees Celsius at which the viscosity of tar is 50 seconds as measured with standard tar efflux viscometer. The temperature range within which "hot mop" roofing must be applied to be effective. *See also* Hot mop. Also known as EVT.

Ethyl acetate Volatile, flammable, slightly water-soluble liquid, characteristic fruity odor. May cause irritation of eyes, nose, and throat, narcosis, dermatitis. Used as a reagent and solvent for varnishes and lacquers.

Ethyl alcohol Mobile, flammable liquid, miscible in water, with a pleasant odor. May cause impaired perception, incoordination, mental excitement or depression, drowsiness. Used as raw material for production of glycol ethers, amines, and as a reagent and solvent. Also known as grain alcohol or ethanol.

Ethyl benzene Flammable, water-insoluble liquid. May cause irritation of eyes and mucous membranes, headache, dermatitis, narcosis. Used in organic synthesis, as a resin solvent, and for conversion to styrene monomer.

Ethylene glycol Alcohol. Constitutes a hazard when ingested. May cause temporary stimulation of central nervous system followed by depression. Used as antifreeze in cooling and heating systems, and in synthesis of alkyd resins, plasticizers, synthetic fibers (Dacron), polyethylene terephthalate (PET), and synthetic waxes. Also known as glycol.

Eutectic salt Salt used for storing heat. At a given temperature, salt melts or changes phase, absorbing large amounts of heat. This heat is then released when the salt solidifies or freezes.

Evaporative cooling The phase change of water from liquid to gas is a heat-absorbing process. The result is effective cooling of the air as water evaporates. This technique can be used to significantly reduce reliance on mechanical refrigeration, particularly in hot, dry climates.

Extrude Force heat-softened polymer through a dye or orifice to produce a continuously formed sheet, rod, bar, tube, etc.

Face fiber The fiber that is exposed on the surface face of the carpet. Typically it is stitched into a backing material.

Feldspar Common silicate mineral consisting primarily of silicates of aluminum with potassium, sodium, and calcium metals.

Ferric oxide Ferric oxide dust and fumes may cause benign pneumoconiosis. Used as pigment for metal polishing, rubber, linoleum, ceramics, glass. Also known as jeweler's rouge, red ochre.

Fetotoxin A toxin with the potential to harm a fetus.

Fiberboard Rigid or semirigid sheet material made from wood or other vegetable fibers. Construction panels made from compressed fibers, including wood, paper, straw, or other cellulose fibers. One common type is medium-density fiberboard (MDF). *See* Formaldehyde.

Fiberglass resin Uncured polyester resin used for fabricating glass-fiber-reinforced and cast plastic products.

Fiberization The process of reducing a material, such as newspaper or cotton, into a loose fiber.

Filament A continuous strand of natural or synthetic fiber. Silk is a natural filament, and synthetic filaments are extrusions of molten or dissolved polymer.

Filler Inert material added to paper, resin, or bituminous material, or used to fill holes in wood, plaster, or other surfaces.

Fire retardant Material that reduces or eliminates the tendency of flammable or combustible materials to burn. Fire retardants may be applied to the surface, impregnated, or incorporated during polymerization of plastics and rubbers. Ammonium sulfate and borax are inorganic flame retardants. Intumescent flame retardants such as ammonium sulfonates swell in fires and block oxygen. Because carbon is less flammable than plastic, flame retardants functioning as catalysts can be added to promote pyrolysis of the polymer structure to a carbonaceous char. Also known as fireproofing compound.

Flame spread The speed at which fire will move through a material; determined using standard laboratory testing methods.

Flash point The lowest temperature at which a substance emits flammable vapor that ignites spontaneously.

Flat plate collector An assembly containing a panel of metal or other suitable material (usually with a flat black color on its sun side) that absorbs sunlight and converts it into heat. This panel is usually in an insulated box, covered with glass or plastic on the sun side to retard heat loss. In the collector, the heat transfers to a circulating liquid or gas, such as air, water, oil, or antifreeze; the heat is either utilized immediately or stored for later use.

Fluorescent lamp   A lamp that produces visible light by emitting electromagnetic radiation. Commonly fluorescent lamps consist of a glass tube whose inner wall is coated with a material that fluoresces when bombarded with secondary radiation generated by a gaseous discharge within the tube. Fluorescent lighting is much more efficient than incandescent, requiring 25–35 percent of the energy to produce an equivalent amount of light. Ordinary fluorescent lamps produce about 65–70 lumens/watt. Recent technical advances have made fluorescent lighting even more energy efficient while improving color rendition. Linear fluorescent tubes are designated as *T* for tubular and *8* for 8/8ths of an inch in diameter. Next-generation T5 lamps are 5/8ths of an inch in diameter and more energy-efficient than standard T9 lamps.

Fluoride   A compound of the very active element fluorine.

Fluorocarbon   Nonflammable, heat-stable hydrocarbon liquid or gas, in which some or all hydrogen atoms have been replaced by fluorine atoms. Formerly used in refrigerants, aerosol propellants, solvents, blowing agents, coatings, monomers. As with CFCs, fluorocarbons are classified as ozone-depleting substances (ODS) and have been banned from use as aerosol propellants.

Fly ash   Fine, noncombustible particulate carried in gas stream from a furnace. Often used in concrete to reduce volume of waste. *See* bottom ash.

Foamed-in-place   An insulating material containing cements or plastics that is installed wet using foaming equipment, and cures in place.

Focusing collector   A collector that has a parabolic or other reflector that focuses sunlight onto a small area for collection. A reflector of this type greatly intensifies the heat at the point of collection, allowing the heat collection fluid to achieve higher temperatures. This type of collector will work only with direct beam sunlight.

Formaldehyde   Poisonous, reactive, flammable gas with pungent suffocating odor. Combines readily with many substances and polymerizes easily. May cause irritation of eyes, nose, throat, and respiratory system, tearing of the eyes, burns of the nose, coughing or bronchial spasm, allergic reaction. Contact may result in sensitization. Carcinogen. Used in wood products, plastics, fertilizer, and foam insulation. Incorporated in synthetic resins by reaction with urea, phenols, and melamine. Urea-formaldehyde (UF) resin is used in particleboard (e.g., for subflooring and shelving and in cabinetry and furniture), hardwood plywood paneling (e.g., decorative wall covering, cabinetry, furniture), and medium-density fiberboard (MDF) (drawer fronts, cabinets, furniture tops). MDF contains a higher resin-to-wood ratio than other UF pressed wood products and is generally the highest formaldehyde-emitting pressed wood product, particularly when the surfaces and edges of these products are unlaminated or uncoated. Softwood plywood and oriented strandboard (OSB) produced for exterior construction contains dark phenol-formaldehyde (PF) resin. Pressed wood products containing PF resin generally emit less formaldehyde than those containing UF resin.

Formaldehyde scavengers   Agents added to products manufactured with formaldehyde to neutralize gases before they escape. Usually sulfite or ammonia compounds, scavengers are sometimes used to treat affected buildings directly by fumigation, or as a coating for air filters. *See also* Ammonia fumigation, Hexamethylene tetramine, *and* Sulfites.

Fossil fuel   Hydrocarbon deposits from plant remnants, including coal, peat, tar sands, shale oil, petroleum, natural gas. *See* Nonrenewable resource.

Freon   Trade name for series of nonflammable, non-explosive fluorocarbon and chlorofluorocarbon products (FCs and CFCs) widely used in refrigeration and air-conditioning, now classified as ozone-depleting substances (ODS) with restrictions from commercial use. Freon sometimes refers to dichlordifluoromethane. *See* Chlorofluorocarbons and Fluorocarbons.

Friable   Capable of being easily rubbed, crumbled, or pulverized into powder.

Fully adhered   A membrane bonding technique for roofing that requires the use of an adhesive material to be distributed evenly between the membrane and the substrate over the entire surface. This technique has excellent long-term strength and wind uplift resistance qualities; however, it is very difficult to remove at the end of its useful life.

Fungicide   An agent that destroys molds, mildews, yeasts. Includes mercurials (e.g., phenyl mercuric acetate). The destruction of fungi does not necessarily destroy its toxic or allergenic properties.

Fungus, *pl.* fungi   Fungi include yeasts, molds, mildews, mushrooms, and puffballs, a group of organisms lacking chlorophyll. Fungi are ubiquitous both outdoors and indoors. The fungi found indoors are commonly referred to as molds (e.g., species of *Penicillium*, *Aspergillus*, and *Cladosporium*). All fungi are allergenic. Exposure to specific types of mold may result in infectious or inflammatory diseases (e.g., inflammation of airways, chronic bronchitis, hypersensitivity pneumonitis, asthma). Since 1982, studies in North America and Europe have proliferated on the association of dampness and mold with respiratory symptoms, demonstrating that the severity of these symptoms is more extensive than those caused by environmental tobacco smoke. Molds producing potent mycotoxins (chemicals produced by fungi that are toxic to humans and animals) include *Aspergillus versicolor* and *Stachybotrys atra*. The spores of *Aspergillus versicolor* contain sterigmatocystin, closely related to aflatoxin, which has been classified as a probable human carcinogen by the International Agency for Research on Cancer (IARC). *Stachybotrys atra* is suspected by some to be the likely cause of pulmonary hemodosiderosis (respiratory tract bleeding) in infants, which has led to fatalities. *Aspergillus versicolor* grows on damp building materials (e.g., condensation under vinyl wall covering). *Stachybotrys atra* requires continuously wet building materials (e.g., soaked wallboard). Moisture is the primary factor to be controlled to prevent mold growth.

Fusion bonding Carpet manufacturing process in which yarn is embedded between two parallel sheets of adhesive-coated backing. The sheets are slit, forming two pieces of cut-pile carpet.

Gas-filled window Double- or multiple-glazed window systems where the air space(s) is (are) filled with a low-conducting gas. Argon is the most commonly used krypton and sulfur hexafluoride are also used, but are more costly. Gas-filled windows must be hermetically sealed and must be able to contain the injected gas over a long period of time. These fills reduce the heat exchange rate associated with windows. Gas-filled windows provide the greatest benefit when used in conjunction with low-emissivity coatings.

Generally Regarded as Safe (GRAS) A classification of food additives. The Food, Drug and Cosmetic Act of 1958 provided grandfather approval for most additives commonly used prior to that time. These additives cannot be removed from use until they are proven harmful to the public by the Food and Drug Administration. Over 600 substances are on the FDA list of GRAS substances. They were placed on this list on the basis of past experience in food use, scientific determination of their safety, or testimony regarding their safety.

Geotextile Fabric manufactured from synthetic fibers or yarns that serves as a continuous membrane between soil and aggregate in earth structures.

Glass fiber Fiberglass, produced by spinning molten glass. Since they are stiff, they must be spun finer than organic fibers. They must be dyed before extrusion and protected against abrasion by coating with a lubricant. Used for fireproof and acid-resistant textiles, in fiber-reinforced plastics, and in insulation. Man-made mineral fibers are suspected carcinogens.

Glazing A covering of transparent or translucent material used to filter radiation through glass or plastic. Glazing retards heat losses from reradiation and convection.

Global warming potential (GWP) The ratio of the warming caused by a material to the warming caused by a similar mass of carbon dioxide (e.g., CFC-12 has a GWP of 8,500).

Glycols Alcohols with two hydroxyl groups, used as raw material for manufacture of polyesters, e.g., ethylene glycol reacts with terephthalic acid to produce PET.

Gray water Domestic wastewater, composed of wash water from kitchen, bathroom, and laundry sinks, tubs, and washers. Does not include human waste.

Green roof Vegetation cover on roof surfaces. There are two types: extensive and intensive. Extensive green roofs (also referred to as eco-roofs or living roofs): thin soil layer with horizontally spreading, low-growing vegetation cover over entire roof surface that adds minimal loads to structure; serves as ecological stormwater management control by eliminating or delaying runoff. Also effectively reduces temperatures of the roof surface by absorbing heat from the sun, which may reduce the urban heat island effect. Intensive green roofs (also referred to as traditional roof garden): thick soil layer or planters with intensive care and maintenance requiring vegetation, such as trees and shrubs; add substantial loads to building structure.

Grout Fluid mixture of cement, water, and possibly sand.

Gypsum/cellulose An interior wallboard product that uses cellulose from recycled newspapers with gypsum and perlite.

Hardwood Deciduous trees with broader leaves and usually slower growth rates than the conifers, or softwoods. Common temperate-region hardwoods include dense, close-grained wood from oak, maple, cherry, walnut, beech, birch, cypress, elm, and hickory. Hundreds of hardwoods are available from both temperate and tropical regions. Used in furniture and flooring, for appearance, excellent durability, and resistance to wear.

Harvested rainwater The rain that falls on a roof or yard and is channeled to a storage tank (cistern). The first wash of water on a roof is usually discarded and the subsequent rainfall is captured for use if the system is being used for potable water. Good-quality water is available by this method in most areas.

Hazardous chemical Any hazardous material requiring a Material Safety Data Sheet under the Occupational Safety and Health Administration's hazard communication standard, including those associated with physical hazards such as fire and explosion, or health hazards such as cancer and dermatitis.

Hazardous air pollutant Air contaminant not included in the ambient air quality standards of the Clean Air Act but which may present a threat of adverse human health or environmental effects. Includes 17 chemical classes: antimony compounds, arsenic compounds (inorganic, including arsine), beryllium compounds, cadmium compounds, cobalt compounds, coke oven emissions, cyanide compounds, glycol ethers, lead compounds, manganese compounds, mercury compounds, fine mineral fibers (includes mineral fiber emissions from facilities manufacturing or processing glass, rock or slag fibers, or other mineral-derived fibers of average diameter 1 micrometer or less), nickel compounds, polycyclic organic matter, radionuclides (including radon), and selenium compounds. Also known as air toxics or toxic air pollutants.

Heat capacity The number of BTU a cubic foot of a material can store with a 1 degree F increase in its temperature.

Heat recovery Heat utilized that would otherwise be wasted. Sources of heat include machines, lights, process energy, and people.

Heat-welded resilient flooring Technique of joining two sheets of resilient flooring by heating and inserting a color-matched welding thread of polyvinyl chloride along the length of the seam. Once cooled, the welding thread is trimmed flush with the floor, creating a waterproof seam.

Heat-welded roofing Technique used to bond plies of membrane roofing together. Hot air welding requires the membrane to contain a thermoplastic material; bituminous heat welding is accomplished with the use of a torch. Neither technique requires the use of chemicals; however, many membrane roofing materials emit noxious gases when heated.

Heating degree day A unit based upon temperature difference and time, used in estimating heating energy consumption. For any one day, when the mean temperature is less than a reference temperature (typically 65 degrees F), there are as many degree days heating as degrees Fahrenheit temperature difference between the mean temperature for the day and the reference temperature. The sum of all degree days over a calendar year is annual heating degree days (HDD).

Heating recovery ventilator *See* Energy recovery ventilator.

Heavy metal An inorganic element whose specific gravity is 5 or more, and of relatively high molecular weight. Includes toxic metals, e.g., arsenic, cadmium, chromium, lead, mercury and zinc. Many are classified as persistent, bioaccumulative toxic pollutants by EPA. *See* PBT.

Hessian Coarse cloth woven from jute fiber. Burlap. Used as backing for carpet or resilient flooring.

Hexamethylene tetramine White crystalline powder formed from ammonia and formaldehyde. Used as curing agent for phenolic and urea resins, and an accelerator for slow-curing rubber vulcanizates. Also known as cystamine.

Hexane Flammable, very volatile liquid with faint odor. Insoluble in water, miscible with alcohol. May cause light-headedness, nausea, headache, numbness of extremities, muscle weakness, irritation of eyes and nose, dermatitis, chemical pneumonia, giddiness. Used as solvent, to thin paints.

High-performance coating An architectural coating formulated to withstand exposure to harsh environmental conditions, including outside weather conditions all the time, temperatures consistently above 95 degrees C or below 0 degrees C, solvents, harsh detergents, abrasives or scouring agents, or corrosive atmosphere or fluids.

Holographic device Uses diffractive structures to control light transmission. Incoming light is redirected as a function of angle of incidence and wavelength of the incoming light. There are two processes for creating holographic devices to date photopolymer process (thick film) and embossing process (thin film relief). The holographic films can be assembled either in series or in parallel. Currently, large polyester sheets with an embossed, diffractive structure are used. These can be attached to the upper portion of any visible transparent aperture facing orientations that receive solar radiation. Direct sunlight falling on the device is diffracted toward the ceiling deep into the space; glare-free, diffuse light is then reflected onto work surfaces. Current prototypes are partially transparent, allowing vision through them, though providing less efficiency. The view remains undistorted but is darkened somewhat.

Hot mop The process by which liquefied asphalt is applied to a roofing surface in order to adhere bituminous roofing membranes.

HVAC system efficiency The ratio of the useful energy output (at the point of use) to the energy input in consistent units for a designated time period, expressed in percent. *See also* AFUE, COP, EER, SEER, *and* Steady state combustion efficiency.

Hydrocarbon Chemical composed only of carbon and hydrogen; petroleum crude oil is largest source of hydrocarbons.

Hydrochlorofluorocarbon (HCFC) Hydrochlorofluorocarbons are generally less detrimental to depletion of the stratospheric ozone than related chlorofluorocarbons; generally used to replace chlorofluorocarbons. However, a total ban on all CFCs and HCFCs is scheduled effective 2030. *See also* Chlorofluorocarbon.

Hydrofluorocarbon (HFC) Hydrofluorocarbons (HFCs) have no ozone depletion potential, but are greenhouse gases, and contribute to global warming. *See also* Chlorofluorocarbon.

Hydrogen sulfide Flammable, highly toxic gas with offensive odor. Irritant and chemical asphyxiant. Insidious poison, since it fatigues the sense of smell. Used in chemical synthesis.

Hydropulp A mechanical method of breaking down wood fiber into pulp using water pressure instead of caustic chemicals. A very-low-emissions pulping method.

Impervious surface area Area that has been sealed and does not allow water to infiltrate, such as roofs, plaza, streets, and other hard surfaces.

Indigenous Native to a region.

Indirect gain system In indirect gain systems, sunlight strikes a thermal mass located between the sun and the space. The sunlight is absorbed by the mass, converted into thermal energy, and transferred into the conditioned spaces. Because conditioned spaces do not receive solar radiation immediately, indirect gain systems offer greater control over temperature swings and overheating. The two basic types of indirect gain systems are thermal storage walls and roof ponds.

Indoor air quality (IAQ) ASHRAE defines acceptable indoor air quality as air in which there are no known contaminants at harmful concentrations as determined by cognizant authorities and with which a substantial majority (80 percent or more) of the people exposed do not express dissatisfaction.

Industrial hygiene The science and art devoted to the recognition, evaluation, and control of those environmental factors or stresses arising in or from work situations that may cause sickness, impaired health and well-being, or significant discomfort and inefficiency among workers or the public. A certified industrial hygienist has demonstrated proficiency through the American Board of Industrial Hygiene.

Industrial waste Materials remaining from industrial operations. Includes liquid, sludge, solid, or hazardous waste.

Inert Inert ingredients listed by a manufacturer are distinct from the product's active ingredients. However, these ingredients may not be inert from a health perspective. For example, in agricultural sprays, the principal toxic ingredient is often the inert vehicle, e.g., kerosene or petroleum oil. Dusts and powders included as inert ingredients may include hydrated lime, calcium carbonate, gypsum, talc.

Infrared radiation Electromagnetic radiation, whether from the sun or a warm body, that has wavelengths longer than the red end of the visible spectrum (greater than 0.75 microns). We experience infrared radiation as heat. Of the radiation emitted by the sun, 49 percent is in the infrared band.

Infrared reflective technology These halogen lamps have a reflective coating on the inner lamp designed to redirect infrared radiation heating the filament to produce more visible light. As a result, lighting energy efficiency compared to standard halogen is improved, as less input power is necessary to keep the filament hot.

Inorganic compound Chemical that does not contain carbon as the principal element (except carbonates, cyanides, and cyanates). Minerals, metals, ceramics, and water are examples of inorganic compounds. Most tend to be very stable because they oxidize slowly or not at all. *See also* Organic compound.

Insecticide A chemical agent that destroys insects. These toxins act on the reproductive or nervous system of larval or adult insects. Use of insecticides is controlled by the Food and Drug Administration.

Insolation The total amount of solar radiation (direct, diffuse, and reflected) striking a surface exposed to the sky. This incident solar radiation is generally measured in BTU per square foot per hour.

Insulation Material having resistance to transfer of energy, e.g., acoustic, electric, thermal, vibrational, or chemical.

Integrated waste management Using a variety of practices, including source reduction, recycling, incineration, and landfilling, to minimize the amount of municipal solid waste.

International Agency for Research on Cancer (IARC) classification A method for evaluating the strength of evidence supporting a potential human carcinogenicity judgment based on human, animal, and other supporting data. Definitions are as follows Group 1 carcinogenic to humans; Group 2A probably carcinogenic to humans; Group 2B possibly carcinogenic to humans; Group 3, not classifiable as to human carcinogenicity; and Group 4, probably not carcinogenic to humans.

Irritant A chemical that is not corrosive but which causes a reversible, inflammatory effect on living tissue by chemical action at the site of contact.

Irritation An inflammatory response, usually of skin, eye, or respiratory tract, induced by direct action of a substance.

Isocyanate One of a group of neutral derivatives of primary amines. Compounds having the general formula $R(N=C=O)_n$. Includes 4,4'-diphenylmethane diisocyanate (MDI) and toluene diisocyanate (TDI). May cause respiratory and skin sensitization and occupational asthma. Used in production of polyurethanes, varnish, foam, paint, concrete sealers, bonding agents, pesticides.

Isocyanurate Produced from isocyanates. Used in flame retardant, resilient, rigid polymers.

Isolated gain system In isolated gain systems, the solar collection and storage elements are separate from the spaces they provided heat. Generally south-facing solariums, greenhouses, and atriums are common examples of sun spaces in isolated gain systems.

Isoparaffinic hydrocarbons Branched-chain version of aliphatic hydrocarbon. A type of highly purified petroleum solvent sold as "odorless" paint thinner. Often used in solvent-based, low-toxicity paints.

Joint compound A wet filler material used to join materials of the same type, to create a uniform surface.

Ketone One of a class of organic compounds. Examples are acetone and methyl ethyl ketone, which are used as solvents.

Kiln-dried A method of drying wood in an oven after sawing that results in 10 percent or less moisture content. This makes the wood more dimensionally stable and better able to resist decay, but results in higher embodied energy associated with production.

Lacquer Manufactured from high-molecular-weight polymers such as cellulose esters, acrylics, polyurethanes, and vinyls, to give a glossy, opaque, or pigmented finish. Lacquers dry rapidly, without oxidation or polymerization, when solvents evaporate.

Laminate A thin layer of material (veneer) bonded to another surface. Wood and plastics are both commonly laminated.

Lanolin Wax from sheep's wool, composed of a complex mixture of esters of higher alcohols and long-chain fatty acids. Used in paints and as base for emollients in shampoos and cosmetics.

Latex Stable water dispersion of synthetic or natural polymers. Milky colloid in which natural or synthetic rubber or plastic is suspended in water. A naturally occurring, sticky resin from rubber tree sap used for rubber products, carpet backings, and paints. Latex is a broad term that also applies to synthetic rubbers, usually styrene butadiene. Styrene is a known toxin and a carcinogen. *See also* Styrene butadiene latex.

Latex paint Water suspension or emulsion of polyvinyl acetate, polyacrylics, and polystyrene butadiene combined with pigments and additives, including binders and suspending agents. They also contain small amounts of coalescing solvents. Latex paints dry by evaporation. As water evaporates from the film, the coalescing solvents allow the particles of resin to fuse together (coalesce), forming a continuous coating. Attributes can include excellent adhesion, color and gloss retention, long-term flexibility, and toughness. Their advantages include ease of application and cleanup, safety during application and occupancy, and VOC compliance. Generally, latex paints must be protected from freezing and applied at a minimum temperature of 50 degrees F.

LD$_{50}$ Measure of toxicity. Amount of a substance that causes death in 50 percent of exposed animals or humans (lethal dose, 50 percent).

Lead Soft, heavy metal. Acute toxicity common in young children, may cause permanent brain damage. Carcinogen. "Lead-free" plumbing may contain up to 8 percent lead, and lead-free solders and flux may contain up to 0.2 percent lead. Used in alloys in pipes, cable sheaths, shields against radioactivity. *See* 33/50 Program. Identified by EPA as a persistent, bioaccumulative toxic pollutant. *See* PBT.

Life cycle assessment (LCA) A process or framework to evaluate the environmental burdens associated with a product, process, or activity by identifying, quantifying, and assessing its energy and material usage and environmental releases, to identify opportunities for environmental improvements. Extraction and processing of raw materials, manufacturing, transportation and distribution, use/reuse/maintenance, recycling and final disposal are all considered.

Life cycle All stages of development, from extraction to production, marketing, transportation, use, and disposal.

Life cycle cost All internal and external costs associated with a product, process, or activity throughout its entire life cycle. The Department of Defense has defined it to mean the amortized annual cost of a product, including capital costs, installation costs, operating costs, maintenance costs, and disposal costs discounted over the life of the product. However, this definition has traditionally excluded environmental costs.

Light shelf   Light shelves are horizontal projections at the building interior that reflect direct sun rays onto the ceiling deep into a space. Light shelves work best on facades that are generally south-facing, since they work for long periods of time each day and also can provide shading of glazing below.

Lighting power density   The installed lighting power in a building, typically measured in watts per square feet.

Lighting power ratio   The ratio of dimmed lighting power with daylighting to undimmed lighting power at the illumination set point. Low lighting power ratios mean lighting energy savings and reductions in cooling loads due to lighting energy dissipation.

Lignin   A substance that in combination with cellulose forms and binds the woody cell walls of plants. Potential biomass material for use in energy production and as a chemical feedstock. Used as an extender in phenolic resins and as a filler in rubber.

Limonene   A terpene with a lemon odor, derived from oils in citrus fruits, peppermint, and spearmint. Skin irritant, sensitizer. Used as solvent, in manufacture of resins, and as a wetting and dispersing agent.

Linoleum   Natural linoleum is made from natural, minimally processed ingredients, including linseed oil, pine rosin, cork dust, wood flour, limestone, mineral pigments, and jute backing. Synthetic materials such as petrochemical plasticizers, PVC, or synthetic rubber are not typically used. Off-gassing will depend primarily on the adhesive used for installation. Some long-term off-gassing will occur with the linoleum due to oxidation of the linseed oil, resulting in emission of a mixture of aldehydes and carboxylic acids, which are not considered hazardous but may affect sensitive individuals.

Linseed oil   Derived from flaxseed by crushing and pressing with or without heat. Used as a vehicle in oil paints and as a component of oil varnishes.

Lithopone   A white pigment made by reacting barium sulfide, zinc sulfide, and zinc oxide. Used in paint and linoleum. Commercial demand for lithopone has decreased since the introduction of titanium pigments. Also known as Griffith's zinc white.

Linseed oil putty   A mixture of linseed oil and finely ground calcium carbonate (chalk) used for woodwork and glazing.

Loose-fill insulation   Insulation made from vermiculite, perlite, glass or mineral wool, shredded wood, or shredded paper, loosely packed to allow pockets of dead air space. For use in wall and ceiling cavities.

Low-impact development   New development that minimizes disturbance on-site due to construction and erosion. Low-impact developments are designed to blend well into their environmental setting to preserve natural features and the maximum amount of open space.

Lumen (lm)   A unit of measurement of the rate at which a lamp produces light. A lamp's light output rating expresses the total amount of light emitted in all directions per unit time.

Lumen method   The most widely used method in the United States to evaluate the contribution of daylight to room illumination. Many different variables are taken into account, including sky condition, position of sun, room size, glazing area, and transmission characteristics (such as overhangs, shades, and blinds).

Magnesium oxide   Very fine, slightly water-soluble, odorless powder. Combines with water to form magnesium hydroxide, an alkaline compound. Exposure to fumes may cause irritation of eyes and nose, metal fume fever. Used as lining in refractory ovens, fertilizer, chemical reagent. Also known as magnesia.

Makeup air   Outdoor air supplied to replace exhaust air and exfiltration.

Mastic   Mixture of finely powdered rock and asphaltic material used in highway construction. Mastic gum is a natural solid resin used in adhesives and lacquers.

Material Safety Data Sheet   A compilation of information required under the OSHA hazard communication standard, including a listing of hazardous chemicals, health and physical hazards, exposure limits, and handling precautions.

Mechanically adhered (roofing)   A method of attaching a roofing material to its underlying substrate through the use of mechanical fasteners. The frequency of these fasteners can be increased or decreased depending on wind loading. This is a fast and easy method for installing modular roofing types. Mechanical fasteners allow for easy material recovery at the end of their useful life.

Medium-density fiberboard (MDF)   Composite panel product generally made from lignocellulosic (wood) fibers combined with a synthetic resin or other bonding system and joined together under heat and pressure. May contain additives. Used in kitchen cabinets, paneling (as core material with veneers, printed surfaces, vinyl or low pressure laminates), doors, jambs and millwork, and laminate flooring. *See* Formaldehyde.

Melamine resin   Thermosetting resin made from formaldehyde and melamine. Lower-molecular-weight resins are used for impregnating paper and in laminating. In textile finishing, they provide soil and wrinkle resistance. High-molecular-weight resins are used for tableware. When fully cured, melamine resin is inert, meaning that no formaldehyde is emitted under normal conditions. Melamine resin is generally used as the bonding agent in adhesives and in plastic laminate manufacture.

Mercury   A heavy metal that at room temperature is a silvery, heavy, mobile liquid. Readily absorbed by all routes of exposure, and symptoms of overexposure may include personality changes, excessive salivation, kidney damage, muscle tremors, depression, irritability. Used in fluorescent lamps, in mirrors, in antifouling paints. Also known as quicksilver. See 33/50 Program. Identified by EPA as a persistent, bioaccumulative toxic pollutant. *See* PBT.

Methane   Odorless, nonpoisonous, light, flammable gas. Chief component of natural gas (about 85 percent). Contributes to the greenhouse effect. Functions as a simple asphyxiant, physically displacing oxygen in the lungs. Used in manufacturing of ammonia, acetylene, formaldehyde, and organic synthesis. Atmospheric methane holds in heat radiating from the Earth and is a more effective greenhouse gas than carbon dioxide. Also known as marsh gas.

Methanol   Flammable, poisonous, mobile liquid, miscible with water, ether, and alcohol. Poisoning may occur from any route of exposure, and symptoms include headache, fatigue, nausea, and visual impairment. Used in manufacture of formaldehyde, in chemical synthesis, in gasoline antifreeze, and as a solvent. Also known as methyl alcohol or wood alcohol.

Methyl cellulose   A grayish-white powder from cellulose, which swells in water to a colloidal solution. Used in water-based paints and ceramic glazes as an adhesive. Used as a substitute for water-soluble gums, to render paper greaseproof. Also known as cellulose methyl ether.

Methyl ethyl ketone (MEK)   An organic, colorless liquid with a minty odor. Flammable, water-soluble liquid, miscible in oil. May cause irritation of eyes and nose, headache, dizziness, and vomiting. Used as a solvent in vinyl films, as a reagent in organic synthe-

sis, in the surface coating industry, and in synthetic resins. *See* 33/50 Program. *See also* Methyl ethyl ketone peroxide.

Methyl ethyl ketone peroxide   Unstable organic that, like hydrogen peroxide, releases oxygen. Like many peroxides, it is extremely toxic. Concentrated solutions are corrosive to skin and mucous membrane. Used as a catalyst for polymerizing plastics and as a hardener for fiberglass resin. *See also* Methyl ethyl ketone.

Methyl isobutyl ketone   Flammable, colorless organic liquid with pleasant aroma. Methyl isobutyl ketone has a slower evaporation rate than methyl ethyl ketone. Moderately toxic, methyl ethyl ketone is an eye and nose irritant, and can cause headaches, dizziness, and nausea. Used as a solvent and chemical intermediate. *See* 33/50 Program.

Methyl methacrylate   Flammable, colorless liquid. Used as a monomer for polymethacrylate resins.

Methylene chloride   Nearly nonflammable, nonexplosive liquid. May cause fatigue, weakness, sleepiness, light-headedness, numbness or tingling of limbs, nausea, irritation of eyes and skin. Carcinogen. Used as a refrigerant in compressors, as a solvent, and in paint removers, aerosol propellant, insecticide. Used in cleaners, paint strippers, and foam-blowing agents. Also known as dichloromethane. *See* 33/50 Program.

Methylene bisphenyl isocyanate (MDI)   Also called MDI, is an organic compound used in binding resins. Associated with occupational asthma and sensitization.

Mica   A group of minerals, crystalline silicates, with sheetlike structures. Used as fillers in thermosetting resins.

Microbial   Pertaining to microorganisms, such as bacteria, protozoans, yeasts, mold, viruses, and algae.

Mineral wool   A fibrous glass made from molten slag, rock, and/or glass, produced by blowing or drawing, used for insulation and fireproofing. Also known as rock wool.

Modified bitumen   An asphalt-based material that is a composite of styrene butadiene styrene (SBS), atactic polypropylene (APP), or polyalphaolefin (PAO) with a polyester or fiberglass matting material. This is a built-up roofing system.

Monomer   A simple molecule that can be linked to other like molecules to form a polymer. Commercially important monomers include acrylonitrile, bisphenol A, epichlorohydrin, ethylene, ethylene glycol, ethylene oxide, formaldehyde, isocyanates, methyl methacrylate, phenol, propylene glycol, styrene, terephthalic acid, vinyl acetate, and vinyl chloride.

Mothproofing A treatment applied to fibers to resist damage by moths. Mothproofing agents are typically skin irritants and may cause adverse reactions on contact. Wool is the fiber most prone to moth attack.

Multiple chemical sensitivity (MCS) A set of symptoms that may include a burning sensation in the eyes or throat, difficulty breathing, cough, fatigues, headache, rashes, and neurological complaints following exposure to an inciting agent or agents. Those experiencing it report that it can be debilitating and can arise from exposure to chemicals that are generally considered innocuous to most people. Also known as idiopathic environmental intolerance.

Mutagenic Raises the frequency of genetic mutations above the spontaneous rate.

Mylar Trademark for a polyester sheet used for decorative and industrial purposes. Tough, heat resistant, and chemically stable.

Naphthalene Volatile, water-insoluble crystals with coal tar aroma. May cause nausea, vomiting, headache, fever. Used for moth repellents, fungicides, lubricants, and resins and as a solvent.

National Institute for Occupational Safety and Health (NIOSH) Federal division of the U.S. Department of Health and Human Services that develops and periodically revises recommendations or limits of exposure to potentially hazardous substances or conditions in the workplace. It also recommends preventative measures to reduce or eliminate adverse health hazards.

Neoprene Generic name for polychloroprene, synthetic rubber with resistance to ozone, weathering, various chemicals, oil, flame, and elevated temperatures. Suitable for general-purpose uses in paints, putties, adhesives, rubber gaskets, caulking, wire and cable coatings, waterproof membranes, shoe heels.

Neurotoxicity Any toxic effect on any part of the central or peripheral nervous system. These changes can be expressed as functional changes (e.g., behavioral or neurological abnormalities) or as neurochemical, biochemical, physiological, or morphological changes.

Nickel An inorganic, corrosion-resistant metallic element used in electroplating, batteries, and welding. May cause sensitization dermatitis, allergic asthma, pneumonitis. Carcinogen. *See* 33/50 Program. Identified by the EPA as a persistent, bioaccumulative toxic pollutant. *See* PBT.

Nitric oxide Poisonous gas with a sharp, sweet odor (brown at very high concentrations). Overexposure may cause irritation of eyes, nose, and throat, drowsiness, unconsciousness. Used as stabilizer for propylene and in bleaching of rayon. Also called nitrogen monoxide.

Nitrogen dioxide Dark brown poisonous gas with a pungent, acrid odor. Damaging component of photochemical smog and a by-product of gas combustion. Overexposure to this insidious gas may cause coughing, mucoid frothy sputum, chest pain, delayed pulmonary edema, cyanosis, and eye irritation.

Nonrenewable energy Sources of energy such as oil, coal, or natural gas that are not replaceable after they have been used.

Nonrenewable resource A resource that cannot be replaced in the environment. Fossil fuels (coal, petroleum, natural gas) are examples of nonrenewable energy sources.

Nontoxic Not injurious to human health or the environment when used for its intended, normal use in specified concentrations.

Nylon Synthetic thermoplastic melt-spun fiber in the polyamide resin family. Crystalline solid characterized by high strength, elasticity, durability, high flexibility, low water absorption, resistance to abrasion, rot, and mildew. Used in manufacture of synthetic fibers, rope, carpet, and molded plastics. Some nylons are recyclable, though very little recycling is currently done.

Nylon 6 Polymer derived from caprolactam. It is a very durable fiber among synthetics, second only to nylon 6,6. Used for textiles. It is made from a single polymer and thus can be 100 percent recycled back into carpet fiber. Also called Zeftron (trademark for product manufactured by BASF). *See also* Nylon *and* Nylon carpet.

Nylon 6,6 Polymer which is exceptionally resistant to heat. Used in fibers and plastics by melt extrusion. One of most durable of the synthetic fibers. At this point in time, it is recyclable only into low-grade noncarpet items. Also called Antron (trademark for product manufactured by Dupont) or Ultron (Monsanto). *See also* Nylon *and* Nylon carpet.

Nylon carpet Nylon fibers are considered to be the strongest synthetic carpet fibers with the best resistance to abrasion and stains; however, the fiber generates a large amount of static electricity, will degrade and fade over time, and will decompose if put in contact with mineral acids. The most common nylons used for carpeting are nylon 6 and nylon 6,6. As of 1992, nylon represented 80 percent of the U.S.

market share for carpet, and some carpet manufacturers are trying to make fiber recycling more viable.

Occupancy sensor A device that detects the presence or absence of people within an area and causes any combination of lighting, equipment, or appliances to be turned on, turned off, or adjusted accordingly.

Off-gassing The releasing of gases or vapors into the air.

Old growth Wood from trees found in mature forests. In many cases, the trees have never been exposed to logging operations. In the northwest United States, only about 10 percent of these biologically rich areas are left.

Olefin Synthetic thermoplastic melt-spun fiber. It is based on polypropylene, manufactured from propane (a gas by-product of oil refining), combined with ethylene. Olefin rates as high as nylon in abrasion resistance, durability, and strength, while also resisting stains, chemicals, fading, and the generation of static electricity; however, olefin lacks resiliency, has poor texture retention, and is susceptible to scarring.

Organic compound Chemical compound based on carbon chains or rings, and containing hydrogen with or without oxygen, nitrogen, or other elements. Organic compounds are the basis of all living things; they are also the foundation of modern polymer chemistry. There are several million known organic compounds, and their characteristics vary widely. *See also* Inorganic compound *and* Volatile organic compound.

Organic waste Natural materials, such as food and yard waste, that decompose naturally.

Organically grown Agricultural products that are grown with minimal use of synthetic fertilizers or pesticides. Various state and industry definitions are used to determine which products can be sold as organically grown.

Organochlorine Organic compounds formed with chlorine, bromine, or fluorine in their structure. Organochlorines exhibit a range of effects; some are very toxic (dioxins, PCBs, DDT) and others are chemically stable (Teflon).

Organophosphates The most widely used class of insecticides, e.g., parathion and malathion. Toxic to humans.

Oriented-strand board (OSB) A manufactured wood product, mainly used in construction, composed of strands of wood laid in the same direction and glued together with a binder. This process produces a very high-strength product from low-grade waste material from the wood milling industry.

Oxidant Oxidation reactions indoors may be potential sources of complex mixtures of chemically reactive compounds, which also may be potent mucous membrane irritants. Most oxidizing agents (e.g., ozone) are also strong irritants.

Ozone Unstable blue gas with pungent odor, a powerful oxidant. Irritating and injurious to the lungs, irritates eyes and mucous membranes, and may cause pulmonary edema and chronic respiratory disease. **1.** In the stratosphere, 5 to 30 miles above the earth's surface, ozone protects the earth from harmful ultraviolet radiation from the sun. This protective shield is thought to be depleted by chemically active species, leading to effects that include increased incidence of cataracts, skin cancer, and immunosuppression. Chlorofluorocarbons (CFCs), which are stable in the atmosphere and may reach the stratosphere, are cleaved by UV radiation to yield chlorine radicals. Chlorine radicals interfere with ozone formation and destroy and deplete stratospheric ozone. Several international agreements have led to reduced usage of CFCs, which are being replaced by hydrochlorofluorocarbons (HCFCs) and hydrofluorocarbons (HFCs). **2.** While stratospheric ozone is protective, ground-level ozone is associated with photochemical smog and public health advisories. **3.** "Ozonation" is sometimes used to remove the smoky odor from fire-damaged structures. **4.** Ozone is itself an irritant, and it reacts with hydrocarbons to produce additional irritating substances. Ozone in outdoor air and that generated by electrostatic equipment (copiers, laser printers, air cleaners) may react with VOCs emitted indoors to create irritating aldehydes and other problematic VOCs. Use of ozone-resistant and chemically stable polymeric building products would avoid such chemical reactions. *See also* Chlorofluorocarbon *and* Ultraviolet radiation.

Ozone depletion potential A relative measure of the potency of chemicals in depleting the stratospheric ozone; the ozone depletion factor is set relative to the depletion potential of CFC-11, which is designated 1.0. The ozone depletion factor potential depends upon the chlorine and the bromine content and atmospheric lifetime of the chemical.

Paint Protective coating material that includes pigments suspended in a liquid medium. Properties may include stability, resistance to water and environmental stress, gloss, color, opacity, hardness, flexibility. Paints are formulated from finely ground pigment, a volatile solvent (water or hydrocarbons), binders (resins, drying oils, latexes) and additives (stabilizers, defoamers, pesticides, dispersants, fire retardants, UV absorbers, coalescing agents). Modern binders are resins that include alkyds, acrylics, and epoxies. Concerns about smog formation from VOCs in paints have increased use of water-based latex paints and resulted in federal limits on VOC content in paints. More stringent VOC limits have been set by regional air quality management districts in California and elsewhere. Alternatively, VOC and paint aerosol misting can be reduced by other methods of application, including use of spray equipment in which paint is atomized by pressure, steam, or heat; electrostatic spraying, in which paint is attracted to a conductive surface; electrodeposition, in which paint is deposited onto a conductive surface from a water bath; and powder coating, in which dry pigment is applied and then fused to the surface.

Paraffin wax Solid, crystalline hydrocarbon mixture derived from the paraffin distillate portion of crude petroleum. Low toxicity and approved as a food additive. Used to waterproof wood and cork, and in the manufacture of varnishes.

Particulates Fine solid particles of dust, spores, pollens, dander, skin flakes, mite allergens, cell debris, mold, mildew, mineral fibers, or solids escaping from combustion processes that are small enough to become suspended in air. Very small particulates (<.005 mm) can be inhaled deep into the lungs. Particulates containing plant or animal proteins (pollens, dust mites, and fungal spores) are allergenic, while those containing mineral fiber (silica, asbestos) can cause lung disease or cancer.

Passive solar cooling Building design that avoids unneeded solar heat, utilizes natural ventilation, and employs thermal mass (especially in hot, dry climates) to retain coolness.

Passive solar heating Building design that uses natural processes to collect, store, and distribute heat for a building. Most passively solar-heated buildings require an auxiliary heating system for periods when solar heat is unavailable or insufficient.

Payback analysis Evaluation of the period of time in which initial expenditures are recovered through subsequent savings. Simple payback can be calculated as follows: simple payback period = initial cost ÷ annual savings.

PBT Persistent, bioaccumulative toxic pollutant. Highly toxic, long-lasting substances that can build up in the food chain to levels harmful to human and environmental health. Associated with a range of adverse health effects, including effects on the nervous system, reproductive and developmental problems, cancer, and genetic impacts. EPA has developed a strategy to reduce priority PBT pollutants as part of its source reduction and recycling initiative. The first

12 priority PBT pollutants identified by EPA consist of aldrin/dieldrin, benzo(a)pyrene, chlordane, DDT, hexachlorobenzene, alkyl lead, mercury and compounds, mirex, octachlorstyrene, PCBs, dioxins and furans, and toxaphene. A total of 53 chemicals have been identified on the Resource Conservation and Recovery Act (RCRA) PBT list at the end of 1998 as being of greatest concern: 1,1-dichloroethane, 1,1,1-trichloroethane, 1,2-dichlorobenzene, 1,2,4-trichlorobenzene, 1,2,4,5-tetrachlorobenzene, 1,3-dichlorobenzene, 1,4-dichlorobenzene, 2-methylnaphthalene, 2,4,5-trichlorophenol, 4-bromophenyl phenyl, acenaphthene, acenaphthylene, anthracene, antimony, arsenic, benzo(g,h,i) perylene, beryllium, bis(2-ethylhexyl)phthalate, butyl benzyl phthalate, cadmium, chloroform, chromium, copper, cyanide, dibutyl phthalate, dioxins (PCDD), alpha-endosulfan, beta-endosulfan, fluoranthene, fluorene, furans (PCDF), heptachlor, heptachlor epoxide, hexachlorobenzene, hexachlorobutadiene, γ-hexachlorocyclohexane, lead, mercury, methoxychlor, naphthalene, nickel, nitrobenzene, octachlorostyrene, pentachlorobenzene, pentachloronitrobenzene, pentachlorophenol, phenanthrene, 2,4,6-*tris*(1,1-dimethylethyl)-phenol, phenol, polycyclic aromatic compounds, pyrene, selenium, and zinc.

Peak electrical demand The peak electrical demand is the maximum instantaneous load or the maximum average load over a designated interval of time, usually fifteen or thirty minutes measured by meter by the utility or power provider. Also known as peak power.

Peak load shedding Peak load shedding defers system loads from peak periods to periods of low demand. The result is a flattening of the system load schedule, thus decreasing demand charges from the electric utility. Design strategies that reduce the peak load are often referred to as "peak shaving."

Penetrating sealer A finish that is absorbed into wood, concrete, or other porous materials, and protects not only the surface but the entire upper layer of the material.

Pentane Flammable water-insoluble hydrocarbon liquid, with gasoline odor. May cause drowsiness, irritation of eyes and nose, dermatitis, chemical pneumonia. A CFC replacement as the blowing agent for some foam insulations. Used as chemical intermediate and solvent.

Perlite Volcanic glass, low-density filler that expands when heated and transforms into a fluffy form that can be used as a plaster additive and for insulation purposes.

Pervious paving Paving material that allows water to penetrate to the ground below.

Pesticide Lethal chemical that destroys pests, e.g., insects, rodents, nematodes, fungi, seeds, viruses, or bacteria. Term includes insecticides, herbicide, rodenticide, and fungicide. Chemical pesticides include organochlorine, organophosphorus, carbamates, chlorophenoxy compounds, dinitrophenols, and paraquat. The active ingredients are semivolatile, and some, particularly the organochlorine insecticides, are persistent in the environment. The carrier solvents and inert ingredients may exhibit similar or greater toxicity than the active ingredients, and can include volatile ingredients that off-gas into indoor air. May cause central nervous system effects (dizziness, nausea). Direct indoor applications can subject building occupants to VOCs and pesticide residue. Alternative, safe forms of controlling pests include use of sticky or mechanical traps. Also known as biocide. Many pesticides have been identified by the EPA as persistent, bioaccumulative toxic pollutants. *See* PBT.

Petrochemical Chemical made from petroleum or natural gas feedstock, such as ethylene, butadiene, most major plastics, and resins. Also known as petroleum chemicals. *See* Hydrocarbon.

pH A term used to describe the hydrogen ion activity of a system. A solution of pH 0 up to 7 is acid, pH of 7 is neutral, and pH over 7 to 14 is alkaline. The lower the pH, the stronger the acid. The higher the pH, the stronger (more alkaline) the base.

Phenol Poisonous and caustic water-soluble crystals with sharp, burning taste derived from crude oil or coal. Phenol is produced by reacting benzene and propylene. Phenol is rapidly absorbed through the skin and from the stomach and lungs. Systemic toxicity can result, characterized by an initial excitatory phase, rapidly progressing to CNS depression. Direct contact may cause irritation and dermatitis. Used to make synthetic resins and weed killers, as a solvent, adhesives, dyes, and chemical intermediate.

Phenol formaldehyde resin Thermosetting resin made by reaction of phenol and formaldehyde, with good strength and chemical resistance. Both phenol and formaldehyde are toxic chemicals; however, the phenolic resin is said to be inert as a fully cured polymer and a relatively low emitter of formaldehyde compared to urea formaldehyde resin. Used as adhesive for particleboard, decorative laminate backing, coatings, insulation. *See* Formaldehyde.

Phenol resorcinol formaldehyde A resin produced by reacting phenol with formaldehyde and then adding resorcinol to cure to a solid. Phenol resorcinol

formaldehyde is less costly than resorcinol formaldehyde but may not have equivalent bonding qualities. Generally used as the adhesive for interior composite wood products. *See also* Formaldehyde *and* Resorcinol formaldehyde.

Phenolic resin Thermosetting resins made from reaction of phenols and aldehydes, one example of which is phenol-formaldehyde resin.

Phenolic resin insulation foam Insulation manufactured by foaming phenolic resin using HCFC-141b. All components of phenolic foam are derived from crude oil and natural gas. HCFCs have been substituted in response to the general phase-out of CFCs due to concern for ozone layer depletion. While HCFCs are far less dangerous to the ozone layer, they are strong greenhouse gases. *See also* Hydrochlorofluorocarbon *and* Phenolic resin.

Phenyl mercuric acetate Toxic organic mercurial compound. May cause nerve damage. Previously used as a fungicide in paints. It has been banned since 1991 for use in most interior paints. Banned from use in food products. Used as antiseptic, fungicide, herbicide, and mildewcide.

Phosgene Highly toxic colorless gas that condenses to a fuming liquid. Diluted in air, odor resembles moldy hay. Vapors strongly irritating to eyes. Extreme pulmonary irritant, once used as war gas. Initial symptoms are mild and transient, with delayed effects 6 to 24 hours after exposure. Under intense heat, some chlorinated solvents, e.g., carbon tetrachloride, trichloroethylene, methylene chloride, may decompose to phosgene and contribute to toxic effects of fires. Effects include choking, constricted feeling in chest, coughing, painful breathing, bloody sputum. Used in manufacture of some foam insulations and organic chemicals, such as production of isocyanates by reaction with amines.

Photochromic Exhibits reversible color change when exposed to visible or near-visible radiant energy. Photochromic glazing incorporates metal halides, allowing the glazing to change optical properties when exposed to light and revert to its original state in the dark. For a window application, the glass lowers its transmissivity as outdoor light levels increase. Photochromic glass is widely used in sunglasses; however, it is still experimental and very expensive for building applications.

Photovoltaic Capable of generating a voltage as a result of exposure to visible or other radiation. Solid-state cells (typically made from silicon) directly convert sunlight to electricity. The electricity can be used immediately, stored in batteries, or sold to a utility. Costs continue to drop and efficiency is improving for this technology. *See also* Building integrated photovoltaics.

Phthalates A large family of hydrocarbon compounds added to plastics to keep them soft and supple. In 1985 a scientific panel reported to the Consumer Product Safety Commission that bis- or di(2-ethylhexyl)phthalate (also known as bis(2-ethylhexyl)phthalate) caused cancer in animals and may do so in humans. Preliminary studies in Norway suggest that childhood asthma may be associated with phthalates such as DEHP, used in PVC flooring and PVC-coated wall coverings. DEHP produces mono(2-ethylhexyl) phalalate, which has been shown to produce bronchial asthma in lab animals. DEHP was replaced by diisononyl phthalate, or DINP, in toys; however, it has also been found that DINP causes tumors in rats. In addition to their use as plasticizers, phthalates are also used as solvents and catalysts. *See also* Plasticizers. Bis(2-ethylhexyl) phthalate, butyl benzyl phthalate and dibutyl phthalate have been identified by EPA as persistent, bioaccumulative, toxic pollutants. *See* PBT.

Piece dyeing A process by which carpets are fabricated with undyed yarn and dyed after manufacture. It is mainly used for tufted carpet and solid colors.

Pigment Water-insoluble natural or synthetic coloring matter, used to impart color to other materials such as textiles, paints, stains, and plastics. In pigment dyeing, dispersions are applied to the fabric surface and bonded by heating. To obtain dull or matte yarns, small amounts of titanium dioxide are added to polymer solution or melt before extrusion. Historically derived from clays and other earthen minerals or plants, modern pigments are mostly synthetic, and many are derived from heavy metals.

Plastic glazing Originally developed as safety glazings, for their greater strength and impact resistance over glass. Plastics are now widely used for other advantages, including sound abatement, thermal insulation, and ease of manipulation into curved shapes.

Plasticizer A nonvolatile organic liquid or low-melting-paint solid additive that gives an otherwise rigid plastic flexibility, including phthalate esters, epoxy, and phosphate esters. Two common plasticizers are di(2-ethylhexyl)phthalate (DEHP) and 2,2,4-trimethyl-1,3-pentanediol-diisobutyrate (TXIB). Most plasticizers off-gas slowly and, in flooring, are a major source of VOC emissions.

Plastic Material that contains one or more organic polymeric substances of large molecular weight, is solid in its finished state, and at some stage in its manufacture or processing into a finished article can be shaped by flow. Includes polymers, plasticizers, stabilizers, fillers, and other additives. Many toxic chemicals are used in plastics manufacturing (e.g., benzene, cadmium compounds, carbon tetrachloride, lead compounds, styrene, vinyl chloride).

Plywood Material composed of thin sheets of wood glued together, with the grains of adjacent sheets oriented at right angles to each other.

Pollution prevention Source reduction and other practices that reduce or eliminate the creation of pollutants through increased efficiency in the use of raw materials, energy, water, or other resources, or protection of natural resources by conservation. May include reduction of substance volumes; substitution for toxic substances; implementation of clean technology; and/or installation of in-process recovery equipment (recycling). Example replacing VOC-based solvents and lubricants with water-based formulations.

Polyamide resin Synthetic resin, produced from polymerization of amino acid or condensation of a polyamine with a polycarboxylic acid. Nylons are polyamide resins. *See also* Nylon.

Polychlorinated biphenyl (PCB) One of a group of highly stable chlorinated isomers of biphenyl. Commercial PCBs are mixtures of various isomers and congeners. Highly persistent in the environment. The composition of PCB mixtures changes in the environment; the more carcinogenic components tend to bioaccumulate in fish and bind to sediments. PCBs are probable human carcinogens and are associated with other serious health effects, including those affecting the immune, reproductive, nervous, and endocrine systems. PCBs are currently being studied for their effects as environmental contaminants on the endocrine system of humans and animals. PCBs are known to affect thyroid hormone levels in humans; these levels are critical for normal growth and development. Due to their nonflammability, chemical stability, high boiling point, and electrical insulating properties, PCBs had wide use, e.g., in electrical, heat transfer, and hydraulic equipment and as plasticizers in paints, plastics, and rubber products. Concern over their toxicity and environmental persistence led to federal prohibitions on PCB manufacturing in 1976. PCBs may still be used in closed systems, e.g., electrical capacitors and transformers, vacuum pumps, and turbines, and in equipment not replaced since 1977. Identified by EPA as persistent, bioaccumulative toxic pollutants. *See* PBT.

Polyester Thermosetting and thermoplastic polymers made from esters of alcohols and formed in fibers, as a solid, or in sheets of plastic. Examples are polyethylene terephthalate, polybutyleneterephthalate. Used for fibers, laminates, moldings, and in composites. Many plastics are classified as polyester. *See also* Polyester fiber, Polyethylene terephthalate.

Polyester fiber   Fiber filament made from a material that is primarily thermoplastic polyester resin, such as Dacron or Mylar, which has high strength and resistance to moisture and soil resistance when cured but is not as durable as nylon. It can also be composed of PET recycled plastic. In carpeting, its use is mostly limited to light-traffic, residential applications.

Polyethylene   Thermoplastic material composed of polymers of ethylene. Used for films, coatings, flexible containers. There are high-density (HDPE) and low-density (LDPE) forms. These are relatively low-toxicity materials. *See also* Polyolefin.

Polyethyleneterephthalate (PET)   Thermoplastic polyester resin made from ethylene glycol and terephthalic acid. Used to make films or fibers. High tensile and impact strength, high stiffness, high flex life and toughness. Used in blow molding of soft-drink bottles, photographic film, electrical insulation. Common recycled polyester plastic resin used to produce polyester fiber and sheet plastics.

Polymer   Substances made of molecules formed by union of simple molecules (monomers), e.g., polymerization of ethylene forms polyethylene, condensation of phenol and formaldehyde yields phenol-formaldehyde resins. Cellulose and proteins are naturally occurring polymers, while plastics (such as acrylic, polyester, polyamides, etc.) are synthetic polymers. In paint, polymers are used as a supplemental resin aiding hardness and durability, and increasing elasticity to reduce cracking. *See also* Monomer *and* Copolymer.

Polymeric material   Includes a wide range of building products, e.g., adhesives, caulks, paints, sealants, varnishes, thermal insulation, waterproofing membranes, bituminous emulsions, wall covering, wood-based products, cleaners, carpets, and carpet underlays. These generate a wide range of VOC emissions indoors.

Polymeric methylene diisocyanate (PMDI)   A urea resin, one of a group of thermosetting amino resins and plastics and urea formaldehyde resins. A polyol that can be produced from waste-stream petrochemicals, particularly PET bottles. PMDI is a component of foams such as polyurethane and polyisocyanurate. The polyisocyanurate production industry recycles 30 million pounds of colored plastic bottles per year. PMDI is potentially toxic and requires special handling in manufacturing.

Polyolefin   A class of common, synthetic thermoplastic materials including polyethylene and polypropylene. Polyolefin can be spun into fibers to produce a tough exterior weather barrier fabric for construction. *See also* Polypropylene *and* Polyethylene.

Polypropylene   Thermoplastic resin made by polymerization of propylene. Product is hard and tough, resists moisture, oils, and solvents, and is heat resistant. Used in molded articles, fibers, film, toys. Melt-extruded polypropylene is used in indoor-outdoor carpets, outdoor furniture, nonwoven materials, "hard elastic" materials, carpet yarn, rope, artificial turf, packaging, and primary carpet backing. *See also* Polyolefin.

Polystyrene   Tough thermoplastic polymer, made by polymerization of styrene. Soluble in aromatic and chlorinated hydrocarbon solvents. Extruded polystyrene (XPS) rigid insulation has high insulation value and a void-free structure, making it largely impervious to water. XPS is manufactured using HCFCs as the blowing agent; HCFCs are strong greenhouse gases. Expanded polystyrene (EPS) board is sometimes used as an alternate to XPS to avoid use of HCFCs; however, EPS has a slightly lower insulating value, and gaps between beads of EPS may allow moisture intrusion, which may require additional flashing or moisture barrier films. Used in injection molding, extrusion, or casting for electrical insulation, fabric lamination, rigid foam, and molding of plastic objects. *See also* Styrene.

Polyurethane   Thermoplastic and thermosetting polymers. Used in rubbers with high abrasion resistance, foams, binders for paints to provide flexibility.

Polyurethane resin   Resin formed by reaction of diisocyanate (e.g., toluene diisocyanate) with a phenol, amine, or hydroxylic or carboxylic compound to produce a polymer with free isocyanate groups. Isocyanates used in production must be handled with care during manufacturing; they have been associated with occupational asthma and sensitization. Used as protective coating, potting or casting resin, adhesives, rubbers and foams, in paints, varnishes, and adhesives. *See* Isocyanate.

Polyvinyl aetate (PVA)   Thermoplastic polymer, insoluble in water, gasoline, oils and fats, soluble in ketones, alcohols, chlorinated hydrocarbons. Used in adhesives, for emulsifying, suspending, and thickening solutions, and in paints, e.g., water-based emulsion glues. Used as textile finishes for natural and synthetic fibers and nonwoven fabrics.

Polyvinyl chloride (PVC)   Thermoplastic polymer of vinyl chloride. Rigid material with good electrical properties and flame and chemical resistance. Stabilizers are needed to prevent discoloration from light or heat, and plasticizers are needed for flexibility. Vinyl chloride monomer is a known human carcinogen. Due to environmental releases during manufacturing, PVC production is banned in many parts of Europe. The environmental organization Greenpeace has developed an on-line resource guide to PVC alternatives. Hazardous when burned. Used in soft flexible films, including flooring, and in molded rigid products, e.g., pipes, fibers, upholstery, siding and bristles. Identified by a "3" inside a recycling triangle found on packaging.

Porcelain High-grade, vitreous ceramic ware characterized by high strength, low absorption, good translucency, and hard glaze.

Portland cement A kind of cement made by burning limestone and clay in a kiln. When water is added to the cement, the calcium oxide is hydrated to form alkaline calcium hydroxide. Although brief skin contact may be tolerated, some develop extensive skin burns. Cement dermatitis may include skin dryness, rashes, etc. Unhydrated Portland cement is a respirable dust but is not a silica hazard. Used as the base for most grouts for ceramic mosaics, quarry, and paver tiles. Also known as hydraulic cement or cement.

Postcommercial recycled content Material that has been recovered or otherwise diverted from the solid-waste stream during the manufacturing process. Does not include used, reconditioned, or remanufactured components. Also known as preconsumer recycled content.

Postconsumer recycled content Material or finished product that has served its intended consumer use and has been discarded for recovery. This material is part of the broader category of recovered material. Examples include newspaper, magazines, beverage containers, building materials, etc.

Potable water Water suitable for drinking.

Pressure-sensitive adhesive Dry adhesive that develops maximum bonding power when applied by light pressure. Eliminates the need to apply wet adhesives on-site during installation, possibly eliminating some off-gassing.

Pressure-treated wood Wood that is chemically preserved to prevent moisture decay, e.g., with chromated copper arsenate (CCA). Substitutes to CCA have been developed because of concerns about leaching of chromium and arsenic into groundwater and soil over time, and concerns over contact with skin during construction and inhalation of these metals during sawing. Pressure-treated wood containing arsenic and chromates is considered a suspected carcinogen. Ammonium copper quat (ACQ) is one alternate; this type of pressure-treated wood is not classified as a hazardous waste (as are CCA pressure-treated products). Pressure-treated wood products are currently not suitable for recycling.

Primary backing The substance to which the carpet fiber is attached. Primary backings are almost exclusively composed of polypropylene.

Primary treatment In wastewater treatment, the removal of coarse and fine floating and suspended solids from raw sewage. *See also* Secondary treatment *and* Tertiary treatment.

Primer (sealer, undercoat) Any coating intended to be applied to the surface of a substrate to perform one or more of the following functions: provide a firm bond between the substrate and subsequent coats; protect porous substrates; prevent subsequent coatings from being absorbed by the substrate; prevent harm to subsequent coatings by materials in the substrate; provide a smooth surface for subsequent coats; seal fire, smoke, or water damage; neutralize odors; block stains; block efflorescence; condition chalky surfaces; or coat acoustical materials without affecting their acoustical properties.

Proposition 65 Officially known as California's Safe Drinking Water and Toxic Enforcement Act of 1986, Proposition 65 mandates that the governor of California publish a list of chemicals that are known to cause cancer or have developmental or reproductive toxicity. In addition, warnings must be provided by businesses that knowingly or intentionally expose individuals to these chemicals. The governor's list currently includes over 580 chemicals: 420 carcinogens and 160 reproductive toxins. Proposition 65 has spurred industry to develop process modifications, chemical substitutions, and pollution control devices to eliminate or reduce emissions of listed chemicals that would have required warnings.

Propylene glycol Viscous, colorless, oily alcohol liquid, nontoxic, miscible with water, alcohol, solvents. Used as nontoxic antifreeze in breweries and dairies. Substitute for more toxic ethylene glycol and glycerol. Used as chemical intermediate, in polymer synthesis (polypropylene glycol, polyurethane, cellophane), and as an antifreeze, solvent, lubricant, plasticizer, bactericide. Used in paints, waxes, and sealers.

R-value Index of the ability of a substance to retard the flow of heat; the higher the numerical value, the higher the insulating value. The inverse of the rate of heat flow (conductivity) through a material.

Radiant barrier   A layer of metallic foil that reflects thermal radiation without transferring heat to other materials. Preferably, foil may contain high (>90 percent) recycled content.

Radon   Heavy, gaseous radioactive element, produced from decay of radium in soil and rocks (e.g., granite, shale, or phosphate). Radon and its decay products are carcinogens.

Rain sensor   A device that measures rainfall and may be used to prevent unnecessary irrigation.

Rammed earth   A building technique for exterior walls where earth is tamped down between forms. Certain mixtures of moistened earth used in this technique harden under pressure and form a strong, solid wall that is then covered by a waterproofing coat. Rammed-earth buildings maintain a relatively consistent temperature without artificial heating or cooling due to the thermal mass of the earth.

Recovered material   Waste materials and by-products that have been recovered or diverted from solid waste. Excludes those materials and by-products generated from and commonly reused within an original manufacturing process.

Recycled plastic lumber   Structural components fabricated from recycled plastic as a replacement for lumber. Insect and water resistant.

Recycling   The extraction and recovery of valuable materials from scrap or other discarded materials. Metals are separated electrostatically. Recycled mixed plastics are used for products that do not depend on color, clarity, or strength, e.g., carpet backing. Higher-value recycled products require sorting of plastics based on differences such as density, physical properties, solubility, or light sensitivity. True recycling is the conversion of a waste material back into its original form. An alternative is conversion into another material. *See also* Conversion.

Reflective glass   Glass coated with metallic oxide or other material to increase the amount of solar energy reflected. The result is a reduction in the cooling load within the building. Sometimes, however, reflective glass also transfers the heat gain to a surrounding building that is not in need of it.

Reflector   Highly reflective backing inserted behind a light fixture, used to reclaim lighting and improve efficiency.

Regeneration   Restoration of logged forestlands and mined sites. Drainage, soil replacement, replanting, and fertilization are usually involved.

Renewable resources   A resource that is replenished at a rate equal to or greater than its rate of depletion.

Examples of renewable energy resources include solar, wind, hydro, geothermal, and biomass resources. Renewable resources are sometimes referred to as regenerative, nondepletable, or current-income energy.

Resilient flooring   Resilience is the ability of a material to return to its original form after subjection to static or dynamic loads, or sudden impact. Resilient flooring may include rubber, vinyl, or linoleum floor coverings.

Resin   Any solid or semisolid organic product of natural or synthetic origin with no definite melting point. Most resins are polymers. Natural resins are water-insoluble fluids that exude from plants; on exposure to air they initially form soft products and after long periods polymerize to solids or semisolids. Used in varnishes and lacquers; examples include dammar, Canada balsam. Synthetic resins are solid or semisolid materials that have a tendency to flow under stress and usually have a softening or melting range. Commonly, the term *resin* is used synonymously with uncured fluid thermosetting materials, and as a synonym for plastics and polymers.

Resorcinol formaldehyde   Phenol formaldehyde resin, soluble in water, ketones, and alcohol, used to make fast-curing adhesives for wood gluing. When fully cured, it is considered to be highly stable and nontoxic; if not completely cured, remnant resorcinol and formaldehyde monomers remain. *See also* Formaldehyde *and* Phenol resorcinol formaldehyde.

Reuse   The recovery of a material for additional use without reprocessing (e.g., glass bottles reused by a dairy).

Rigid insulation   Insulation, such as foamed plastic, wood, cork, glass, or mineral fibers, pressed into standard-sized boards for easy handling. Used as a surface insulation.

Rock wool   *See* Mineral wool.

Roof pond   A body of water on the roof of a structure that is exposed to solar gain, which it absorbs and stores. The thermal energy is radiated into the building uniformly and at a moderated temperature, in both sunny and cloudy conditions.

Rubberized jute cushion   Carpet cushion made of the natural fiber jute, using the part of the jute plant that cannot be used for weaving other products. The cushion is constructed by alternating layers of aligned strips of jute and polypropylene carrier mesh. SB latex is sprayed on both sides, for a total latex content of 10–15 percent.

Runoff Surface streams that appear after precipitation or irrigation. A lost resource and contributor to nonpoint source pollution.

Runaround coils A runaround coil system is composed of two or more extended surface fin coils installed in air ducts and interconnected by piping. Water, or a heat-exchange fluid of ethylene glycol and water, is circulated through the system by a pump. The fluid absorbs heat from the hot-air stream and releases it into the cold-air stream (or vice versa). A runaround coil system can be used in winter to preheat cold outdoor air and in summer to cool hot outdoor air. Runaround coils are most often used when it is physically difficult to locate the exhaust air duct in close proximity to the makeup air duct. They are substantially less efficient than heat wheels and heat-pipe heat exchangers.

Salvage Recovery and reclamation of damaged, discarded, or abandoned material, e.g., during demolition or renovation.

Sand barrier termite prevention A shallow trench around the perimeter of a building foundation that is filled with sand. Termites cannot pass through the barrier because their tunnels cave in.

Saturated air Air whose vapor pressure is the saturation vapor pressure and whose relative humidity is 100. Air that holds the maximum amount of water vapor at the specified temperature and pressure.

Scheduled switching Scheduled switching is the most basic type of automatic lighting control. Lights are programmed to turn on or off (and brighten or dim) at prescribed times, according to the expected patterns of occupancy.

Sealant A material with adhesive properties and the capability of expansion and contraction that is used primarily to fill, seal, waterproof, or weatherproof gaps or joints between two surfaces. VOC limits for sealants have been established by specific entities, such as California's South Coast Air Quality Management District, to protect against smog formation outdoors. *See* Caulking.

Seasonal energy efficiency ratio *See* SEER.

Secondary backing The material that is bonded to the primary backing of a carpet for added durability, manufactured from, e.g., SB latex, vinyl, thermoplastic, jute, or urethane.

Secondary treatment In wastewater treatment, biological treatment for removing floating and settleable solids, oxygen-demanding substances and suspended solids. Includes trickling filters or activated sludge processes. Disinfection is the final stage of secondary treatment. *See also* Primary treatment *and* Tertiary treatment.

SEER The seasonal energy efficiency rating, which reflects the cooling performance over the entire cooling season. It is the total cooling energy provided over the course of its normal annual usage period divided by the total electric energy input in watt-hours over the same period.

Selective pyrolysis Heating a substance in a controlled manner in the absence of oxygen. Pyrolysis of carpeting can result in reduction of resins to their monomer components. Since resins break down at different temperatures, it is then feasible to recover each one separately.

Sensitization The priming of the immune system following an initial exposure to an antigenic substance. The sensitized individual is now capable of responding to subsequent exposure with a stronger response and the possibility of clinical symptoms.

Shading coefficient The ratio of solar energy transmitted through a window to incident solar energy that is normal to it. Used to express the effectiveness of glazing or a shading device.

Sheathing board Composition board (e.g., fiber or gypsum cement) used instead of wood sheathing, e.g., to cover the framework of buildings or cabinets.

Shellac Natural, alcohol-soluble, water-insoluble flammable resin. Made from lac resin deposited on tree twigs in India by the lac insect and used in wood coatings. Shellac varnish provides a fast-drying, hard finish. Shellac substitutes include rosin-modified maleic resin and a polymer made from phthalic anhydride and polyol.

Sick building syndrome (SBS) A pattern of health complaints related to poor indoor air quality. Unlike building-related illness, sick building syndrome does not have known causation or definite symptoms, nor can it be diagnosed medically. It may be a multifactorial problem (e.g., inadequate ventilation, deficiencies in HVAC operation, exposure to indoor air pollutants such as tobacco smoke, VOCs, mold). Symptoms include nasal stuffiness, dry and irritated eyes, throat, and skin; headaches; generalized lethargy and tiredness leading to poor concentration. Symptoms typically disappear upon leaving the building.

Silica gel Highly absorbent silica used as a dehumidifying and dehydrating agent, as a catalyst or catalyst carrier.

Silicates Inorganic compounds containing silicon, oxygen, and one or more metals. Silicates are hazardous if inhaled but make chemically stable building products.

Siliconate Any of a large family of chemicals based on silica, e.g., silica gel, sodium silicate, silicone.

Silicone Heat-stable, water-repellent, semiorganic polymers of organic radicals attached to the silicones, e.g., dimethyl silicone. Fluid, resin, or elastomer; grease, rubber, or foamable powder. Relatively low toxicity. Use in caulking and flexible plastics, lubricating oils and sealers, defoaming agents, adhesion promoters, water-repellant and heat-resistant coatings, varnishes, and heat-resistant paints.

Silicone alkyd An alkyd coating modified with up to 30 percent silcone resin. Silicone alkyd paints dry, cure, and perform as alkyds, with improved color and gloss retention, for use in areas with intense sunlight. *See also* Alkyd.

Single-ply roofing membrane The generic name for all elastomeric-type roofing membranes, often incorporating polyester or other elastic reinforcing. Thermoplastic membranes are composed of PVC or olefin. Thermosetting membranes are composed of ethylene propylene membranes. They can be applied by mechanical, adhesive, or ballasted methods. *See also* Thermoplastic, Thermosetting, Polyvinyl chloride, *and* Olefin.

Sink effect *or* sink factor The absorption of chemicals into porous materials, e.g., gypsum drywall or ceiling tiles, to be reemitted at a later time.

SIPs *See* Structural insulated panels.

Sisal Coarse, stiff yellow fiber produced by leaves of a plant native to Mexico and Central America. Used for making twine and brush bristles.

Sizing Preliminary application of material to surface to fill pores and limit absorption of adhesive or coating, used for textiles, paper, and other porous materials. Surface treatment applied to glass fibers used in reinforced plastics. Generic term for coating yarns or fabrics to protect them from abrasion and breakage. Sizes are hydrophilic materials such as starch, soluble gums, polymers, and antistatic agents; may also include a temporary, formaldehyde-based fabric treatment that makes fabric stiffer and easier to work.

Slag Nonmetallic by-product of smelting and refining of metals. Used in cement manufacture, lightweight concrete, and rock wool.

Sludge Mud, slime, semisolid waste. In waste disposal, raw sludge is the mass collected in sedimentation tanks from screened wastewater. Sewage sludge has been considered for agricultural land application because of its high nitrogen and phosphorus content; however, concern about heavy metals and other toxic ingredients limit its use.

Slurry Free-flowing, pumpable suspension of fine solid material in liquid.

Soaker hose Low-flow watering device; hose with numerous perforations, used to irrigate plant beds and gardens.

Sodium fluorosilicate Poisonous powder, slightly soluble in water. Used as a rodenticide and insecticide, e.g., as a mothproofing agent for wool, as a preservative, and in dyeing processes, and to fluoridate drinking water.

Sodium silicate Crystal-like pieces of silicates, which are very slightly soluble or almost insoluble in cold water. May cause irritation of skin and mucous membranes on contact. If swallowed, causes vomiting and diarrhea. Used to fireproof textiles, and in corrugated paperboard manufacture. Known as liquid glass, silicate of soda, sodium metasilicate, soluble glass, water glass.

Softwood Wood from a coniferous tree, such as pine, fir, hemlock, spruce, or cedar. Softwoods are fast-growing and primarily used for construction. *See also* Hardwood.

Soil moisture sensor A device that can be attached to any automatic irrigation system that monitors the water available to plants and allows irrigation only when the soil moisture level drops below the desired level.

Solar collector A device designed to gather and store energy from solar radiation, ranging from ordinary windows to complex mechanical devices. The three major types of active solar collectors used in building applications are flat plates, evacuated tubes, and a variety of linear concentrators. Flat plates are the most common type used for heating and hot water. Evacuated and concentrating collectors are often used for applications requiring higher temperatures. *See also* Photovoltaic.

Solar control retrofit film A thin plastic film glued to clear or glazed glass to increase its shading coefficient. Tinted and/or aluminized polyester solar control films for retrofit were first introduced in the early 1960s. Newer coatings have improved in spectral selectivity, and films are also available with low-E characteristics.

Solar heat gain coefficient (SHGC) Preferred terminology for solar heat gain through glazing and fenestration. Weighted average of solar radiation penetrating glass at different angles (typically, 86 percent).

Solar water heater A water heating system in which heat from the sun is absorbed by collectors and transferred by pumps to a storage unit. The heated fluid in the storage unit conveys its heat to the domestic hot water of the building through a heat exchanger. Controls regulating the operation are needed.

Solid waste Solid product or material disposed of in landfills, incinerators, or compost. Can be expressed in terms of weight or volume.

Solution dyeing Adding dye to molten polymer solution before fibers are extruded. Pigments used are inorganic or metallized organic compounds. Solution dyeing is most effective in producing large quantities of single-color carpet fiber. Also known as dope dyeing.

Solvent Compound that is normally liquid in pure state.

Source reduction Any practice that reduces the amount of hazardous substance, pollutant, or contaminant prior to recycling, treatment, or disposal, and reduces the hazards to public health and the environment associated with release of these materials. Includes equipment or technology modifications, process or procedure modifications, reformulation or redesign of products, substitution of raw materials, and improvements in housekeeping, maintenance, training, or inventory control. *See* Pollution prevention.

Source separation Separating waste materials by type at the point of discard so that they can be efficiently recycled.

Soya lecithin A fatty acid phosphate extract of soybean oil, also found in other grains and egg yolk. Used in inks, soaps, plastics, paints, and textiles processing. Safe as a food additive.

Spectrally selective glazing Spectrally selective glazings are those that have been tuned to absorb solar infrared radiation while maintaining visible transmittance. Tint is achieved in glazing by adding materials to the glass during production or by applying a plastic coating film after production. The tinting materials increase absorptance of solar radiation and may change the color appearance of the glass. Blue, green, and aqua are naturally selective for the visible wavelengths. *See* Coolness index.

Sponge rubber cushion Foamed, flexible rubber from unvulcanized latex, or from strongly masticated rubber stock, with gas-producing ingredient such as sodium bicarbonate. For carpeting, the cushion is made of rubber manufactured through a vulcanization process. Rubber resin is mixed with fillers, plasticizers, and other chemicals, and reduced to a thin film; the film is sent through a vulcanizing oven, which expands the rubber into a steel grid. A thin strip of spun, bonded nylon or polyester is placed on top of the hot rippled surface to provide dimensional

stability and to serve as a laminating film. The rubber source is either natural rubber or SB rubber (that does not contain 4-PC). Carpet cushion can be a source of VOC emissions indoors, and may deteriorate due to moisture from below when laid on concrete. Used for comfort cushioning, shock insulation. Also known as foam rubber cushion.

Stack effect Pressure-driven airflow produced by convection, by the difference between confined hot gas in chimney or stack and cool air surrounding the outlet. The stack effect can overpower a building's mechanical system and disrupt ventilation and circulation.

Stack scrubber Air pollution control device, used to wash out or remove entrained liquid droplets or dust, or remove undesired gas from process stream. On coal-fired power plants, wet scrubbers are used to reduce sulfur dioxide emissions to control acid rain, using calcium carbonate (limestone) and in the process creating large volumes of waste gypsum, known as synthetic gypsum, which is usable in drywall.

Steady-state combustion efficiency The percentage of fuel content into the appliance (at full, continuous output) after subtracting losses for exhaust products.

Stock dyeing Dyeing fibers before they are spun into yarn. Cut staple fiber is packed into a vat, and then dye liquid is forced through the fibers continuously while the temperature is increased. Includes use of acid, premetallized, and chrome dyes. Stock dyeing is most commonly used for dyeing wool.

Straw bale A building technique for exterior walls where straw (not hay) bales are stacked, reinforced, and interlocked in a manner that forms a thick, highly insulating wall. This technique was used in early structures in the Plains region of the United States and has been revived in the United States and in Europe.

Straw mud An old building technique for exterior walls where earth material is mixed with straw, moistened, and pressed between forms. This strong wall is then covered with a waterproofing plaster system.

Structural insulated panels (SIPS) Premanufactured load-bearing panels of wood framing, sheathing, and insulation that are hoisted into place within a timber framewood.

Styrene Oily liquid with penetrating odor, produced from benzene. Toxic, very refractive, insoluble in water, soluble in alcohol, polymerizes rapidly. May cause irritation of eyes and nose, drowsiness, weakness and unsteady gait, narcosis, defatting dermatitis. Suspect carcinogen. Used as monomer for thermoplastics, elastomers, and thermosetting resins. Also known as phenylethylene, styrene monomer, and vinylbenzene. *See also* Polystyrene *and* Benzene.

Styrene butadiene latex (SB latex)   Used in carpet backing, adhesives, and binding agents in paint. *See also* Styrene.

Styrene butadiene rubber (SBR)   Styrene butadiene rubber is the most common type of synthetic rubber, made by copolymerization of styrene and butadiene monomers. Characteristic pungent odor; may be irritating. Used in tires, adhesives, binder, sealants, footwear. Also known as SBR. *See also* Styrene.

Substrate   Basic surface on which a material, e.g., architectural coating or finish, is applied.

Sulfites and sulfates   Compounds formed with sulfur oxides. Sulfites and sulfates are generally toxic, have very sharp or "rotten egg" odors, and contribute to acid rain. *See also* Formaldehyde scavengers.

Sulfur dioxide   Nonflammable gas soluble in water, alcohol and ether, with strong, suffocating odor. Highly irritant gas, often cited as dangerous in smog. Primary cause of acid rain, produced during coal combustion. Inhalation produces respiratory tract irritation, sometimes with pulmonary edema, bronchoconstriction. Some people may be more susceptible to the effects of sulfur dioxide than others. Used as chemical intermediate and as a solvent.

Sulfuric acid   Very corrosive strong acid, colorless liquid, miscible with water and dissolves most metals. May cause irritation of eyes, nose, and throat, pulmonary edema, bronchitis, emphysema, conjunctivitis, dental erosion, skin and eye burns. Contributor to acid rain. Used in manufacture of rayon and cellulose, paints and pigments, fertilizers, and explosives.

Sunscreen   A fixed exterior louver that reflects and/or absorbs solar radiation. A sunscreen's effectiveness in shading a window depends on its light absorption properties and its geometry with respect to the window opening.

Sun space   A well-glazed space, generally south-facing, that collects heat and supplies some of it to another space (typically adjoining). Temperatures within sunspaces are normally not controlled and float daily and seasonally.

Surface-area-to-volume ratios   One potential and often misleading indicator of building energy performance. The smallest ratios apply to buildings that are spherical or, more practically, squarish in shape. Disregarded is the fact that surface area can also be very useful if it increases the potential for passive solar heating, natural ventilation, and/or daylighting of buildings.

Surfactant   Surface-active agent, a soluble compound that reduces the surface tension of liquids. Surfactants serve as detergents and as wetting, foaming, emulsifying, dispersing, and penetrating agents. Includes sodium salts of linear alkylate sulfonates, quaternary ammonium salts, ethoxylated alcohols. Used in concrete and cement, paint, textiles, polymers, etc.

Synthetic coal   A product that is made through the carbonization of shredded waste carpet by heating it to 550 degrees F in an oxygen-free environment. This product is then burned as an alternative fuel source that releases more energy per pound than coal and burns more cleanly.

Task lighting   Any form of light that is focused on a specific surface or object. It is intended to provide high-quality lighting (often flexible) for a predetermined activity.

Tedlar   Tough, transparent fluoride plastic sheet used as a protective surface for wall coverings. It imparts resistance to yellowing, staining, corrosive chemicals, solvents, light, and oxygen.

Teratogenic   Causing birth defects by acting on the developing fetus.

Terpene   Flammable, unsaturated hydrocarbon liquid found naturally in essential oils and plant oleoresins, e.g., in conifers. Moderately toxic, irritating. Includes hexanal, alpha and beta pinene, 3-carene, and d-limonene. Can interact with ozone indoors to form irritating compounds, including aldehydes. Terpenes are used in organic synthesis.

Terrazzo   Mosaic flooring surface made from marble, granite, or other stone chips embedded in a binder, whose surface is ground and polished. The binder may be cementitious, resinous, or a combination of both. Resinous binders include epoxy and polyester resins. Terrazzo flooring is sometimes divided with strips of brass, zinc, or plastic.

Tertiary treatment   Final stage in wastewater treatment to remove nitrates and phosphates and fine particles. The process is also known as advanced sewage treatment and follows removal of raw sludge and biological treatment. *See also* Primary treatment *and* Secondary treatment.

Tetrachloroethylene   Stable, nonflammable, and nonexplosive liquid. May cause irritation of eyes, nose, and throat, nausea, flushing of face and neck, vertigo, dizziness, liver and kidney damage. Carcinogen. A solvent used as a degreasing agent and in dry cleaning. Also known as perchloroethylene. *See* 33/50 Program. *See* Design for the Environment.

Textile wall covering Fibers laminated to a backing material that provides stability and adhering qualities. The fibers can be natural or synthetic, or a mix, and woven or laid in parallel strands. Examples include grass cloth, strings, woven wool, linen, jute, and sisal.

Thermal bridging A thermal bridge is a highly conductive element in the building envelope that penetrates or bypasses the insulation and acts as a thermal short circuit through the insulation system. The R-value of a wall area with thermal bridging can be reduced significantly. For example, reductions of 40–60 percent occur in metal-framed exterior walls without insulated sheathing.

Thermal chimney A section of a building where solar heat or thermal currents are controlled in a manner that stimulates an updraft and the exhaust of heated air. This draws fresh air into occupied areas of the building through open windows or vents, providing a passive cooling system.

Thermal envelope The shell of a building that essentially creates a barrier from the elements. A highly insulated thermal envelope allows maximum control of interior temperatures with minimal outdoor influence.

Thermal mass Material that absorbs heat or coolness and releases it slowly over a long period of time. Earth, water, and masonry materials can provide excellent thermal mass in passive heating or cooling system design.

Thermal pollution Discharge of heated effluent into natural waters that may upset the ecological balance of the waterway due to change in temperature, threatening the survival of some types of life or favoring the survival of others.

Thermal storage Thermal storage enables a solar gain system to collect more heat than is immediately required and store it for later use.

Thermal storage wall A masonry or water wall used to store heat from the sun. Typically, the generally south-facing side is painted a dark color to improve absorption.

Thermocirculation The convective circulation of fluid that occurs when warm fluid rises and is displaced by denser, cooler liquid in the same system.

Thermochromic Reversible change in color of a substance as its temperature changes. Thermochromic windows change from clear to opaque when a critical temperature is reached. Current prototypes absorb and/or diffuse solar energy but are not heat reflective.

Thermoplastic resin Plastic that will repeatedly soften when heated and harden when cooled, e.g., styrene, polystyrene, polyesters, linear polyurethanes, acrylics, cellulosics, polyethylenes, vinyls, nylons, fluorocarbons. Thermoplastic polyesters have good physical and electrical properties, toughness, low moisture absorption and thermal stability, good chemical and hydrolytical stability. Thermoplastics have better processing and recycling options for scrap materials than thermoset resins. *See also* Thermosetting resin.

Thermosetting resin Plastic that solidifies when first heated under pressure and cannot be remelted or remolded, e.g., epoxies, melamine, phenolics, ureas. Usually obtained by cross-linking, e.g., phenol formaldehyde resins, polyesters, urea and melamine formaldehyde resins, polyurethane foams. *See also* Thermoplastic resin.

Thixotropic Property of certain gels that liquefy when vibrated and then solidify if left standing. Substances providing thixotropic effects in polymeric materials are fumed silica, precipitated silica, organophilic clays, and some organics. Used in resins, epoxies, acrylics, and urethanes.

Time lag The period of time between the absorption of solar radiation by a material and its release into a space. Time lag is an important consideration in sizing a thermal storage wall or Trombe wall.

Titanium dioxide Water-insoluble metal powder based on titanium, a strong, low-density, corrosion-resistant white metallic element. Slight lung fibrosis may be a result of occupational exposure. Considered a potential occupational carcinogen. Widely used as a white pigment in paint, vitreous enamel, linoleum, rubber, and plastics (including vinyl).

Toluene Aromatic liquid derived from coal tar, insoluble in water, soluble in alcohol, with strong solvent odor. May cause central nervous system, liver, and kidney effects, and defat the skin. Used as chemical intermediate, in paints and coatings, in cleaning agents and plastics, and as a component of fuel. Also known as toluol, methylbenzene. *See* 33/50 Program.

Total lighting power allowance The calculated lighting power allowed for the interior and exterior space areas of a building or facility. *See* Lighting power density.

Toxic substance In very general terms, any material considered to be hazardous to human health or the environment, e.g., benzene, carbon tetrachloride, chloroform, dioxane, ethylene dibromide, methylene chloride, tetrachloroethylene, 1,1,1-trichloroethane, trichloroethylene.

Toxic waste Waste material that is potentially harmful to human health or to the environment if discharged.

Toxicity The nature and degree of a given agent's adverse effects on living organisms.

Trichloroethylene Heavy, stable, toxic liquid with chloroform aroma, slightly soluble in water, soluble in organic solvents. Carcinogen. May affect respiratory system, heart, liver, kidneys, central nervous system, skin. Used in solvent extraction, dry cleaning, and as a fumigant and chemical intermediate. *See* 33/50 Program.

Tropical hardwood Wood products harvested from tropical rainforests. Tropical forests are not being harvested in a well-managed manner except in a few isolated cases. Certification efforts indicate that sustainably harvested woods do exist, and only wood certified from a sustainable source should be utilized.

Tubular skylight New concept in channeling daylight into dimly lit areas for residential and commercial buildings. Tubular skylights spread natural light evenly throughout a desired area.

Tung oil Yellow, combustible drying oil from seed of tung tree. Soluble in ether, chloroform, oils. Used in paint, varnishes, linoleum.

TXIB (2,2,4-trimethyl-1,3-pentanediol diisobutyrate) VOC emission that may be associated with vinyl flooring.

Ultraviolet radiation (UV) Electromagnetic, short-wavelength radiation, in range 4–400 nanometers, beginning just beyond the short-wavelength limit of visible light and overlapping with wavelengths of long X rays. UV causes bleaching and deterioration of products, as well as sunburn, which can lead to skin cancer. The stratospheric ozone layer absorbs much ultraviolet radiation before it reaches the earth's surface. Also known as ultraviolet light.

Underlayment A sheet material laid under finish flooring material to minimize irregularities in the subfloor or to add acoustic separation.

Underwriters Laboratories (UL) The U.S. testing agency responsible for verifying product electrical safety, fire ratings, etc.

Unitary backing In carpeting systems, where the secondary backing is bonded directly to the primary backing, either by heat or by chemical reaction, so that the two substances merge into one.

Urea formaldehyde resin Synthetic thermoset resin made by reaction of urea with formaldehyde or its polymer. May be source of formaldehyde emissions indoors. Used as binder for interior composite wood products. *See also* Formaldehyde.

Urethane Combustible, toxic powder, soluble in water and alcohol. Urethane (polyurethane) coatings contain an active isocyanurate complex. Tough, hard, flexible, chemical-resistant films are formed by either moisture curing or copolymerization. Moisture-cured urethanes dry by solvent evaporation and cure by reacting with moisture in the air. Generally for this to occur, relative humidity levels must exceed 20 percent. Copolymerization involves a two-component (or catalyzed) urethane that cures by the addition of a co-reactant (catalyst) to the isocyanurate-containing component. Mixing, induction time, and pot life vary according to the type of isocyanurate and catalyst used. Urethanes are light stable, gloss retentive, and nonyellowing. Used as a solvent and chemical intermediate. *See also* Isocyanurate.

Vapor retarder A construction component that is impervious to the flow of moisture and air. Used to prevent condensation in walls and other locations of insulation.

Varnish All varnishes are solutions of resinous materials in a solvent. Clear or pigmented surface coating that changes to a hard solid when dried from a liquid.

Ventilation air The portion of supply air that is outdoor air plus any recirculated air that has been treated for the purpose of maintaining acceptable indoor air quality.

Vermiculite Micalike magnesium, iron, and silica mineral that can be expanded by heating into a noncombustible insulating pellet, used in loose-fill insulation.

Vinyl chloride Flammable, explosive gas with ethereal aroma, soluble in alcohol, slightly soluble in water. Monomer for polyvinyl chloride. Highly toxic, damages the liver, affects the central nervous system, blood, respiratory system. Carcinogen. Liquid vinyl chloride can cause frostbite. Used widely in organic synthesis and in adhesives.

Vinyl composition tile (VCT) Flooring system made from polyvinyl chloride resins, usually by injection molding or dispersion coating. VCT may contain about 15 percent PVC and 85 percent calcium carbonate, an inert filler. Pigments and stabilizers may be added. Plasticizers are used in smaller quantities than in sheet vinyl flooring, and so emissions and odors are typically lower. *See also* Vinyl flooring *and* Polyvinyl chloride.

Vinyl flooring Flooring system manufactured from polyvinyl chloride (PVC) resin over a backing material, e.g., paper or foamed plastic. Much higher content of PVC than in VCT. Plasticizers are added for flexibility, and fungicides may also be added. Emissions testing on vinyl flooring has identified the solvents used in the plasticizer, and plasticizer decomposition products. The adhesives used to install the flooring, which may also be flexible products, can continue to emit for a prolonged period. Odorous compounds such as phenol have been identified in emissions from this product. *See also* Polyvinyl chloride.

Vinyl wall covering   Sheets of PVC vinyl, colored and usually embossed, and laminated to a backing that imparts stability and adhering qualities. May include plasticizers and hexane. The backing is usually paper or a loosely woven fabric of polyester or cotton. Vinyl wall coverings and their adhesives may emit VOCs indoors. *See also* Polyvinyl chloride.

Vitrify   Heat treat to produce a glazed surface, as with ceramics. Also known as gasification.

Volatile organic compound (VOC)   Chemicals that contain carbon molecules and have high enough vapor pressure to vaporize from material surfaces into indoor air at normal room temperatures (referred to as off-gassing). VOCs occurring indoors include alkanes (e.g., hexane, decane, tetradecane), alkenes (e.g., terpenes such as alpha-pinene, limonene), aromatic hydrocarbons (toluene, ethyl benzene, styrene, xylenes), alcohols (e.g., ethanol, 2-propanol, butanol, hexanol, 2-phenylethanol), glycols and glycol ethers (dipropopylene glycol, 2-ethoxyethanol, 2-methoxyethanol), ethers (e.g., dioxane), aldehydes (e.g., formaldehyde, acetaldehyde, glutaraldehyde), ketones (e.g., acetone, butanone), acids (e.g., acetic acid), esters (acetates, phthalates, acrylates). Chemists typically define VOCs by their boiling point; e.g., the World Health Organization definition includes organic compounds with boiling points ranging from 50 to 260 degrees C (others have specified a boiling point temperature range from 0 to 400 degrees C). Emissions of a group of VOCs are often expressed as total volatile organic compounds (TVOC), which is the sum of all of the VOCs detected. The EPA definition of VOCs for architectural coatings includes hydrocarbons that are photochemically reactive. Of the VOCs, formaldehyde (a carcinogen) and acrolein (a suspected carcinogen) are known irritants at levels that may be encountered indoors. Most VOCs are relatively inert at typical indoor concentrations, but they can react with oxidants such as ozone and possibly nitrogen oxide and nitrogen dioxide to form reactive species and possibly strong irritants, including various acids and aldehydes. VOCs may cause eye and upper respiratory irritation, nasal congestion, headache, and dizziness. Examples of building materials that contain VOCs include, but are not limited to, solvents, paints, adhesives, carpeting, and particle board.

Volatile solvent   Lay term; solvent that evaporates (off-gasses) at room temperature, and may contribute to poor indoor air quality.

Vulcanize   Chemical reaction to transform a soft or liquid rubber into a tough, heat-resistant rubber. Process uses sulfur or other vulcanizing agent to crosslink rubber or plastic, increasing its strength and resiliency. Other curing agents are organic polysulfides and organic peroxides.

Waste heat   Heat escaping from combustion that can be captured and used for other processes.

Waste-to-fuel process   Burning of industrial waste to provide steam, heat, or electricity.

Wastewater treatment   Water that is discharged from homes and businesses from sinks, toilets, washers, showers, etc., treated through a series of separation and aeration processes.

Water-based paint   Paint in which the vehicle or binder is dissolved in water or in which the vehicle or binder is dispersed as an emulsion. An example is latex paint.

Water budget   **1**. An evaluation of the hydrologic balance in an area. **2**. The calculated amount of water a household should use based on the type and number of fixtures, landscape requirements, and number of occupants.

Water-conserving irrigation   Drip irrigation, soaker hoses, bubblers, and low-trajectory spray heads for water distribution; zoning irrigation for different water-demand plant types; electronic timers with five-day programming and rain override devices; irrigation schedules for early-morning watering every five to seven days; soil moisture sensors.

Water economizer   A system by which the supply air of a cooling system is cooled directly or indirectly or both by evaporation of water or by other appropriate fluid (in order to reduce or eliminate the need for mechanical refrigeration).

Water repellent   Chemical used to treat textiles, leather, paper, or wood to make them resistant to wetting, e.g., resins, aluminum or zirconium acetates, latexes, silicone resin to prevent penetration of rainwater on porous or absorbent masonry surfaces. For textiles, a material that causes water droplets to roll off as they strike the fabric.

Waterproofing   Make impervious to water, e.g., with a resin sealer or asphalt coating.

Weaving Looms are used to weave colored pile yarns and backing yarns into a carpet, to which is added a back coating, usually of latex, to provide stability. A secondary backing is not necessary on a woven carpet. Less adhesive is needed to install a woven carpet compared to one that is tufted.

Wetland Environment characterized by shallow or fluctuating water levels and abundant aquatic and marsh plants. Includes marshes, swamps, bayous, bogs, fens, sloughs, and ponds.

Wind test A test that measures the strength of a material's adherence to the substrate that it is attached to. Samples that undergo this test are ranked by their point of failure: an I-60 rating refers to a sample that loses its adherence under a 60 PSF applied pressure; an I-90 rating loses its adherence under a 90 PSF pressure, etc. This test is identical in requirements for both mechanically and fully adhered roofing systems.

Wind turbine A machine that generates electricity from the wind by turning a generator-connected wind propeller.

Window-to-wall ratio The ratio of glazing area to the gross exterior wall area.

Wing walls Small outside walls on a building set perpendicular to an exterior wall next to a window. A negative pressure zone is created by the wing walls stimulating air movement (breeze) through the windows.

Wool A natural fiber obtained from sheep, characterized by absorbency, resiliency, and insulation. Luxurious, very resilient, and naturally resistant to fire. Wool tends to generate static electricity at low humidities, which can be remedied by adding carbon fiber to the yarn. Wool is also prone to deterioration by moths and insects and so may contain chemical treatments.

Xeriscape Landscaping for water and energy efficiency and lower maintenance. The seven xeriscape principles are good planning and design; practical lawn areas; efficient irrigation; soil improvement; use of mulches; low-water-demand plants; good maintenance.

Xylenes Aromatic hydrocarbon liquid produced from petroleum. May have anesthetic effects, irritate the eyes, nose, and throat, and defat skin. Used for high-octane and aviation gasolines, solvents, chemical intermediates, and in manufacture of polyester resins, in dyes, paints, adhesives. *See* 33/50 Program.

Zinc oxide White-gray metal powder, insoluble in water, soluble in alkalies and acids, resistant to ultraviolet radiation and mold growth. Low toxicity, but dust and fumes are hazardous. Used as white pigment in paints, ointments, plastics, and rubber. Oxide of zinc used as constituent of creams for its astringent and soothing qualities.

Zinc-rich primer Paint containing high proportion of metallic zinc dust (at least 80 percent by volume) in the dry film, applied to iron and steel as an anticorrosive. Because zinc is a more chemically active metal than steel, when exposed to aggressive chemicals or corrosive agents zinc will "corrode" to protect the steel substrate (same reason that hot-dipped galvanizing minimizes steel corrosion). For this cathodic protection to take place, there must be direct contact between the zinc pigment particles and the steel substrate, requiring that the steel be sandblasted (not an environmentally desirable procedure).

Top 10 Sustainable Design Internet Resources

A select list of Web sites that provide a wealth of information as well as a listing of related resources

1 **Center of Excellence for Sustainable Development**

http://www.sustainable.doe.gov

The Web site lists conferences and meetings, funding opportunities, and information about land use and planning, transportation, green buildings, municipal energy, sustainable business, measuring progress, financing, and resource efficiency for air, water, and materials.

The Web page also provides links to top sustainable development Web pages, including:

Web Site Links	Web Page Address
Energy Efficiency and Renewable Energy Network	http://www.eren.doe.gov
Center for Renewable Energy and Sustainable Technology	http://solstice.crest.org/index.shtml
Public Technology, Inc.	http://www.pti.org

2 **Energy Efficiency and Renewable Energy Network (EREN)—Department of Energy**

http://www.eren.doe.gov

The page offers information on a comprehensive range of energy-related technologies, featured sites, and specialized resources. The site provides publications, responses, and referrals to other organizations. For instance:

- *Software Tools:* Link to the Office of Building Technology, State and Community Programs includes valuable tools, including energy-related software tools, for buildings with an emphasis on using renewable energy and achieving energy efficient and sustainable buildings.

- *Economic Analysis Tools:* Link to the Office of Federal Energy Management Program includes analytical software tools for life cycle costing and other methods of economic analysis. The tools help project designers choose conservation measures that are the most cost-effective and environmentally friendly.

Web Site Links	Web Page Address
Building Energy Software Tool Directory	http://www.eren.doe.gov/buildings/tools_directory/
Economic Analysis Tools	http://www.eren.doe.gov/femp/greenfed/2.2/ 2_2_economic_analysis.htm

③ United States Green Building Council (USGBC)

http://www.usgbc.org

Promotes the understanding, development, and implementation of green building policies, technologies, and design practices. The site provides information about programs, resources, and the council's activities.

- *LEED Green Building Rating System:* Leadership in Energy and Environmental Design (LEED) site provides guidance to the owner, planners, architects, landscape architects, and engineers. Site helps evaluate environmental performance from a whole building perspective over a building's life cycle, providing a definitive standard for what constitutes a green building.

- *Green Building Forum:* Site takes user to articles about the most currently discussed green building topics and issues. See also Environmental Building News for additional listings and links.

Web Site Links	Web Page Address
LEED Green Building Rating System	http://www.usgbc.org/resource/

④ Center for Renewable Energy and Sustainable Technology (CREST)

http://solstice.crest.org/index.shtml

A good site for sustainable energy and development information. The page features documents, databases, publications, and articles to circulate new information regarding sustainable living, energy efficiency, and renewable energy. CREST's software and Internet services provide access to a broad range of topics: innovative public policy reports, interactive media, renewable energy success stories, and informative on-line discussion groups.

- *Solstice Organizations:* Site lists unique organizations and nonprofit, research, and outreach institutes, such as the Rocky Mountain Institute, that focus on sustainable design.

- *Rocky Mountain Institute:* A nonprofit research and educational foundation with a goal to foster the efficient and sustainable use of resources. Site publications can be reviewed on the publication list. The Web site also features the newsletter, published three times a year, with reports for a nonspecialist audience on the institute's recent work.

Web Site Links	Web Page Address
Solstice Organizations	http://solstice.crest.org/orgs.shtml
Rocky Mountain Institute	http://www.rmi.org

 ## Environmental Protection Agency (EPA)

http://www.epa.gov

Site provides access to listings of programs and initiatives, research, newsletters, publications, and software. Various links lead to specific topics such as indoor air quality (IAQ), Office of Water, Office of Wetlands, and State, Local and Tribal Projects, that promote the understanding, development, and implementation of green building policies, technologies, and design practices.

- *IAQ:* Web page features information regarding objectives for indoor air quality characteristic to schools, offices, and homes, and also provides a good reference to common sources of indoor pollutants. Links are provided to the Consumer Product Safety Commission, Department of Housing and Urban Development, American Society of Heating, Refrigerating, and Air-Conditioning (ASHRAE), Occupational Safety and Health Administration, Tennessee Valley Authority, and World Health Organization.

- *Water Conservation Glossary:* Summary of terms frequently used in sustainable planning and site design issues related to water conservation. Site also provides links to various topics such as drinking water protection and ecosystem protection and to publications and organizations, and includes a comprehensive reference list.

- *Wetlands and Watersheds:* Site offers specific information on wetland and watershed protection, restoration, nonpoint source pollution prevention, databases, and publications, including the Index of Watershed Indicators. It is a unique site, as a user can locate a watershed by zip code and will be able to retrieve valuable information such as land use, habitats, tributaries, underlying aquifer, and rock type.

- *Emissions Tools:* E-Grid site provides tools that allow the user to convert energy generation into emissions, and differentiates between power generation from different sources, such as coal, natural gas, nuclear, hydro, solar, and wind.

- *Environmental Communities:* Site provides links to the Web pages of Community-based Environmental Protection, Enviroene, Green Communities, Sustainable Development Challenge Grants, and others. They serve as tools for planning and building livable communities.

Web Site Links	Web Page Address
Indoor Air Quality (IAQ)	http://www.epa.gov/iaq/
Office of Water	http://www.epa.gov/ow/
Water Conservation Glossary	http://www.epa.gov/watrhome/you/glossref.html
Wetlands, Oceans, Watersheds	http://www.epa.gov/owowwtr1/
Emission Tools	http://www.epa.gov/acidrain/egrid/egrid.htm
Environmental Communities	http://www.epa.gov/epahome/partners.htm
Global Warming	http://www.epa.gov/globalwarming

⑥ Lawrence Berkeley National Laboratory

http://eande.lbl.gov/btp/btp.html

Site features the Building Technologies Department of the Lawrence Berkeley National Laboratory, which conducts research on all aspects of energy efficiency in buildings. The site provides information on past and current research activities and software tools for energy efficient building design. Especially valuable links are:

- *Windows and Daylighting:* Site provides information about glazing materials, DOE's Electrochromic Initiative, fenestration products for commercial buildings, and technical support to help architects, engineers, and other specifiers choose energy-efficient and cost-effective windows.

- *Related Web Sites:* Comprehensive collection of Web pages sorted by building-related resources, windows and glazing resources, energy-related resources, international resources, and telephone directories of other national laboratories.

Web Site Links	Web Page Address
Windows and Daylighting	http://windows.lbl.gov/
Related Web sites	http://eande.lbl.gov/btp/links.html

⑦ Environmental Building News

http://ebn@www.buildinggreen.com

These articles, reviews, and news stories are a prime source on energy-efficient, resource-efficient, and healthy building practices. Material selection, siting, indoor air quality, daylighting, and other subjects relating to green building practices are addressed. The complete Environmental Building News with searchable database requires a paid subscription.

- *Product Reviews:* Site provides information regarding green building products and manufacturers. It also lists workshops on green building products.

- *Big Green:* The site features an e-mail discussion group for green design and construction professionals. The intent of this forum is to discuss and promote green building principles and practices on projects larger than single-family houses.

Web Site Links	Web Page Address
Product Review	http://www.buildinggreen.com/products/productslist.html
Big Green	http://www.buildinggreen.com/elists/bg_signup.html

⑧ Public Technology, Inc. (PTI)

http://pti.nw.dc.us

This site features products and services for local and state governments on its Web page. The focus is on improving the quality and availability of new technologies and reducing its costs. PTI publications cover a wide range of technology topics, from fuel-cell technology, to intelligent transportation systems to geographic information systems.

- *Publication Catalog:* Especially resourceful. Site lists new technologies and related Web sites by category, i.e., sustainable strategies; electric utility; cooling, heating, and motor efficiency; shedding light on lighting; water; waste—gas and solids; and best practices.

- *Energy Information Administration:* Features information on all forms of energy, including petroleum, natural gas, coal, nuclear, renewables, and alternative fuels. Also provides environmental, international, and forecast information about electricity.

Web Site Links	Web Page Address
Publication Catalog	http://pti.nw.dc.us/publications/
Energy Information Administration	http://www.eia.doe.gov/

 ## Green Building Resources Center

http://www.geonetwork.org

The GEO site features green design news and events as well as a searchable link library and Green Bookstore, which contain hundreds of resources on sustainable topics.

- *Green Design Network:* The network is a tool for finding products, case studies, experts, publications, regional resource directories, and Web links.
- *Green Bookstore:* Searchable list of books related to sustainable design categories, including sustainable development, biodiversity, site design and landscape, and sustainable economics.
- *Web Link Library:* Green Building Resources Center also publishes a booklet, *Web Links and Descriptions,* which lists related Web sites with short descriptions, organized alphabetically and also by topic areas. The booklet is available through the Web site.

Web Site Links	Web Page Address
Green Design Network	http://www.greendesign.net/
Green Bookstore	http://www.geonetwork.org/bookstore/index.html
Web Link Library	http://www.geonetwork.org/links/index.html

 ## American Planning Association Smart Growth

http://www.planning.org/plnginfo/growsmar/gsindex.html

Growing Smart is a service mark of the American Planning Association. Site features Growing Smart Newsletter with summaries from all fifty states, research publications, planning advisory services and legislative and policy issues.

- *Smart Growth:* Site provides valuable overarching information regarding creating communities, growing a sustainable economy, protecting natural resources, governing sustainably, and living sustainably. Site also features tools, technologies, contacts, and case studies for each topic.
- *Smart Growth and Neighborhood Conservation:* Site features Smart Growth Initiative in the state of Maryland and provides useful links to other sites through Smart Growth Resources.

Related Web Sites	Web Page Address
Smart Growth	http://www.sustainable.org
Smart Growth and Neighborhood Conservation	http://www.op.state.md.us/smartgrowth/index.html

Sustainable Design Resources in Print

A select list of resources we have found to be especially helpful . . .

General

Ray Anderson. *Mid-Course Correction: Toward a Sustainable Enterprise: The Interface Model.* White River Junction, VT: Chelsea Green Publishing Company, 1999.

> The personal story of Ray Anderson's realization that businesses need to embrace principles of sustainability, and of his efforts, often frustrating, to apply these principles within a billion-dollar corporation that is still measured by the standard scorecards of the business world. While the path has proved to have many curves, Interface is demonstrating that the principles of sustainability and financial success can coexist within a business and can lead to a new prosperity that includes human dividends as well.

Paul Ekins. *The Gaia Atlas of Green Economics.* New York: Anchor Books, 1992.

> The book shows a way out of the destructive obsession with economic growth. It explores a new concept of wealth and wealth creation; it describes a new economics synthesis between the market, state, families, and communities; it sets out what governments and people can do to build a sustainable society—to create prosperity and a fairer world in a healthy environment.

Paul Hawken, Amory B. Lovins, and L. Hunter Lovins. *Natural Capitalism: Creating the Next Industrial Revolution.* Boston: Little, Brown and Company, 1999.

> Three top strategists show how leading-edge companies are practicing "a new type of industrialism" that is more efficient and profitable while saving the environment and creating jobs. The authors write that in the next century, cars will get 200 miles per gallon without

compromising safety and power, manufacturers will relentlessly recycle their products, and the world's standard of living will jump without further damaging natural resources.

Dianna Lopez Barnett with William D. Browning. *A Primer on Sustainable Building*. Snowmass, CO: Rocky Mountain Institute, Green Development Services, 1995.

A primer on the logistics of sustainable development and its economic benefits to developers, builders, consumers, and government. The book is an introductory guide to sustainable building principles.

Public Technology and U.S. Green Building Council. *Sustainable Building Technical Manual: Green Building Design, Construction, and Operations*. Washington, DC: Public Technology, Inc., 1996.

A manual offering guidelines on building design, siting, material selection, energy efficiency, and indoor air quality, including substantial annotated resource lists. Also addresses construction administration and actions for local governments. Provides sample specifications for construction waste reuse and recycling, energy-efficiency incentive program participation, on-site environmental impact minimization, and ventilation for indoor air quality.

Mathis Wackernagel and William Rees. *Our Ecological Footprint: Reducing Human Impact on the Earth*. Philadelphia: New Society Publications, 1995.

The book provides useful charts and thought-provoking illustrations, and introduces a revolutionary new way to determine humanity's impact on the Earth. It presents a tool for measuring and visualizing the resources required to sustain households, communities, regions, and nations.

Site

Richard A. Clayton and Thomas R. Schueler. *Design of Stormwater Filtering Systems*. Silver Spring, MD: The Center for Watershed Protection, 1996.

A design manual for stormwater filtering systems to remove pollutants from urban runoff. The manual presents detailed engineering guidance on eleven different filtering systems, including sand filters, bioretention, and vegetated filter strips.

Bruce K. Ferguson. *Introduction to Stormwater: Concept, Purpose, Design*. New York: John Wiley & Sons, 1998.

Professional reference combines basic principles of hydrology with the latest applications for wetlands construction, groundwater recharge, water harvesting, and so on.

Wesley A. Groesbeck and Jan Streifel. *Sustainable Landscapes and Gardens: The Resource Guide*. Salt Lake City, UT: Environmental Resources, Inc., 1996.

A detailed listing of information, materials, and products for sustainable landscape design.

Jacklyn Johnston and John Newton. *Building Green*. London: London Ecology Unit, 1992.

A pictorial guide to using plants on roofs, walls, and pavements.

J. T. Lyle. *Regenerative Design for Sustainable Development*. New York: John Wiley & Sons, 1994.

A design guide and information resource on sustainable building and planning in the context of living systems.

Maryland Department of the Environment. *Maryland Stormwater Design Manual*. Baltimore: Maryland DOE, 1999.

A design manual addressing stormwater management strategies to reduce stream channel erosion, pollution, siltation, and sedimentation, and local flooding to protect water and land resources.

J. William Thompson and Kim Sorvig. *Sustainable Landscape Construction: A Guide to Green Building Outdoors*. Washington, DC: Island Press, 2000.

A practical, professional guide to alternatives in landscape construction, design, and maintenance, organized around ten key principles, as well as balanced discussion of attitudes and controversies that help or hinder stewardship of the land. Over a hundred projects from around the world illustrate sustainable methods.

U.S. Environmental Protection Agency, Policy, Planning and Evaluation. *Cooling Our Communities: A Guidebook on Tree Planting and Light-Colored Surfacing*. Washington, DC: EPA, 1992.

A practical guide published by the US EPA Climate Outreach and Innovation Division in collaboration with the Department of Energy's Lawrence Berkeley Laboratory. The publication presents the environmental potential and economic benefits of strategic landscape planning to reduce urban heat islands and also considers the resulting potential to significantly reduce energy use for cooling.

U.S. Department of the Interior, National Park Service. *Guiding Principles of Sustainable Design*. Denver, CO: DOI, 1993.

An excellent statement of the vision for sustainable development, particularly for site design of parks and recreational facilities. Environmental challenges are balanced with opportunities and guidelines for architects and planners.

Energy

N. Greene, A. Gupta, and J. Bryan. *Choosing Clean Power: Bringing the Promise of Fuel Cells to New York*. New York: Natural Resources Defense Council, Inc., 1997.

Fuel cells are poised to substantially improve the way that we generate electricity. This report describes the role that fuel cells can play in providing clean energy sources and includes policy recommendations for this emerging clean power technology. See http://www.nrdc.org.

Othmar Humm and Peter Toggweiler. *Photovoltaics in Architecture: The Integration of Photovoltaic Cells in Building Envelop.* Basel: Birkhäuser Verlag, 1993.

A multilanguage book (in German, French, Italian, and English) that presents the technical and design requirements for photovoltaic facades and roofs to make use of solar energy. The book demonstrates how these elements can be integrated into the architecture of buildings while embracing ecological, technical, and aesthetic aspects.

Illumination Engineering Society of North America. *Illumination Engineering Society of North America (IESNA) Lighting Handbook.* 8th ed. New York: IESNA, 1993.

Professional handbook of lighting.

Passive Solar Industry Council, National Renewable Energy Laboratory, Lawrence Berkeley National Laboratory, Berkeley Solar Group. *Designing Low Energy Buildings.* Washington, DC: Passive Solar Industry Council, 1997.

Workbook format with Energy 10 software for integrating day-lighting, energy-efficient equipment, and passive solar design into commercial, institutional, and residential buildings.

Adrian Tuluca. *Energy Efficient Design and Construction Commercial Buildings.* New York: McGraw-Hill, 1997.

Clear, nontechnical discussions describe available energy-saving techniques for commercial, institutional, education, health care, and high-rise residential buildings from the architect/designer's perspective with expected dollar savings, practical considerations, and locations where the techniques have been applied.

Donald Watson, ed. *The Energy Design Handbook.* Washington, DC: AIA Press, 1993.

An extensive text on energy design providing a clear introduction to design issues, system options, and energy and cost analysis.

Material Resources

American Institute of Architects. *Environmental Resource Guide.* New York: John Wiley & Sons, 1997.

An extensive volume of in-depth reports on building materials and components. Reports present information both by material and by application, including life-cycle flow charts and tables listing environmental stressors by phase (material acquisition and preparation; manufacturing and fabrication; construction, use, and maintenance; recycling, reuse, or disposal). Also includes case studies of several green buildings.

Good Wood Alliance. *Good Wood Directory.* Burlington, VT: Good Wood Alliance, 1996.

A printed directory listing sources of sustainably harvested wood and reclaimed wood in the following categories: certified sources (i.e., forestry operations); certified manufacturers; certified distributors; noncertified distributors; noncertified recycled sources, manufacturers, and distributors. Lists species and wood products, where applicable.

E Build. GreenSpec. *The Environmental Building New Product Directory and Guideline Specifications.* Brattleboro, VT: E Build, Inc., 1999.

A comprehensive guide offering detailed information about environmentally preferable materials and products. The guide provides a 300-page product directory and manufacturers' product literature, organized in sixteen different divisions for easy access.

Kalin and Associates, Inc. *Greenspec.* Newton Centre, MA: Kalin and Associates, Inc., 1996.

A manual offering product listings and brief manufacturer descriptions of environmental features, as well as product-specific environmental specification language. Organized by specification section, including a brief section on construction waste management and recycling. Includes specification language on disk.

Kim Leclair and David Rousseau. *Environmental by Design: A Sourcebook of Environmentally Aware Material Choices.* Vancouver, BC: Hartley & Marks, 1992.

Defines the health and environmental issues surrounding the use of interior materials and finishes and provides recommendations. Identifies building materials in fourteen categories, including Canadian, U.S., and European products.

Tracey Mumma, ed. *Guide to Resource-Efficient Building Elements.* 6th ed. Missoula, MT: Center for Resourceful Building Technology, 1997.

A sustainable design guidebook, national in scope, offering general discussions of building materials by category as well as selected product listings. Updated yearly.

Sally Small, ed. *Sustainable Design and Construction Database.* Denver, CO: National Park Service, 1995.

A database listing environmentally responsible building materials by category and providing general research sections on many building material categories. Version 2.0 is available on-line at www.nps.gov/dsc/dsgncnstr/susdb.

Tree Talk, Inc. *Woods of the World.* Burlington, VT: Tree Talk, Inc., 1996.

An extensive searchable database, international in scope, displaying alternatives to currently endangered or unsustainably harvested tree species. Species are searchable by appearance, workability, strength, and other characteristics, as well as by location and conservation status. Graphic files provide images of wood grain and color, maps illustrate species concentrations, and videos illustrate forestry and woodworking techniques. Also included is a searchable directory of wood products listed in the *Harris Directory* (by B. J. Harris). Most versions available as a CD-ROM.

Triangle J Council of Governments, Design Harmony Architects, and Abacot Architecture. *WasteSpec: Model Specifications for Construction Waste Reduction, Reuse and Recycling.* Research Triangle Park, NC: Triangle J Council of Governments, 1995.

A guidance manual offering specification language for environmentally responsible construction waste management.

Indoor Environment

Sheet Metal and Air Conditioning Contractors' National Association (SMACNA). *Indoor Air Quality Guidelines for Occupied Buildings under Construction.* Chantilly, VA: SMACNA, 1995.

Guidelines for protecting indoor air quality in retrofit, renovation, or phased construction.

U.S. Environmental Protection Agency, Office of Air and Radiation. *Building Air Quality: A Guide for Building Owners and Facility Managers.* Washington, DC: EPA, 1991.

An in-depth resource from the U.S. EPA and NIOSH providing information on indoor air quality problems and how to correct them. It offers advice on developing an IAQ building profile, creating an IAQ management plan, identifying causes and solutions for IAQ problems, and deciding whether outside technical assistance is necessary.

B. C. Wolverton. *How to Grow Fresh Air: 50 Houseplants That Purify Your Home or Office.* New York: Penguin Books, 1996.

Based on twenty-five years of research at the National Aeronautics and Space Administration (NASA), this book discusses how houseplants can purify air by removing chemical vapors and further improve indoor air by balancing the humidity level. Individual plant species are rated based on their effectiveness.

Water

Donald A. Hammer, ed. *Constructed Wetlands for Wastewater Treatment: Municipal, Industrial and Agricultural.* Chelsea, MI: Lewis Publishers, Inc., 1989.

This book provides general information about constructed wetlands and their potential to provide relatively simple and economical solutions for wastewater treatment. Included are principles about wetland ecology, hydrology, soil chemistry, vegetation, and wildlife as well as management guidelines, policies and regulations, siting and construction requirements.

Robert H. Kadlec and Robert L. Knight. *Treatment Wetlands*. Boca Raton: Lewis Publishers, Inc., 1996.

A comprehensive book that describes all major wetland configurations, wastewater sources, and combinations of climatic conditions, as well as design approaches that can be tailored to specific wetland treatment projects. It examines the planning, design, construction, and operation of wetlands used for water quality treatment as a promising and efficient technology. The book also includes detailed information on wetland ecology, wetland water quality, selection of appropriate technology, design for consistent performance, construction guidance, and operational control through effective monitoring.

Gerald A. Moshiri. *Constructed Wetlands for Water Quality Improvement*. Boca Raton, FL: Lewis Publishers, Inc., 1993.

The book assembles contributions from prominent scientists and serves as an encyclopedia of information on the use of constructed wetlands for improving water quality.

National Association of Plumbing-Heating-Cooling Contractors. *Assessment of On-Site Graywater and Combined Wastewater Treatment and Recycling Systems*. Falls Church, VA: NAPHCC, 1992.

A free-of-charge publication produced for the U.S. Environmental Protection Agency that provides information to develop a better understanding of on-site wastewater treatment and recycling technology, including associated costs, regulatory and institutional constraints, and health and safety issues. To order call (800) 490-9198. Order no. EPA832-R-92-900.

U.S. Environmental Protection Agency, Office of Water. *Subsurface Flow Constructed Wetlands for Wastewater Treatment: A Technology Assessment*. Washington, DC: EPA, 1993.

A free-of-charge U.S. EPA publication that provides information for better understanding this technology. To order call (800) 490-9198. Order no. EPA832-R-93-008.

Economics

Alphonse J. Dell'Isola and Kirk J. Stephen. *Life Cycle Costing for Design Professionals*. New York: McGraw-Hill, 1981.

Book discusses theory, history, and application of life cycle costing. Includes step-by-step worksheets for analyzing material, maintenance, labor, and other costs incurred in the construction and operation of buildings. It includes how to evaluate methods and materials in the design stage for their long-range cost implications.

Case Studies

David Lloyd Jones. *Architecture and the Environment: Bioclimatic Building Design*. Woodstock, NY: Overlook Press, 1998.

> An international survey of contemporary architecture built green. Fifty buildings are examined, explaining how they all respond to the need to achieve harmony with their settings, to conserve energy, and to provide for the health and well-being of their occupants.

Rocky Mountain Institute. *Green Development: Integrating Ecology and Real Estate*. New York: John Wiley & Sons, Inc., 1997.

> A guidebook on environmentally sustainable development based upon eighty case studies drawn from RMI's extensive worldwide research and consulting work.

James Steele. *Sustainable Architecture: Principles, Paradigms, and Case Studies*. New York: McGraw-Hill, 1997.

> The book sets forth a strategy for redefining the post-industrial role of architecture and urbanism, illustrated by case histories from both industrialized and nonindustrialized nations.

U.S. Environmental Protection Agency, Office of Wastewater Management, Municipal Technology Branch. *Constructed Wetlands for Wastewater Treatment and Wildlife Habitat: 17 Case Studies*. Washington, DC: EPA, 1993.

> A free-of-charge U.S. EPA publication that summarizes extensive research efforts providing insight into the design, operation and performance of natural and constructed wetlands treatment systems. To order call (800) 490-9198. Order no. EPA832-R-93-005.

Brenda Vale and Robert Vale. *Green Architecture: Design for an Energy-Conscious Future*. Boston: Little, Brown and Company, 1991.

> Book provides an illustrated overview of resource-conscious building and the relationship between the built environment and common challenges, such as power supply, waste and recycling, food production, and transportation, by looking at case studies from around the world.

Periodicals

Advanced Buildings Newsletter. Royal Architectural Institute of Canada, Ottawa, Ontario.

> The journal is published intermittently together with CANMET, Natural Resources Canada, and PERD (Program on Energy R&D). It reviews the most recent advances in sustainable building materials and technologies in Canada.

Choose Green Reports. Green Seal.

> Monthly reports present the research findings of Green Seal, an independent, nonprofit standard-setting organization that creates standards for the "eco-labeling" of products. *Choose Green Reports* are available on-line at the U.S. Department of the Interior Web site: http://www.doi.gov/oepc/gseal.html.

Environmental Building News. Brattleboro, VT: E Build, Inc.

> A monthly journal reviewing the most recent advances in sustainable building materials and technologies in the United States and abroad. Topics range from product reviews and news briefs to in-depth reporting on selected topics. Many articles are available on-line at the Environmental Building News Web site: http://www.ebn@buildinggreen.com.

Environmental Design and Construction: The Magazine for Successful Building—Economically and Environmentally. Troy, MI: Business New Publishing Company.

> A bimonthly journal reviewing the most recent advances in sustainable building materials and technologies worldwide. It also publishes a buyers' guide for environmentally preferable materials on an annual basis.

Indoor Air Bulletin. Hal Levin, Indoor Air Information Service, Inc., Santa Cruz, CA.

> A comprehensive monthly journal reviewing technical issues related to design for indoor air quality.

Interiors and Sources. North Palm Beach, FL, L.C. Clark Publishing Company.

> Published nine times a year, this journal reviews the most recent advances in commercial and residential interior design from lighting through appliances. See http://www.isdesignet.com.

The Green Business Letter: The Hands-On Journal for Environmentally Conscious Companies. Tilden Press, Inc. Washington, DC.

> A monthly journal that focuses on environmental business topics. Visit on-line at http://www.greenbiz.com.

Index

Smithsonian Institution, National Air and Space Museum, Dulles Center, 280
Trees
    endangered species, 224
    preservation, 62, 199
    species diversity, 56
    survey of, 49
    transplanting existing, 44
    in wildlife habitat, 58
    wind shield, 55
Trellis, green, 83, 196, 201, 202–203, 268
Trichloroethylene, 131
TRNSYS (TRaNsient System Simulation Program), 79
T*Sol, 81
Turner Feature Animation Office and Production Facility, 212–213

U

Ultraviolet light (UV) disinfection, 113
University of Technology, Sydney, 317
University of Wisconsin, Green Bay, Academic Building, 7, 16, 25, 290–300
University of Wisconsin, Milwaukee, 261
Urban heat island effect, 55
Urban infill site, 46
Urinals. See Toilets and urinals
U.S. Army Corps of Engineers, 53
U.S. Green Building Council (USGBC), xiii, 39, 222, 384
Utility incentive programs, 16
Utility rebates, 76

V

Value Engineering (VE) reviews, 264
Vapor barrier, 127
Vapor retarder, 90, 127, 282
Variable air volume (VAV) system, 181, 203, 225, 226, 270, 282
Variable-frequency drives (VFDs), 181
Varnish, 166
Vegetated rooftops, 4, 8, 10, 55, 56, 128, 189
Vegetated swales, 8, 53, 54
Vehicle emissions, 125
Veneer woods, 155
Venetian blinds, 84
Ventilation, 5, 10, 82, 90, 182, 259, 286
    computer-controlled, 333–334
    during construction, 273–274
    displacement, 283, 309–310, 333
    evaluation, 120
    natural, 126
    occupancy-controlled, 284, 294
    parking garage, 181
    passive system, 318–319
    preoccupancy flush-out, 132, 133
    rates, 74, 124, 125, 204, 312
    standards, 123, 124
    temporary, 131

Videoconferencing, 204, 213, 230, 232
Villa Erques Eco-Resort, 321–330
Vines
    native, 201
    on trellis structure, 196, 201, 202–203, 268
Vinyl chloride, 131
Vinyl tile, 163
Virginia Alliance for Solar Energy, 226, 279
Visual comfort protection (VCP), 85
VisualDOE, 79
VOCs. See Volatile organic compounds
Volatile organic compounds (VOCs), 28, 128, 129, 130, 131
    low-VOC materials, 141, 147, 156, 164, 165, 166, 182, 228, 235, 261, 299, 307, 330

W

Walls
    acoustical panels, 164–165
    climate wall, 236–237, 333–334
    coverings, 164, 218
    double envelope concept, 236–237
    gypsum board, 160–161, 206, 213, 299
    insulating value, 282
    movable partitions, 146
    permeable, 328–329
    window, 191, 236, 241
    wood paneling, 216
Washing machines, water-efficient, 115, 169
Waste management
    reduction strategies, 319, 330
    separation, 319
    See also Composting; Recycling
Waste stream, building user's, 143
Wastewater treatment
    constructed wetlands, 5, 11, 105, 111–112, 327–328, 332
    for irrigation, 106, 110, 328
    on-site, 62, 106, 110, 170
    permits, 58, 108
    soil amendments from, 152
    types of, 111
    See also Water management
WasteWise program, 141
Water analysis, 109, 113
Water closets. See Toilets and urinals
Water conservation, 5, 10–11, 213, 226–227, 271
    appliances, 115, 169
    education, 116
    incentive programs, 108
    irrigation, 14, 43, 57–58, 63–64, 106, 110, 114, 151
    rainwater collection, 5, 11, 105, 108, 109–110, 204, 298, 317, 318
    swimming pools, 113, 327
    See also Plumbing fixtures; Wastewater treatment; Water reuse
Watergy, 80